BEGINNING

GAME PROGRAMMING

Michael Morrison

SAMS   800 East 96th St., Indianapolis, Indiana, 46240 USA

Beginning Game Programming

International Standard Book Number: 0-672-32659-0

Library of Congress Catalog Card Number:

Printed in the United States of America

First Printing: July 2004

07   06   05   04   4   3   2   1

Trademarks

Warning and Disclaimer

Associate Publisher
Michael Stephens

Acquisitions Editor
Loretta Yates

Development Editor
Mark Renfrow

Managing Editor
Charlotte Clapp

Project Editor
George E. Nedeff

Copy Editor
Rhonda Tinch-Mize

Indexer
Erika Millen

Proofreaders
Tonya Fenimore
Suzanne Thomas

Technical Editor
David Franson

Team Coordinator
Cindy Teeters

Designer
Gary Adair

Page Layout
Brad Chinn

Contents at a Glance

Table of Contents

About the Author

Michael Morrison is a writer, developer, toy inventor, and author of a variety of computer technology books and interactive Web-based courses. In addition to his primary profession as a writer and freelance nerd for hire, Michael is the creative lead at Stalefish Labs, an entertainment company he co-founded with his wife, Masheed. The first commercial debut for Stalefish Labs is a traditional social/trivia game called *Tall Tales: The Game of Legends and Creative One-Upmanship* (www.talltalesgame.com). When not glued to his computer, playing hockey, skateboarding, or watching movies with his wife, Michael enjoys hanging out by his koi pond. You can visit Michael on the Web at www.michaelmorrison.com.

About the Technical Editor

David Franson has been a professional in the field of networking, programming, and computer graphics since 1990. In 2000, he resigned from his position as Information Systems director of one of the largest entertainment law firms in New York City to pursue a full-time career in game development. He wrote *2D Artwork* and *3D Modeling for Game Artists*, which were published November 2002.

Dedication

To my late friend, Randy Weems, who taught me practically everything I know about game programming and who lives on in every game I create.

Acknowledgments

Thanks to Mike Stephens, Loretta Yates, Mark Renfrow, David Franson, and the rest of the gang at Sams Publishing for making this such a pleasurable writing experience. Also, I owe an enormous thanks to my wife, Masheed, for being my best friend and biggest supporter.

We Want to Hear from You!

As the reader of this book, *you* are our most important critic and commentator. We value your opinion and want to know what we're doing right, what we could do better, what areas you'd like to see us publish in, and any other words of wisdom you're willing to pass our way.

As an associate publisher for Sams, I welcome your comments. You can email or write me directly to let me know what you did or didn't like about this book—as well as what we can do to make our books better.

Please note that I cannot help you with technical problems related to the *topic* of this book. We do have a User Services group, however, where I will forward specific technical questions related to the book.

When you write, please be sure to include this book's title and author as well as your name, email address, and phone number. I will carefully review your comments and share them with the author and editors who worked on the book.

Email: feedback@samspublishing.com
Mail: Michael Stephens
           Associate Publisher
           Sams Publishing
           800 East 96th Street
           Indianapolis, IN 46240 USA

Reader Services

For more information about this book or others from Sams Publishing, visit our Web site at www.samspublishing.com. Type the ISBN (0672326590) or the title of the book in the Search box to find the book you're looking for.

Introduction

Television shows such as *Junkyard Wars* and *American Chopper* have enjoyed great success largely due to the fact that they reveal the creative process behind the construction of interesting machines such as submarines, battering rams, and motorcycles. Educational television shows have been around since the dawn of the television age, but it's taken until recently for education to be considered in the realm of legitimate entertainment. These shows have succeeded because they show how fun and challenging it can be to take an idea in your head and turn it into a reality. Yes, they are educational; but more importantly, they are fun. A similar degree of challenging fun is awaiting you in this book as you learn how to construct your own video games. No, you won't be able to ride your games down the street revving the engine, but you will be able to share them with your friends and family and show off your newly acquired game development skills.

Although it's kind of hard to imagine now, there was a time not so long ago when the concept of a video game was a "pie in the sky" idea. Computers were barely seen as useful tools in business and were viewed as having even less potential for entertainment. Technology has a way of changing the way we think about things, and it wasn't long before early video games captured the minds and quarters of an entire generation. Yes, I am a child of the '80s, and I feel fortunate to have spent part of my childhood in the decade when video games went from a pipe dream to a cultural phenomenon.

Video games are interesting in that they represent the first form of interactive digital entertainment. Perhaps more importantly, video games represent the first truly interactive art form. When you think about it, there aren't many paintings, sculptures, or musical compositions that allow you to interact with them and change them in any way. Video games allow creators to share something more with the game player by giving players a chance to put part of themselves into a game and then see what comes out. In fact, the best games are the ones that allow players to express their own unique styles and techniques when playing the game, while at the same time being entertained by the game designer's vision of an imaginary world portrayed by the game.

If you think this introduction is setting you up for a book filled with nostalgia and artsy video game talk, think again. Although I appreciate the history of video games, as well as the artistry that goes into their design, I realize that you're interested in creating your own games. The trick is to learn from the past while equipping yourself to create a new future. So, I'll use past video games to explain game construction techniques and give you ideas, but my ultimate goal is to empower you with the game programming knowledge to realize your own vision of the perfect computer game.

I'm sure you already know that computer programming is a challenging, yet rewarding endeavor that gives you the freedom to do some interesting things within the context of a computer. Unfortunately, game programming has often been somewhat of a mysterious discipline within computer programming. Although there are a lot of games, there really aren't all that many game programmers. The reason is primarily because game programming is a uniquely challenging area of software development that requires a mastery of several different disciplines. To create even a simple game, you must understand how to write code to draw bitmapped graphics, carry out sprite animation, play sampled digital sound effects, and process user input from a keyboard, mouse, and/or joystick. If these tasks sound somewhat overwhelming, it's because they are if you aren't properly prepared to tackle them.

This book tackles each game programming discipline one at a time and in a way that allows you to build one skill on top of the previous one you just learned. The end result is that you start with a few fundamental game programming skills and slowly build up a base of knowledge that allows you to tackle increasingly more complex games. The significance of this approach is that it allows you to ease into game programming a step at a time, with a focus on ramping up your skills throughout the book to tackle more challenging projects.

Will this book make you a game programming guru? Not exactly. The idea here is to provide you with a solid foundation in game programming skills that you can use to create interesting games of your own. This book does not cover DirectX, which is Microsoft's advanced game programming library. DirectX is a complex technology used to create commercial games. You should definitely aspire to learn DirectX if you decide to get more serious about game programming, but the purpose of this book is to show you how to create fun games with a minimal amount of pain. DirectX has a significant learning curve, so I decided that it was best left to more advanced game programming books. The good news is that you don't need DirectX to create interesting and highly entertaining games of your own, as you learn throughout this book.

How This Book Is Structured

This book is organized into eight parts; each of which tackles a different facet of game programming:

▶ Part I, "Getting Started"—In this part, you learn the basics of video game development and what goes into creating a game. You create a reusable software engine for games, as well as find out how to draw basic graphics, including bitmapped images.

▶ Part II, "Interacting with Game Players"—In this part, you learn how to interact with players through input devices such as the keyboard, mouse, and joysticks. This part of the book also guides you through the development of your first complete game, which is a tile matching memory game called Brainiac. You don't stop there, however, because you also develop your second complete game in this part, an ode to the classic Tron arcade game called Light Cycles.

▶ Part III, "Animating Games with Sprites"—In this part, you learn the ropes of sprite animation, which is the cornerstone of two-dimensional game programming. You uncover the basics of game animation and then build classes to support animation in games. You also develop your third complete game in this part of the book, which is a game called Henway that is influenced by the classic Frogger arcade game.

▶ Part IV, "Making Noise with Sound and Music"—In this part, you get acquainted with music and sound effects as they apply to games. More specifically, you find out how to create wave sound effects and then play them in games, as well as how to play MIDI music. With a solid foundation in sound under your belt, you move on to create Battle Office, which is your fourth complete game.

▶ Part V, "Taking Animation to the Next Level"—In this part, you go beyond the basics of sprite animation to learn some advanced animation techniques that are valuable in action games. You learn how to animate the appearance of sprites, as well as how to create animated backgrounds. You then put this new knowledge to work in another complete game called Meteor Defense, which is roughly similar to the Missile Command arcade game.

▶ Part VI, "Adding Brains to Your Games"—In this part, you learn the fundamentals of artificial intelligence (AI) and why it is important to games. AI can be a daunting topic, so I focus on some basic AI techniques that are easy to understand and apply in your own games. This part of the book also includes the development of another complete game, Space Out, which is a space shoot-em-up that incorporates virtually everything you've learned throughout the book.

▶ Part VII, "Spicing Up Your Games"—In this part, you explore some interesting game programming techniques that allow you to add a professional touch to your games. You learn how to create a splash screen, a demo mode, and a high score list that is stored to disk. Along the way, you spice up the Space Out game with each new technique to make it a more professional quality game. This provides you with a good game to use as a starting point for your own game programming projects.

▶ Part VIII, "One for the Road"—In this part, you wrap up the book by working through the design and development of an adventure simulation and one more complete game. The adventure simulation, Wanderer, takes advantage of scrolling backgrounds to allow you to guide an adventuresome person around a virtual world. The Stunt Jumper game is a side-scrolling motorcycle jumping game in which you ride a stunt motorcycle and attempt to jump over buses.

What You'll Need

This book assumes that you have knowledge and understanding of the C++ programming language. Although the program examples and games you develop throughout the book are Windows programs, you aren't required to have a background in Windows programming. In truth, I really don't rely on any complex C++ programming constructs, so a basic understanding of C++ is all you need. If your C++ skills are a bit rusty, you can get a refresher by reading Appendix B, "A C++ Programming Primer." Similarly, Appendix C, "A Windows Game Programming Primer," provides you with the bare essentials of Windows programming as it applies to games, which is definitely worth reading if you have no prior knowledge of the Win32 API (Application Programming Interface).

Although prior knowledge of Windows programming isn't critical, it is very important that you understand how to build a C++ program using a development environment on the Windows platform, such as Visual C++ (Visual Studio), Borland C++Builder, or Dev-C++. If you already have a favorite C++ development environment, that's great. If not, you'll probably want to check out Appendix A, "Selecting a Game Development Tool," which describes some of the more popular Windows C++ development tools.

All the examples in the book are available on the accompanying CD-ROM, along with project files for Visual C++, C++Builder, and Dev-C++. I encourage you to try and use one of these three tools in combination with the projects I've provided because creating a new project from scratch for a Windows game can often be tricky.

If you decide to go with a development tool different from these three, you'll need to create a new project for each example and then add the source code files. Your development tool might allow you to import one of the projects I've provided, so take a look before creating new projects by hand. If you have trouble building a project, make sure that you're linking in the appropriate standard libraries because there are a couple of libraries (winmm.lib and msimg32.lib) that you must import in most of the program examples and games. Also make sure that the project is set to create a "Windows application," not a "console application."

Beyond some C++ knowledge and a good C++ development tool, all you really need are an open mind and a bit of creativity to get the most out of this book. They will serve you well as you embark on this journey into the world of game creation. Have fun!

PART I

Getting Started

CHAPTER 1

Learning the Basics of Game Creation

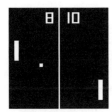

Arcade Archive

Having been fortunate enough to have grown up during the video game revolution, it was Pong that first introduced me to the interactive digital art form that we now call video games. Pong was created in 1972 by Nolan Bushnell, who founded Atari, one of the first companies to establish the Silicon Valley technological counterculture that sparked the computer industry. Pong was painfully simple in design, yet addictive enough to a generation of youth who were entranced by the ability to compete with each other through an electronic medium. Although Pong started out as an arcade game, it wasn't until it was released as the first home video game console that it became a household name. Although many people think Pong was the first video game ever, that distinction goes to a lesser-known game called Computer Space, also by Nolan Bushnell, which was released in 1971.

If you're familiar with Pong, you can certainly appreciate the advancements made over the last 30+ years that allow us to now have video games that literally rival movies in audiovisual appeal. If you've ever been curious about how these games work, you've certainly come to the right place. I started my journey into video game development through this same sense of amazement and curiosity that I had the power to create my own little virtual world that lived by its own rules, my rules. Armed with a little programming knowledge and a desire to see where my imagination could take me, I learned the essentials of video game creation. Unfortunately, I had to learn it the hard way by inventing my own solutions and using trial and error to solve even the simplest of problems. Fortunately for you, this painful approach is no longer necessary. This chapter introduces you to the fundamentals of game creation.

In this chapter, you'll learn

▶ About the different kinds of video games

▶ The main things to consider when designing a new game

▶ Why object-oriented programming (OOP) is important for game development

▶ What kinds of tools you'll use as a game developer

Getting to Know Video Games

It's worth starting this discussion by pointing out that video games haven't always enjoyed the kind of respect they are given nowadays as legitimate forms of entertainment. From its early days as a niche entertainment business that was never taken seriously, the video game industry has grown into a very important sector of global business. Video games are now funded in a manner and on a scale comparable to Hollywood movies, and they often involve famous actors, actresses, screenwriters, musicians, and other entertainment professionals whom we previously only associated with movies. In fact, the production of a modern video game is in many ways like producing a movie. There are pitches, story-boards, and market tests, and those are just to get a game financed. Once a game rolls into production, there are teams of designers, animators, and program-mers—not to mention various other talented individuals and companies—who pitch in to help make a finished game. Modern games cost millions of dollars to produce and can reap enormous rewards for those willing to put up the time and money.

You're probably reading this book because you don't have a few million extra dollars lying around to throw into a video game project, or maybe you'd just rather spend your pile of cash elsewhere. Either way, you may have had a faint hope that it's still possible for one person to create a highly entertaining video game with little more than elbow grease. It's not only possible, it's also highly rewarding and quite empowering. However, video games have traditionally repre-sented one of the most complex and mysterious facets of programming and, therefore, have likely scared away many a curious would-be game creator. My goal is to demystify the game development process and show you that you don't have to be a genius to have fun creating your own games. However, if you happen to be a genius, it certainly won't hold you back!

Even with the skills you develop throughout this book, I have to come clean and admit that it isn't very realistic to think that a single person can conceive and develop a video game comparable to many of the popular commercial games on the market today. It's no more feasible than for a would-be filmmaker to embark on the next *Star Wars* by himself. However, plenty of aspiring filmmakers have broken into the business with less ambitious projects to begin with, and that's my recommendation to you—cut your teeth on simple games that you can complete on your own, and then move on to more ambitious projects as your skills and resources increase. Who knows? You might decide to go to work for a game company or even launch your own.

Why Video Games?

If you're an avid game player, you might already know the answer to this question, but it's worth asking anyway: Why are video games so popular, and why are so many people interested in learning how to create their own? I think it has something to do with the allure of creating a little world all your own, where the limits are only your technical skills and your imagination. The goal of this book is to strengthen one while sparking the other.

To better understand why so many people gravitate toward video games, consider how popular movies are in modern cultures. Few of us are able to watch a great movie without at some point envisioning ourselves right there taking part in a scene. Video games enable us to step beyond the role of an audience member and become a participant in an interactive story. Essentially, all video games enable you to step into a world and take part in it, even if that world consists solely of an outer space background and a few aliens. When walking through a video game arcade, it's as if each screen is a window into another reality just begging you to come inside and see what's going on.

That's enough of the dreamy talk. What do video games mean to the would-be game programmer? From a development perspective, video games are quite interesting in that they require such a wide range of talents. Video games provide us with all the usual technical challenges associated with software development (usually more) along with illustration, animation, sound effects, and music, and those don't even touch on the story aspect of games—where entire screenplays are often developed. By developing a video game from start to finish, you'll practically become a modern renaissance person, acquiring some degree of expertise in many disciplines. You'll also successfully merge many divergent interests into a greater medium enjoyable by others. It's for this reason that so many of us are intrigued by the endless possibilities associated with video game design and development.

Types of Video Games

Speaking of creating your own games, you might be wondering why I keep referring to "video games" when the games created in this book are played on a computer. Although I hate to split hairs over terminology, it's worth pointing out that
a *video game* is an interactive electronic entertainment medium that uses a video
screen as its primary display. In other words, the term video game applies to all
games with a screen and a joystick or some other controller. Contrast this with a
traditional pinball machine, for example, which is certainly played, but doesn't
rely on a video screen for output. Video games can be further classified into three
categories: arcade games, console games, and computer games.

Arcade Games

Arcade games are video games that are built into hefty cabinets with payment
mechanisms that require you to pay in order to play the games. Arcade games
represent the birth of video games and are responsible for separating quite a few
'80s American (and Japanese) youths from their hard-earned (or hard-begged)
quarters. Arcade games often rely on custom hardware components and unique
physical controls to separate them from other types of video games. Although
arcade games certainly still exist, they are a minor component of the video game
market these days, and they aren't the bastion of innovation they once were.
Don't get me wrong; some really cool new arcade games are out there, but you
have to look beyond arcade games to get to the really active portion of the video
game market.

Console Games

Console games followed quickly on the coattails of arcade games. They represent
home gaming systems from the classic Pong, Atari 2600, and Intellivision systems
to today's Sony Playstation 2, Microsoft Xbox, and Nintendo GameCube. Console
game systems are designed from the ground up as consumer game machines and
rival arcade games in terms of game quality. We are currently in the midst of a
convergence of digital entertainment technologies that is quite capable of placing
console games at the center of the home entertainment equation. In fact,
Microsoft has plans for its Xbox console game system to become an all-
encompassing digital entertainment device. The Windows operating system
itself is now offered in a Media Center Edition, which is the first major step
toward establishing Windows as an all-encompassing operating system for digital
entertainment. The next few years should be interesting in terms of seeing how
console games merge with traditional entertainment equipment.

Handheld game platforms, such as Nintendo's GameBoy Advance, are also considered console games—at least in the sense that they have well-defined hardware
specifications geared exclusively toward gaming. A rapidly growing area of handheld gaming is that of mobile communication devices, such as mobile phones
and pocket-sized computers. Although most of these devices can be classified as
either phones or personal digital assistants (PDAs) that happen to support games,
a few are starting to appear with an obvious focus toward gamers. Nokia's N-
Gage mobile game deck is somewhat of a GameBoy on steroids and is leading a
technological charge toward combining mobile communication with personal
gaming.

I have to muddy the waters a little here by clarifying that developing games for a
mobile phone or PDA is more akin to developing a computer game, as opposed to a
console game. This is because mobile phones and PDAs tend to use more "open"
operating systems, such as Windows Mobile, whereas proprietary devices, such as
the GameBoy Advance, rely on "closed" systems that require special tools and
licensing agreements.

Computer Games

Computer games represent the third classification of video games and were last to
the video game show simply because it took longer for personal computers to
become technically capable of doing enough interesting things with graphics and
sound to make good games possible. Computer games now represent a massive
segment of the video game industry and rival console games in terms of popularity and sales. There was a time when console games competed with computer
games, but most popular games are now available in both console and computer
versions, so you have the option of deciding whether to use a computer or a dedicated console gaming system to play games. The Xbox system is somewhat
unique among consoles in that it shares a software game development platform
with computer games. I'm referring to DirectX, which is Microsoft's game development toolkit that originated on PCs and now carries over to the Xbox.

I'll go ahead and let you know up front that this book doesn't cover game programming using the DirectX game development toolkit. This is because DirectX is very
complex technology with a painfully steep learning curve not suited to beginning
game development. In fact, most of the benefits of using DirectX aren't realized until
you move on to building complex games. Rather than spending half the book on the

basics of how DirectX works, I decided to spend the entire book teaching you how to create games. If, after reading this book, you decide to move forward and learn DirectX, I highly recommend Clayton Walnum's *Teach Yourself Game Programming with DirectX in 21 Days*. I'm not against DirectX in any way. I just think it's a bit of overkill for learning the basics of game programming.

Assessing the Different Types of Games

I want to clarify the different types of video games because there is a great deal of difference in developing each type. For example, arcade games rely on specialized hardware and proprietary development tools that are expensive and difficult to obtain for a startup game programmer. Console games run a close second in terms of presenting a significant barrier to entry for new game programmers. Not only are the tools expensive and difficult to get your hands on, but they also often require a very specialized set of programming skills that are usually learned on the job while working for a game company. Additionally, you typically must pay hefty licensing fees and have your game tested and approved by console manufacturers before being allowed to release a game for a console.

Computer games (including mobile phone and PDA games) are really the only video games that are accessible to the individual from a development perspective. Tools for computer game programming are readily available and are either free or relatively inexpensive. Not only that, but you can leverage existing knowledge in a mainstream programming language such as C++ to develop computer games. This book focuses on the development of computer games using C++, although most of the concepts and techniques also apply to arcade and console games.

I've deliberately left out one classification of video games that really doesn't quite compare to the three types you just learned about: *Web games*. You know those little miniature golf games that pop up as advertisements and all the various trivia games scattered around the Web? Although some interesting Web games are out there, most of them don't compare to other types of video games—at least with respect to how they are developed. Most Web games are developed using a multimedia authoring tool such as Macromedia Flash, which relies on scripted programming and insulates you significantly from common game programming tasks. I'm not saying that there is anything wrong with this approach if you can get away with using it for a particular game, but you'll find that you can do so much more with a full-blown programming language.

Learning Game Design Essentials

Now that you have some perspective on the types of video games and the viability of each from a development view, you're ready to start learning about designing games. Do you have some ideas of games you'd like to create, or are you clueless about where to begin? Regardless of which camp you're in, I'm here to help. Keep in mind that coming up with a good game idea is often the easy part; taking the concept to reality is where the difficulty arises and many of us fall short. As long as you take things a step at a time and don't get overwhelmed by the details, you'll do just fine.

The first step in taking a game from the drawing board to the keyboard is to get a solid idea of what you want the game to be. I'm not saying that you have to create an itemized list of every screen, creature, and minute interaction. However, it is very important to establish some minimal ground rules about the big picture of what you envision for the final game. The following are the key items you should focus on when putting together the overall concept of your game:

- Basic idea
- Story line
- Graphics
- Sound
- Controls
- Play modes

The next few sections explore these game design considerations in more detail.

Coming Up with the Basic Idea

The most important design step in creating a game is to determine the basic idea behind the game. Is it a shoot-em-up, a maze game, a role-playing game (RPG), a driving game, a puzzle game, a simulation, or some combination of these? On the other hand, do you have a truly original game idea that doesn't neatly fit into an existing genre? Is the object to rescue good guys, eliminate bad guys, or just explore a strange environment? What time frame is your game set in, or does it even have a time frame? These are just a few of the questions you need to ask yourself when developing the basic idea for a new game. Think about it and write everything down. Whatever comes to mind, write it down because brainstorms come and go, and you don't want to forget anything. Forcing yourself to formalize your ideas and get them on paper causes you to think about it more and usually clears up a lot of uncertainties.

If you're having trouble coming up with a basic game idea, think about the influences of some of the more popular games around. Many games are based on movies, some are based on historical events, and others are based on sports. Some games are so popular that there are movies based on the games (Tomb Raider, Final Fantasy, Resident Evil, and so on). Ultimately, most computer games are models of the world around us, whether fantasy or real, so look no further when dreaming up your game. Movies in particular can provide a lot of good, creative settings and story lines for games—just be careful not to "borrow" too much.

Regardless of your inspiration, remember that your game has to be fun. No matter how fancy the graphics are or how immersive the sound, the overriding design goal of any game is always to maximize fun. Who wouldn't want to spend all day trying to figure out the best way to have fun? That, my friend, is the real allure of game programming. If your game isn't fun to play, no amount of fancy graphics, sound, or celebrity voice-overs will save it. Some of the best games of all time have weak graphics and sound by modern standards, but their fun factor has never diminished. A testament to this fact is the recent resurgence of classic arcade games, including the re-release of the upright arcade games Galaga and Ms. Pac-Man.

A good example of a painfully simple game that is surprisingly fun is the classic Atari 2600 Combat game. This game came with most Atari 2600 console systems, so most Atari gamers got a chance to try it out. Combat suffered from the severely limited technology of the time, and its graphics and sound show it. However, the game play of Combat is great and, in my opinion, rivals modern games. When you think about it, the one aspect of game development that hasn't changed much over the years is the user input side of the equation. Granted, there are fancier joysticks and some new gadgety features, such as force feedback, but at the end of the day it's still just an interface to your hands. This helps explain why arcade games created in 1982 still can be quite fun, even though they are technically far inferior to modern games. The creators of those games didn't have the luxury of 3D rendered graphics and spatial THX sound, so they went to work on the way their games played. Although the games you develop throughout this book will be technically superior to the classics of 1982, you'll use a similar development approach by foregoing complex bleeding-edge technology for playability.

The point I'm trying to make is that you must make fun the priority when designing your game. After you have a basic idea of what your game will be and have decided that you're going to make it fun at all costs, you can then move on to developing a story line.

Putting Together the Story Line

Aren't story lines just for movies and complicated cinematic games? Absolutely not. Even if your game is a simple action game with a couple of characters fighting it out, developing a story line helps you establish the mood and landscape and also think up creatures to populate the game world. Putting your game in the context of a story also brings the game player closer to your world. Remember the classic Pong game mentioned at the opening of this chapter? Although it succeeded without a good story, it would have been much more interesting if it had been designed with a story in mind. Maybe the ball is an atom bouncing around in a damaged nuclear reactor, and if it goes off the screen, the whole thing will melt down. It's up to you and your friend to control the "atomic deflectors" and keep the atom from escaping. Now that I think about it, maybe Pong was better off just being a blip and some lines, but you get the idea.

If you get really serious about a story line for your game, you might want to consider creating a storyboard. Commonly used to pitch movies, a *storyboard* tells a story scene by scene using rough sketches of each scene. Storyboards are important visual tools because they enable you to visualize a game based on a story line. Having a storyboard to reference helps ensure that you don't lose sight of the story when you get heavily into development. Figure 1.1 shows a simple storyboard of a popular movie you might recognize. Can you guess what it is?

FIGURE 1.1
Even a stick figure storyboard can convey a recognizable story.

Give up? This is my stick figure interpretation of the movie Jaws, which is probably my favorite movie of all time. As you can see in the figure, even my limited artistic abilities and love of stick figures can convey the basics of a story. Of course, a storyboard for a real game or movie would likely consist of more than four frames.

It's worth pointing out that storyboards aren't appropriate for all games. For example, most sports games don't benefit from storyboards because the objectives of the games are fairly concrete. On the other hand, maybe you want to simulate the trials and tribulations of modern athletes in your sports game—in which case, a story might creep back into the equation.

Visualizing the Graphics

My stick figure artistry is the perfect segue into the next major component of game design: graphics. Although games can certainly be fun without fancy graphics, you can significantly improve any game with the graphics you use. It's important to select a level of graphics consistent with your design goals and resources. There was a time when you also had to factor in the graphics capabilities of computers, but these days, even relatively low-end computers are powerful enough for games of moderate to medium complexity.

**Construction
        Cue**

Some amazing graphics tools are out there that make it possible to create surprisingly cool graphics without necessarily being an artist. On the other hand, if you have a friend with more artistic ability than you, it might be worth it to recruit him to help you out with your game.

Screen resolution is an important consideration for most games. If you've ever noticed your screen flickering and your monitor making a strange noise when you first start a commercial game, you're familiar with different screen resolutions; the game is switching to a resolution different from what you were using. The most common resolution these days for Windows PCs is 800×600, which means that there are 800 *pixels* (colored graphical squares) across the screen and 600 down the screen. If you have a monitor larger than 15 inches or a graphics card with a lot of memory, your resolution can be set much higher; mine is currently set at 1280×1024. The significance of resolution is that it directly affects the size of the graphics in games. Most commercial games are designed to run at several different resolutions, but you might not want to hassle with that for your own games. In fact, in this book, I opted to stick with a fixed size for the game screen in each example game, which is an approach that works fairly well and simplifies the game graphics.

Another design decision worth considering in regard to graphics is the player's perspective of the game. Will the playfield be 2D, 3D, or some combination of the two? Will the player be able to see his character onscreen, or will everything be first-person as if looking through the character's field of vision? These considerations have an enormous impact on the programming complexity of a game and, therefore, should be decided very early in the design phase.

Choosing the Right Sound for Your Game

Sound is one element of games that might not seem as significant as graphics until you try playing a game without it. Seriously, just turn off the speakers while playing one of your favorite games and notice how it impacts the overall experience. On the other hand, if the game play and graphics alone are enough to make your game appealing, the sound will be the icing on the cake. It's important to use sound everywhere you can; sound effects are a bare minimum, and if you really want to do it right, you'll consider using some sort of music soundtrack.

The first thing to decide regarding sound is the quality of sounds in a game, which can dramatically impact memory requirements and overall game performance. For sound effects, you'll be dealing with sampled sounds in the form of *wave* (WAV) files. You must select a sampling rate, whether you want mono or stereo sound, and whether the sound uses 8 bits or 16 bits to store each sample. You learn much more about what these sound properties mean in Chapter 12, "Playing Digital Sound Effects," but for now, just understand that they directly impact both the quality and performance of sounds. For example, CD-quality sound is sampled at 44KHz in 16-bit stereo. CD-quality sound provides the best quality at the expense of a huge storage overhead; a typical music CD holds about 80 minutes and requires more than 700MB of storage space. You will more than likely settle on a lower sound quality in games to minimize storage space and improve performance.

> *Sampling* refers to the process of converting sound waves into a digital format that can be stored and played on a computer. You learn more about how sampling works in Chapter 12.

Gamer's Garage

In games, music is often handled differently from sound effects. Although it is possible to record music as a sampled sound, this can take up a lot of space. For this reason, a good alternative to sampled music is *MIDI (Musical Instrument Digital Interface)* music, which is the standard for arranging and playing musical compositions on computers. Unlike sampled music, MIDI music involves specifying the individual musical notes in a piece of music and associating them with virtual musical instruments. Creating a MIDI soundtrack can be difficult if you have no music background, but you might be able to find existing MIDI music to meet your needs. Fortunately, all you really need to know at this stage of a game's design is that you should consider developing programming code that can play a MIDI soundtrack. Chapter 13, "Playing MIDI Music," shows you how to play MIDI music in your games.

Dictating Game Play with the Controls

The controls used to interface with the game player make up an extremely important part of a game's design, and they shouldn't be taken lightly. It's important to support as many input devices (mouse, keyboard, joystick, and so on) as possible so that people with a preference for certain devices can use them. Game players use a wide variety of controls, and it's your job to decide which ones you think are worth supporting and how they will be used to control the game. It never hurts to support extra input devices.

At the very least, you can count on supporting the keyboard and mouse. You might as well plan on supporting joysticks in most games, too, providing it makes sense to use a joystick in the context of the game. Beyond those three input devices, it's up to you to decide whether it's worth the extra effort to support other devices. Some input devices might not even be applicable to your game; in which case, the decision is easy. With steering wheels, virtual reality helmets, touch-sensitive gloves, and dance pads, there are plenty of advanced input options if you want to go the distance in supporting input devices. In addition, who knows what other kinds of revolutionary input devices are on the horizon?

Gamer's Garage

Game pads work similarly to joysticks; therefore, these devices don't usually require any special design considerations; a game that works with a joystick will likely work with most game pads.

Deciding on the Play Modes

The last consideration to make in regard to the overall design of a game is that of play modes. Will the game be a one-player or a two-player game, or will it be networked to allow a lot of players? If it supports multiplayer mode, is it competitive play, cooperative play, or some of both? These important decisions can dramatically impact both the fun factor and the technical difficulties of developing the game. For one thing, networking a multiplayer game presents some pretty serious technical hurdles at the programming level. I'm not trying to scare you away from networking; I just want to point out that it's a fairly advanced area of game programming.

To better understand the considerations that can go into determining play modes for a game, allow me to give you a practical example. I once developed a simple action game called Combat Tanks that was loosely based on the old Atari 2600 Combat game. When designing the game, I initially envisioned two players fighting each other head-to-head (see Figure 1.2). At the time, I had no interest in adding networking support, which was very difficult to program then, so the players played at the same computer using keys on different sides of the keyboard to control their respective tanks. After some testing, it became apparent that a one-player mode for the game would be fun too. I mistakenly thought it would be easy to design a computer tank that could think and react like a human player. I was seriously naïve about that idea.

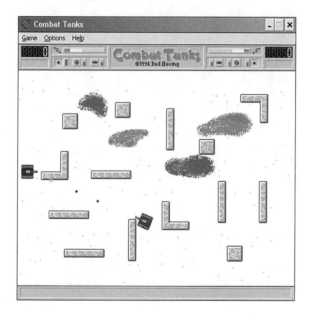

FIGURE 1.2
My Combat Tanks game was originally developed as a two-player tank battle game.

I learned pretty quickly that adding intelligence to computer opponents is a tricky business; all the little strategic decisions we make as humans while playing a game are very difficult to program into a mindless computer opponent. Therefore, I figured out a workaround. Rather than have a single intelligent computer opponent, I opted for an onslaught of stupid computer opponents (see Figure 1.3). The resulting game played as a head-to-head tank game in two-player mode and as a one-against-all shoot-em-up in one-player mode. It still turned out to be quite fun as a one-player game, and I didn't have to deal with the complexities of "teaching" the computer tank how to be as crafty as a human.

FIGURE 1.3
By adding hordes of "dumb" computer enemies, I was able to add a much needed one-player mode to the game.

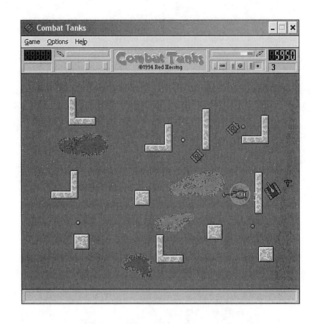

Gamer's Garage

Although my tank game is now more than 10 years old, it's still fun in a nostalgic kind of way. If you'd like to try it out, you can download it from my Web site at `http://www.michaelmorrison.com/`. I actually cowrote Combat Tanks with my late friend, Randy Weems, whom I gladly credit for a great deal of my knowledge of game programming.

Please understand that I'm not advocating taking the easy way out when it comes to determining the play modes of your games, like I did. I'm only trying to make the point that there are many ways to arrive at a desired result. For me, the simplest solution ended up working out great because it allowed me to inject some interesting enemies into the game, such as foot soldiers, bombers, and helicopters. A little creativity can often go a long way toward overcoming technical hurdles in game programming.

Object-Oriented Programming and Games

Because you have some experience with C++, you've no doubt heard of object-oriented programming. *Object-oriented programming* or *OOP* is a programming technique in which you treat parts of a program as *objects,* as opposed to chunks of programming code. OOP is particularly useful in games because games are actually easier to understand when you break them down into objects. For this reason, programming languages such as C++ are ideal for developing games. The next two sections provide you with an OOP refresher and then put OOP in the context of game development.

Understanding OOP

The idea behind OOP is to make programming more akin to the way people think, as compared to the way computers think. People tend to think in terms of meaningful things (objects). As an example, if you were to describe a hockey game, you might talk about the rink, the players, the nets, and the puck. From a computer's perspective, a computer hockey game is no different from any other program—it's just a bunch of ones and zeros. Programming languages allow programmers to avoid having to think in terms of ones and zeros. OOP languages take things a step further by allowing you to think in terms of objects.

Classes of objects make up an important part of OOP. A *class* is a category of objects. Another way to say this is that an object is an *instance* of a class. If you were creating a computer hockey game, you might create a single hockey player class; the actual players in the game are *instances* of this class. Figure 1.4 shows how the hockey player objects are related to the single player class.

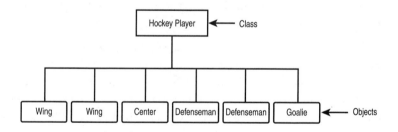

FIGURE 1.4
Several hockey player objects can be created from a single player class.

The figure reveals how several objects are created from a single class, which serves as a template for the objects. Using a food analogy instead of hockey, you can think of the class as a cookie cutter and the objects as the cookies. Another important feature of classes is that they allow you to create *subclasses*, which add to the properties and features in a class to make it more specific. A subclass *inherits* the properties and features from its *parent class* and then adds some of its own. In this way, a subclass is similar to a human child in that it inherits traits from its parent, but also has its own new traits. Going back to the hockey analogy, a goalie class might be designed as a subclass of the hockey player class that uses extra equipment (chest pad, blocker, and so on) and has a limited range of motion near the net.

Applying OOP to Games

In order to understand the benefits that OOP offers in terms of game development, it's helpful to think of a game as a type of abstract simulation. If you think about most of the games you've seen or played, it's almost impossible to think of one that doesn't simulate something. All the adventure games and sports games are clearly simulations, and even the most far-out space games are modeling objects that exist in some kind of virtual world. Knowing that games are models of worlds, you can make the connection that most of the things in games (landscapes, creatures, and so on) correspond to things in these worlds. Once you can resolve a game into a collection of "things," you can apply OOP techniques to the design. This is possible because things can easily be translated into objects in an OOP environment.

To better understand what I'm talking about, consider the OOP design of a simple fantasy adventure game. The object representing the world for this game might contain information such as its map and images that represent the visualization of the map, as well as time and weather. All other objects in the game would include positional information that describes where in the world they are located. This positional information could be a simple XY value that pinpoints the object's location on the world map or possibly a three-dimensional XYZ value that also takes into account the elevation of the object with respect to the ground or sea level.

The object for the main character in the game would include information such as life points and any items picked up during the game (weapons, lanterns, keys, and so on). The game itself would interact with the character object by telling it to move in different directions based on user input. The items carried by the character would also be created as objects. For example, the lantern object would probably keep track of how much fuel is left in the lantern and whether it is on or off. Interactions with the lantern would simply include turning it on or off; the lantern object would be smart enough to reduce its fuel supply when the lantern is turned on.

Creatures in the game could all be based on a single creature class that describes general characteristics shared by all creatures, such as life points, aggression, and how much damage they inflict when fighting. Specific creature objects would then be created and turned loose in the virtual world. The creature objects and the main character object could all be subclassed from the same organism object. Unlike the character object, which is driven by user interactions, the creature objects would be controlled by some type of intelligence programmed into the game. For example, more aggressive creatures might always chase after the main character when they are on the screen together, whereas passive creatures might have a tendency to hide and avoid contact. You could create creature subclasses that enhance the basic creature with unique capabilities, such as the ability to fly, swim, or breathe fire. Figure 1.5 shows how the different classes in this hypothetical adventure game might be organized.

I mentioned that creature objects in this hypothetical adventure game would be controlled by some kind of artificial intelligence, while the main character object is controlled by user interactions. Although this is true, it's important to point out that you should carefully design objects so that you can easily alter them for either human or computer control. In other words, it should be possible to allow a human player to play as a creature without having to alter the game code dramatically. In this way, all organism objects would likely have common "commands" for actions such as walking, running, attacking, and so on. Whether these commands are issued by an artificial intelligence algorithm or a human pressing buttons on a game pad isn't really important from the perspective of the organism object.

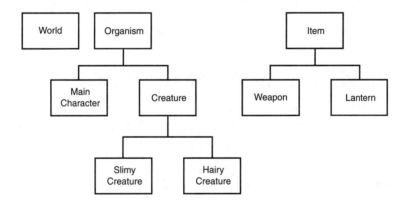

FIGURE 1.5
Classes in a hypothetical adventure game are built on one another to establish a virtual world of objects.

Don't forget that classes are templates for objects, which means that the classes shown in the figure are designed as blueprints for creating objects in the game. However, it's not until you actually create the objects themselves that they are able to exist in the virtual world and interact with one another. Again, the class is the cookie cutter, and the object is the cookie. So, the development of a game using OOP first involves designing classes for the various "things" in the game and then creating objects using those classes.

The beauty of the OOP approach to game development is that the game more or less runs itself once everything is in place. In other words, each object is responsible for handling its own business, so the game doesn't have to concern itself too much with what each object is doing; the game is just providing a framework in which the objects exist. This framework primarily consists of a game screen for the objects to be drawn on and a main game loop or update loop that tells the objects some time has passed. For creatures, this update would entail determining the direction in which to move and whether they should attack or run. For the main character, an update involves performing an action based on user input. The main point I'm trying to make is that objects are independent entities that basically know how to take care of themselves.

A more practical benefit of OOP design in games has to do with reusing code. Let's say that you've completed your fantasy adventure game we just talked about and would like to create a similar game set in outer space. Instead of starting over from scratch, you could take the objects you developed for the first game and reuse them in the new game. Granted, some changes would be in order, but many of the changes could be made by creating new subclasses, as opposed to rewriting the originals. Code reuse is certainly one of the most dramatic benefits to using an OOP approach to game development.

Exploring the Tools of the Trade

Before embarking on any game development project, it's important to assemble a set of tools that you will use to construct the game. Although there are a variety of different tools that could feasibly factor into the development of a complex game, the most critical tools are as follows:

- ▶ Compilers and development environments
- ▶ Graphics tools
- ▶ Sound and music tools

The next few sections take a look at these tools in greater detail.

Compilers and Development Environments

Regardless of what programming language you're using to develop games, you will likely need a compiler to turn the programming code into an executable game application. Because this book focuses on using C++ as the programming language for creating games for Windows, you'll need a C++ compiler that is capable of creating Windows applications using the Win32 API (Application Programming Interface). C++ compilers range from high-powered commercial development environments, such as Microsoft Visual Studio .NET and Borland C++BuilderX, to free compilers, such as Bloodshed Dev-C++ and DJGPP. Appendix A, "Selecting a Game Development Tool," provides more details on selecting a compiler for game development. The example games presented throughout the book can be compiled using any of these compilers.

Choosing a Graphics Tool

Similar to compilers, graphics tools range from high-end commercial tools to tools that you can download free; you can also use graphics tools built into Windows, such as Paint. If you decide to draw your graphics by hand, you will need to scan in the artwork and clean it up in a special tool. Of course, you'll need a scanner to scan in artwork, but those are fortunately very affordable. Even if you don't plan on drawing game graphics by hand, you'll need an image editing program or paint program, as they are often called. Paint is the standard image editor built into Windows, which is surprisingly useful for creating and editing basic game images.

At the other end of the spectrum are tools, such as Adobe Photoshop, which are used by graphics professionals to perform extremely powerful special effects on images. Middle-of-the-road options include Adobe Photoshop Elements, Jasc Paint Shop Pro, and Microsoft Digital Image Pro and offer many of the features of Photoshop at a more affordable price and a lesser learning curve. If you have Microsoft Office installed on your computer, you also likely have Microsoft Photo Editor installed, which is another useful image editing program.

Selecting Sound and Music Tools

You learned earlier in the chapter that sound effects used in games are typically sampled, which means that you record them using a microphone or maybe from an audio CD. The sound card on your computer has a line-in port and a microphone port—both of which can be used to sample sounds. You can use the built-in Sound Recorder application in Windows to sample sounds, or you can invest in a fancier commercial tool, such as Cool Edit Pro. Either way, the process is very straightforward: just hook up the sound source (microphone, CD player, and so on) and start recording using the sound editing software. You'll need to perform some cleanup on the sound after recording, such as removing extra noises that appear before and after the sound.

In addition to sampled sound effects, you might want to experiment with creating your own MIDI music. To do so, you must use another special tool known as a MIDI authoring tool. This kind of tool is different from a sound editor in that it is designed so that you enter musical compositions similar to what you see on a sheet of written music. You then assign instruments to different notes as if a band were playing the tune. A more intuitive approach to using a MIDI authoring tool is to connect a MIDI music keyboard to your computer and play the music on it. If your sound card has a MIDI port, and most of them do, the music you play will be recorded by the MIDI software and saved. You can then further arrange the music and alter the way it sounds.

Summary

Although you didn't get to wrap your hands around any example code, this chapter served as an important starting point for learning the basics of game development. The goal of this chapter was to help you direct your brain power toward the primary issues involved in designing a game at a conceptual level. You found out about the essential game design concepts required to get started down the path to creating your own games. You also learned about object-oriented programming (OOP) and why it is important for game development. The chapter concluded by introducing you to the different kinds of development tools commonly found in the arsenal of the game programmer.

Chapter 2, "Creating an Engine for Games," leads you straight into the development of a game engine that you will continue to enhance and reuse throughout the entire book. If you are new to Windows programming, I encourage you to take a timeout and read Appendix C, "A Windows Game Programming Primer," before moving on to Chapter 2. Fortunately, one of the goals behind creating the game engine is to allow you to focus only on the game-specific parts of your game programs, as opposed to the overhead code that is only there to satisfy Windows. However, your Windows programming knowledge is still important as you assemble the game engine and put it through its paces.

Field Trip

For your first field trip, it only makes sense to make a visit to your local computer store and explore the current offerings in the way of computer games. Granted, most commercial games are significantly more complex than the games you'll be creating in this book, but nevertheless, they represent what you should be ultimately striving for in terms of game creation. As you study the games on the shelf, pay particular attention to the different genres and how some games rely heavily on story, whereas others simply promote a particular type of game play. Don't be afraid to buy a game if you like it and have some fun playing it before you move on to the next chapter. Although I consider creating games to be more fun than playing them, you'll have a better idea of what makes a game fun if you continue to play games as you work your way toward becoming a seasoned game developer.

CHAPTER 2

Creating an Engine for Games

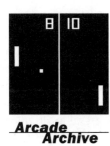

Arcade Archive

While Pong gets credit for being the first publicly identifiable video game, I think it's safe to say that Space Invaders was the first video game to really captivate the world's imagination. Released in 1978 by Taito, Space Invaders was the original vertical shooter that set the stage for many an alien shoot-em-up to come. Space Invaders enjoyed such frenzied popularity in Japan that the country encountered a coin shortage and had to quadruple its supply of yen. Space Invaders still lives on today in quite a few modern games, as well as in revamped 3D versions of the classic original. In 2004, the original stand-up Space Invaders arcade game was re-released so that it could be enjoyed by a new generation of gamers—to ensure that the game would continue to rake in quarters, the cost was increased to 50 cents per play.

A game is a specialized type of program, but it is still just a program written in a programming language. This means that you can create a game just as you would any other Windows program; for an example of a minimal graphical Windows program, check out the Skeleton application in Appendix C, "A Windows Game Programming Primer." Certain game-specific tasks must be carried out in all games. Therefore, it would be quite helpful to organize the code in your games so that the game-specific code is isolated from the general Windows application code. In isolating this code, it might also be useful to build in some cool features that apply solely to games. The idea I'm suggesting is that of a *game engine*, which is a grouping of program code that performs tasks common to games. This chapter guides you through the design and development of a game engine that you'll build on throughout the remainder of the book.

In this chapter, you'll learn

- ▶ The importance of a game engine in game development
- ▶ How to design and develop a basic game engine for Windows game programming
- ▶ How to create an example that demonstrates the power of the game engine

What Is a Game Engine?

Think about a few different games you like, and try to think of them in terms of how they might be designed under the hood. More importantly, see if you can figure out any common design elements that would apply to all the games. For example, do all the games have a background, a title screen, a geographical map, and background music? If so, it's possible that they are designed around the concept of a game engine. Game engines are particularly useful in situations in which you plan on creating more than one game, and you don't want to have to reinvent the wheel each time around. The idea is that you figure out what common functionality all games use, and you write it once and stick it in the game engine.

Another significant benefit of a game engine for Windows games is that it allows you to hide the messy details of Windows-specific code that doesn't necessarily have anything to do with a game. For example, virtually all the code in the Skeleton application in Appendix C has nothing to do with a game, but it's required of every Windows application. Rather than have you cut and paste this generic code to create a new game, I prefer hiding it in a game engine where you never have to fool with it again. You know it's there, but by not having to look at it, you're free to focus on the more important and fun parts of your game code.

In case you're wondering, there's nothing magical or mysterious about a game engine. A game engine represents an organization of the code for a game so that general application tasks are separated from game-specific tasks. The benefit to the game developer is that you can add features to a game engine that you will be able to reuse in all of your future games. Additionally, using a game engine allows you to simplify the code for your games and focus your attention on the game code that matters most. Once you get accustomed to using a game engine, you'll wonder how games could be created any other way. In reality, most commercial game developers do have their own custom game engines that they've developed over years of learning what common features most games require.

Your own game engine will likely improve and expand upon the game engine in this book as you design and develop more demanding games.

Pondering the Role of a Game Engine

It is the responsibility of a game engine to handle the chores of setting up a game, making sure that it runs properly, and then shutting it down. Although it is true that these tasks are required of any program, certain aspects of initializing, running, and cleaning up after games are truly unique to games. Therefore, it is important for a game engine to address the unique needs of games and help make the process of building games around the engine as simple and straightforward as possible. With a well-designed game engine, you'll find that creating a game requires a lot less code than if you had not relied on a game engine. The idea is to develop certain core game routines once, stick them in the game engine, and then never bother with them again unless absolutely necessary. For example, once you've written code to load an image and draw it on the screen, there is never a reason to rewrite the code again. Loading and drawing images is a basic feature required of all game engines.

> As time and resources allow, you might choose to optimize certain algorithms within your game engine to help make it run more efficiently. Generally speaking, the first goal is to get a game feature working properly and then worry about optimizing it later as you have time.

Construction Cue

Breaking a Game Down into Events

Every Windows program can be broken down into events, which are things that take place while a program is running, such as mouse clicks and window resizes. Just as Windows programs have events that they must handle, games have their own unique set of events that must be taken into consideration during development. The initialization process of a game can be considered an event, and its responsibilities are to load graphics and sounds for the game, clear the playing field, zero out the score, and so on. Similarly, user input carries over to games as well, meaning that mouse clicks and key presses are events that games certainly must concern themselves with. Additionally, keep in mind that, in Windows, it's possible for some games to be minimized or otherwise placed into the background, which means that you'll probably want to pause the game. This activation and reactivation process can be represented by a couple of events.

Gamer's Garage

Many commercial Windows games run only in full-screen mode, which means that they can't be tiled visually with other running Windows applications. Even so, these games are technically still running alongside other programs and, therefore, must be able to pause themselves if another application takes center stage.

Although many other events could certainly factor into a game engine, the following are some of the core events applicable to just about any game:

▶ Initialization

▶ Start

▶ End

▶ Activation

▶ Deactivation

▶ Paint

▶ Cycle

The initialization event occurs when a game is first launched and gives a game a chance to perform critical initial setup tasks, including creating the game engine itself. The start and end events correspond to the start and end of a game, and they provide good places to perform initialization and cleanup tasks associated with a specific game session. The activation and deactivation events come into play when a game is minimized or sent to the background and then later restored. The paint event is sent when a game needs to draw itself and is similar to the Windows WM_PAINT message. Finally, the cycle event enables a game to perform a single game cycle, which is very important, as you learn next.

Establishing the Timing for Games

If you've never taken a look at a game from a programming perspective, it might surprise you to learn how all the movement and the animation in a game are orchestrated. You will learn all the details of animated graphics in Chapter 9, "Making Things Move with Sprite Animation," but for now, I want to touch on the importance of game timing as it applies to animation and other facets of games. Every game, except extremely simple card games, relies on some sort of timing mechanism to enable the game to break down its execution into frames or cycles. A *cycle* of a game is one slice of time, which usually corresponds to a snapshot of the game's graphics and data. If you think of a game as a movie playing on a VCR or DVD player, pressing Pause allows you to view a single cycle. Stepping forward one frame in the video is like moving to the next cycle of the game. In any given cycle, a game takes care of updating its graphics, as well as performing any other calculations and processing related to how characters and objects are moving and interacting with each other.

A good way to get a grasp on the importance of game cycles is to take a practical game as an example. The classic Space Invaders game was mentioned in the opener of this chapter, so let's use it as an example to demonstrate game cycles. When Space Invaders first starts, the ship is created, along with several rows of alien invaders. Each of these objects has an initial position and velocity. If Space Invaders had no timing or game cycles, the game would be forever frozen in its initial state, as if you had pressed a permanent Pause button when the game started. We know that this isn't the case, however, because the game starts out with the aliens slowly moving across the screen. If you were to view Space Invaders a cycle at a time, you would notice that, in each cycle, the aliens are only moved slightly. This is because there happen to be quite a few cycles taking place in a given period of time, which gives the effect of smooth motion. Figure 2.1 shows a few hypothetical cycles of Space Invaders and how the aliens move ever so slightly, along with a shot fired by the player's ship.

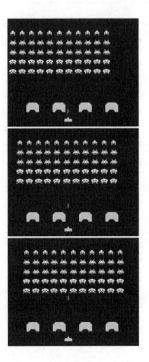

FIGURE 2.1
A few cycles of a hypothetical Space Invaders game reveals how the objects in the game change slightly with each cycle.

Figure 2.1 reveals how each cycle of the Space Invaders game reflects a small change in the state of the objects in the game. Therefore, the role of a game cycle is to update the status of all the objects in the game and then reflect these changes by updating the graphics shown on the screen. Judging by how fast things are visibly changing in most games, can you guess how often game cycles take place? Even the most sluggish of games includes no less than 12 cycles per second, which is incidentally the minimum rate required to trick your eyes into thinking that they are seeing movement instead of a series of changing images. As a comparison, televisions display 30 different images (cycles) per second, whereas motion pictures rely on 24 images per second. You learn much more about the significance of different rates of animation in Chapter 9. For now, it's important to understand that just about every game is highly dependent on periodic cycles.

Gamer's Garage

A single screen of graphics in a game is known as a *frame*. Because a new screen of graphics is drawn during each game cycle, the speed of games is often measured in *frames per second*, or *fps*. Because the discussion in this chapter is centered on cycles, as opposed to frames, I refer to game speeds in *cycles per second*. However, cycles per second, frames per second, and even images per second are really the same measurement.

The more cycles a game can run through in a given amount of time, the smoother the game appears to run. As an extreme example, compare the "smoothness" of a slideshow to a motion picture. The slideshow abruptly moves from one still image to another with no transition or sense of smooth movement, whereas a motion picture shows fluid motion as if you were experiencing it in real-time. Similarly, a game with only a few cycles per second will appear choppy, whereas a higher number of cycles per second will result in a much smoother game. A larger number of cycles per second also gives you more flexibility in speeding up or slowing down a game to arrive at a perfect speed.

Knowing that more cycles result in smoother graphics and better flexibility, you might think that you could crank up the cycles per second really high. As with most things in life, there is a trade-off when it comes to game cycles and game efficiency. The problem lies in the fact that the amount of processing taking place in a game in each cycle is often considerable, which means that to perform numerous cycles per second, your computer's processor and graphics card have to be able to keep up. Even with the blazingly fast computers prevalent these days, there are practical limitations as to how fast most computers can perform game processing. In reality, most games will fall in the range of 15 to 20 cycles per second, with a maximum speed surpassing that of a motion picture at 30 cycles per second. Except for some rare situations, the minimum speed you should shoot for is 12 cycles per second.

Commercial 3D games are always pushing the envelope of what is possible given the current computer hardware available. The number of cycles per second for a modern 3D game is the most common measurement used to determine if the game is being too ambitious in terms of how much it is taxing the processing capabilities of the computer. In an ideal world, you would design games with beautifully detailed graphics and not worry about whether the game brings a user's system to a screeching halt. In reality, game designers are always walking a tight rope to make games look incredibly good yet still maintain a decent frame rate (ideally, 30fps or more).

Now that you understand how the timing of a game is expressed in terms of cycles, you can probably see why a cycle is a type of game event. It works like this: When a game first starts, you initialize the game engine with the game speed in cycles per second. Let's say that you go with 12 cycles per second. The game engine is then responsible for setting up and managing a timer that fires a cycle event 12 times each second. The game code receives these cycle messages and handles them by updating the objects in the game and redrawing the game screen. You can think of a cycle event as a snooze alarm that keeps going off over and over; except in this case, it's going off 12 times a second. Your game clearly isn't getting much sleep!

Speaking of sleep, another role of a game engine is to put a game to sleep whenever it is no longer the active window. In practical terms, putting a game to sleep simply means that the game engine stops sending cycle messages. Because no cycle messages are being sent, the game is effectively paused.

Developing a Game Engine

You now understand enough about what a game engine needs to accomplish that you can start assembling your own. In this section, you create the game engine that will be used to create all the games throughout the remainder of the book. Not only that, but also you'll be refining and adding cool new features to the game engine as you develop those games. By the end of the book, you'll have a powerful game engine ready to be deployed in your own game projects.

If you're accustomed to reading books that give you every little piece of code to type in and try out as you go, I should caution you that I don't list every line of code in this book. Certain pieces of code just aren't that important in the context of game programming (but are nonetheless required of all Windows programs), and I'd rather not burden you with long code listings when you can learn what you need to learn from a smaller snippet of code. The CD-ROM accompanying the book has the complete source code for every example in the book, so the code is there for you to sift through if you want to explore every little nuance. You'll also need the complete source code to build the examples; more on this later.

The point to this little discussion is that it isn't necessary for you to take in every line of code in order to learn how to reuse the code in this book to create your own games. Therefore, understand as you work through the rest of the book that the focus is on showing you the most interesting and significant code so that you have the knowledge to run with it and carry out your own game creations. Having said all of this, I do show you all the code for the game engine once I've presented the bits and pieces that go into it.

The Game Event Functions

The first place to start in creating a game engine is to create handler functions that correspond to the game events mentioned earlier in the chapter. When an event occurs in a game, the corresponding event handler function will be called, which gives your game a chance to respond accordingly. The following are these functions, which should make some sense to you because they correspond directly to the game events:

```
BOOL GameInitialize(HINSTANCE hInstance);
void GameStart(HWND hWindow);
void GameEnd();
void GameActivate(HWND hWindow);
void GameDeactivate(HWND hWindow);
void GamePaint(HDC hDC);
void GameCycle();
```

The first function, GameInitialize(), is probably the only one that needs special explanation simply because of the argument that gets sent into it. I'm referring to the hInstance argument, which is of type HINSTANCE. This is a Win32 data type that refers to an application instance. An *application instance* is basically a program that has been loaded into memory and is running in Windows. If you've ever used Alt+Tab to switch between running applications in Windows, you're familiar with different application instances. The HINSTANCE data type is a handle to an application instance, and it is very important because it enables a program to access its resources since they are stored with the application in memory.

The GameEngine Class

The game event handler functions are actually separated from the game engine itself, even though there is a close tie between them. This is necessary because it is organizationally better to place the game engine in its own C++ class. This class is called GameEngine and is shown in Listing 2.1.

Construction Cue

If you were trying to adhere strictly to object-oriented design principles, you would place the game event handler functions in the GameEngine class as virtual methods to be overridden. However, although that would represent good OOP design, it would also make it a little messier to assemble a game because you would have to derive your own custom game engine class from GameEngine in every game. By using functions for the event handlers, you simplify the coding of games at the expense of breaking an OOP design rule. Such are the trade-offs of game programming.

LISTING 2.1 The GameEngine Class Definition Reveals How the Game Engine Is Designed

```
class GameEngine
{
protected:
  // Member Variables
  static GameEngine*  m_pGameEngine;
  HINSTANCE           m_hInstance;
  HWND                m_hWindow;
  TCHAR               m_szWindowClass[32];
  TCHAR               m_szTitle[32];
  WORD                m_wIcon, m_wSmallIcon;
  int                 m_iWidth, m_iHeight;
  int                 m_iFrameDelay;
  BOOL                m_bSleep;

public:
  // Constructor(s)/Destructor
          GameEngine(HINSTANCE hInstance, LPTSTR szWindowClass, LPTSTR szTitle,
              WORD wIcon, WORD wSmallIcon, int iWidth = 640, int iHeight = 480);
  virtual ~GameEngine();

  // General Methods
  static GameEngine*  GetEngine() { return m_pGameEngine; };
  BOOL                Initialize(int iCmdShow);
  LRESULT             HandleEvent(HWND hWindow, UINT msg, WPARAM wParam,
                        LPARAM lParam);

  // Accessor Methods
  HINSTANCE GetInstance() { return m_hInstance; };
  HWND      GetWindow() { return m_hWindow; };
  void      SetWindow(HWND hWindow) { m_hWindow = hWindow; };
  LPTSTR    GetTitle() { return m_szTitle; };
  WORD      GetIcon() { return m_wIcon; };
  WORD      GetSmallIcon() { return m_wSmallIcon; };
```

The game engine member variables keep track of important information such as the game's title, icons, width, height, frame delay, and sleep status.

The game engine constructor creates a game with a default screen size of 640x480, which is the actual game playing area.

continues

*You specify the
frame rate in
frames per second,
which means that a
value of 30 results
in the game run-
ning at 30 frames
per second (fps).*

LISTING 2.1   Continued

```
int        GetWidth() { return m_iWidth; };
int        GetHeight() { return m_iHeight; };
int        GetFrameDelay() { return m_iFrameDelay; };
void       SetFrameRate(int iFrameRate) { m_iFrameDelay = 1000 /
                iFrameRate; };
BOOL       GetSleep() { return m_bSleep; };
void       SetSleep(BOOL bSleep) { m_bSleep = bSleep; };
};
```

The GameEngine class definition reveals a subtle variable naming convention that you might or might not be familiar with. This naming convention involves naming member variables of a class with an initial m_ to indicate that they are class members. Additionally, global variables are named with a leading g_ to indicate that they are globals. This convention is useful because it helps you to immediately distinguish between local variables, member variables, and global variables in a program. The member variables for the GameEngine class all take advantage of this naming convention.

The GameEngine class defines a static pointer to itself, m_pGameEngine, which is used for outside access by a game program. The application instance and main window handles of the game program are stored away in the game engine using the m_hInstance and m_hWindow member variables. The name of the window class and the title of the main game window are stored in the m_szWindowClass and m_szTitle member variables. The numeric IDs of the two program icons for the game are stored in the m_wIcon and m_wSmallIcon members. The width and height of the game screen are stored in the m_iWidth and m_iHeight members. It's important to note that this width and height correspond to the size of the game screen, or play area, not the size of the overall program window, which is larger to accommodate borders, a title bar, menus, and so on. The m_iFrameDelay member variable indicates the amount of time between game cycles in milliseconds. Finally, m_bSleep is a Boolean member variable that indicates whether the game is sleeping (paused).

Construction Cue

If the naming convention of preceding variable names with characters to indicate their variable type is unfamiliar to you, take a quick look at "Unconventional Coding Conventions" in Appendix C. The idea is to use one or two characters to convey the data type of a variable; for example, m_iWidth is a member variable of type integer (i), whereas m_szTitle is a member variable that is a null-terminated string (string with a trailing zero).

The `GameEngine` constructor and destructor are defined after the member variables, as you might expect. The constructor is very important because it accepts arguments that dramatically impact the game being created. More specifically, the `GameEngine()` constructor accepts an instance handle, window classname, title, icon ID, small icon ID, width, and height. Notice that the `iWidth` and `iHeight` arguments default to values of `640` and `480`, respectively, which is a reasonable minimum size for game screens. The `~GameEngine()` destructor doesn't do anything, but it's worth defining in case you need to add some cleanup code to it later.

I mentioned that the `GameEngine` class maintains a static pointer to itself. This pointer is accessed from outside the engine using the static `GetEngine()` method. The `Initialize()` method is another important general method in the `GameEngine` class, and its job is to initialize the game program once the engine is created. The `HandleEvent()` method is responsible for handling standard Windows events within the game engine and is a good example of how the game engine hides the details of generic Windows code from game code.

The remaining methods in the `GameEngine` class are *accessor methods* used to access member variables; these methods are all used to get and set member variables. The one accessor method to pay special attention to is `SetFrameRate()`, which sets the frame rate or number of cycles per second of the game engine. Because the actual member variable that controls the number of game cycles per second is `m_iFrameDelay`, which is measured in milliseconds, it's necessary to perform a quick calculation to convert the frame rate in `SetFrameRate()` to milliseconds.

The source code for the `GameEngine` class provides implementations for the methods described in the header that you just saw, as well as the standard `WinMain()` and `WndProc()` functions that tie into the game engine. The `GameEngine` source code also initializes the static game engine pointer, like this:

```
GameEngine *GameEngine::m_pGameEngine = NULL;
```

Listing 2.2 contains the source code for the game engine's `WinMain()` function.

LISTING 2.2   The `WinMain()` Function in the Game Engine Makes Calls to Game Engine Functions and Methods and Provides a Neat Way of Separating Standard Windows Program Code from Game Code

```
int WINAPI WinMain(HINSTANCE hInstance, HINSTANCE hPrevInstance,
  PSTR szCmdLine, int iCmdShow)
{
  MSG         msg;
  static int  iTickTrigger = 0;
  int         iTickCount;
```

continues

LISTING 2.2   Continued

First, initialize the game with a call to GameInitialize().

```
if (GameInitialize(hInstance))
{
  // Initialize the game engine
  if (!GameEngine::GetEngine()->Initialize(iCmdShow))
    return FALSE;

  // Enter the main message loop
  while (TRUE)
  {
    if (PeekMessage(&msg, NULL, 0, 0, PM_REMOVE))
    {
      // Process the message
      if (msg.message == WM_QUIT)
        break;
      TranslateMessage(&msg);
      DispatchMessage(&msg);
    }
    else
    {
      // Make sure the game engine isn't sleeping
      if (!GameEngine::GetEngine()->GetSleep())
      {
```

This section of code is where the timing of the game is established.

```
        // Check the tick count to see if a game cycle has elapsed
        iTickCount = GetTickCount();
        if (iTickCount > iTickTrigger)
        {
          iTickTrigger = iTickCount +
            GameEngine::GetEngine()->GetFrameDelay();
          GameCycle();
        }
      }
    }
  }
  return (int)msg.wParam;
}
```

Wrap things up with a call to GameEnd().

```
// End the game
GameEnd();

return TRUE;
}
```

Although this WinMain() function is similar to those found in every Windows application, there is an important difference. The difference has to do with the fact that this WinMain() function establishes a game loop that takes care of generating game cycle events at a specified interval. The smallest unit of time measurement in a Windows program is called a *tick*, which is equivalent to one millisecond and is useful in performing accurate timing tasks. In this case, WinMain() counts ticks in order to determine when it should notify the game that a new cycle is in order. The iTickTrigger and iTickCount variables are used to establish the game cycle timing in WinMain().

The first function called in WinMain() is GameInitialize(), which gives the game a chance to be initialized. Remember that GameInitialize() is a game event function provided as part of the game-specific code for the game; therefore, it isn't a direct part of the game engine. A method that is part of the game engine is Initialize(), which is called to get the game engine itself initialized. From there, WinMain() enters the main message loop for the game program. The else part of the main message loop is where things get interesting. This part of the loop first checks to make sure that the game isn't sleeping and then uses the frame delay for the game engine to count ticks and determine when to call the GameCycle() function to trigger a game cycle event. WinMain() finishes up by calling GameEnd() to give the game program a chance to wrap up the game and clean up after itself.

The other standard Windows function included in the game engine is WndProc(), which is very simple because the HandleEvent() method of the GameEngine class is responsible for processing Windows messages:

```
LRESULT CALLBACK WndProc(HWND hWindow, UINT msg, WPARAM wParam, LPARAM lParam)
{
  // Route all Windows messages to the game engine
  return GameEngine::GetEngine()->HandleEvent(hWindow, msg, wParam, lParam);
}
```

All WndProc() really does is pass along all messages to HandleEvent(), which might at first seem like a waste of time. However, the idea is to allow a method of the GameEngine class to handle the messages so that they can be processed in a manner that is consistent with the game engine.

Speaking of the GameEngine class, now that you have a feel for the support functions in the game engine, we can move right along and examine specific code in the GameEngine class. Listing 2.3 contains the source code for the GameEngine() constructor and destructor.

LISTING 2.3 The `GameEngine::GameEngine()` Constructor Takes Care of Initializing Game Engine Member Variables, Whereas the Destructor is Left Empty for Possible Future Use

```
GameEngine::GameEngine(HINSTANCE hInstance, LPTSTR szWindowClass,
  LPTSTR szTitle, WORD wIcon, WORD wSmallIcon, int iWidth, int iHeight)
{
  // Set the member variables for the game engine
  m_pGameEngine = this;
  m_hInstance = hInstance;
  m_hWindow = NULL;
  if (lstrlen(szWindowClass) > 0)
    lstrcpy(m_szWindowClass, szWindowClass);
  if (lstrlen(szTitle) > 0)
    lstrcpy(m_szTitle, szTitle);
  m_wIcon = wIcon;
  m_wSmallIcon = wSmallIcon;
  m_iWidth = iWidth;
  m_iHeight = iHeight;
  m_iFrameDelay = 50;   // 20 FPS default
  m_bSleep = TRUE;
}

GameEngine::~GameEngine()
{
}
```

A speed of 20 frames per second is a reasonable default for most games, although you can certainly fine-tune it if you want.

The `GameEngine()` constructor is relatively straightforward in that it sets all the member variables for the game engine. The only member variable whose setting might seem a little strange at first is `m_iFrameDelay`, which is set to a default frame delay of 50 milliseconds. You can determine the number of frames (cycles) per second for the game by dividing 1,000 by the frame delay, which in this case results in 20 frames per second. This is a reasonable default for most games, although specific testing might reveal that it needs to be tweaked up or down. Keep in mind that you should always shoot for the highest frame rate (lowest frame delay) possible that allows your game to run smoothly; you don't want to see a game slowing down because it can't keep up with a high frame rate.

The `Initialize()` method in the `GameEngine` class is used to initialize the game engine. More specifically, the `Initialize()` method now performs a great deal of the messy Windows setup tasks, such as creating a window class for the main game window and then creating a window from the class. Listing 2.4 shows the code for the `Initialize()` method.

LISTING 2.4   The `GameEngine::Initialize()` Method Handles Some of the Dirty Work that Usually Takes Place in `WinMain()`

```
BOOL GameEngine::Initialize(int iCmdShow)
{
  WNDCLASSEX    wndclass;

  // Create the window class for the main window
  wndclass.cbSize        = sizeof(wndclass);
  wndclass.style         = CS_HREDRAW | CS_VREDRAW;
  wndclass.lpfnWndProc   = WndProc;
  wndclass.cbClsExtra    = 0;
  wndclass.cbWndExtra    = 0;
  wndclass.hInstance     = m_hInstance;
  wndclass.hIcon         = LoadIcon(m_hInstance,
    MAKEINTRESOURCE(GetIcon()));
  wndclass.hIconSm       = LoadIcon(m_hInstance,
    MAKEINTRESOURCE(GetSmallIcon()));
  wndclass.hCursor       = LoadCursor(NULL, IDC_ARROW);
  wndclass.hbrBackground = (HBRUSH)(COLOR_WINDOW + 1);
  wndclass.lpszMenuName  = NULL;
  wndclass.lpszClassName = m_szWindowClass;

  // Register the window class
  if (!RegisterClassEx(&wndclass))
    return FALSE;

  // Calculate the window size and position based upon the game size
  int iWindowWidth = m_iWidth + GetSystemMetrics(SM_CXFIXEDFRAME) * 2,
      iWindowHeight = m_iHeight + GetSystemMetrics(SM_CYFIXEDFRAME) * 2 +
        GetSystemMetrics(SM_CYCAPTION);
  if (wndclass.lpszMenuName != NULL)
    iWindowHeight += GetSystemMetrics(SM_CYMENU);
  int iXWindowPos = (GetSystemMetrics(SM_CXSCREEN) - iWindowWidth) / 2,
      iYWindowPos = (GetSystemMetrics(SM_CYSCREEN) - iWindowHeight) / 2;

  // Create the window
  m_hWindow = CreateWindow(m_szWindowClass, m_szTitle, WS_POPUPWINDOW |
    WS_CAPTION | WS_MINIMIZEBOX, iXWindowPos, iYWindowPos, iWindowWidth,
    iWindowHeight, NULL, NULL, m_hInstance, NULL);
  if (!m_hWindow)
    return FALSE;

  // Show and update the window
  ShowWindow(m_hWindow, iCmdShow);
  UpdateWindow(m_hWindow);

  return TRUE;
}
```

This code allows you to specify the exact size of the actual game screen, as opposed to the size of the overall application window.

This code is similar to the Skeleton program example found in Appendix C, and it should be familiar to you if you've done any Windows programming using the Win32 API. An important thing to note in this code is how it determines the game application window size, which is calculated based on the size of the game client area. The GetSystemMetrics() Win32 function is called to get various standard window sizes, such as the width and height of the window frame, as well as the menu height. The position of the game application window is then calculated so that the game is centered on the screen.

The window styles used to describe the main game window are WS_POPUPWINDOW, WS_CAPTION, and WS_MINIMIZEBOX, which result in a window that is not resizable and can't be maximized; however, it does have a menu and can be minimized.

The Initialize() method is a perfect example of isolating generic Windows program code and moving it into the game engine. Another example of this approach is the HandleEvent() method, which is shown in Listing 2.5.

LISTING 2.5   The GameEngine::HandleEvent() **Method Receives and Handles Messages that Are Normally Handled in** WndProc()

```
LRESULT GameEngine::HandleEvent(HWND hWindow, UINT msg, WPARAM wParam,
  LPARAM lParam)
{
  // Route Windows messages to game engine member functions
  switch (msg)
  {
    case WM_CREATE:
      // Set the game window and start the game
      SetWindow(hWindow);
      GameStart(hWindow);
      return 0;

    case WM_SETFOCUS:
      // Activate the game and update the Sleep status
      GameActivate(hWindow);
      SetSleep(FALSE);
      return 0;

    case WM_KILLFOCUS:
      // Deactivate the game and update the Sleep status
      GameDeactivate(hWindow);
      SetSleep(TRUE);
      return 0;

    case WM_PAINT:
      HDC         hDC;
      PAINTSTRUCT ps;
      hDC = BeginPaint(hWindow, &ps);

      // Paint the game
```

Start the game in response to the WM_CREATE message.

```
      GamePaint(hDC);

      EndPaint(hWindow, &ps);
      return 0;

    case WM_DESTROY:
      // End the game and exit the application
      GameEnd();
      PostQuitMessage(0);
      return 0;
  }
  return DefWindowProc(hWindow, msg, wParam, lParam);
}
```

Paint the game in response to the WM_PAINT message.

End the game in response to the WM_DESTROY message.

The HandleEvent() method contains a switch statement that picks out Windows messages and responds to them individually. The HandleEvent() method also makes calls to game engine functions whose implementations are specific to each different game. First, the WM_CREATE message is handled, which is sent whenever the main game window is first created. The handler code for this message sets the window handle in the game engine and then calls the GameStart() game event function to get the game initialized.

The WM_SETFOCUS and WM_KILLFOCUS messages inform the game whenever its window receives (activated) or loses (deactivated) the input focus, respectively. If the game window is being activated (gains focus), the GameActivate() function is called, and the game is awoken. Similarly, if the game window is being deactivated (loses focus), the GameDeactivate() function is called, and the game is put to sleep.

The remaining messages in the HandleEvent() method are pretty straightforward in that they primarily call game functions. The WM_PAINT message handler calls the standard Win32 BeginPaint() function followed by the GamePaint() function. The EndPaint() function is then called to finish up the painting process; you learn a great deal more about BeginPaint() and EndPaint() in the next chapter. Finally, the WM_DESTROY handler calls the GameEnd() function and then terminates the whole program.

To help put all this game engine code into perspective, check out Listings 2.6 and 2.7, which contain the complete GameEngine.h header and GameEngine.cpp source code files. Please note that you don't need to understand every little nuance of this code in order to build games based on it. It will make much more sense as you get comfortable using it to build games throughout the book.

LISTING 2.6   The Complete GameEngine.h Header Code

```
#pragma once

//------------------------------------
// Include Files
//------------------------------------
#include <windows.h>

//------------------------------------
// Windows Function Declarations
//------------------------------------
int WINAPI        WinMain(HINSTANCE hInstance, HINSTANCE hPrevInstance,
                     PSTR szCmdLine, int iCmdShow);
LRESULT CALLBACK  WndProc(HWND hWnd, UINT msg, WPARAM wParam, LPARAM lParam);

//------------------------------------
// Game Engine Function Declarations
//------------------------------------
BOOL GameInitialize(HINSTANCE hInstance);
void GameStart(HWND hWindow);
void GameEnd();
void GameActivate(HWND hWindow);
void GameDeactivate(HWND hWindow);
void GamePaint(HDC hDC);
void GameCycle();

//------------------------------------
// GameEngine Class
//------------------------------------
class GameEngine
{
protected:
  // Member Variables
  static GameEngine*  m_pGameEngine;
  HINSTANCE           m_hInstance;
  HWND                m_hWindow;
  TCHAR               m_szWindowClass[32];
  TCHAR               m_szTitle[32];
  WORD                m_wIcon, m_wSmallIcon;
  int                 m_iWidth, m_iHeight;
  int                 m_iFrameDelay;
  BOOL                m_bSleep;

public:
  // Constructor(s)/Destructor
        GameEngine(HINSTANCE hInstance, LPTSTR szWindowClass, LPTSTR szTitle,
            WORD wIcon, WORD wSmallIcon, int iWidth = 640, int iHeight = 480);
  virtual ~GameEngine();

  // General Methods
  static GameEngine*  GetEngine() { return m_pGameEngine; };
  BOOL                Initialize(int iCmdShow);
  LRESULT             HandleEvent(HWND hWindow, UINT msg, WPARAM wParam,
                        LPARAM lParam);

  // Accessor Methods
```

The specific implementations of these functions are game-specific and must be provided by each game that uses the game engine.

```
HINSTANCE GetInstance() { return m_hInstance; };
HWND      GetWindow() { return m_hWindow; };
void      SetWindow(HWND hWindow) { m_hWindow = hWindow; };
LPTSTR    GetTitle() { return m_szTitle; };
WORD      GetIcon() { return m_wIcon; };
WORD      GetSmallIcon() { return m_wSmallIcon; };
int       GetWidth() { return m_iWidth; };
int       GetHeight() { return m_iHeight; };
int       GetFrameDelay() { return m_iFrameDelay; };
void      SetFrameRate(int iFrameRate) { m_iFrameDelay = 1000 /
            iFrameRate; };
BOOL      GetSleep() { return m_bSleep; };
void      SetSleep(BOOL bSleep) { m_bSleep = bSleep; };
};
```

LISTING 2.7   The Complete `GameEngine.cpp` Source Code

```
#include "GameEngine.h"

//---------------------------------------·
// Static Variable Initialization
//---------------------------------------·
GameEngine *GameEngine::m_pGameEngine = NULL;

//---------------------------------------·
// Windows Functions
//---------------------------------------·
int WINAPI WinMain(HINSTANCE hInstance, HINSTANCE hPrevInstance,
  PSTR szCmdLine, int iCmdShow)
{
  MSG        msg;
  static int iTickTrigger = 0;
  int        iTickCount;

  if (GameInitialize(hInstance))
  {
    // Initialize the game engine
    if (!GameEngine::GetEngine()->Initialize(iCmdShow))
      return FALSE;

    // Enter the main message loop
    while (TRUE)
    {
      if (PeekMessage(&msg, NULL, 0, 0, PM_REMOVE))
      {
        // Process the message
        if (msg.message == WM_QUIT)
          break;
        TranslateMessage(&msg);
        DispatchMessage(&msg);
      }
      else
      {
        // Make sure the game engine isn't sleeping
        if (!GameEngine::GetEngine()->GetSleep())
```

continues

LISTING 2.7   Continued

```
      {
        // Check the tick count to see if a game cycle has elapsed
        iTickCount = GetTickCount();
        if (iTickCount > iTickTrigger)
        {
          iTickTrigger = iTickCount +
            GameEngine::GetEngine()->GetFrameDelay();
          GameCycle();
        }
      }
    }
  }
  return (int)msg.wParam;
}

// End the game
GameEnd();

return TRUE;
}

LRESULT CALLBACK WndProc(HWND hWindow, UINT msg, WPARAM wParam, LPARAM lParam)
{
  // Route all Windows messages to the game engine
  return GameEngine::GetEngine()->HandleEvent(hWindow, msg, wParam, lParam);
}

//--------------------------------------
// GameEngine Constructor(s)/Destructor
//--------------------------------------
GameEngine::GameEngine(HINSTANCE hInstance, LPTSTR szWindowClass,
  LPTSTR szTitle, WORD wIcon, WORD wSmallIcon, int iWidth, int iHeight)
{
  // Set the member variables for the game engine
  m_pGameEngine = this;
  m_hInstance = hInstance;
  m_hWindow = NULL;
  if (lstrlen(szWindowClass) > 0)
    lstrcpy(m_szWindowClass, szWindowClass);
  if (lstrlen(szTitle) > 0)
    lstrcpy(m_szTitle, szTitle);
  m_wIcon = wIcon;
  m_wSmallIcon = wSmallIcon;
  m_iWidth = iWidth;
  m_iHeight = iHeight;
  m_iFrameDelay = 50;    // 20 FPS default
  m_bSleep = TRUE;
}

GameEngine::~GameEngine()
{
}

//--------------------------------------
```

```
// Game Engine General Methods
//— — — — — — — — — — — — — — — — — — — — — — — — — — — — — — —·
BOOL GameEngine::Initialize(int iCmdShow)
{
  WNDCLASSEX    wndclass;

  // Create the window class for the main window
  wndclass.cbSize         = sizeof(wndclass);
  wndclass.style          = CS_HREDRAW | CS_VREDRAW;
  wndclass.lpfnWndProc    = WndProc;
  wndclass.cbClsExtra     = 0;
  wndclass.cbWndExtra     = 0;
  wndclass.hInstance      = m_hInstance;
  wndclass.hIcon          = LoadIcon(m_hInstance,
    MAKEINTRESOURCE(GetIcon()));
  wndclass.hIconSm        = LoadIcon(m_hInstance,
    MAKEINTRESOURCE(GetSmallIcon()));
  wndclass.hCursor        = LoadCursor(NULL, IDC_ARROW);
  wndclass.hbrBackground  = (HBRUSH)(COLOR_WINDOW + 1);
  wndclass.lpszMenuName   = NULL;
  wndclass.lpszClassName  = m_szWindowClass;

  // Register the window class
  if (!RegisterClassEx(&wndclass))
    return FALSE;

  // Calculate the window size and position based upon the game size
  int iWindowWidth = m_iWidth + GetSystemMetrics(SM_CXFIXEDFRAME) * 2,
      iWindowHeight = m_iHeight + GetSystemMetrics(SM_CYFIXEDFRAME) * 2 +
        GetSystemMetrics(SM_CYCAPTION);
  if (wndclass.lpszMenuName != NULL)
    iWindowHeight += GetSystemMetrics(SM_CYMENU);
  int iXWindowPos = (GetSystemMetrics(SM_CXSCREEN) - iWindowWidth) / 2,
      iYWindowPos = (GetSystemMetrics(SM_CYSCREEN) - iWindowHeight) / 2;

  // Create the window
  m_hWindow = CreateWindow(m_szWindowClass, m_szTitle, WS_POPUPWINDOW |
    WS_CAPTION | WS_MINIMIZEBOX, iXWindowPos, iYWindowPos, iWindowWidth,
    iWindowHeight, NULL, NULL, m_hInstance, NULL);
  if (!m_hWindow)
    return FALSE;

  // Show and update the window
  ShowWindow(m_hWindow, iCmdShow);
  UpdateWindow(m_hWindow);

  return TRUE;
}

LRESULT GameEngine::HandleEvent(HWND hWindow, UINT msg, WPARAM wParam,
➥ LPARAM lParam)
{
  // Route Windows messages to game engine member functions
  switch (msg)
  {
    case WM_CREATE:
```

continues

LISTING 2.7   Continued

```
    // Set the game window and start the game
    SetWindow(hWindow);
    GameStart(hWindow);
    return 0;

  case WM_SETFOCUS:
    // Activate the game and update the Sleep status
    GameActivate(hWindow);
    SetSleep(FALSE);
    return 0;

  case WM_KILLFOCUS:
    // Deactivate the game and update the Sleep status
    GameDeactivate(hWindow);
    SetSleep(TRUE);
    return 0;

  case WM_PAINT:
    HDC        hDC;
    PAINTSTRUCT ps;
    hDC = BeginPaint(hWindow, &ps);

    // Paint the game
    GamePaint(hDC);

    EndPaint(hWindow, &ps);
    return 0;

  case WM_DESTROY:
    // End the game and exit the application
    GameEnd();
    PostQuitMessage(0);
    return 0;
  }
  return DefWindowProc(hWindow, msg, wParam, lParam);
}
```

You've now seen all the code for the game engine, which successfully hides generic Windows code while providing a basic framework for games. Let's now take a look at an example that puts this embryonic game engine to work.

Construction Cue

If you're a bit intimidated by seeing this much code in only the second chapter of the book, let me ease your concerns by explaining that building games on top of the game engine is more straightforward than building the game engine itself. You'll find that game code is made much simpler thanks to the work put into the game engine.

Building the Blizzard Example

The game engine you created in this chapter allows you to create games without having to repeat boilerplate Windows code that is required of every Windows program. In this section, you use the game engine to create a new example called Blizzard that demonstrates the absolute minimum requirements of a Windows game. You'll quickly realize that the Blizzard example is very easy to understand because the game engine hides most of the mess associated with Windows programs.

You'll be glad to know that the Blizzard example isn't just a remake of the Skeleton example from Appendix C with the game engine thrown in. Because the game engine includes support for establishing a game loop complete with timed game cycles, it only makes sense to take advantage of that feature. Therfore, the Blizzard example demonstrates the power of game cycles and how they make it possible to get interesting graphical effects with little effort. More specifically, you find out how to rapidly draw graphical icons (snowflakes) at random locations on the game screen and see firsthand how the speed of the game loop impacts the performance of the game.

Construction Cue

All the code for the Blizzard example—including project files for Visual Studio/C++ .NET, Borland C++Builder, and Bloodshed Dev-C++—is located on the accompanying CD-ROM. I encourage you to use the project files that I've provided because they contain the necessary settings for the examples to compile and link properly. Windows programs (especially games) can sometimes be tricky to set up in terms of getting the compiler and linker settings just right.

Writing the Program Code

The Blizzard example is divided into two source files: the Blizzard.h header file and the Blizzard.cpp source code file. Listing 2.8 contains the code for the Blizzard.h header file, which is relatively simple. Keep in mind that all the code for the Blizzard example is available on the accompanying CD-ROM.

Construction Cue

If you haven't yet installed a C++ development environment for Windows, please take a look at Appendix A, "Selecting a Game Development Tool." The accompanying CD-ROM includes source code files and project files for several popular development environments, such as Microsoft Visual C++ .NET, Borland C++Builder, and Bloodshed Dev-C++. It also includes executable versions of all the examples found in the book so that you can run them and test them out, even if you don't have a development tool installed yct.

LISTING 2.8   The Blizzard.h Header File Simply Imports a Few Header Files and Declares the Important Global Game Engine Pointer

```
//-------------------------------.
// Blizzard Application
// C++ Header - Blizzard.h
//-------------------------------.

#pragma once

//-------------------------------.
// Include Files
//-------------------------------.
#include <windows.h>
#include "Resource.h"
#include "GameEngine.h"

//-------------------------------.
// Global Variables
//-------------------------------.
GameEngine* g_pGame;
```

Every game based on the game engine requires a global game engine pointer.

This header file includes the familiar windows.h, as well as Resource.h and GameEngine.h. After importing these header files, a global game engine pointer, g_pGame, is defined. This pointer is very important because it will provide the Blizzard example access to the game engine.

The Resource.h header file is somewhat of a helper file that establishes identifiers for all the resources used throughout the program. In this case, the only resources are two icons of different sizes (16x16 and 32x32). Listing 2.9 contains the code for the Resource.h header file for the Blizzard example.

LISTING 2.9   The Resource.h Header File Declares Identifiers for Icons Used in the Blizzard Example

```
//-------------------------------.
// Icons                  Range : 1000 - 1999
//-------------------------------.
#define IDI_BLIZZARD        1000
#define IDI_BLIZZARD_SM     1001
```

Resources are typically numbered in certain ranges to make it easier to distinguish them from each other and to help ensure that they have unique values. As you get into more interesting examples throughout the book, you'll be adding additional types of resources to the Resource.h header file, such as bitmap images and wave sound resources.

Speaking of resources, the icons in the Blizzard example are listed in the Blizzard.rc resource script, which is shown in Listing 2.10.

LISTING 2.10   The Blizzard.rc Resource Script Lists Icon Resources Used in the Blizzard Example

```
#include "Resource.h"

//— — — — — — — — — — — — — — — — — — — — — — — — — — — — — —·
// Icons
//— — — — — — — — — — — — — — — — — — — — — — — — — — — — — —·
IDI_BLIZZARD       ICON       "Res\\Blizzard.ico"
IDI_BLIZZARD_SM    ICON       "Res\\Blizzard_sm.ico"
```

The Blizzard.rc resource script is where the resource identifiers in the Resource.h file are linked to actual resource files. In this example, the resource files are icon files, which is evident by their .ICO file extension. When you compile the Blizzard example, the resources listed in the Blizzard.rc resource script are compiled into binary form and are linked into the Blizzard.exe executable.

Now that you've gotten a look at the helper files that go into the Blizzard example, let's move on to the main source code. The main Blizzard program is fleshed out in the Blizzard.cpp source code file, which is shown in Listing 2.11

LISTING 2.11   The Blizzard.cpp Source Code File Reveals how Straightforward the Program Code for a Minimal Windows Program (Game) Becomes when a Game Engine Is Used

```
//— — — — — — — — — — — — — — — — — — — — — — — — — — — — —·
// Blizzard Application
// C++ Source - Blizzard.cpp
//— — — — — — — — — — — — — — — — — — — — — — — — — — — — —·

//— — — — — — — — — — — — — — — — — — — — — — — — — — — — —·
// Include Files
//— — — — — — — — — — — — — — — — — — — — — — — — — — — — —·
#include "Blizzard.h"

//— — — — — — — — — — — — — — — — — — — — — — — — — — — — —·
// Game Engine Functions
//— — — — — — — — — — — — — — — — — — — — — — — — — — — — —·
BOOL GameInitialize(HINSTANCE hInstance)
{
  // Create the game engine
  g_pGame = new GameEngine(hInstance, TEXT("Blizzard"),
    TEXT("Blizzard"), IDI_BLIZZARD, IDI_BLIZZARD_SM);
  if (g_pGame == NULL)
    return FALSE;

  // Set the frame rate
```

continues

LISTING 2.11   Continued

A framerate of 15 frames per second is a sufficient frame rate for this example, as opposed to the default setting of 20 fps.

If a game ever needs to call the standard rand() function to generate random numbers, you should always call the srand() function to seed the random number generator.

All the painting in this example takes place within the GameCycle() function, so there is no need to do anything in GamePaint()—this is a fairly rare scenario.

```cpp
  g_pGame->SetFrameRate(15);

  return TRUE;
}

void GameStart(HWND hWindow)
{
  // Seed the random number generator
  srand(GetTickCount());
}

void GameEnd()
{
  // Cleanup the game engine
  delete g_pGame;
}

void GameActivate(HWND hWindow)
{
  HDC   hDC;
  RECT  rect;

  // Draw activation text on the game screen
  GetClientRect(hWindow, &rect);
  hDC = GetDC(hWindow);
  DrawText(hDC, TEXT("Here comes the blizzard!"), -1, &rect,
    DT_SINGLELINE | DT_CENTER | DT_VCENTER);
  ReleaseDC(hWindow, hDC);
}

void GameDeactivate(HWND hWindow)
{
  HDC   hDC;
  RECT  rect;

  // Draw deactivation text on the game screen
  GetClientRect(hWindow, &rect);
  hDC = GetDC(hWindow);
  DrawText(hDC, TEXT("The blizzard has passed."), -1, &rect,
    DT_SINGLELINE | DT_CENTER | DT_VCENTER);
  ReleaseDC(hWindow, hDC);
}

void GamePaint(HDC hDC)
{
}

void GameCycle()
{
  HDC   hDC;
  HWND  hWindow = g_pGame->GetWindow();

  // Draw the snowflake icon at random positions on the game screen
    hDC = GetDC(hWindow);
```

```
DrawIcon(hDC, rand() % g_pGame->GetWidth(), rand() % g_pGame->GetHeight(),
    (HICON)(WORD)GetClassLong(hWindow, GCL_HICON));
ReleaseDC(hWindow, hDC);
}
```

Because you haven't learned how to draw bitmap images yet, this code draws icons instead.

The really interesting thing about the code for the Blizzard example is how the only functions present in the code are the game event functions described in GameEngine.h (refer to Listing 2.6). The first of these functions is GameInitialize(), whose responsibility is to get the program started off on the right foot. More specifically, the GameInitialize() function creates a GameEngine object and assigns it to the g_pGame global variable. The GameInitialize() function then sets the frame rate for the game to 15 frames per second, which is a little slower than the default setting of 20 frames per second. This change is primarily to demonstrate how you will often change the default frame rate for games depending on their specific needs.

The GameStart() function is next, and its job is to initialize game data and start a game. In the case of the Blizzard example, there really isn't any game data, so the only code in GameStart() is code to seed a random number generator. I mentioned earlier that the Blizzard example draws snowflake icons at random positions on the screen. In order to successfully generate random numbers for these positions, you have to seed the random number generator. This is accomplished with a call to the standard C library function, srand().

> Random number generators don't truly generate random numbers. Instead, they generate a pattern of numbers that has the appearance of being random if you make sure that the pattern is selected differently each time a program is run. This is accomplished by seeding the random number generator with an unpredictable value. It turns out that the internal Windows tick count changes so rapidly that if you look at it at any given instant, you will generally get a unique value, which is sufficient to seed the random number generator and get "random" results.

Construction Cue

Similar to the GameStart() function, the GameEnd() function is designed to clean up game data once a game is over. In this case, the GameEnd() function is only required to clean up the game engine.

The GameActivate() and GameDeactivate() functions are very similar to each other in the Blizzard example. Both are here just to demonstrate how you can respond to game activations and deactivations, and they do so by drawing text on the game screen. For example, the GameActivate() function obtains the client rectangle for the game window and then uses it as the basis for drawing a line of text centered on the game screen. I realize that some of this graphics code probably looks a little strange, but don't worry too much about it because the next chapter gives you the whole scoop on how to draw graphics in Windows. Speaking of strange graphics code, the GamePaint() function is responsible for painting the game screen, but in this case, all the painting takes place in the GameCycle() function, so GamePaint() does nothing.

The GameCycle() function is the last function in the Blizzard example and is, without a doubt, the most interesting. The job of this function is to draw a snowflake icon at a random location on the game screen. This might not seem like a big deal, but keep in mind that you set the frame rate to 15 frames per second, which means that the GameCycle() function is getting called 15 times every second; this means that 15 icons get drawn in random locations every second! The first step in the GameCycle() function is to obtain a window handle for the main game window; this window handle is important because it allows you to draw on the game screen. The drawing actually takes place when the Win32 DrawIcon() function is called to draw the Blizzard icon. The standard rand() function is called to determine a random location on the game screen, and the icon is extracted from the game window class using the Win32 GetClassLong() function.

Construction Cue

I used a little trick in this example to avoid the task of loading and drawing bitmap images. Because a Windows application's icon is automatically loaded into its window class, I chose to draw the icon, as opposed to loading a bitmap image and drawing it. You learn how to load and draw a bitmap image in Chapter 4, "Drawing Graphical Images," but for now, drawing an icon proved much simpler.

Although I admittedly threw you a few curves with the graphics code in the Blizzard example, hopefully, you were able to follow along with most of the code. You were also hopefully able to see the benefit of relying on the game engine to take care of a lot of the dirty work associated with Windows game programming.

Testing the Finished Product

When you run the Blizzard example, you are presented with a game screen that rapidly fills up with snowflake icons, as shown in Figure 2.2.

It doesn't take too long for the Blizzard screen to fill up with snowflake icons. This has a lot to do with the fact that you have the game set up so that it runs through 15 game cycles per second. You could dramatically slow down or speed up the icons being drawn by altering the frame rate of the game in the GameInitialize() function.

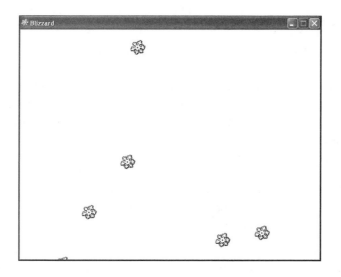

FIGURE 2.2
The Blizzard example demonstrates how the game engine makes it possible to focus solely on the game-specific aspects of a Windows program.

Another interesting point to make about the Blizzard example is how it isn't smart enough to repaint the snowflake icons if the window gets invalidated, as shown in Figure 2.3. In other words, if you minimize the program or activate another window in front of it, the game screen will get cleared. This happens because the GamePaint() function doesn't have any code to redraw the snowflake icons in response to the game screen needing a repaint. The repaint problem in the Blizzard example is addressed in the next chapter when you explore Windows graphics in more detail.

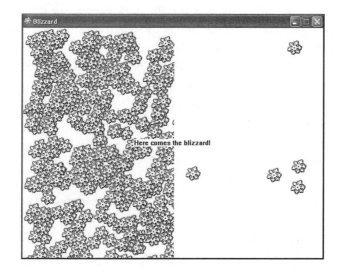

FIGURE 2.3
The timing aspect of the game engine causes the Blizzard example to fill up quite quickly with randomly placed Blizzard icons.

Summary

This chapter took an important leap forward in your game development path by guiding you through the design and development of a basic game engine for Windows games. You learned about the importance of a game engine, as well as what code goes into creating a fully functioning game engine. Although features certainly need to be added to the game engine to make it more useful in the context of games, the elements are in place for creating Windows games with much less effort than if you didn't create the engine. It's okay if you don't yet fully appreciate the role of the game engine in making your life easier as a game programmer. But trust me; you will eventually come to appreciate the game engine for how it simplifies game development and allows you to focus on the most important facets of game design.

Chapter 3, "Learning to Draw Basic Graphics," explains the mysteries behind the graphics code that you saw in the Blizzard example. You learn some of the fundamental graphics techniques that will carry you forward throughout the rest of the book. You also create a pretty neat example that demonstrates your new graphics knowledge.

Extreme Game Makeover

Many of the chapters throughout the book contain this section, which includes ideas about how to improve upon the program examples and games. You might be thinking that the Blizzard example is about as limited as an example can be, but part of an "extreme makeover" is showing how to turn one thing into something unexpectedly different. In the case of the Blizzard example, you can turn it into a uniquely different program by changing the snowflake icon and the manner in which the icon is drawn in the GameCycle() function. Just follow these steps:

1. Modify the Blizzard.ico and Blizzard_sm.ico to a completely different theme, such as a fireball.

2. Add a POINT global variable to the program that is used to "remember" the position of the fireball; this position can initially be randomly calculated.

3. Each time through the GameCycle() function, alter the position of the fireball so that it appears to move in a particular direction over time.

The end result of these changes is a program that shows a fireball gracefully moving across the screen leaving trails of fire, as opposed to randomly appearing snowflakes.

CHAPTER 3

Learning to Draw Basic Graphics

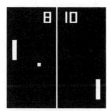

Arcade Archive

1979 was a critical milestone in the evolution of video games because it brought us Asteroids, which is one of the most enduring games ever. Created by Atari, Asteroids was one of the first vector graphics games, which means that it relied solely on lines to draw graphics, as opposed to little square pixels. Asteroids demonstrated that a very simple concept, with even simpler graphics and a soundtrack that gradually builds tension, creates a mix for success. In fact, Asteroids was so successful that arcade operators had to build larger coin boxes for the games—not a bad problem to have!

A computer game consists of many different pieces, all of which must come together to form a unique entertainment experience for the player. By far, the most important pieces of any game are the graphics. Graphics are used to represent the characters and creatures in a game, as well as background worlds and other interesting objects that factor into the overall game design. Granted, games have certainly done well because of factors outside of graphics, such as game play and sound quality, but those games are very rare. Besides, nowadays game players expect to see high-quality graphics just as we all expect to see high-quality visual effects in Hollywood movies. So, it's important to develop a solid understanding of graphics programming and how to use graphics wisely in your games.

In this chapter, you'll learn

- ▶ The basics of drawing graphics using the Windows Graphics Device Interface

- ▶ What a device context is and why it's important to GDI graphics

- ▶ How to paint text and primitive graphics in Windows

- ▶ How to create a sample program that demonstrates GDI graphics in the context of the game engine

Graphics Essentials

Before jumping into the details of how graphics work in Windows and how they are applied to games, it's important to establish some ground rules and gain an understanding of how computer graphics work in general. More specifically, you need to have a solid grasp on what a graphics coordinate system is, as well as how color is represented in computer graphics. The next couple of sections provide you with this knowledge, which you'll put to practical use a little later in the chapter.

Understanding the Graphics Coordinate System

All graphical computing systems use some sort of *graphics coordinate system* to specify how points are arranged in a window or on the screen. Graphics coordinate systems typically spell out the *origin* (0, 0) of the system, as well as the axes and directions of increasing value for each of the axes. If you're not a big math person, this simply means that a coordinate system describes how to pinpoint any location on the screen as an XY value. The traditional mathematical coordinate system familiar to most of us is shown in Figure 3.1.

FIGURE 3.1
The traditional XY coordinate system is commonly used in math.

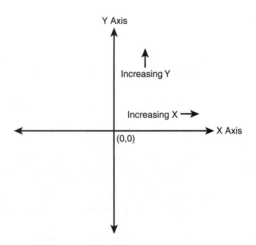

Windows graphics relies on a similar coordinate system to specify how and where drawing operations take place. Because all drawing in Windows takes place within the confines of a window, the Windows coordinate system is applied relative to a particular window. The Windows coordinate system has an origin that is located in the upper-left corner of the window, with positive X values increasing to the right and positive Y values increasing down. All values in the Windows coordinate system are positive integers. Figure 3.2 shows how this coordinate system looks.

When I talk about drawing graphics in a window, I'm actually referring to the *client area* of a window, which doesn't include the title bar, menus, scrollbars, and so on. In the case of games, you can think of the client area of the main game window as the game screen. You learn more about the client area of a window later in this chapter in the section titled, "Painting Windows."

Gamer's
Garage

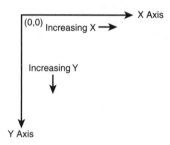

If the Windows graphics coordinate system sounds a little complicated, just think of it in terms of a classic game of Battleship. In Battleship, you try to sink enemy ships by firing torpedoes at specific locations on a grid. Battleship uses its own coordinate system to allow you to specify locations on the grid where ships might be located. Similarly, when you draw graphics in Windows, you specify locations in the client area of a window, which is really just a grid of little squares called *pixels*.

Learning the Basics of Color

A topic that impacts almost every area of game graphics is color. Fortunately, most computer systems take a similar approach to representing color. The main function of color in a computer system is to accurately reflect the physical nature of color within the confines of a computer. This physical nature isn't hard to figure out; anyone who has experienced the joy of Play-Doh can tell you that colors react in different ways when they are combined with each other. Like Play-Doh, a computer color system needs to be capable of mixing colors with accurate, predictable results.

Color computer monitors provide possibly the most useful insight into how software systems implement color. A color monitor has three electron guns: red, green, and blue. The output from these three guns converges on each pixel on the screen, stimulating phosphors to produce the appropriate color. The combined intensities of each gun determine the resulting pixel color. This convergence of different colors from the monitor guns is very similar to the convergence of different colored Play-Doh.

Gamer's Garage

Technically speaking, the result of combining colors on a monitor is different from that of combining similarly colored Play-Doh. The reason for this is that color combinations on a monitor are *additive*, meaning that mixed colors are added together to become white; Play-Doh color combinations are *subtractive*, meaning that mixed colors are subtracted from each other to become black. Whether the color combination is additive or subtractive depends on the physical properties of the particular medium involved.

The Windows color system is very similar to the physical system used by color monitors; it forms unique colors by using varying intensities of the colors red, green, and blue. Therefore, Windows colors are represented by the combination of the numeric intensities of the primary colors (red, green, and blue). This color system is known as *RGB (Red Green Blue)* and is standard across most graphical computer systems.

Gamer's Garage

RGB isn't the only color system used by computers. Another color system used heavily in desktop publishing applications is *CMYK*, which stands for Cyan-Magenta-Yellow-Black. Colors in the CMYK color system are expressed in terms of the color components cyan, magenta, yellow, and black, as opposed to red, green, and blue in RGB. The CMYK color system is used heavily in printing because CMYK printing inks are subtractive in nature, making it easier to print using a four-color ink combination (cyan, magenta, yellow, and black); hence the term four-color printing.

Table 3.1 shows the numeric values for the red, green, and blue components of some basic colors. Notice that the intensities of each color component range from 0 to 255 in value.

TABLE 3.1 Numeric RGB Color Component Values for Commonly Used Colors

Color	Red	Green	Blue
White	255	255	255
Black	0	0	0
Light Gray	192	192	192
Medium Gray	128	128	128
Dark Gray	64	64	64
Red	255	0	0
Green	0	255	0
Blue	0	0	255
Yellow	255	255	0
Purple	255	0	255

The Win32 API defines a structure named COLORREF that combines the red, green, and blue components of an RGB color into a single value. The COLORREF structure is important because it is used throughout the Win32 API to represent RGB colors. To create a color as a COLORREF structure, you use the RGB() macro, which accepts red, green, and blue color components as arguments. Here is an example of creating a solid green color using RGB():

```
COLORREF green = RGB(0, 255, 0);
```

The color created in this line of code is green because the green component (the middle argument) is specified as 255, whereas the red and blue components are specified as 0. Changing the values of these three arguments alters the mix of the color—with lower numbers resulting in darker colors and higher numbers resulting in brighter colors.

You can experiment with RGB color combinations in the standard Paint program that comes with Windows. Double-click one of the colors in the color palette in the lower left corner of the Paint window. Then, click the Define Custom Colors button in the Edit Colors dialog box. You can then either type numbers into the Red, Green, and Blue edit fields or click to select a color and intensity (see Figure 3.3).

FIGURE 3.3
The standard Windows Paint program allows you to specify colors via RGB values.

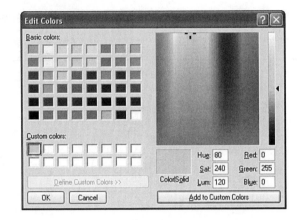

Examining Graphics in Windows

In order to seamlessly support a wide range of graphical output devices, Windows handles the painting of graphics a little differently than you might expect. Instead of allowing you to draw directly to the screen, a layer called the *Graphics Device Interface* or *GDI* is used to separate drawing operations from physical graphics devices, such as monitors and printers. The role of the GDI is to provide a programmatic interface for painting graphics in a generic manner. GDI operations work in concert with Windows graphics drivers to communicate with physical graphics devices. Figure 3.4 shows the architecture of GDI.

FIGURE 3.4
The GDI in Windows provides a layer between graphics operations at the application (game) level and physical graphics devices.

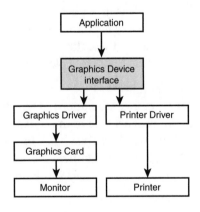

Keep in mind that although I use the term "generic" to describe GDI graphics, the Win32 API provides a broad range of GDI graphics operations. In fact, the remainder of this chapter is devoted to showing you some of the interesting things you can do with GDI graphics.

Working with Device Contexts

The key component in GDI graphics is the graphics context or *device context*, which acts as a gateway to a physical graphics device. You can think of a device context as a generic drawing surface to which graphics are painted. In other words, a device context is like a piece of paper that you can draw on—except once you've drawn on it, the resulting image can be displayed on a variety of different devices. Device contexts are very important in Windows programming because they make it possible to have device-independent graphics.

A device context is really just a way to allow you to draw in a generic manner without worrying about where the drawing is physically taking place. Device contexts are necessary so that the same graphics routines can be used regardless of whether you are drawing to the screen, to memory, or to a printer. Granted, in game programming you'll always be drawing to the screen, but that doesn't mean you can just ignore the GDI. You have to go through a device context in order to draw graphics using the GDI, so you might as well get comfortable with them. The important thing to remember is that all the drawing you do in Windows is actually done to a device context. It is then up to Windows to make sure that the drawing on the device context gets properly displayed on the screen.

You normally obtain a device context by calling the Win32 BeginPaint() function. BeginPaint() is paired with EndPaint() to form a graphics drawing pair, like this:

```
PAINTSTRUCT ps;
HDC hDC = BeginPaint(hWindow, &ps);
*** GDI drawing operations go here ***
EndPaint(hWindow, &ps);
```

The BeginPaint() function requires a window handle and a PAINTSTRUCT structure. The PAINTSTRUCT structure is filled with information pertaining to the device context and is rarely used in game programming. The BeginPaint() function returns a handle to a device context, which is all you need to start drawing graphics using the GDI. The EndPaint() function is then responsible for releasing the device context once you're finished with it.

It's also possible to paint outside of the BeginPaint()/EndPaint() function pairing—in which case, you have to obtain a device context in a slightly different manner. This is done using the GetDC() function, which only requires a window handle to obtain a device context. You must match the GetDC() function with the ReleaseDC()function to release the device context when you're finished using it. The following is an example of how these two functions are used together:

```
HDC hDC = GetDC(hWindow);
*** GDI drawing operations go here ***
ReleaseDC(hWindow, hDC);
```

In addition to device contexts, the GDI also supports the following common graphics components that you'll find useful in developing game graphics:

▶ Pens

▶ Brushes

▶ Bitmaps

▶ Palettes

The next few sections look at these graphics components in more detail and help you to understand how they fit into the GDI, as well as game graphics.

Writing with Pens

Pens in the GDI are analogous to ink pens in the real world; they are used to draw lines and curves. Pens can be created with varying widths and different colors. There are two kinds of pens: cosmetic and geometric. A *cosmetic pen* draws lines of fixed width and lines that need to be drawn quickly. A *geometric pen* draws scaleable lines, lines that are wider than a single pixel, and lines with unique styles. Given that cosmetic pens offer the speediest approach to drawing, they are the pen type most commonly used in game programming.

Painting with Brushes

Brushes in GDI are analogous to paint brushes in the real world; they are used to paint the interior of polygons, ellipses, and paths. Although you might commonly think of a paint brush as using a solid color, GDI brushes can also be defined based on a bitmap pattern, which means that they paint in a pattern, instead of as a solid. Brushes and pens go hand in hand when drawing graphics using the GDI. For example, if you were to draw a circle, a pen would be used to draw the outline of the circle, whereas a brush would be used to paint its interior.

Drawing Images with Bitmaps

A *bitmap* is a graphical image stored as an array of pixels. If you've ever used a digital camera or seen pictures on a Web site, you are already familiar with bitmaps. Bitmaps are rectangular, so the number of pixels in a bitmap is the width of the bitmap multiplied by its height. Bitmaps can contain multiple colors and are often based on a specific palette or set of colors. Bitmaps are, without a doubt, the most important graphics components in game programming because they provide the most flexibility in terms of using high-quality artwork. Unfortunately, bitmaps are a little more complex to use at the programming level, which is why I don't go into detail with them until the next chapter.

Managing Color with Palettes

A *palette* is a set of colors used by the GDI when rendering a bitmap. As an example, many images (bitmaps) are stored as 256-color images, which means that they use colors from a palette of 256 colors. Depending on the specific settings of your screen in Windows, the GDI might have to map the color palette for a bitmap to the color palette used by the screen. Most of the complexities of palette management are handled automatically by Windows.

Bitmap images can be stored in a variety of different formats ranging from 1 bit per pixel to 32 bits per pixel. 256-color bitmaps require 8 bits per pixel and are therefore referred to as 8-bit images. A pure black and white bitmap requires only one bit per pixel because each pixel is either on (black) or off (white); these are called 1-bit images. The most popular images in use today are 24-bit images, and they are capable of doing an excellent job of representing highly detailed images with millions of different colors.

Nowadays, it's safe to assume that most desktop PCs are set to a color mode higher than 256 colors (8-bit). In fact, most PCs are now set to 24-bit color, which supports more than 16 million different colors. This is important because if you assume that the target computer system for your game uses a 16-bit or higher color mode, you don't have to fool with palettes. You can simply create all of your game graphics as 24-bit images and load them without worrying about the complexities of mapping bitmap colors to screen colors. The next chapter shows you how to carry out this task.

Painting Windows

The Win32 API includes a special message that is delivered to a window whenever it needs to be painted. This message is called WM_PAINT, and it serves as one of the main ways in which graphics are drawn to a window. A window might need to be repainted when the window is first created, when the window is uncovered from behind other windows, or for a variety of other reasons. The bottom line is that you must handle the WM_PAINT message in order to paint the inside (client area) of a window.

When I refer to painting or drawing to a window, I'm really referring to the *client area* of a window. This is the rectangular part of a window inside the window's border that doesn't include the window frame, caption, menu, system menu, or scrollbars. Figure 3.5 reveals how the coordinates of the client area begin in the upper-left corner of the window and increase down and to the right, as you learned earlier in the chapter. This coordinate system is very important because most GDI graphics operations are based on it.

FIGURE 3.5
Most graphics in a Windows program are drawn to the client area of a window, which uses the Windows graphics coordinate system.

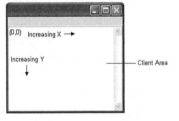

As you might recall, message handling takes place in the WndProc() function for a window. However, we were smart enough to make things simpler with the game engine you created in the previous chapter. More specifically, a WndProc() function is hidden in the game engine that handles the WM_PAINT message and calls the GamePaint() function. However, the call to the GamePaint() function is sandwiched between calls to the Win32 BeginPaint() and EndPaint() functions. This allows you to place graphics code in the GamePaint() function of your game without having to worry about obtaining a device context. The following is the

WM_PAINT message handler in the WndProc() function, which shows how the GamePaint() function is called:

```
case WM_PAINT:
  HDC        hDC;
  PAINTSTRUCT ps;
  hDC = BeginPaint(hWindow, &ps);

  // Paint the game
  GamePaint(hDC);

  EndPaint(hWindow, &ps);
  return 0;
```

The device context obtained from BeginPaint() is passed into the GamePaint() function to delegate the specifics of drawing graphics to each individual game. The following is an example of a simple GamePaint() function:

```
void GamePaint(HDC hDC)
{
  *** GDI drawing operations go here ***
}
```

GDI painting operations are performed on a device context or DC, which is passed into the function via the hDC argument. The following is an example of drawing a line in the GamePaint() function:

```
void GamePaint(HDC hDC)
{
  MoveToEx(hDC, 0, 0, NULL);
  LineTo(hDC, 50, 50);
}
```

This code shows how to draw a line using GDI functions. You learn more about how these functions work in a moment, but first, let's take a look at how to draw text.

Painting Text

In Windows, text is treated no differently from graphics, which means that text is painted using GDI functions. The primary GDI function used to paint text is TextOut(), which looks like this:

```
BOOL TextOut(HDC hDC, int x, int y, LPCTSTR szString, int iLength);
```

The following are the meanings of the different arguments to the `TextOut()` function:

- `hDC`—Device context handle
- `x`—X coordinate of text position
- `y`—Y coordinate of text position
- `szString`—The string to be painted
- `iLength`—Length of the string to be painted

The first argument to `TextOut()` is a handle to a device context, which is provided by the `BeginPaint()` function. All GDI functions require a handle to a device context, so you should get comfortable with seeing it in graphics code. The x and y arguments specify the position of the upper-left corner of the first string character relative to the client area (see Figure 3.6), whereas the last two arguments are a pointer to a string and the length of the string, in characters.

FIGURE 3.6
Text is drawn at the upper-left corner of the first character with respect to the client area of a window.

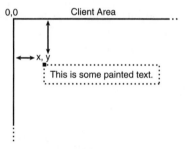

The following is an example of how to use the `TextOut()` function to draw a simple string of text:

```
void GamePaint(HDC hDC)
{
  TextOut(hDC, 10, 10, TEXT("Michael Morrison"), 16);
}
```

Another text-related function that you might consider using is `DrawText()`, which allows you to draw text within a rectangle, as opposed to drawing it at a specified point. As an example, you can use `DrawText()` to center a line of text on the screen by specifying the entire client window as the rectangle in which to draw the text. The following is an example of using the `DrawText()` function in place of `TextOut()`:

```
void GamePaint(HDC hDC)
{
  RECT rect;
  GetClientRect(hWindow, &rect);
  DrawText(hDC, TEXT("Michael Morrison"), -1, &rect,
    DT_SINGLELINE ¦ DT_CENTER ¦ DT_VCENTER);
}
```

In this example, the text is drawn centered both horizontally and vertically in the entire client area of the window. Notice that the length of the text string isn't necessary; this is because -1 is provided as the length, which means that the length should be automatically determined because the string is null-terminated. The flags in the last argument of DrawText() are used to determine how the text is drawn, which in this case, causes the text to be centered both horizontally and vertically.

Painting Primitive Graphics

Graphics primitives form a fundamental part of GDI and consist of lines, rectangles, circles, polygons, ovals, and arcs. You can create pretty impressive graphics by using these primitives in conjunction with each other. If you think graphics primitives sound somewhat limiting, keep in mind that some of the most enduring arcade games of all time were created solely through graphics primitives. Lunar Lander, Asteroids, Tempest, Gravitar, and Space Duel are a few of the classic vector arcade games whose graphics consisted solely of primitives.

The following are the major graphics primitives you can paint with GDI functions:

- ▶ Lines
- ▶ Rectangles
- ▶ Ellipses
- ▶ Polygons

The next few sections demonstrate how to draw each of these graphics primitives, along with how to use pens and brushes to add color to them.

Lines

Lines are the simplest of the graphics primitives and are therefore the easiest to draw. Lines are painted using the MoveToEx() and LineTo() functions, which set the current position and draw a line connecting the current position to a specified end point, respectively. The idea is that you use `MoveToEx()` to move the pen to a certain point and then use `LineTo()` to draw a line from that point to another point. You can continue to draw lines connecting points by calling `LineTo()` again. The following are what these functions look like:

```
BOOL MoveToEx(HDC hDC, int x, int y, LPPOINT pt);
BOOL LineTo(HDC hDC, int x, int y);
```

Construction Cue

> An XY coordinate in Windows is referred to as a *point* and is often represented by the Win32 `POINT` structure. The `POINT` structure is used throughout Windows to represent coordinates for a variety of different operations. The `POINT` structure consists solely of two long integer fields, x and y.

Both functions accept a handle to a device context and an X and Y value for the point of the line. The `MoveToEx()` function also allows you to provide an argument to store the previous point. In other words, you can pass a pointer to a point as the last argument of `MoveToEx()` if you're interested in finding out the last point used for drawing. The following is an example of using `MoveToEx()` and `LineTo()` to draw a couple of lines:

```
void GamePaint(HDC hDC)
{
  MoveToEx(hDC, 10, 40, NULL);
  LineTo(hDC, 44, 10);
  LineTo(hDC, 78, 40);
}
```

In this code, the drawing position is first set by calling `MoveToEx()` and providing the XY position of a point. Notice that the final argument is passed as `NULL`, which indicates that you aren't interested in finding out the previous point. The `LineTo()` function is then called twice, which results in two connected lines being drawn.

Rectangles

Rectangles represent another type of graphics primitive that is very easy to draw. The `Rectangle()` function enables you to draw a rectangle by specifying the upper-left corner and the lower-right corner of the rectangle. The following is the prototype for the `Rectangle()` function, which helps to reveal its usage:

```
BOOL Rectangle(HDC hDC, int xLeft, int yTop, int xRight, int yBottom);
```

Construction Cue

To draw a perfect square using the `Rectangle()` function, just specify a rectangle that has an equal width and height.

The `Rectangle()` function is straightforward in that you pass it rectangular dimensions of the bounding rectangle for the rectangle to be painted. The following is an example of how to draw a couple of rectangles:

```
void GamePaint(HDC hDC)
{
  Rectangle(hDC, 16, 36, 72, 70);
  Rectangle(hDC, 34, 50, 54, 70);
}
```

There isn't really anything remarkable about this code; it simply draws two rectangles of differing sizes and positions. Don't forget that the last two arguments to the `Rectangle()` function are the X and Y positions of the lower-right corner of the rectangle, not the width and height of the rectangle.

Another handy rectangle function is `FillRect()`, which is used to simply fill a rectangular area with a particular color. The color used for the filling is determined by the brush passed into the function. The following is the prototype for the `FillRect()` function:

```
int FillRect(HDC hDC, CONST RECT *lprc, HBRUSH hbr);
```

Unlike the `Rectangle()` function, the `FillRect()` function accepts a pointer to a `RECT` structure instead of four separate rectangle values. You'll also notice that the `FillRect()` function accepts a brush handle as its third argument. The `FillRect()` function is put to good use later in the chapter when you build the Crop Circles example.

Ellipses

Although they are curved, ellipses are drawn in a manner very similar to rectangles. An ellipse is simply a closed curve, and therefore, it can be specified by a bounding rectangle. The circular explosions in the classic Missile Command game provide a very good example of a filled ellipse. Ellipses are painted using the `Ellipse()` function, which looks like this:

```
BOOL Ellipse(HDC hDC, int xLeft, int yTop, int xRight, int yBottom);
```

Construction Cue

To draw a perfect circle using the `Ellipse()` function, just specify a rectangle that has an equal width and height.

The Ellipse() function accepts the rectangular dimensions of the bounding rectangle for the ellipse to be painted. The following is an example of drawing an ellipse using the Ellipse() function:

```
void GamePaint(HDC hDC)
{
  Ellipse(hDC, 40, 55, 48, 65);
}
```

Not surprisingly, this code draws an ellipse based on four values that specify a bounding rectangle for the ellipse.

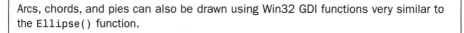

Construction Cue

> Arcs, chords, and pies can also be drawn using Win32 GDI functions very similar to the Ellipse() function.

Polygons

The trickiest of graphics primitives is the polygon, which is a closed shape consisting of multiple line segments. The asteroid shapes in the popular Asteroids game offer a great example of polygons. Polygons are painted using the Polygon() function, which follows:

```
BOOL Polygon(HDC hDC, CONST POINT* pt, int iCount);
```

As you can see, the Polygon() function is a little more complex than the other graphics primitives functions in that it takes an array of points and the number of points as arguments. A polygon is painted by connecting each of the points in the array with lines. The following is an example of how to draw a polygon shape using the Polygon() function:

```
void GamePaint(HDC hDC)
{
  POINT points[3];
  points[0] = { 5, 10 };
  points[1] = { 25, 30 };
  points[2] = { 15, 20 };
  Polygon(hDC, points, 3);
}
```

The key to this code is the creation of the array of points, points, which contains three POINT structures. These three POINT structures are initialized with XY pairs, and the whole array is then passed into the Polygon() function, along with the total number of points in the array. That's all that is required to draw a polygon shape consisting of multiple line segments.

Working with Pens and Brushes

It's one thing to simply draw graphics primitives in their default mundane black and white style. It's quite another to control the line and fill colors of the primitives to get more interesting results. This is accomplished by using pens and brushes, which are standard GDI objects used in drawing graphics primitives. Whether you realize it or not, you're already using pens and brushes when you draw graphics primitives. It's just that the default pen is black, and the default brush is the same color as the window background.

Creating Pens

If you want to change the outline of a graphics primitive, you need to change the pen used to draw it. This typically involves creating a new pen, which is accomplished with the CreatePen() function:

```
HPEN CreatePen(int iPenStyle, int iWidth, COLORREF crColor);
```

The first argument is the style of the pen, which can be one of the following values: PS_SOLID, PS_DASH, PS_DOT, PS_DASHDOT, PS_DASHDOTDOT, or PS_NULL. All but the last value specify different kinds of lines drawn with the pen, such as solid, dashed, dotted, or a combination of dashed and dotted. The last value, PS_NULL, indicates that no outline is to be drawn; in other words, the pen doesn't draw. The second argument to CreatePen() is the width of the pen in logical units, which typically corresponds to pixels when drawing to the screen. The final argument is the color of the pen, which is specified as a COLORREF value. To help make things clear, the following is an example of how to create a solid blue pen that is one-pixel wide:

```
HPEN hBluePen = CreatePen(PS_SOLID, 1, RGB(0, 0, 255));
```

Keep in mind that simply creating a pen isn't enough to begin drawing with it. In a moment, you learn how to select a pen into a device context and begin drawing with it. However, let's first learn how to create brushes.

Creating Brushes

Although several different kinds of brushes are supported in the GDI, I'd like to focus on solid brushes, which allow you to fill in graphics shapes with a solid color. You create a solid brush using the Win32 CreateSolidBrush() function, which simply accepts a COLORREF structure. The following is an example of creating a purple brush:

```
HBRUSH hPurpleBrush = CreateSolidBrush(RGB(255, 0, 255));
```

Notice in this code that a value of 255 is used to set the red and blue components of the color, which is how you are achieving purple in the final mixed color; try out this color combination in Paint to see how it results in purple. Now that you have a handle to a brush, you're ready to select it into a device context and begin painting with it.

Selecting Pens and Brushes

In order to use a pen or brush you've created, you must select it into a device context using the Win32 SelectObject() function. This function is used to select graphics objects into a device context and applies to both pens and brushes. The following is an example of selecting a pen into a device context:

```
HPEN hPen = SelectObject(hDC, hBluePen);
```

In this example, the hBluePen you just created is selected into the device context. Also notice that the previously selected pen is returned from SelectObject() and stored in hPen. This is important because you will typically want to restore GDI settings to their original state when you're finished painting. In other words, you want to remember the original pen so that you can set it back when you're finished. The following is an example of restoring the original pen using SelectObject():

```
SelectObject(hDC, hPen);
```

Notice that it is no longer important to remember the return value of SelectObject() because you are restoring the original pen.

One more important task related to creating pens is that of deleting graphics objects that you create. This is accomplished with the DeleteObject() function, which applies to both pens and brushes. It is important to delete any graphics objects that you create after you've stopped using them and they are no longer selected into a device context. The following is an example of cleaning up the blue pen:

```
DeleteObject(hBluePen);
```

Selecting and deleting brushes is very similar to selecting and deleting pens. The following is a more complete example to illustrate:

```
HBRUSH hBrush = SelectObject(hDC, hPurpleBrush);
// *** Do some drawing here! ***
SelectObject(hDC, hBrush);
DeleteObject(hPurpleBrush);
```

In this example, the purple brush from the previous section is selected into the device context, some drawing is performed, and the old brush is restored. The purple brush is then deleted to clean up everything.

Building the Crop Circles Example

At this point, you've seen bits and pieces of GDI graphics code, and you've learned how to carry out basic drawing operations with a variety of different graphics shapes. You've also learned how to tweak the appearance of those shapes by creating and using different pens and brushes. You're now ready to put what you've learned into a complete example program that demonstrates how to draw graphics in the context of a game. Okay, you're not really creating a game in this chapter, but you are using the game engine to draw some pretty neat graphics. The example I'm referring to is called Crop Circles, and its name comes from the fact that it displays a random series of connected circles similar to those that have mysteriously appeared on rural English farm land. In the case of the Crop Circles example, I can assure you there is no alien involvement.

The idea behind the Crop Circles example is to draw a line connected to a circle at a random location in each cycle of the game engine. Although the lines and circles are drawn outside of the GamePaint() function in response to a game cycle, it is still important to demonstrate how to draw within GamePaint() so that the drawing isn't lost when the window is minimized or hidden. For this reason, Crop Circles draws a dark yellow background in GamePaint() to demonstrate how graphics drawn in this function are retained even if the window must be repainted. The actual lines and circles are drawn in GameCycle(), which means that they are lost if the window is repainted. Let's take a look at how the code actually works for this example program.

Writing the Program Code

The fun begins in the Crop Circles example with the header file, CropCircles.h, which is shown in Listing 3.1. All the code for the Crop Circles example is available on the accompanying CD-ROM.

LISTING 3.1 The CropCircles.h Header File Declares the Global Game Engine Pointer and the Rectangular Position of the Previous Circle that Was Drawn

```
#pragma once

//————————————————————————————————·
// Include Files
//————————————————————————————————·
#include <windows.h>
#include "Resource.h"
#include "GameEngine.h"

//————————————————————————————————·
// Global Variables
//————————————————————————————————·
GameEngine* g_pGame;
RECT        g_rcRectangle;
```

Although this global variable is a rectangle, it's actually being used to store the dimensions of a circle.

This code isn't too mysterious. In fact, the only real difference between this header and the one you saw for the Blizzard example in the previous chapter is the declaration of the g_rcRectangle global variable. This rectangle stores the rectangular dimensions of the previously drawn circle, which allow you to connect it to the next circle with a line. The end result is that the circles all appear to be interconnected, which is roughly similar to real-world crop circles.

Moving right along, remember that we're now taking advantage of the game engine to simplify a great deal of the work in putting together programs (games). In fact, all that is really required of the Crop Circles example is to provide implementations of the core game functions. Listing 3.2 contains the code for the first of these functions, GameInitialize().

LISTING 3.2 The GameInitialize() Function Creates the Game Engine and Sets the Frame Rate to 1 Cycle Per Second

```
BOOL GameInitialize(HINSTANCE hInstance)
{
  // Create the game engine
  g_pGame = new GameEngine(hInstance, TEXT("Crop Circles"),
    TEXT("Crop Circles"), IDI_CROPCIRCLES, IDI_CROPCIRCLES_SM);
  if (g_pGame == NULL)
    return FALSE;

  // Set the frame rate (yes, it's deliberately slow)
  g_pGame->SetFrameRate(1);

  return TRUE;
}
```

An unnaturally slow frame rate of 1fps results in crop circles that gradually appear on the game screen.

The GameInitialize() function is responsible for creating the game engine and setting the frame rate for it. In this case, the frame rate is set at 1 cycle per second (frame per second), which is extremely slow by any game standard. However, this frame rate is fine for viewing the crop circles being drawn; feel free to raise it if you want to see the circles drawn faster.

Following up on GameInitialize() is GameStart(), which actually gets things going. Listing 3.3 shows the code for the GameStart() function.

LISTING 3.3 The GameStart() Function Seeds the Random Number Generator and Establishes an Initial Rectangle for the First Circle

```
void GameStart(HWND hWindow)
{
  // Seed the random number generator
  srand(GetTickCount());

  // Set the position and size of the initial crop circle
  g_rcRectangle.left = g_pGame->GetWidth() * 2 / 5;
  g_rcRectangle.top = g_pGame->GetHeight() * 2 / 5;
  g_rcRectangle.right = g_rcRectangle.left + g_pGame->GetWidth() / 10;
  g_rcRectangle.bottom = g_rcRectangle.top + g_pGame->GetWidth() / 10;
}
```

Any program that makes use of random numbers is responsible for seeding the built-in random number generator. This is accomplished with the call to srand(). You'll see this line of code in virtually all the example programs throughout the book because most of them involve the use of random numbers; random numbers often play heavily into the development of games. The remainder of the GameStart() function is responsible for setting the position and size of the initial rectangle for the first circle to be drawn. This rectangle is sized proportionally to the client area of the main program window and is positioned centered within the client area.

As I mentioned earlier, part of the Crop Circles example demonstrated the difference between drawing graphics in the GamePaint() function, as opposed to drawing them in GameCycle(). Listing 3.4 shows the code for GamePaint(), which in this case is responsible for drawing a solid colored (dark yellow) background behind the crop circles.

LISTING 3.4   The GamePaint() Function Draws a Dark Yellow
Background that Fills the Entire Client Area

```
void GamePaint(HDC hDC)
{
  // Draw a dark yellow field as the background for the crop circles
  RECT    rect;
  GetClientRect(g_pGame->GetWindow(), &rect);
  HBRUSH hBrush = CreateSolidBrush(RGB(128, 128, 0));    // dark yellow color
  FillRect(hDC, &rect, hBrush);
  DeleteObject(hBrush);
}
```

The FillRect() function you learned about in this chapter is used to draw a dark
yellow rectangle that fills the entire client area. Because the rectangle is being
drawn in GamePaint(), it is not lost when the window is repainted. You can easily
alter the color of the background by changing the RGB values of the solid brush
used to fill the rectangle.

The GameCycle() function is where the actual crop circles are drawn, as shown in
Listing 3.5.

LISTING 3.5   The GameCycle() Function Randomly Alters the Size and
Position of the Crop Circle and Then Draws It

```
void GameCycle()
{
  RECT       rect;
  HDC        hDC;
  HWND       hWindow = g_pGame->GetWindow();

  // Remember the location of the last crop circle
  int iXLast = g_rcRectangle.left +
    (g_rcRectangle.right - g_rcRectangle.left) / 2;
  int iYLast = g_rcRectangle.top +
    (g_rcRectangle.bottom - g_rcRectangle.top) / 2;

  // Randomly alter the size and position of the new crop circle
  GetClientRect(g_pGame->GetWindow(), &rect);
  int iInflation = (rand() % 17) - 8; // increase or decrease size by up to 8
  InflateRect(&g_rcRectangle, iInflation, iInflation);
  OffsetRect(&g_rcRectangle,
    rand() % (rect.right - rect.left) - g_rcRectangle.left,
    rand() % (rect.bottom - rect.top) - g_rcRectangle.top);

  // Draw a line to the new crop circle
  hDC = GetDC(hWindow);
  HPEN hPen = CreatePen(PS_SOLID, 5, RGB(192, 192, 0)); // light yellow color
  SelectObject(hDC, hPen);
```

*A random inflation
value is used to
determine the size
of the next crop
circle based on the
size of the previous
circle.*

```
MoveToEx(hDC, iXLast, iYLast, NULL);
LineTo(hDC,
  g_rcRectangle.left + (g_rcRectangle.right - g_rcRectangle.left) / 2,
  g_rcRectangle.top + (g_rcRectangle.bottom - g_rcRectangle.top) / 2);

// Draw the new crop circle
HBRUSH hBrush = CreateSolidBrush(RGB(192, 192, 0));    // lighter yellow color
SelectObject(hDC, hBrush);
Ellipse(hDC, g_rcRectangle.left, g_rcRectangle.top,
  g_rcRectangle.right, g_rcRectangle.bottom);
ReleaseDC(hWindow, hDC);
DeleteObject(hBrush);
DeleteObject(hPen);
}
```

The GameCycle() function is interesting in that it does a few things you haven't
seen before. First of all, it uses two new Win32 functions, InflateRect() and
OffsetRect(), to randomly alter the size and position of the new crop circle. A
random inflation value is first calculated, which is in the range of -8 to 8. This
value is then used as the basis for shrinking or growing the rectangular extents of
the circle using the InflateRect() function. The rectangle is then offset by a random amount between -9 and 9 using the OffsetRect() function.

With the new crop circle size and position figured out, the GameCycle() function
moves on to drawing a line connecting the previous circle to the new one. A 5-
pixel wide, light yellow pen is created and selected into the device context prior to
drawing the line. The line is then drawn using the familiar MoveToEx() and
LineTo() functions.

After drawing a line connecting the new crop circle, you're ready to determine a
new fill color for it; this is accomplished by creating a dark yellow, solid brush.
You then simply select the brush into the device context and draw the crop circle
with a call to the Ellipse() function. After drawing the circle, the device context
is released, and the brush and pen are deleted.

Testing the Finished Product

Now that you've worked through the code for the Crop Circles example, I suspect
that you're ready to see it in action. Figure 3.7 shows the program running with
several crop circles in full view, but unfortunately, no alien presence.

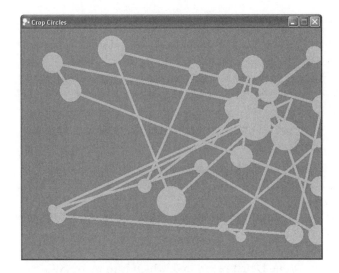

If you recall from the code, the Crop Circles example is smart enough to redraw the dark yellow background if the window is minimized or resized, but it doesn't take into account redrawing the circles and lines. You can test this out by covering part of the window with another window and then revealing the window again. The portion of circles and lines not covered will be erased because of the repaint, but the part of the window that was visible will remain untouched. This redraw problem is not too difficult to fix. In fact, you solve the problem in the next chapter when you build a slideshow example program using bitmap images.

Summary

This chapter laid the groundwork for the game graphics that you develop and use throughout the remainder of the book. I know; you're no doubt getting antsy because you've yet to touch on anything terribly game-specific. However, keep in mind that game programming, especially in Windows, involves a variety of different programming disciplines that must come together before a complete game can be built. Even so, hopefully, you're feeling a significant sense of accomplishment now that you know how to draw graphics with a little animated pizzazz using the GDI.

Chapter 4, "Drawing Graphical Images," continues along in the exploration of GDI graphics programming by uncovering the most important game development concept: graphical images. You find out about bitmap images, specifically how they work and how to load and display them in a Windows program. You also put your image-handling skills to work by creating a slideshow that you can use to display storyboards for your games or maybe just pictures from your last vacation.

Field Trip

I was very tempted to send you on a trip to England to experience firsthand the real-life crop circle phenomenon up close; some of the more publicized crop circles have been in England, although crop circles have actually appeared all over the world. Because a trip to England might not be convenient for you, let's instead take a field trip to learn more about primary colors and how they are used in varying combinations to form other colors. More specifically, I want you to visit your local toy store and buy some Play-Doh or other suitable colored clay. Experiment with creating different colors by combining primary colors of Play-Doh, which in this case, will likely be red, blue, and yellow, as opposed to the red, green, and blue colors used in RGB computer graphics. As you squish together different colors, keep in mind that Play-Doh color combinations are subtractive, which means that mixed colors are subtracted from each other to become black; in other words, the more colors you mix, the darker the result. Computer graphics are additive and therefore have the opposite effect when combined; they get lighter as you combine them.

CHAPTER 4

Drawing Graphical Images

Pac-Man, without a doubt one of the most beloved video games of all time, made its debut in 1980. Pac-Man was responsible for establishing the maze game as a standard genre of early video games. The Pac-Man character was created by Toru Iwatani, a Namco game developer, who observed the shape of a pizza he was eating that was missing a piece. The shape of Pac-Man, a circle with a missing wedge for a mouth, is now a solid fixture in video game history. Interestingly enough, Atari turned down rights to Pac-Man in America because they thought the game was too easy, so Midway reaped the rewards instead.

We've all heard that a picture is worth a thousand words, and when it comes to computer games, pictures might be worth even more than that. To translate it into nerd talk, a 640×480 image is worth 307,200 pixels. Okay, maybe nerd talk is something I should avoid. The point is that pictures (images) are extremely important in computer games because they provide the only means of incorporating artwork into the games. Sure, it's nice to be able to draw lines, rectangles, and ellipses using GDI functions, but it would take a great deal of effort to draw a menacing creature out of graphics primitives. With a few classic vector graphics games providing an exception, game developers use graphical images as a means of visualizing graphical parts of games. This chapter is all about showing you how to load and display graphical images.

In this chapter, you'll learn

- ▶ The fundamentals of bitmap images and why they are important in game programming

- ▶ About the inner workings of bitmap images

▶ How to develop an all-purpose bitmap class for use in games

▶ How to use the bitmap class to represent slide images in a slideshow program

The Basics of Bitmap Images

Images in Windows games are represented by *bitmaps*, which are rectangular graphics objects containing rows and columns of little squares called *pixels*. The name bitmap comes from the fact that the rows and columns determine how to map the pixels to the screen; the pixels themselves are composed of bits. Each pixel in a bitmap is a solid color. In fact, the only information associated with a pixel is its color. Therefore, you can think of a bitmap as a rectangular arrangement of little colored squares. If you prefer a movie analogy, a bitmap is a *matrix* of pixels. If you're old enough to remember the popular Lite Brite toy, you definitely have an understanding of how a bitmap works. Lite Brite, which is still manufactured today by Hasbro, allows you to plug colored pegs into a black plastic grid to draw pictures.

Gamer's Garage

> Two types of bitmaps are supported in Windows: *device-dependent bitmaps* and *device-independent bitmaps*. Device-dependent bitmaps are stored in a manner determined by a specific device, whereas device-independent bitmaps are stored in such a way that they can be displayed on any device. All the bitmaps you work with in this book are device-independent bitmaps, which are sometimes referred to as *DIBs*. Just keep in mind that when I refer to "bitmaps" from here on, I'm really referring to DIBs.

You are probably familiar with bitmaps from the popular .BMP file type that is used throughout Windows. BMP is the standard image format used in Windows, and it is also the format you'll be using to work with bitmaps throughout this book. Although GIF and JPEG have certainly surpassed BMP as image formats for use on the Web, BMP is still used a great deal by Windows users. Not only that, but the BMP image format is considerably simpler and easier to work with at a programming level than GIF and JPEG. You can use the standard Paint program built into Windows to create and edit BMP files, or you can use Microsoft Photo Editor, which offers more features for working with photographic images.

If you're fortunate enough to have access to a higher-powered image editor, such as Photoshop, Paint Shop Pro, or Microsoft Digital Image Pro, you'll have a leg up when it comes to creating your own high-quality bitmap images.

Gamer's Garage

Although there is only one bitmap image format, not all bitmap images are created equal. First of all, the bitmap image format allows you to create bitmaps with varying numbers of colors. More specifically, you can create 8-bit bitmaps that use 256 (palettized) colors or 24-bit bitmaps that use more than 16 million colors. You can also create bitmaps that use a technique known as *compression* to help reduce the size of the bitmap file. To help keep the code simple, the bitmaps you use throughout the book are all 24-bit, uncompressed bitmaps. This is very important to remember because other types of bitmaps won't work with the bitmap code you develop in this chapter.

Regardless of how you create a bitmap, it ultimately ends up as a file with a .BMP file extension. To use such a bitmap in a Windows program, you have two options:

▶ Read the bitmap directly from the file

▶ Store the bitmap as an application resource and read it from memory

In the first option, the Windows program opens the bitmap file from disk and reads in the image data. It then uses the bitmap image data to create a GDI bitmap graphics object that can be drawn to a device context. The second option involves storing a bitmap as a resource within the executable program, which means that you don't have to include the bitmap file with the program once it is compiled. The advantage to this option is that you are able to distribute your game as a single program file. The bitmap class you create later in this chapter supports both approaches to using bitmaps.

Looking Inside a Bitmap

In order to use bitmaps in your games, you must have a basic understanding of how they are put together. More specifically, you need to have knowledge of the inner structure of a bitmap because you must write code that reads this structure and extracts information about the bitmap. This is necessary so that you can create a bitmap object that can be drawn in your games. You'll be glad to know that bitmaps aren't too terribly complicated, as is evident in Figure 4.1.

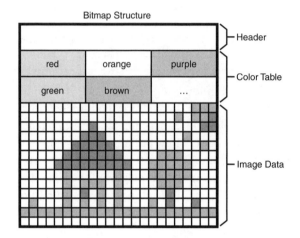

The figure reveals that every bitmap consists of three basic parts:

- ▶ Header
- ▶ Color table
- ▶ Image data

The header contains information pertaining to the overall makeup of the bitmap, such as its width, height, number of bits per pixel (8 or 24, for example), and so on. The color table contains the palette for the bitmap, which is the list of colors used throughout the image. The color table is extremely important for 8-bit bitmaps because it describes up to 256 colors used by pixels in the image. Conversely, 24-bit bitmaps don't need a color table because their colors are sufficiently described by the pixels themselves. More specifically, the 24 bits in a 24-bit image are divided into three 8-bit values—one for each of the color components—red, green, and blue.

The image data is where the actual pixels of the bitmap are stored. For example, if a bitmap is 10x12, it is 10 pixels across and 12 pixels down for a total of 120 pixels. If it is an 8-bit image, each pixel requires 8 bits (1 byte) to describe its color, whereas a 24-bit image requires 24 bits per pixel. Therefore, the image data for an 8-bit version of the 10×12 bitmap would consist of 120 bytes, whereas the 24-bit version would take up 360 bytes. To determine the color of each 8-bit pixel, you would look up the byte value in the color table to see what color the pixel is; there is no color table for 24-bit images because each pixel directly specifies its own color.

Of course, all this image data stuff takes place automatically after you load an image and start using it with GDI functions. In other words, you only have to worry yourself with the inner workings of bitmaps when you first load the bitmap from a file or resource. Once loaded, you use a handle to a bitmap to draw it to a device context in much the same way as you drew graphics primitives to a device context in Chapter 3, "Learning to Draw Basic Graphics."

Developing a Bitmap Class

Although I could provide you with a handful of bitmap functions and set you on your way, bitmaps provide a perfect opportunity to take advantage of object-oriented programming. More specifically, you can create a class that includes all the code required to load and draw bitmaps and then use the class to create bitmap objects that are much easier to use than if you had created several functions. Knowing this, the next couple of sections are devoted to the design and development of a bitmap class that you will use throughout the book in just about every example program from here on. Although the bitmap class is admittedly a little tricky in places, once created, it is unbelievably easy to use. The idea is to create the class once with the knowledge that it will make your life incredibly easier in coming chapters.

How the Bitmap Class Will Work

The idea behind the Bitmap class is to provide a means of loading bitmaps from a file or resource, as well as drawing bitmaps to a device context. By incorporating these capabilities into a class, you'll be able to create Bitmap objects in your games that are very easy to use and that hide the messy aspects of working with bitmaps. The Bitmap class has the following requirements:

- ▶ Loads a bitmap from a file
- ▶ Loads a bitmap from a resource
- ▶ Creates a blank bitmap in a solid color
- ▶ Draws a bitmap to a device context
- ▶ Obtains the width and height of a bitmap

The first two requirements are fairly obvious from the earlier discussion. The third requirement isn't terribly important just yet, but you might find yourself wanting to create a blank bitmap for some reason, so why not have that capability?

Besides, in Chapter 9, "Making Things Move with Sprite Animation," you'll see how bitmaps are important for solving a flicker problem associated with animation; the solution requires blank bitmaps. The final requirement isn't terribly important, but you might encounter a situation in which it's necessary to determine the width and height of a bitmap. The information is readily available when you load a bitmap, so you might as well make it accessible from the Bitmap class.

Putting the Code Together

The code for the Bitmap class is admittedly complex in places, so I'm not suggesting that you expect to understand every nuance of it immediately. In fact, my goal isn't really to make you a bitmap expert, which is practically a requirement in order to fully understand the Bitmap class. Even so, I don't like the idea of accepting code at face value without any explanation, so I'd like for you to have a general understanding of what is going on in the Bitmap class. If I gloss over a section of code, just understand that the goal here is to get you using bitmaps in as little time as possible so that you can quickly move on to drawing them in games.

The Class Definition

Win32 defines several data structures that pertain to bitmaps, so you'll see several different ones throughout the Bitmap class code. One of these structures is BITMAPINFOHEADER, which is a structure that stores the header information associated with a bitmap. When you read a bitmap from a file or resource, you will store its header in a BITMAPINFOHEADER structure.

It's worth pointing out that our Bitmap class will be designed solely for loading 24-bit uncompressed bitmap images in the BMP file format. This not only simplifies the code for the class, but it also focuses on the highest-quality bitmap images, which you will no doubt want to use in your games. With that in mind, let's take a look at the Bitmap class definition, which is shown in Listing 4.1.

LISTING 4.1 The Bitmap Class Definition Includes the Member Variables and Methods Used to Manage Bitmaps

```
class Bitmap
{
protected:
  // Member Variables
```

```
HBITMAP m_hBitmap;
int     m_iWidth, m_iHeight;

// Helper Methods
void Free();
public:
  // Constructor(s)/Destructor
  Bitmap();
  Bitmap(HDC hDC, LPSTR szFileName);
  Bitmap(HDC hDC, UINT uiResID, HINSTANCE hInstance);
  Bitmap(HDC hDC, int iWidth, int iHeight, COLORREF crColor = RGB(0, 0, 0));
  virtual ~Bitmap();

  // General Methods
  BOOL Create(HDC hDC, LPSTR szFileName);
  BOOL Create(HDC hDC, UINT uiResID, HINSTANCE hInstance);
  BOOL Create(HDC hDC, int iWidth, int iHeight, COLORREF crColor);
  void Draw(HDC hDC, int x, int y);
  int  GetWidth() { return m_iWidth; };
  int  GetHeight() { return m_iHeight; };
};
```

Every bitmap object must keep track of its handle because the Windows GDI requires a bitmap handle for drawing bitmaps.

This listing reveals the overall makeup of the Bitmap class, including its member variables, constructors, destructor, and methods. The m_hBitmap member variable is used to store a handle to the bitmap, which is extremely important for drawing the bitmap to a device context using the GDI. The m_iWidth and m_iHeight member variables store the width and height of the bitmap, respectively.

The Constructors and Destructor

Notice in Listing 4.1 that there are three constructors in the Bitmap class in addition to the default constructor—each of which corresponds to one of the different approaches to creating bitmaps. Each Bitmap() constructor has a corresponding Create() method that is used to handle the work of loading the bitmap data and creating it as a GDI object. The Free() method is a helper method used within the Bitmap class to free up the memory associated with the bitmap. The Draw() method shouldn't be too surprising because it provides a means of drawing the bitmap to a device context. Finally, the GetWidth() and GetHeight() methods are simply used to obtain the width and height of the bitmap, respectively.

To help keep the focus on game programming and move you along as quickly as possible, I opted not to delve too deeply into the code for the Bitmap class. You'll find that the CD-ROM for this book contains the complete code for the Bitmap class, including all the Bitmap() constructors, as well as the destructor and the Create() and Free() methods.

Construction Cue

The Bitmap() constructors are all very simple in that they call a corresponding Create() function to carry out the specifics of creating a bitmap based on a file, a resource, or a solid color. The default constructor doesn't do much of anything other than initialize member variables; the idea behind this constructor is that you will eventually call the Create() method directly to load the Bitmap object with data. The destructor calls the Free() method to release the memory associated with the bitmap and clear the bitmap handle.

The Free() method first checks to see if the bitmap handle, m_hBitmap, is valid—in which case, it deletes the GDI bitmap object and clears out the handle. This is all that's required to free the memory associated with the bitmap.

Three Ways to Create a Bitmap

There are three Create() methods in the Bitmap class that are fairly long, but you can access them from the CD-ROM. The first Create() method is responsible for loading a bitmap from a file.

The method starts out by calling Free() to make sure that any previous bitmap data is cleaned up; this would apply if the same Bitmap object was being reused for a different bitmap. The file is then opened, and the resulting file handle is checked to make sure that the open proceeded without a hitch. The file header for the bitmap is then read from the file, and some checks are made to ensure that it was read without any problems. The file header contains information about the bitmap file itself, whereas the info header contains information about the bitmap. The info header is read next, and another error check is performed.

With the headers properly read from the file, the Create() method is ready to get down to the real business of reading the bitmap image data. It is worth pointing out the usage of the CreateDIBSection() Win32 function, which is used to obtain a handle to a GDI bitmap object from raw bitmap data. This function ultimately makes it possible to read a bitmap and prepare it for use with the GDI. The last step in the Create() method is to free the bitmap memory if an error occurred while reading its data.

The second Create() method supported by the Bitmap class is used to load a bitmap from a resource.

This method roughly follows the same pattern as the first Create() method—except, in this case, the bitmap information is retrieved from a resource in memory, as opposed to being read from a file. The first step is to find the bitmap resource, load the resource into memory, and then lock the resource so that you can access its raw data. The width and height of the bitmap are stored next, and the image data is copied and used as the basis for obtaining a bitmap handle using CreateDIBSection(). Finally, the method concludes by performing some cleanup in case an error occurred.

The last of the Create() methods is the one that creates a blank bitmap in a solid color.

This method is considerably different from the other two Create() methods because it has the luxury of not having to involve itself with any existing bitmap data. Instead, it uses a Win32 function called CreateCompatibleBitmap() to create an entirely new bitmap based on the supplied device context. Because the width and height are provided as arguments to the method, they are easy to store. Most of the work in the method has to do with filling the bitmap with a solid color. A compatible device context is first created to hold the bitmap for drawing, and then a solid brush in the specified color is created. The bitmap is then selected into the device context and filled with the solid brush. The graphics objects are then cleaned up to finish the job of this Create() method .

Drawing the Bitmap

The three Create() methods are, by far, the toughest parts of the Bitmap class, so the Draw() method will be a welcome relief.

The Draw() method is actually similar to the third Create() method because it involves drawing a bitmap. However, in this case, the bitmap is being drawn to an outside device context, as opposed to you drawing on the bitmap itself. The Draw() method accepts a device context and an XY coordinate as arguments. This reveals how simple it is to use the method to draw a bitmap. The first step in drawing the bitmap is ensuring that the bitmap handle is valid. If the handle checks out okay, a compatible device context is created to temporarily store the bitmap, and the bitmap is selected into the device context. This is an important step because drawing images always takes place from one device context to another.

The bitmap is actually drawn using the Win32 BitBlt()function, which draws an image from a source device context to a specified location on a destination device context. Drawing a bitmap image is sometimes referred to as *blitting*, which is where the name BitBlt() comes from; you are blitting the image bits when you draw the image. The Draw() method finishes by cleaning up the temporary device context.

Construction Cue

> The x and y arguments to the `Bitmap::Draw()`method are specified relative to the device context the bitmap is being drawn on, and they indicate the upper-left corner of the bitmap image.

You now have a complete, fully working `Bitmap` class that is ready to be used in games to load and draw bitmap images. Let's move on and take a look at a program example that puts the `Bitmap` class through its paces.

Building the Slideshow Example

Because you haven't learned about how to process user input, such as key strokes and mouse clicks, it still isn't quite possible to create a game yet. However, the remainder of the chapter guides you through the creation of a surprisingly practical example that happens to serve as a great demonstration of the `Bitmap` class. I'm referring to the Slideshow program, which uses a series of bitmap images to present a slideshow. The Slideshow program takes advantage of the timing mechanism built into the game engine to provide a delay between moving to each successive image in a slideshow. The `Bitmap` class proves to be quite useful as a means of loading and drawing bitmap images from both files and resources.

Before looking at the code for the Slideshow program, let's quickly go over what it is supposed to accomplish:

▶ Create several bitmaps from files

▶ Create several bitmaps from resources

▶ Create a blank bitmap in a solid color

▶ Draw the bitmaps one at a time as part of a slideshow

▶ Time the presentation of the slides in the slideshow appropriately

These requirements for the Slideshow program make it pretty clear what is supposed to happen. The only thing worth mentioning is that you wouldn't normally mix the two approaches of loading bitmaps from files and resources. Generally speaking, it makes sense to commit to one approach or the other. In the case of a slideshow, it probably makes more sense to load bitmaps from files because you might want to change the images without recompiling the program. However, in this case, it's important to demonstrate the different uses of the `Bitmap` class.

Writing the Program Code

The header for the Slideshow example is the best place to start in terms of getting acquainted with how it works. Check out Listing 4.2 to get a feel for what the header is all about. Don't forget that you can access all of the code for the Slideshow program on the accompanying CD-ROM.

LISTING 4.2 The Slideshow.h Header File Imports a Few Header Files and Declares Several Global Variables

```
#pragma once

//—————————————————————————————————————————————·
// Include Files
//—————————————————————————————————————————————·
#include <windows.h>
#include "Resource.h"
#include "GameEngine.h"
#include "Bitmap.h"

//—————————————————————————————————————————————·
// Global Variables
//—————————————————————————————————————————————·
HINSTANCE    g_hInstance;
GameEngine*  g_pGame;
const int    g_iNUMSLIDES = 6;
Bitmap*      g_pSlides[g_iNUMSLIDES];
int          g_iCurSlide;
```

To create your own slideshows with more or fewer slides, just change this constant to a different number.

Other than declaring a few global variables, there aren't really any surprises here. The g_hInstance variable is necessary because a program instance handle must be used to load bitmaps as resources. An *instance* is simply a program loaded into memory; all the programs you have open and running in Windows are considered instances. An *instance handle* is a reference to an instance, which allows you to interact with the instance and do things such as load resources that are stored in the executable program file. Because you're going to be loading bitmaps as resources, it's important to store away an instance handle for the Slideshow program.

The g_pGame global variable is used to store a pointer to the game engine, which should be familiar to you by now. The remaining member variables relate specifically to the slideshow functionality. The global constant g_iNUMSLIDES is used to set the number of slides in the slideshow, and it should be changed if you modify the number of slides in the slideshow. The g_pSlides variable is perhaps the most important because it stores away pointers to the Bitmap objects; these objects correspond to the slides in the slideshow. Finally, the g_iCurSlide variable represents the array index of the current slide, which is the slide currently being displayed. This variable is important because it keeps track of where the slideshow is in the slide sequence.

The global variables in the Slideshow header file are somewhat revealing, but you obviously have to look at the code for the game functions to really get a feel for what's going on. Listing 4.3 contains the code for the GameInitialize() function, which is the first of the Slideshow game functions.

LISTING 4.3 The GameInitialize() **Function Creates the Game Engine, Sets the Frame Rate to One Cycle Per Second, and Stores Away the Instance Handle for the Program**

```
BOOL GameInitialize(HINSTANCE hInstance)
{
  // Create the game engine
  g_pGame = new GameEngine(hInstance, TEXT("Slideshow"),
    TEXT("Slideshow"), IDI_SLIDESHOW, IDI_SLIDESHOW_SM);
  if (g_pGame == NULL)
    return FALSE;

  // Set the frame rate
  g_pGame->SetFrameRate(1);

  // Store the instance handle
  g_hInstance = hInstance;

  return TRUE;
}
```

1fps is still too fast for the slideshow, so we'll have to tweak the timing again later in the code.

The GameInitialize() function is pretty basic in terms of doing things you'd expect to see in a program that makes use of the game engine. Notice, however, that the frame rate for the game engine is set to 1, which means that there is only one game cycle per second. This is important because it helps to establish the timing of the slideshow. The problem is that one second is still too short a period to flip between slides, so we'll have to trick the game engine into displaying each slide a little longer; you tackle this problem in a moment. The only other task carried out in GameInitialize() is storing away the instance handle, which is very important for loading bitmaps from resources.

Although GameInitialize() creates and initializes the game engine, it's the GameStart() function that really gets the Slideshow program on track. Its counterpart is GameEnd(), which cleans up the bitmaps created in GameStart(). The code for both functions is shown in Listing 4.4.

LISTING 4.4 The `GameStart()` and `GameEnd()` Functions Take Care of Initializing and Cleaning Up the Slide Bitmaps

```
void GameStart(HWND hWindow)
{
  // Create and load the slide bitmaps
  HDC hDC = GetDC(hWindow);
  g_pSlides[0] = new Bitmap(hDC, TEXT("Image1.bmp"));
  g_pSlides[1] = new Bitmap(hDC, TEXT("Image2.bmp"));
  g_pSlides[2] = new Bitmap(hDC, TEXT("Image3.bmp"));
  g_pSlides[3] = new Bitmap(hDC, IDB_IMAGE4, g_hInstance);
  g_pSlides[4] = new Bitmap(hDC, IDB_IMAGE5, g_hInstance);
  g_pSlides[5] = new Bitmap(hDC, 640, 480, RGB(0, 0, 0));

  // Set the first slide
  g_iCurSlide = 0;
}

void GameEnd()
{
  // Cleanup the slide bitmaps
  for (int i = 0; i < g_iNUMSLIDES; i++)
    delete g_pSlides[i];

  // Cleanup the game engine
  delete g_pGame;
}
```

This code demonstrates the three approaches to creating bitmaps, but in your own slideshows, you'll likely opt for creating bitmaps from files.

The slide array is zero-indexed, which means that the first slide is actually slide number 0.

The `GameStart()` function takes on the responsibility of creating the slide bitmaps. It first obtains a device context, which is necessary to create any bitmaps. It then loads several bitmaps from files, as well as loading a few bitmaps as resources. The final bitmap is a solid color (black) bitmap that is created using the third `Bitmap()` constructor. After creating the bitmaps, the `GameStart()` function sets the current slide to the first bitmap.

The `GameEnd()` function simply cleans up the slide bitmaps by stepping through the array and deleting them one at a time. This is an important part of the Slideshow program because you definitely want to clean up after yourself.

The current slide is drawn to the game screen in the Slideshow program thanks to the `GamePaint()`function, which is shown in Listing 4.5.

LISTING 4.5 The `GamePaint()` Function Simply Draws the Current Slide Bitmap

```
void GamePaint(HDC hDC)
{
  // Draw the current slide bitmap
  g_pSlides[g_iCurSlide]->Draw(hDC, 0, 0);
}
```

The GamePaint() function is probably simpler than you might have expected. Here, you're really getting to see how helpful the Bitmap class is because it allows you to draw a bitmap image with a very simple call to the Draw() method of the Bitmap object. The g_iCurSlide global variable is used to make sure that the appropriate slide is drawn.

The GameCycle() function is responsible for moving to the next slide after imposing a small delay, as shown in Listing 4.6.

LISTING 4.6   The GameCycle() **Function Steps Through the Slides After Waiting a Few Seconds**

```
void GameCycle()
{
  static int iDelay = 0;

  // Establish a 3-second delay before moving to the next slide
  if (++iDelay > 3)
  {
    // Restore the delay counter
    iDelay = 0;

    // Move to the next slide
    if (++g_iCurSlide == g_iNUMSLIDES)
      g_iCurSlide = 0;

    // Force a repaint to draw the next slide
    InvalidateRect(g_pGame->GetWindow(), NULL, FALSE);
  }
}
```

The slide is only advanced every fourth time through this function, which slows down the slideshow to 1/4 fps or 1 frame every 4 seconds.

Because the game engine is limited to a minimum frame rate of one second, it's necessary to slow down the slideshow further by imposing a delay in the GameCycle() function. Three seconds is a reasonable delay for viewing each slide, so the GameCycle() function uses a static variable, iDelay, to delay each slide for three seconds before moving to the next one. This works because the frame rate is set at one cycle per second, and you only update the slide on every third cycle or every three seconds. In order to move to the next slide, the iCurSlide variable is incremented; if it is incremented past the last slide, the slideshow starts over at the first slide.

Just because you increment the current slide variable doesn't mean that the slideshow updates to show the new slide bitmap. Keep in mind that the current slide bitmap is drawn in the GamePaint() function, which is called whenever the client area of the Slideshow window needs to be repainted. The trick is to force a repaint of the window, which is possible using the Win32

InvalidateRect()function. The GameCycle() function calls InvalidateRect() to force a repaint and display the new slide bitmap. The second argument to InvalidateRect() indicates that the entire client area is to be repainted, whereas the last argument indicates that it isn't necessary to erase the client area before repainting.

Assembling the Resources

You've now seen the vast majority of the code for the Slideshow example, which hopefully wasn't too overwhelming, seeing as how the Bitmap class removed a great deal of the work required to display images. The only remaining code to address involves the bitmap resources used in the program. To demonstrate how to use bitmaps as resources, I decided to go ahead and include all the slide bitmaps as resources, even though the program only loads three of them as resources. Listing 4.7 contains the code for the Resource.h header file, which defines unique resource IDs for the bitmaps.

> Don't forget that all the bitmaps used in the Slideshow example, as well as all the bitmaps used throughout this book, are stored as 24-bit, uncompressed bitmaps.

Construction Cue

LISTING 4.7   The Resource.h Header File Contains Resource IDs for the Icons and Bitmap Images in the Slideshow Example

```
//-------------------------------------------------.
// Icons                  Range : 1000 - 1999
//-------------------------------------------------.
#define IDI_SLIDESHOW      1000
#define IDI_SLIDESHOW_SM   1001


//-------------------------------------------------.
// Bitmaps                Range : 2000 - 2999
//-------------------------------------------------.
#define IDB_IMAGE1         2000
#define IDB_IMAGE2         2001
#define IDB_IMAGE3         2002
#define IDB_IMAGE4         2003
#define IDB_IMAGE5         2004
```

The standard Windows naming convention is to name bitmap resources with an IDB_ prefix.

This code reveals how resources are typically organized according to type. It also shows how the numbers used to distinguish between resources are specified as ranges for each resource type. This is primarily an organizational issue, but it does help to keep things straight. Notice that there is no ID for the sixth bitmap, the solid color bitmap, because it is a blank bitmap that doesn't derive from a resource.

The bitmap resource IDs come into play in the Slideshow.rc resource script, which is shown in Listing 4.8.

LISTING 4.8   The Slideshow.rc Resource Script Contains the Resources for the Slideshow Example, Including the Bitmap Resourcese

```
//--------------------------------.
// Include Files
//--------------------------------.
#include "Resource.h"


//--------------------------------.
// Icons
//--------------------------------.
IDI_SLIDESHOW       ICON         "Res\\Slideshow.ico"
IDI_SLIDESHOW_SM    ICON         "Res\\Slideshow_sm.ico"


//--------------------------------.
// Bitmaps
//--------------------------------.
IDB_IMAGE1          BITMAP       "Res\\Image1.bmp"
IDB_IMAGE2          BITMAP       "Res\\Image2.bmp"
IDB_IMAGE3          BITMAP       "Res\\Image3.bmp"
IDB_IMAGE4          BITMAP       "Res\\Image4.bmp"
IDB_IMAGE5          BITMAP       "Res\\Image5.bmp"
```

Bitmap resources are specified just like other resources in the RC file, except that they are listed as type BITMAP.

This resource script reveals how bitmap resources are included using the BITMAP resource type. Including bitmaps in a resource script is similar to including icons and involves specifying the resource ID, resource type, and image file for each bitmap. By including bitmaps in the resource script, you are alleviating the need to include separate bitmap image files with the completed program.

Construction Cue

If you're using the Borland C++Builder Command Line Tools, be aware that a memory problem with the tool might cause the Slideshow example to not compile properly. This is because the large image files are compiled directly into the Slideshow executable, which causes the compiler to run out of memory and stop with an error. Hopefully, a newer version of the compiler will solve the problem, but as of this writing, the problem still exists.

Testing the Finished Product

The Slideshow example is definitely the most practical program you've seen thus far. You can use the program to display any kind of slideshow of images you want, provided that you store the images as 24-bit bitmaps with no compression. To demonstrate the practicality of the program, I decided to put together a slideshow of photos from a recent trip I took with some friends of mine to the Louisville Extreme Park in Louisville, Kentucky. Figure 4.2 shows a photo of yours truly, and it happens to be the opening slide in the slideshow.

FIGURE 4.2
The Slideshow example demonstrates how to display bitmap images and also serves as a good way to relive a vacation.

You'll notice that every three seconds, the slide will change, eventually leading to the end of the slideshow; after which, it wraps around and begins with the first image again. Figure 4.3 shows another slide in the slideshow (my friend, Darin Masters) to demonstrate how the slides are changed.

FIGURE 4.3
Each successive slide in the Slideshow example is separated by a three-second delay.

Whether or not you decide to place your family album of digital photographs into a Slideshow program of your own, you've hopefully gained an appreciation of bitmaps and how to work with them at the programming level. You also now have the `Bitmap` class, which you will be using heavily throughout the remainder of the book.

Summary

This chapter tackled one of the most important topics of game development by introducing you to bitmap images, as well as how they are loaded and displayed in a Windows program. You first analyzed the inner structure of a bitmap, which was necessary in order to gain an understanding of what it takes to write code that can load a bitmap from a file or resource. You then used this knowledge to assemble a bitmap class that handles the messy details of creating bitmaps based on files, resources, or solid colors. The chapter concluded by demonstrating how to use the bitmap class in a practical example program.

This chapter concludes the first part of the book, which has laid the groundwork for game programming in Windows. The next part of the book addresses the all-important topic of interacting with game players. You find out how to receive and process user input from a keyboard, mouse, and joystick, as well as create two complete games.

Extreme Game Makeover

You can use the Slideshow example in this chapter to do more interesting things than just show a sequence of pictures. For example, you could create a visual presentation by mixing in images that contain text. Microsoft PowerPoint is regularly used for such presentations, but you can use the Slideshow program as your own "poor man's" PowerPoint just by carefully creating the image slides. Follow these steps to create your own informative slideshow:

1. Decide what photographic images you'd like in the slideshow.

2. Using a graphics editing tool, create an image corresponding to each photo that contains a text description or any other text notes you'd like to point out with regard to the photo.

3. Number the images alternating so that each text image appears before its corresponding photographic image.

4. Change the Slideshow code to use this new set of images.

Voila! Now you have a slideshow that can convey useful information, complete with text explanations and descriptions. Whether you're sharing vacation tips at a travel seminar or doctoring family photos with humorous anecdotes, you've just doubled the fun of the Slideshow program.

PART II

Interacting with Game Players

CHAPTER 5

Controlling Games with the Keyboard and Mouse

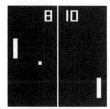

Arcade Archive

Defender is perhaps the most popular side-scrolling game ever made, which means that the game play flows sideways across the screen. Defender also shares the distinction of being one of the most difficult classic video games. Created by Williams in 1980, Defender is also unique in that it is one of two arcade games to have grossed more than one billion dollars. Can you guess the other? Pac-Man! Defender is a great example of a game whose controls were so well integrated into the game play that the game took a lot of experience to master. If you somehow manage to master Defender, its sequel, Stargate, is even tougher.

All the graphics in the world wouldn't save a game if you couldn't interact with it. There's a name for a game with no user interaction—it's called a screensaver! User interaction can come from several different places, but you can generally break it down into a short list of user input devices: the keyboard, the mouse, and joysticks. The keyboard and mouse are, by far, the two most standard user input devices on computers and are just about guaranteed to be supported on all personal computers. Joysticks are also quite common, but aren't nearly as commonplace as keyboards and mouse devices. Therefore, you should consider the keyboard and mouse the two most important game input devices, with joysticks following behind in third place. This chapter focuses on interacting with the user via the keyboard and mouse, whereas joysticks are covered in Chapter 7, "Improving Input with Joysticks."

In this chapter, you'll learn

- ▶ Why user input is so important in games
- ▶ How each of the major types of input devices impact games

▶ How to efficiently detect and respond to keyboard input

▶ How to handle mouse input

▶ How to create a program with an animated graphical object that you can control with the keyboard and mouse

Gaming and User Input

User input is the means by which a user interacts with a game. Considering the fact that user input encompasses all communications between a player and a game, you would think that designing an intuitive, efficient interface for user input would be at the top of the list of key game design elements. However, that isn't always the case. With all the hype these days surrounding real-time, lifelike 3D graphics engines and positional 3D audio in games, effective user input support is often overlooked. In fact, user input is perhaps the most overlooked aspect of modern game design, which is truly a tragedy. It's a tragedy because user input support in a game directly impacts the playability of the game, and when the user input isn't effective, the play suffers.

You see, I'm from the old school of game players, and I still remember paying homage to the gods of gaming with my hard-earned allowance in arcades well before there was an option of playing anything other than Pong at home. (See the opener for Chapter 1, "Learning the Basics of Game Creation.") In return for my quarter offerings, the game gods usually provided me with incredibly fun games that usually had to survive on their playability alone. Because the hardware at that time simply couldn't provide a very high level of graphic and sound intensity, game developers were forced to make up for it with game play. Of course, they didn't consider their focus on playability as making up for anything; with the limited graphics and sound capabilities at the time, they didn't have an option.

Let me give you a quick example of what I'm talking about with regard to playability and user input. One of my all-time favorite games is Ring King, which is a boxing game for the original Nintendo Entertainment System (NES). Ring King is definitely considered "old" by current gaming standards—possibly even ancient. Compared to current games, it has weak graphics, animation, and sound. However, I still play the game simply because it plays so well. That playability is largely based on how the game handles user input; it allows for very subtle timing when you punch and dodge, which goes a long way in a boxing game! Ring King certainly has its limitations, but its designers got it right when they came up with the punch-dodge timing—try to throw a straight lunge punch, and you'll see what I mean. Since then, I've tried to find a modern replacement for Ring King, but with no luck. Although plenty of modern games contain fancy graphics and sound, anything comparable to the responsiveness of the controls in my old favorite is tough to find. I'm still looking, though.

Lest you think I'm being overly critical of current games, plenty of recent games have incredible user input support, along with awesome graphics and sound. However, an equal number of recent games have killer graphics and sound, but little substance when it comes to playability and user input. These types of games might be visually stunning and fun to listen to, but they rarely have any lasting appeal beyond the initial "Wow!"

Gamer's Garage

> Since I'm playing the role of critic for a moment, I'd like to point out a trend in movies that has paralleled video games in many ways: replacing substance with eye candy. Using science fiction and horror movies as a couple of example genres, compare some of the great movies from 20 years ago with some of the popular, recent movies. By and large, you see better storytelling and a more innovative use of special effects in the older movies; their creators didn't have a choice. Since the maturation of computer-generated effects, too many filmmakers rely on wowing us with over-the-top effects when they're not always necessary. I love special effects as much as anyone else, but the "less is more" adage often holds true. The same rule applies to video games.

Now, let me step down from the soapbox and get to the real point, which is that you should carefully plan the user input for your games just as you carefully plan the graphics, sound, and game logic. This doesn't mean only deciding between supporting a keyboard or a mouse for the user interface. It means putting some real thought into making the user interface as intuitive as possible. You want the controls for the game to feel as natural as possible to the player. If you really want to see how well your user interface works, create an alternate set of really awful graphics with little or no sound and see if your game is still fun to play.

Taking a Look at User Input Devices

An *input device* is the physical hardware that allows a user to interact with a game. Input devices all perform the same function: converting information provided by the user into a form understandable by the computer. Input devices establish the link between the user and your game. Even though you can't directly control the input device hardware, you can certainly control how it is interpreted in your game. As I mentioned earlier, there are three primary types of user input devices:

- ▶ The keyboard
- ▶ The mouse
- ▶ Joysticks

Gamer's Garage

In case you're wondering, trackballs are functionally very similar to mouse devices and are often treated just like mouse devices from a software perspective. In fact, the Win32 API doesn't discern between trackballs and mouse devices, so the mouse support in your games indirectly supports trackballs as well. Similarly, game pads are classified as joysticks and are treated no differently than joysticks from a programming perspective.

The next few sections get you acquainted with these devices and their relationship to game user input.

Accepting Keyboard Input

The keyboard has been the computer input device of choice since its inception. Although mouse devices, joysticks, flight sticks, game pads, virtual reality gloves, and many other user input devices have brought extended input capabilities to the game player, none is as established as the keyboard. At the bare minimum, you can always count on a game player having a keyboard.

The keyboard is a surprisingly useful input device for a wide range of games. The sheer number of keys alone gives the keyboard appeal for games that require a wide variety of user input. Even more useful with the keyboard is the natural feel of pressing keys for games requiring quick firing and movement. This usefulness is evident in the number of arcade games that still use buttons, even when powerful digital joysticks are readily available. Keys (or buttons) simply are easier to use in many games, including those with many input combinations.

When assessing the potential use of the keyboard in a game, try to think in terms of the most intuitive user interface possible. For example, any game involving the player moving an object around would benefit from using the arrow keys. A good example is the classic 3D-shooter Doom, which makes creative use of a keyboard-specific feature that greatly enhances the playability of the game. The left and right arrow keys, when used alone, rotate the player left and right in the game world. However, when the Shift key is held down, the same left and right arrow keys cause the player to *strafe*, meaning that the player moves sideways without changing direction. This seemingly small enhancement to the keyboard controls goes a long way when playing the game.

When you're deciding on specific keys to use for keyboard controls in your game, consider the potential limitations on players using other platforms or hardware configurations. For example, I primarily use a Windows XP PC equipped with a Microsoft Natural keyboard. If you aren't familiar with these keyboards, they are split down the middle for ergonomic reasons. If you don't use one of these keyboards, it might not occur to you that key combinations near the center of the keyboard will be separated a few inches for people like me. So, remember that if you use the G and H keys (or other middle keys) in your game, and it plays well for you, it might not work out so well for players with different keyboards.

In Chapter 1, I mentioned a game called Combat Tanks that I co-developed nearly 10 years ago. Back then, there were no keyboards with split key configurations, so that particular game suffers from keys that are uncomfortably spread out on keyboards such as the Microsoft Natural keyboard. Fortunately, we designed the game with customizable keys, so you can change around the control keys for the game. This is an example of a nice game feature having future unintended significance...always a good thing!

Gamer's Garage

The most common keys used in games are the arrow keys. If you're writing an action game, you might also have keys for firing and selecting between weapons. When you're deciding on the keys to use, keep in mind things such as the creative usage of the Shift key in Doom. If you can limit the number of primary game control keys by making use of a secondary key, such as Shift, you've made the game controls that much easier to use.

Just in case you think I'm a bit behind the times by referring to Doom repeatedly, I realize that numerous newer and better first-person shooters are around now. However, I like to point out which games added a new or unique feature to a genre, and in this case, Doom was the first major game I know of that used the strafing feature for moving from side to side.

Gamer's Garage

Responding to the Mouse

Although the keyboard is firmly in place as the most necessary of user input devices, the graphical nature of modern computers establishes the mouse or a similar pointing device as a standard input device as well. The mouse, however, doesn't share the wide range of input applications to games that the keyboard has. This stems from its primary usage as a point-and-click device; if you haven't noticed, a lot of games don't follow the point-and-click paradigm.

In regard to gaming, the usefulness of the mouse is totally dependent on the type of game and, therefore, the type of user interaction dictated by the game. However, as quickly as some people write off the mouse as being a useless interface in some games, others praise the fine control it provides. Again, a good example is Doom. Personally, I think the keyboard is much more responsive than the mouse, and the keyboard enables me to get around faster and with more control. But I have friends who feel lost playing the game without a mouse.

Clearly, this is a situation in which the game designers saw a way to provide support for both the keyboard and mouse. With the exception of the most extreme cases, this should be your goal as well. Different game players like different things, and the safest solution is to hedge your bets and support all input devices whenever possible. By following this simple rule, you can develop games that can be appreciated and enjoyed by a broader group of game players.

Interacting with Joysticks

Although not quite as standard as keyboards and mouse devices, joysticks nonetheless represent a very common component of modern computer systems. Joysticks are in many ways a throwback to video games of old—many of which relied heavily on joysticks for controlling characters, spaceships, and other game objects. Joysticks come in both digital and analog form, although the difference between the two isn't terribly important from a programming perspective. The primary thing to consider when assessing the role of joysticks in games is whether it makes sense to play the game with a joystick. In other words, does the movement in the game lend itself to being carried out with a vertical stick (or flat game pad), as opposed to using keyboard keys or a mouse? Of course, it's not a bad idea to support multiple input devices—in which case, you might opt to include joystick support just to be flexible. Most game pads count as joysticks because they provide a similar functionality in terms of providing a multidirectional control for movement, as well as several buttons.

It's worth mentioning that some games out there seem to be expressly designed for being played with joysticks. For one, the extremely popular game Halo (and its successor Halo 2) on the Xbox console system uses a unique feature that would be difficult to replicate with a keyboard or mouse. Halo allows you to press the joystick inward to activate a rifle scope on your gun. So, if you see some bad guys off in the distance, you can push in on the joystick to zoom with the scope and pick them off one by one. The scope/zoom feature in Halo is an excellent example of an ingenious game feature made possible by a specific type of input device. Of course, the Xbox controller had to include a joystick with the push feature in order for Halo to work, so Microsoft deserves some credit on the hardware side of things.

Assessing Keyboard Input for Games

You know that messages are used heavily throughout the Win32 API to deliver notifications regarding things such as window creation, window destruction, window activation, window deactivation, and so on. You might be glad to find out that this same messaging system is used to deliver notifications regarding key presses on the keyboard. More specifically, the Win32 API defines messages called WM_KEYDOWN and WM_KEYUP that inform you whenever a key has been pressed or released, respectively. These two messages are quite easy to handle in a Windows program, and I'd love to show you how to use them, but there's a problem. The problem is that the standard Windows messaging system is painfully slow when it comes to delivering keyboard messages. Because games rely heavily on responsive controls, it simply isn't acceptable to work with the Windows keyboard messages.

The bottom line is that none of your games can support keyboards. Okay, I'm kidding. The truth is that there is always a workaround in game programming, and the slow keyboard messaging problem presents a perfect opportunity for a workaround. If you recall, the timing for the Game Engine was established back in Chapter 2, "Creating an Engine for Games," in the WinMain() function. The WinMain() function includes a program loop that repeats over and over, processing messages for the program. When the function isn't processing messages, it spends its time running through cycles of the game engine. In other words, the game engine takes advantage of *idle time* in the main program loop to carry out its game-related tasks. This idle time is what you can use to your advantage when processing key presses and releases on the keyboard.

The concept of "idle time" with respect to the WinMain() function is a little misleading. When you consider that games don't typically process very many messages from Windows, the vast majority of the time spent by a game program is idle time or time when it's not responding to standard Windows messages. This time can therefore be put to use running the game engine, which is what I mean when I talk about running through the game cycles during idle time.

Construction Cue

The idea behind this juiced up approach to keyboard event handling is that instead of sitting around waiting for Windows to eventually send you a keyboard message, you constantly check the keyboard to see if any of the keys you're interested in have been pressed. If so, the game instantly springs into motion and efficiently responds to the key press. If no key is pressed, the game engine hums along with no interruptions. The strategy here is to basically take keyboard processing into your own hands and bypass the standard Windows approach, which ultimately results in much more responsive keyboard controls for your games. You learn how to implement this speedy keyboard handler in code a little later in the chapter. For now, let's take a look at how to respond to mouse events.

Tracking the Mouse

When you move the mouse, a series of events is set off that is very similar to those set off by the keyboard. In fact, the Win32 API includes a series of mouse messages that are used to convey mouse events, similar to how keyboard messages convey keyboard events. In the previous section, you learned that the Win32 keyboard messages aren't up to the task of providing efficient input for games. Fortunately, the same cannot be said of the mouse messages. It turns out that the built-in Win32 approach to handling mouse events via messages works out just fine for games. The following are the mouse messages used to notify Windows programs of mouse events:

- ▶ WM_MOUSEMOVE—Any mouse movement
- ▶ WM_LBUTTONDOWN—Left mouse button pressed
- ▶ WM_LBUTTONUP—Left mouse button released
- ▶ WM_RBUTTONDOWN—Right mouse button pressed
- ▶ WM_RBUTTONUP—Right mouse button released
- ▶ WM_MBUTTONDOWN—Middle mouse button pressed
- ▶ WM_MBUTTONUP—Middle mouse button released

The first mouse message, WM_MOUSEMOVE, lets you know whenever the mouse has been moved. The remaining messages relay mouse button clicks for the left, right, and middle buttons, respectively. Keep in mind that a mouse button click consists of a button press followed by a button release; you can implement a mouse dragging feature by keeping track of when a mouse button is pressed and released and watching for mouse movement in between.

A WM_MOUSEWHEEL message is also sent whenever the user rotates the wheel that is located on the top of some mouse devices. Although the mouse wheel could certainly prove useful in some game scenarios, I opted to focus on the core mouse input messages in this discussion. By all means, explore adding support for the WM_MOUSEWHEEL message to the game engine if you have a game in mind that would benefit from it.

Regardless of whether you're interested in mouse movement or a mouse button click, the important factor regarding the mouse is where the mouse cursor is located. Fortunately, the mouse cursor position is provided with all the previously mentioned mouse messages. It's packed into the lParam argument that gets sent to the GameEngine::HandleEvent() method. The following is the prototype for this method, just in case you forgot:

```
LRESULT GameEngine::HandleEvent(HWND hWindow, UINT msg, WPARAM wParam,
  LPARAM lParam);
```

If you recall, the wParam and lParam arguments are sent along with every Windows message and contain message-specific information. In the case of the mouse messages, lParam contains the XY position of the mouse cursor packed into its low and high words. The following is an example of a code snippet that extracts the mouse position from the lParam argument in a WM_MOUSEMOVE message handler:

```
case WM_MOUSEMOVE:
  WORD x = LOWORD(lParam);
  WORD y = HIWORD(lParam);
  return 0;
```

The wParam argument for the mouse messages includes information about the mouse button states, as well as some keyboard information. More specifically, wParam lets you know if any of the three mouse buttons are down, as well as whether the Shift or Control keys on the keyboard are being pressed. In case you don't see it, the wParam argument—used in conjunction with WM_MOUSEMOVE—provides you with enough information to implement your own Doom strafing feature! The following are the constants used with the mouse messages to interpret the value of the wParam argument:

▶ MK_LBUTTON—Left mouse button is down

▶ MK_RBUTTON—Right mouse button is down

▶ MK_MBUTTON—Middle mouse button is down

▶ MK_SHIFT—Shift key is down

▶ MK_CONTROL—Control key is down

You can check for any of these mouse constants to see if a button or key is being pressed during the mouse move. The constants are actually *flags*, which means that they can be combined together in the wParam argument. To check for the presence of an individual flag, you must use the bitwise AND operator (&) to see if the flag is present. The following is an example of checking wParam to see if the right mouse button is down:

```
if (wParam & MK_RBUTTON)
  // Yep, the right mouse button is down!
```

This code shows how to use the bitwise AND operator (&) to check for individual flags. This is a technique you use in Chapter 7 to check the state of a joystick.

Revamping the Game Engine for Input

Because we've already built a game engine for use in carrying out the various tasks associated with game management, it only makes sense to incorporate user input handling into the game engine. Granted, a certain aspect of handling user input is game-specific and therefore must be handled in the code for each individual game. However, there are some general aspects of keyboard and mouse handling that you can incorporate into the game engine to simplify the work required of specific game code.

If you recall, the idea behind the game engine is to provide a certain degree of game functionality in a self-contained class and then delegate game-specific tasks to a series of functions that each game is responsible for providing. For example, the GamePaint() function must be provided in a game to draw the game screen. Although the game engine doesn't technically provide code for the GamePaint() function, it does make sure that it gets called whenever the game window needs to be painted; it's up to each game to provide the actual code for GamePaint(), which makes sense because every game draws itself differently. Similar functions need to be added to the game engine to provide games with a means of handling user input.

The next couple of sections guide you through modifications to the game engine to add support for keyboard and mouse input handling.

Adding Keyboard Support

Earlier in this chapter, you found out that the standard Windows approach to keyboard handling with messages simply isn't good enough for games. A much better way to handle keyboard input is to repeatedly check the state of the keyboard for specific key presses and then react accordingly. Using this strategy, much of the burden of keyboard input handling is passed on to the game code, which means that the game engine is primarily responsible only for calling a keyboard handler function to give the game a chance to respond to key presses. The following is what this function looks like:

```
void HandleKeys();
```

The HandleKeys() function must be provided as part of the game code, and therefore, it isn't included in the game engine. If you don't want your game to support keyboard input, you can just leave the HandleKeys() function blank. Of course, the game engine must make sure that the HandleKeys() function gets called rapidly enough to give your games a responsive feel. This is accomplished in the WinMain() function within the game engine code. The following is the change made to this function:

```
if (iTickCount > iTickTrigger)
{
  iTickTrigger = iTickCount +
    GameEngine::GetEngine()->GetFrameDelay();
  HandleKeys();
  GameCycle();
}
```

The only change to the WinMain() code is the new call to the HandleKeys() function. Notice that this call occurs just before the GameCycle() function, which means that a game gets a chance to respond to keyboard input before every game cycle. Don't forget; the specifics of handling keyboard input are carried out in each specific game when you create your own HandleKeys() function. You find out how to do this later in the chapter.

Even if you don't plan on using keyboard input in your games, you must provide a HandleKeys() function—just leave it empty if you don't want any keyboard controls. This same rule applies to the mouse input functions you learn about next, as well as all the game engine functions that are called on a game for game-specific event handling.

Construction Cue

Adding Mouse Support

Although keyboard input in games is admittedly non-standard in terms of deviating from how things are typically handled in Windows programming, mouse input is handled the old-fashioned way—with messages. It's not that mouse messages are more efficient than keyboard messages; it's just harder to notice sluggish mouse input. In other words, mouse messages appear to be fast enough to allow you to create a responsive mouse interface, whereas keyboard messages do not.

In order to support mouse input, games must support the The following three functions, which are called by the game engine to pass along mouse events:

```
void MouseButtonDown(int x, int y, BOOL bLeft);
void MouseButtonUp(int x, int y, BOOL bLeft);
void MouseMove(int x, int y);
```

In order to connect mouse messages with these mouse handler functions, the game engine must look for the appropriate mouse messages and respond accordingly. The following code includes the new portion of the GameEngine::HandleEvent() method that is responsible for handling mouse messages delivered to the main game window.

```
case WM_LBUTTONDOWN:
  // Handle left mouse button press
  MouseButtonDown(LOWORD(lParam), HIWORD(lParam), TRUE);
  return 0;

case WM_LBUTTONUP:
  // Handle left mouse button release
  MouseButtonUp(LOWORD(lParam), HIWORD(lParam), TRUE);
  return 0;

case WM_RBUTTONDOWN:
  // Handle right mouse button press
  MouseButtonDown(LOWORD(lParam), HIWORD(lParam), FALSE);
  return 0;

case WM_RBUTTONUP:
  // Handle right mouse button release
  MouseButtonUp(LOWORD(lParam), HIWORD(lParam), FALSE);
  return 0;

case WM_MOUSEMOVE:
  // Handle mouse movement
  MouseMove(LOWORD(lParam), HIWORD(lParam));
  return 0;
```

This code handles the following mouse messages: WM_LBUTTONDOWN, WM_LBUTTONUP, WM_RBUTTONDOWN, WM_RBUTTONUP, and WM_MOUSEMOVE. Each piece of message handler code simply calls one of the mouse functions with the appropriate arguments. The first and second arguments to all the mouse functions include the X and Y position of the mouse cursor at the moment the message is delivered. The last argument to the mouse button functions is a Boolean value that identifies whether the left (TRUE) or right (FALSE) mouse button is involved in the event.

As you can hopefully tell from the code, the idea behind the mouse functions is to enable games to simply provide MouseButtonDown(), MouseButtonUp(), and MouseMove() functions, as opposed to getting involved with message handling. So, to support the mouse in your games, all you have to do is provide code for these three functions.

Sprucing Up the Bitmap Class

You've now made the necessary changes to the game engine to prepare it for keyboard and mouse input. However, there is another minor change you need to make that doesn't technically have anything to do with input. I'm referring to bitmap *transparency*, which enables bitmaps to not always appear as square graphical objects. Don't get me wrong; bitmaps definitely are square graphical objects, but they don't necessarily have to be drawn that way. The idea behind transparency is that you can identify a color as the *transparent color*, which is then used to indicate parts of a bitmap that are transparent. When the bitmap is drawn, pixels of the transparent color aren't drawn, and the background shows through.

Why is there a discussion of bitmap transparency in a chapter focused on keyboard and mouse input? The answer has to do with the fact that I want you to view the game engine as a work in progress that is constantly evolving and picking up new features. In this case, the example at the end of this chapter benefits greatly from bitmap transparency, so it only makes sense to add the feature here. You'll continue to make small improvements to the game engine throughout the book, even if they don't tie in directly to the topic at hand. The end result will be a game engine with a lot of slick little features that will make your games all the more fun.

Construction Cue

From a graphics creation perspective, you create bitmaps with transparency by selecting a color that isn't used in your graphics, such as "hot purple," which is also known as magenta. You then use magenta to fill areas of your bitmaps that need to appear transparent. It's then up to the revamped game engine to make sure that these transparent regions don't get drawn with the rest of the bitmap. You obviously don't want magenta borders around your images!

The game development community is mixed in its use of transparency colors. In the old days, magenta (RGB: 255, 0, 255) was the "standard" color to denote transparency. It turns out that it is such an obnoxious color that it is rarely used in game graphics, which is exactly what you need in a "transparent color." However, magenta can be problematic when it comes to blending in a graphic with a background because image editors tend to "feather" the edges of an image to smooth it into its background. Most commercial 3D games use pure black (RGB: 0, 0, 0), pure blue (RGB: 0, 0, 255), or medium gray (RGB: 128, 128, 128) as their transparency color, or they use alpha transparency, which is a whole different can of worms. I've stuck with magenta as the transparency color for the examples throughout the book, but as long as you're consistent within the graphics for a particular game, you can select any unused color you want.

The trick to making bitmap transparency work in the game engine is to expand the existing `Bitmap::Draw()` method so that it supports transparency. This is accomplished by adding two new arguments:

▶ `bTrans`—A Boolean value that indicates whether the bitmap should be drawn with transparency

▶ `crTransColor`—The transparent color of the bitmap

It's important to try to make changes to the game engine that don't cause problems with programs we've already written. Therefore, rather than add these two arguments to the `Draw()` method and require them of all bitmaps, it's much better to add them and provide default values:

```
void Draw(HDC hDC, int x, int y, BOOL bTrans = FALSE,
  COLORREF crTransColor = RGB(255, 0, 255));
```

If you notice, the default value of `bTrans` is `FALSE`, which means that if you leave off the argument, transparency isn't used. This works great for existing code because it doesn't change the way the `Draw()` method already works. You'll notice that the default color specified in `crTransColor` (`RGB(255, 0, 255)`) is magenta, so if you stick with that color as your transparent color, you won't have to specify a transparent color in the `Draw()` method.

The only significant changes to the `Draw()` method involve checking the transparency argument and then drawing the bitmap with transparency using the Win32 `TransparentBlt()` function if the argument is `TRUE`. Otherwise, it's business as usual with the `BitBlt()` function being used to draw bitmaps without transparency.

Although the `TransparentBlt()` function is part of the Win32 API, it isn't as widely supported as the traditional `BitBlt()` function. More specifically, the function isn't supported in versions of Windows prior to Windows 98, such as Windows 95.

Construction Cue

The `TransparentBlt()` function is part of the Win32 API, but it requires the inclusion of a special library called msimg32.lib in order for your games to compile properly. This is a standard library that should be included with your compiler, but you'll need to make sure that it is linked in with any programs that use the `TransparentBlt()` function. If you aren't familiar with altering linker settings for your compiler, just take a look at the compiler documentation and find out how to add additional libraries to a project; it typically involves simply entering the name of the library, msimg32.lib in this case, in a project settings window. Or, if you happen to be using Microsoft Visual Studio, you can follow these steps:

1. Open the project in Visual Studio (Visual C++).

2. Right-click on the project's folder in Solution Explorer and click Properties in the pop-up menu.

3. Click the Linker folder in the left pane of the Properties window and then click Input.

4. Click next to Additional Dependencies in the right pane and type **msimg32.lib**.

5. Click the OK button to accept the changes to the project.

If you're using Microsoft Visual Studio 6, you can accomplish the same task of adding the msimg32.lib file to your project by first right-clicking on the Resource Files project folder. Then, select Add Files to Folder from the pop-up menu and browse to the \LIB directory. Finally, select MSIMG32.LIB and click OK.

Construction Cue

After completing these steps, you can safely compile a program and know that the msimg32.lib library is being successfully linked into the executable program file. You'll know if you didn't edit the linker settings properly because a game build will fail with linker errors if it doesn't link in the msimg32.lib library.

The source code for the examples in the book is located on the accompanying CD-ROM and includes Visual C++, Borland C++Builder, and Dev-C++ project files with the appropriate msimg32.lib linker settings already made.

Construction Cue

Building the UFO Example

In order to really get a feel for how keyboard and mouse input works in games, it's helpful to work through a complete example. The remainder of this chapter focuses on an example called UFO, which is a suitable follow-up to the Crop Circles example from Chapter 3. Although this program isn't technically a game, it's by far the closest thing you've seen to a game yet. It involves a flying saucer that you control with the keyboard and/or mouse. You're able to fly the flying saucer around a bitmap background image. Perhaps most important is the fact that the UFO program demonstrates how good of a feel you can create for game controls. More specifically, the arrow keys on the keyboard are surprisingly responsive in the UFO program.

Although you haven't really learned about animation yet, the UFO example makes use of animation to allow you to fly the flying saucer. Fortunately, the program is simple enough that you can get by without knowing the specifics about animation. All you really need to know is that you can alter the position of a bitmap image to simulate movement on the screen. This occurs thanks to the game engine, which redraws the bitmap every game cycle. So, by altering the position of an image and redrawing it repeatedly, you create the effect of movement. The UFO example reveals how this task is accomplished, as well as how the keyboard and mouse fit into the picture.

Gamer's Garage

> You learn the details of how animation works in Chapter 9, "Making Things Move with Sprite Animation."

Writing the Program Code

The header file for the UFO example lays the groundwork for the meat of the program, which carries out the details of the flying saucer animation and user input. Listing 5.1 contains the code for the UFO.h header file, which declares global variables used to control the flying saucer.

LISTING 5.1   The UFO.h Header File Declares Global Variables Used to Keep Track of the Flying Saucer

```
#pragma once

//------------------------------------------------
// Include Files
//------------------------------------------------
```

```
#include <windows.h>
#include "Resource.h"
#include "GameEngine.h"
#include "Bitmap.h"

//----------------------------------------
// Global Variables
//----------------------------------------
HINSTANCE     g_hInstance;
GameEngine*   g_pGame;
const int     g_iMAXSPEED = 8;
Bitmap*       g_pBackground;
Bitmap*       g_pSaucer;
int           g_iSaucerX, g_iSaucerY;
int           g_iSpeedX, g_iSpeedY;
```

The maximum speed of the flying saucer indicates the maximum number of pixels the saucer can move in the X and/or Y directions in each game cycle.

The first thing of interest in this code is the g_iMAXSPEED constant, which establishes the maximum speed of the flying saucer. The speed of the flying saucer is how many pixels it can travel in a given direction in each game cycle. So, the value of the g_iMAXSPEED constant means that the flying saucer can never travel more than 8 pixels in a horizontal or vertical direction in a game cycle.

The g_pBackground and g_pSaucer global variables store the two bitmaps used in the program, which correspond to a night sky background image and the flying saucer image. The remaining variables pertain to the flying saucer and include its XY position and XY speed. The XY position of the flying saucer is specified relative to the game screen. The XY speed, on the other hand, simply tells the program how many pixels the flying saucer should be moved per game cycle; negative values for the speed variables indicate that the flying saucer is moving in the opposite direction.

With the global variables in place, we can move on to the game functions. The first game function to consider is GameInitialize(), which creates the game engine and establishes the frame rate. The frame rate for the program is set to 30 frames per second. This is a relatively high frame rate for games, but it results in much smoother motion for the flying saucer, as you soon find out.

Next on the game function agenda is the GameStart() function, which creates and loads the flying saucer bitmaps, as well as sets the initial flying saucer position and speed (Listing 5.2).

LISTING 5.2 The `GameStart()` Function Performs Startup Tasks for the UFO Example

```
void GameStart(HWND hWindow)
{
  // Create and load the background and saucer bitmaps
  HDC hDC = GetDC(hWindow);
  g_pBackground = new Bitmap(hDC, IDB_BACKGROUND, g_hInstance);
  g_pSaucer = new Bitmap(hDC, IDB_SAUCER, g_hInstance);

  // Set the initial saucer position and speed
  g_iSaucerX = 250 - (g_pSaucer->GetWidth() / 2);
  g_iSaucerY = 200 - (g_pSaucer->GetHeight() / 2);
  g_iSpeedX = 0;
  g_iSpeedY = 0;
}
```

The saucer is initially placed stationary in the middle of the game screen.

The `GameStart()` function is used to initialize data pertaining to the program, such as the bitmaps and other global variables. The flying saucer position is initially set to the middle of the game screen, and then the speed of the saucer is set to 0 so that it isn't moving.

You might think that a program with an animated flying saucer cruising over a background image would require a complex `GamePaint()` function. However, Listing 5.3 shows how this simply isn't the case.

LISTING 5.3 The `GamePaint()` Function Draws the Background and Flying Saucer Bitmaps

```
void GamePaint(HDC hDC)
{
  // Draw the background and saucer bitmaps
  g_pBackground->Draw(hDC, 0, 0);
  g_pSaucer->Draw(hDC, g_iSaucerX, g_iSaucerY, TRUE);
}
```

As the code reveals, the `GamePaint()` function for the UFO program is painfully simple; all the function does is draw the background and flying saucer bitmaps. The background bitmap is drawn at the origin (0, 0) of the game screen, whereas the flying saucer is drawn at its current position. Notice that TRUE is passed as the last argument to the `Draw()` method when drawing the flying saucer, which indicates that the saucer is to be drawn with transparency using the default transparent color (magenta).

Figure 5.1 shows the flying saucer bitmap image, including the transparent color filled around the saucer; I realize that you're seeing this image in black and white on the printed page, but you can either visualize the hot purple transparent color or open the Saucer.bmp file for yourself from the accompanying CD-ROM.

FIGURE 5.1
The flying saucer bitmap image uses the default transparent color (magenta) in the filled area around the saucer to indicate where the image is transparent.

The GameCycle() function is a little more interesting than the others you've seen because it is actually responsible for updating the position of the flying saucer based on its speed. Listing 5.4 shows how this is accomplished in the code for the GameCycle() function.

LISTING 5.4 The GameCycle() Function Updates the Saucer Position and then Repaints the Game Screen

```
void GameCycle()
{
  // Update the saucer position
  g_iSaucerX = min(500 - g_pSaucer->GetWidth(), max(0, g_iSaucerX + g_iSpeedX)
  g_iSaucerY = min(320, max(0, g_iSaucerY + g_iSpeedY));

  // Force a repaint to redraw the saucer
  InvalidateRect(g_pGame->GetWindow(), NULL, FALSE);
}
```

The min() and max() functions are used to ensure that the saucer stays within the confines of the game screen.

The GameCycle() function updates the position of the flying saucer by adding its speed to its position. If the speed is negative, the saucer will move to the left and/or up, whereas positive speed values move the saucer right and/or down. The seemingly tricky code for setting the position must also take into account the boundaries of the game screen so that the flying saucer can't be flown off into oblivion. Granted, the concept of flying off the screen might sound interesting, but it turns out to be quite confusing! Another option would be to wrap the saucer around to the other side of the screen if it goes over the boundary, which is how games such as Asteroids solved this problem, but I opted for the simpler solution of just stopping it at the edges. After updating the position of the flying saucer, the GameCycle() function forces a repaint of the game screen to reflect the new saucer position.

The flying saucer is now being drawn and updated properly, but you still don't have a way to change its speed so that it can fly. This is accomplished first by handling keyboard input in the HandleKeys() function, which is shown in Listing 5.5.

LISTING 5.5 The HandleKeys() Function Checks the Status of the Arrow Keys, Which Are Used to Control the Flying Saucer

```
void HandleKeys()
{
  // Change the speed of the saucer in response to arrow key presses
  if (GetAsyncKeyState(VK_LEFT) < 0)
    g_iSpeedX = max(-g_iMAXSPEED, --g_iSpeedX);
  else if (GetAsyncKeyState(VK_RIGHT) < 0)
    g_iSpeedX = min(g_iMAXSPEED, ++g_iSpeedX);
  if (GetAsyncKeyState(VK_UP) < 0)
    g_iSpeedY = max(-g_iMAXSPEED, --g_iSpeedY);
  else if (GetAsyncKeyState(VK_DOWN) < 0)
    g_iSpeedY = min(g_iMAXSPEED, ++g_iSpeedY);
}
```

The HandleKeys() function uses the Win32 GetAsyncKeyState() function to check the status of the arrow keys (VK_LEFT, VK_RIGHT, VK_UP, and VK_DOWN) and see if any of them are being pressed. If so, the speed of the flying saucer is adjusted appropriately. Notice that the newly calculated speed is always checked against the g_iMAXSPEED global constant to make sure that a speed limit is enforced. Even flying saucers are required to stay within the speed limit!

Construction Cue

> The GetAsyncKeyState() function is part of the Win32 API, and it provides a means of obtaining the state of any key on the keyboard at any time. You specify which key you're looking for by using its *virtual key code*; Windows defines virtual key codes for all the keys on a standard keyboard. Common key codes for games include VK_LEFT, VK_RIGHT, VK_UP, VK_DOWN, VK_CONTROL, VK_SHIFT, and VK_RETURN.

If you thought handling keyboard input in the UFO program was easy, wait until you see how the mouse is handled. To make things a little more interesting, both mouse buttons are used in this program. The left mouse button sets the flying saucer position to the current mouse cursor position, whereas the right mouse button sets the speed of the flying saucer to 0. So, you can use the mouse to quickly get control of the flying saucer; just right-click to stop it and then left-click to position it wherever you want. Listing 5.6 shows the code for the MouseButtonDown() function, which makes this mouse magic possible.

LISTING 5.6 The MouseButtonDown() Function Uses the Left and Right Mouse Buttons to Move the Flying Saucer to the Current Mouse Position and Stop the Flying Saucer, Respectively

```
void MouseButtonDown(int x, int y, BOOL bLeft)
{
  if (bLeft)
  {
```

```
  // Set the saucer position to the mouse position
  g_iSaucerX = x - (g_pSaucer->GetWidth() / 2);
  g_iSaucerY = y - (g_pSaucer->GetHeight() / 2);
}
else
{
  // Stop the saucer
  g_iSpeedX = 0;
  g_iSpeedY = 0;
}
}
```

Without this code, the saucer would appear with its upper-left corner at the mouse position upon a left button click, as opposed to being centered on the mouse position.

The first step in this code is to check and see which one of the mouse buttons was pressed—left or right. I know, most PC mouse devices these days have three buttons, but I wanted to keep the game engine relatively simple, so I just focused on the two most important buttons. If the left mouse button was pressed, the function calculates the position of the flying saucer so that it is centered on the current mouse cursor position. If the right button was pressed, the speed of the flying saucer is set to 0.

The right button stops the saucer dead in its tracks.

Construction Cue

If you determine that supporting two mouse buttons isn't enough for the game engine, considering that three-button mouse devices are sometimes used, feel free to modify it on your own. It primarily involves changing the third argument of the `MouseButtonDown()` function so that it can convey more than two values—one for each of the three mouse buttons.

Testing the Finished Product

The UFO example is the closest thing you've seen to a game thus far and is quite interesting in terms of allowing you to fly around an animated graphical object. Hopefully, you'll be pleasantly surprised by the responsiveness of the program's keyboard controls. Figure 5.2 shows the UFO program in action as the flying saucer does a flyby of some desert cacti.

If you guide the flying saucer to the edge of the game screen, it will stop, which is to be expected given the program code you just worked through. There are a variety of different ways to tweak this program and make it more intriguing, such as wrapping the flying saucer from one side of the screen to the other, which is why I hope you spend some time tinkering with the code.

FIGURE 5.2
The UFO example
demonstrates how
to control an ani-
mated graphical
object with the key-
board and mouse.

Summary

The ability to effectively communicate with the people who play your games is a critical factor of game design and development. In one direction, a game communicates by displaying graphics and playing sounds and music, but in the other direction, the user responds by interacting with a physical input device of some sort. It's very important for game developers to master the fine art of responding to user input through a variety of different user input devices. The keyboard and mouse are the two fundamental user input devices that you can count on all people having. This chapter showed you how to handle and respond to keyboard and mouse input in an efficient manner specifically suited to games.

Beyond the keyboard and mouse, it's up to your resources and the specific needs of each game to determine whether you should support additional input devices. Chapter 7 tackles the subject of joystick input, which is the next most important input device for games. However, before you get to that, it's time to get down to business and create a real game; the next chapter guides you through the design and development of your first game.

Field Trip

Quick! Forget everything you just learned in this chapter! If you haven't already played it, beg, borrow, or maybe even consider purchasing the game LifeLine by Konami, which is billed as the world's first "voice action adventure." Although LifeLine might be old news to some gamers, it has charted new territory in the way of game user interfaces. LifeLine is very unique in that it relies solely on voice commands to play the game, which means that you don't really use any input device other than a microphone. Although this might sound strange at first, in the context of the game, it works very well because the storyline involves you being stuck in a room communicating with a robot via a microphone. If you already have the game, consider this field trip a day off. Otherwise, I encourage you to check out LifeLine and analyze how it turns traditional game input on its ear. Incidentally, I have no connection to Konami or the game LifeLine, so this isn't a deviously clever plug.

CHAPTER 6

Example Game: Brainiac

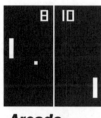

Arcade Archive

Although Tempest is, in many ways, one of those love it or hate it kind of games, most classic video game connoisseurs, myself included, are in the "love it" camp. Released in 1980 by Atari, Tempest represents Atari's first foray into color vector graphics. The idea for Tempest came about when one of the game's creators had a dream about monsters crawling up out of a hole in the ground. Not surprisingly, the game was originally created as a 3D monster game, but 1980 was a little too early for true 3D graphics, so the game was tweaked into the form we now know. Tempest has a known bug that allows you to get 40 free credits upon reaching certain scores. By the way, if you're interested in downloading and playing classic games on your computer, visit http://www.classicgaming.com/.

What good is a game book without any games? I have to admit to feeling kind of bad for spending five chapters getting you primed for game programming. I'd have loved to have hit you with a complete game in the first chapter, but you'd probably have ended up wanting to hit me. The reality is that it's taken five chapters to give you enough knowledge for you to create a complete game, which is the purpose of this chapter. In this chapter, you create a tile game called Brainiac that is similar to the classic Concentration memory game in which you match pairs of hidden tiles. Okay, so the game isn't quite a 3D shoot-em-up, but it is a complete game that you can show off to your buddies. In fact, you can plug in your own tile images to customize the game with embarrassing pictures of your friends and family.

In this chapter, you'll learn

▶ How to dream up the concept for a new game

▶ How to take a game concept and turn it into a game design

▶ How to use the game engine and a game design to build a working game from scratch

▶ That testing a game is the best part of the game development process

How Does the Game Play?

The idea behind the Brainiac game that you design and develop in this chapter is to present a grid of paired tiles. More specifically, a 4×4 grid contains 16 tiles, so 8 pairs of tiles are randomly placed on the grid. Each of the pairs of tiles has a unique image that you use to match up the pairs during the game. The unique image on the tiles is hidden when you start the game and is only revealed as you click tiles and attempt to match them. So, when tiles are unmatched, you see a common tile image that makes the different tiles indistinguishable. It's sort of like having a bunch of playing cards laid out face down. Figure 6.1 shows the grid of tiles in the Brainiac game and how they might be arranged for matching in pairs.

FIGURE 6.1
The Brainiac game consists of a 4[ts]4 grid of randomly arranged tiles that are matched in pairs.

The game proceeds by allowing you to pick one tile and then another. If the two tiles match, they are left visible, and you move on to try to find two more matching tiles. If they don't match, they are flipped back over to remain hidden again. Your job is to remember the positions of unmatched tiles as you turn them over so that you can match them up. The game keeps track of how many attempts it takes to finish matching all the tiles and reports the total to you when you finish. This total is essentially your score for the game, and it is a good incentive to play more and work on your memory skills.

In case you haven't thought about it, the Brainiac game is a perfect game for mouse input. The most intuitive way to play this kind of game is by pointing and clicking the tiles with the mouse, so in this chapter, the only user interface you'll build into the game is mouse input. It wouldn't be a terrible idea to add keyboard (and maybe even joystick) support as an enhancement, but I didn't want to add unnecessary code at this point. Keep in mind that both the keyboard and joystick would have to use an additional graphical component in order to work. For example, you would have to come up with some kind of selection or highlighted graphic to indicate which tile is currently selected. The mouse doesn't require such a component because you already have the mouse cursor to use as the basis for selecting tiles.

I realize that this probably isn't the most fanciful game you might have envisioned as your first complete game, but it is pretty cool when you consider that it presents a challenge for the player and provide a means of scoring how well you play. Additionally, the Brainiac game is a fun little game for incorporating your own images into the tiles and personalizing it.

Designing the Game

The Brainiac game probably sounds reasonably simple from the perspective of a player, but you'll find that it still requires some effort from a programming perspective. Games generally are not simple programs to write, and Brainiac represents probably the simplest game you'll ever develop. Even so, if you take your time and think through the design of your games, you'll be much farther ahead of the curve when you sit down to crank out the code.

As with most games, the key to designing the Brainiac game is to figure out how to accurately store the state of the game at any given moment. In other words, how will you reflect what's going on in the game in variables? Because the game is arranged as a 4×4 grid of tiles, it makes sense that the first thing you'll need is a two-dimensional array of bitmaps that identifies the tile image to be displayed for each tile. Of course, the bitmap images alone don't say anything about whether a match has been made. Therefore, you also need another two-dimensional array that keeps track of whether a tile has been matched. Together, these two arrays have most of the knowledge required to indicate the state of the game at any given moment.

The other missing pieces to the Brainiac puzzle primarily involve variables to support the tile-matching process. More specifically, you need to keep up with the two tiles the user has currently selected so that you can display them properly, as well as perform a match test on them. If the tiles match, you just update their status in the tile state array so that they remain turned over; if not, you make sure that they get returned to their hidden state. Most of the logic in the Brainiac game takes place in the mouse handling code because mouse clicks are the primary means through which the user selects tiles and attempts to make matches.

The two remaining pieces of information critical to the design of the game are the number of matches and the number of tries. The number of matches is extremely important because it determines when the game is over; because there are eight pairs of tiles, getting eight matches constitutes winning the game. The number of tries has more to do with keeping up with how well you did—it's sort of a score-keeping piece of information.

To recap, the design of the Brainiac game has led us to the following pieces of information that must be managed by the game:

▶ A two-dimensional array (4×4) of tile bitmaps

▶ A two-dimensional array (4×4) of tile states

▶ The tiles selected by the user as a potential match

▶ The number of matches

▶ The number of tries

With this information in mind, you're now ready to move on and put the code together for the Brainiac game.

Building the Game

In previous chapters, you've seen how the game engine that you've built thus far has made it possible to create interesting programs with a relatively small amount of code. You're now going to see the true value of the game engine as you assemble the code for the Brainiac game. The next couple of sections explore the code development for the Brainiac game, which is surprisingly straightforward considering that you're creating a fully functioning game. The complete source code and project files for the Brainiac game, not to mention all the examples throughout the book, are located on the accompanying CD-ROM.

Writing the Game Code

As you might have suspected, the code for the Brainiac game is divided between a header file (Brainiac.h) and a source code file (Brainiac.cpp), not to mention the code for the Bitmap class (Bitmap.h and Bitmap.cpp) and the game's resource file (Brainiac.rc). The Brainiac.h header file is the best file to start with in terms of figuring out how the game is assembled, and it is shown in Listing 6.1.

LISTING 6.1   The Brainiac.h Header File Declares Global Variables that Are Used to Manage the Game

```
#pragma once

//-----------------------------------
// Include Files
//-----------------------------------
#include <windows.h>
#include "Resource.h"
#include "GameEngine.h"
#include "Bitmap.h"

//-----------------------------------
// Global Variables
//-----------------------------------
HINSTANCE    g_hInstance;
GameEngine*  g_pGame;
Bitmap*      g_pTiles[9];
BOOL         g_bTileStates[4][4];
int          g_iTiles[4][4];
POINT        g_ptTile1, g_ptTile2;
int          g_iMatches, g_iTries;
```

The first array stores whether a tile has been matched, whereas the second array stores an integer reference (1-9) to the bitmap for the tile.

This code is where the design work you carried out earlier in this chapter directly plays out. More specifically, the pieces of information that were mentioned as critical components of the game are now realized as global variables. The g_pTiles variable stores away the tile images. You might be wondering why the array contains nine bitmaps when there are only eight different tile images for matching. The reason is because there is an extra tile image to represent the backs of the tiles when they are hidden. Speaking of the tile images, Figure 6.2 shows one of the tile bitmaps, which contains an image of a fish within a bordered graphic. Eight of the tile images contain uniquely different looking fish, whereas the ninth image is a blank tile.

FIGURE 6.2
The tile images in the Brainiac game consist of different fish framed by common borders; you can plug in any tile images you choose to replace the fish.

Construction Cue

> You might have noticed in the code that a data type called POINT is being used for the tile selections. This is a standard Win32 data type that stores two pieces of information: an X value and a Y value. The POINT data structure is quite handy and can be used in any situation in which you need to store a point, coordinate, or other numeric data consisting of two integer parts. The X and Y values in the structure are named x and y.

The tile states are stored in a two-dimensional array of Boolean values named g_bTileStates. The idea behind this variable is that a value of TRUE for a tile indicates that it has already been matched, whereas FALSE means that it is still hidden and unmatched. The bitmap associated with each tile is stored in the g_iTiles array, which might seem strange because it doesn't actually reference Bitmap objects. This is because you already have the Bitmap objects available in the g_pTiles array, so all the g_iTiles array has to do is reference each tile bitmap as an index into the g_pTiles array.

The two tile selections are stored in the g_ptTile1 and g_ptTile2 variables. These variables are important because they keep track of the user's tile selections; therefore, they are used to determine when a successful match takes place. The last two variables, g_iMatches and g_iTries, are used to keep track of the number of matches made and the number of match attempts, respectively. The g_iMatches variable will be used a little later in the code to determine if the game is over.

The GameInitialize() function for the Brainiac game is similar to what you've seen in previous examples. In fact, the only change to this function from earlier examples is that the frame rate is set to 1. This means that the GameCycle() function is only called once per second, which is painfully slow for most games. However, the frame rate theoretically could be zero for Brainiac because there is nothing to update on a regular basis. This is because you know when game updates are necessary—when the user clicks a tile. Therefore, because it's not a big deal to have a high frame rate, you might as well minimize its effect on the game.

The Brainiac game is an example of a turn-based game, which means that the game play proceeds according to one or more players taking discrete turns, as opposed to the game responding to events that can occur at any time (event-based games). Most action games are event-based games, whereas most card games are turn-based games. The frame rate is incredibly important for event-based games, whereas it usually plays little or no role in turn-based games.

Gamer's Garage

The GameStart() and GameEnd() functions are responsible for initializing and cleaning up the game data, as shown in Listing 6.2.

LISTING 6.2 The GameStart() Function Creates and Loads the Tile Bitmaps, Whereas the GameEnd() Function Cleans Up the Bitmaps

```
void GameStart(HWND hWindow)
{
  // Seed the random number generator
  srand(GetTickCount());

  // Create and load the tile bitmaps
  HDC hDC = GetDC(hWindow);
  g_pTiles[0] = new Bitmap(hDC, IDB_TILEBLANK, g_hInstance);
  g_pTiles[1] = new Bitmap(hDC, IDB_TILE1, g_hInstance);
  g_pTiles[2] = new Bitmap(hDC, IDB_TILE2, g_hInstance);
  g_pTiles[3] = new Bitmap(hDC, IDB_TILE3, g_hInstance);
  g_pTiles[4] = new Bitmap(hDC, IDB_TILE4, g_hInstance);
  g_pTiles[5] = new Bitmap(hDC, IDB_TILE5, g_hInstance);
  g_pTiles[6] = new Bitmap(hDC, IDB_TILE6, g_hInstance);
  g_pTiles[7] = new Bitmap(hDC, IDB_TILE7, g_hInstance);
  g_pTiles[8] = new Bitmap(hDC, IDB_TILE8, g_hInstance);
```

The blank tile bitmap image is displayed for all unmatched tiles.

LISTING 6.2　Continued

All tiles are initially unmatched, which means that their state is set to FALSE.

```
// Clear the tile states and images
for (int i = 0; i < 4; i++)
  for (int j = 0; j < 4; j++)
  {
    g_bTileStates[i][j] = FALSE;
    g_iTiles[i][j] = 0;
  }
```

This code randomly fills up the tile array with pairs of integer bitmap references in the range 1-9.

```
// Initialize the tile images randomly
for (int i = 0; i < 2; i++)
  for (int j = 1; j < 9; j++)
  {
    int x = rand() % 4;
    int y = rand() % 4;
    while (g_iTiles[x][y] != 0)
    {
      x = rand() % 4;
      y = rand() % 4;
    }
    g_iTiles[x][y] = j;
  }
```

-1 indicates that no tile is currently selected.

```
// Initialize the tile selections and match/try count
g_ptTile1.x = g_ptTile1.y = -1;
g_ptTile2.x = g_ptTile2.y = -1;
g_iMatches = g_iTries = 0;
}

void GameEnd()
{
  // Cleanup the tile bitmaps
  for (int i = 0; i < 9; i++)
    delete g_pTiles[i];

  // Cleanup the game engine
  delete g_pGame;
}
```

Construction
Cue

> If you happen to get a "multiple initialization" compiler error while compiling the Brainiac program, you can easily fix it by removing the `int` variable declaration in the second group of `for` loops in the `GameStart()` function where the tiles are randomly initialized. This error stems from the fact that some compilers don't fully support the standard C++ approach of declaring loop initializer variables local to the loop. So, the `int` variable `i` is mistakenly interpreted as being declared twice. Just remove the second `int` declaration, and everything will work fine.

The `GameStart()` function contains a fair amount of code because all the variables in the game must be carefully initialized for the game to play properly. The function begins by seeding the random number generator, which is necessary because you'll be randomly placing tiles in a moment. The tile bitmaps are then loaded into the g_pTiles array. From there, the real work of initializing the game data begins to take place.

Because a value of FALSE indicates that a tile has not yet been matched, it's necessary to initialize each element in the g_bTileStates array to FALSE. Similarly, the elements in the g_iTiles array are initialized to 0, but for a different reason. When the tiles are randomly placed in the g_iTiles array in a moment, it's important to have the elements initialized to 0 so that you can tell which tile spaces are available for tile placement. The actual tile placement isn't as complicated as it looks. What's happening is that a tile space is randomly selected and tested to see if it has been filled with a tile. If so, the code continues to select random tiles until an empty one is found. When an empty space is found, the tile is set.

The last few steps in the GameStart() function involve setting the g_ptTile1 and g_ptTile2 variables to -1. Because these variables are POINT structures, each of them contains an X and Y value. So, you're actually initializing two pieces of information for each of the tile selection variables. The value of -1 comes into play because it's a good way to indicate that a selection hasn't been made. In other words, you can tell that the user hasn't made the first tile selection by simply looking at the values of g_ptTile1.x and g_ptTile1.y and seeing if they are set to -1. The g_iMatches and g_iTries variables are initialized to 0, which makes sense given their purpose.

The GameEnd() function is responsible for cleaning up the tile bitmaps, as well as the game engine.

The Brainiac game screen is painted in the GamePaint() function, which is shown in Listing 6.3.

LISTING 6.3 The GamePaint() Function Draws the Tiles for the Game According to the Tile States Stored in the Game State Member Variables

```
void GamePaint(HDC hDC)
{
  // Draw the tiles
  int iTileWidth = g_pTiles[0]->GetWidth();
  int iTileHeight = g_pTiles[0]->GetHeight();
  for (int i = 0; i < 4; i++)
    for (int j = 0; j < 4; j++)
      if (g_bTileStates[i][j] ¦¦ ((i == g_ptTile1.x) && (j == g_ptTile1.y)) ¦¦
        ((i == g_ptTile2.x) && (j == g_ptTile2.y)))
        g_pTiles[g_iTiles[i][j]]->Draw(hDC, i * iTileWidth, j * iTileHeight,
          TRUE);
```

continues

LISTING 6.3   Continued

If the tile isn't matched or selected, just draw the blank tile image.

```
    else
      g_pTiles[0]->Draw(hDC, i * iTileWidth, j * iTileHeight, TRUE);
}
```

The job of the GamePaint() function is to draw the 4×4 grid of tile bitmaps on the game screen. This is primarily accomplished by examining each tile state and either drawing its associated tile image (if it is already matched) or drawing a blank tile image (if it isn't matched). One interesting thing to note in this code is that you have to look at more than the tile state when drawing the tiles because it's important to draw the two selected tiles properly even though they might not match. This test for matching a tile pair takes into account both the tile selection values and the tile state.

Although GamePaint() is important in providing the visuals for the Brainiac game, the bulk of the game logic is in the MouseButtonDown() function, which is shown in Listing 6.4.

LISTING 6.4   The MouseButtonDown() Function Carries Out the Majority of the Game Logic for the Brainiac Game

This code cleverly uses the mouse click coordinates to determine which tile was clicked.

```
void MouseButtonDown(int x, int y, BOOL bLeft)
{
  // Determine which tile was clicked
  int iTileX = x / g_pTiles[0]->GetWidth();
  int iTileY = y / g_pTiles[0]->GetHeight();

  // Make sure the tile hasn't already been matched
  if (!g_bTileStates[iTileX][iTileY])
  {
    // See if this is the first tile selected
    if (g_ptTile1.x == -1)
    {
      // Set the first tile selection
      g_ptTile1.x = iTileX;
      g_ptTile1.y = iTileY;
    }
    else if ((iTileX != g_ptTile1.x) || (iTileY != g_ptTile1.y))
    {
      if (g_ptTile2.x == -1)
      {
        // Increase the number of tries
        g_iTries++;

        // Set the second tile selection
        g_ptTile2.x = iTileX;
        g_ptTile2.y = iTileY;

        // See if it's a match
```

```
      if (g_iTiles[g_ptTile1.x][g_ptTile1.y] ==
        g_iTiles[g_ptTile2.x][g_ptTile2.y])
      {
        // Set the tile state to indicate the match
        g_bTileStates[g_ptTile1.x][g_ptTile1.y] = TRUE;
        g_bTileStates[g_ptTile2.x][g_ptTile2.y] = TRUE;

        // Clear the tile selections
        g_ptTile1.x = g_ptTile1.y = g_ptTile2.x = g_ptTile2.y = -1;

        // Update the match count and check for winner
        if (++g_iMatches == 8)
        {
          TCHAR szText[64];
          wsprintf(szText, "You won in %d tries.", g_iTries);
          MessageBox(g_pGame->GetWindow(), szText, TEXT("Brainiac"), MB_OK);
        }
      }
    }
    else
    {
      // Clear the tile selections
      g_ptTile1.x = g_ptTile1.y = g_ptTile2.x = g_ptTile2.y = -1;
    }
  }

  // Force a repaint to update the tile
  InvalidateRect(g_pGame->GetWindow(), NULL, FALSE);
  }
}
```

*Because there are
16 tiles, 8 matches
constitutes a win.*

The first step in the `MouseButtonDown()` function is to determine which tile was clicked. This determination involves using the mouse cursor position provided in the x and y arguments passed into the function. After you determine which tile was clicked, you can quickly check and see if it has already been matched; if so, there is no reason to do anything else because it doesn't make sense to "turn over" a tile that has already been matched. Assuming that the tile hasn't already been matched, the next test is to see if this is the first tile selected; if so, all you have to do is store the tile position in `g_ptTile1`. If not, you have to move on and make sure that it isn't the first tile being reselected, which wouldn't make much sense. If you pass that test, you have to check and see if this is indeed the second tile selection; if so, it's time to go to work and see if there is a match. If this isn't the second tile selection, you know it must be the third click in an unsuccessful match, which means that the tile selections need to be cleared so that the selection process can be repeated.

Getting back to the second tile selection, when you know that the user has just selected the second tile, you can safely increment the number of tries, as well as store away the tile selection. You can then check for a match by comparing the two tile selections to each other. If there is a match, the tile states are modified for each tile, and the tile selections are cleared. The match count is then incremented and checked to see if the game is over. If the game is over, a window is displayed that notifies you of winning, as well as how many tries it took.

The last step in the MouseButtonDown() function is to force a repaint of the game screen with a call to InvalidateRect(). This code is extremely important because it results in the user's action (the tile selection with a mouse click) being visually carried out on the screen.

Tweaking Your Compiler for the Brainiac Program

Similar to the UFO example in the previous chapter, the Brainiac example relies on the standard msimg32.lib library for the TransparentBlt() function used in the Bitmap class. Before you attempt to compile the Brainiac program, make sure that you change the link settings for the program so that the msimg32.lib library file is linked into the final executable. Refer to the documentation for your specific compiler for how this is done or follow these steps if you're using Microsoft Visual Studio .NET:

1. Open the project in Visual Studio (Visual C++).

2. Right-click on the project's folder in Solution Explorer and click Properties in the pop-up menu.

3. Click the Linker folder in the left pane of the Properties window and then click Input.

4. Click next to Additional Dependencies in the right pane and type **msimg32.lib**.

5. Click the OK button to accept the changes to the project.

After completing these steps, you can safely compile a program and know that the msimg32.lib library is being successfully linked into the executable program file. If you're using Visual C++ 6 or some other development environment, the steps will be different, but the general idea is the same. Otherwise, you can make it easy on yourself and just use the project files I've provided on the CD-ROM; there are project files for every example in the book for Visual Studio .NET, Borland C++Builder, and Bloodshed Dev-C++.

Testing the Game

The most rewarding part of the game development process is seeing the end result of all your toiling over game code. In fact, one of the most exciting aspects of game programming is how you can experiment with tweaking the code and seeing how it impacts the game play. Admittedly, there isn't a whole lot to be tweaked on the Brainiac game other than maybe the tile images, but it's nonetheless a neat game to try out now that the code is complete. Figure 6.3 shows the game upon initially starting out, with all the tiles hidden and ready for you to attempt a match.

FIGURE 6.3
The Brainiac game begins with all the tiles hidden, waiting for you to make the first tile selection.

When you click to select a tile, its image is revealed, as shown in Figure 6.4.

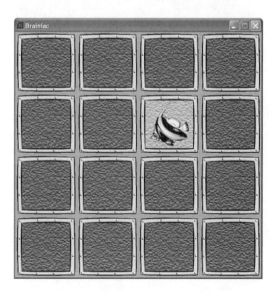

FIGURE 6.4
Clicking a tile reveals its underlying image, which lets you know what you're attempting to match.

After making your first move, the next step is to try to make a match by selecting another tile. Of course, on the first round of the game, this is essentially a shot in the dark. When you fail to make a match, you have to click once more to return the tiles to their hidden state and attempt another match. This gives you time to memorize the locations of the tiles you attempted to match. Making a match simply involves selecting the same two tiles, as shown in Figure 6.5.

Construction Cue

Don't forget that you can substitute any graphics theme you want in place of my fish theme. Just make sure that your tile images are the same size as the fish tile images, or if you want, change your tiles to a larger size—just make sure that you increase the size of the game screen accordingly.

FIGURE 6.5
Matching tiles involves selecting two tiles with the same bitmap image.

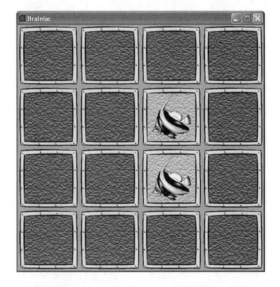

If you're one of those people who can recall the name of every classmate in your kindergarten class, you'll probably find the Brainiac game easy to master. Otherwise, you might just end up clicking aimlessly until you luck out with a few matches. Either way, the game will eventually end, and you'll be able to judge how well you've done by the number of tries it took to match all the tiles. Figure 6.6 shows the window that is displayed upon completing the game.

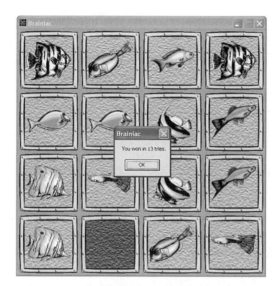

FIGURE 6.6
Upon completing a game of Brainiac, you are presented with a window that lets you know how many tries it took.

If you're the obsessive, competitive type, you will no doubt spend hours trying to get the number of tries down to a ridiculously low number. Or you might decide that Brainiac is nothing more than a light diversion on your path toward creating new and more interesting games. Either way, it's a good example of how to pull together a variety of different skills for the creation of a complete game.

Summary

Up until this chapter, you focused on individual aspects of game development ranging from drawing basic graphics to handling user input. This chapter represents the first attempt at incorporating everything you've learned thus far into the development of a complete game that you can play and share with your friends. By most standards, the Brainiac game is a simple game without too many frills, but it does demonstrate what it takes to put together a working game from start to finish. Perhaps more importantly, you got to experience firsthand what it's like to start with an idea, move forward with a design, and then realize that design in actual code. You'll be repeating this process numerous times throughout the book as you construct more powerful and exciting games, so this experience will serve you well.

The next chapter continues where the previous chapter left off by looking deeper into user input and how it is handled in games. More specifically, you learn how to process joystick input. Fortunately, joysticks really wouldn't be terribly useful in the Brainiac game, which is why I opted to steer you through the development of a working game before tackling joystick input.

Extreme Game Makeover

The simplest and most obvious way to make over the Brainiac game is to swap out the graphics with graphics of your own. To keep things simple, you should make sure that each of your new tiles is the same dimension as the fish tiles in the example (132×128). You could really make things interesting by making your tiles smaller or larger and altering the size of the game screen to accommodate the new tile size. If you really wanted to take the game to a new level, you could change the number of tiles to be matched. For example, you could increase the size of the tile grid from 4×4 to 6×6 or 8×8. The following are the changes you need to make to the game code to move to a different tile grid size:

1. Add new tile graphics to support the required number of tiles (width×height/2). For example, if you change the game to use an 8x8 grid, you'll need 32 different tile images, plus the blank image.

2. Change the size of the game screen in the `GameInitialize()` function to make room for the newly sized tile grid.

3. Change the global two-dimensional tile states and tile arrays to your new tile grid size.

4. Change the `GameStart()` function so that it initializes the tiles based on the new tile grid. More specifically, the first loop's i and j counters correspond to the width and height of the tile grid, respectively. The second loop's j counter must be set to one higher than the total number of unique tile images (33 for an 8×8 grid). All the `rand()` method calls should be adjusted to account for the new grid size (`rand() % 8` for an 8×8 grid).

5. Change the `GamePaint()` function so that it paints the tiles based on the new grid width and height.

6. Change the `MouseButtonDown()` method so that the g_iMatches global variable is checked against a larger number of matches (32 in the case of an 8×8 grid).

Granted, these changes aren't exactly trivial, but they do alter the game significantly. Perhaps of more interest from a game play perspective, increasing the size of the tile grid in the game makes it significantly more difficult to play.

CHAPTER 7

Improving Input with Joysticks

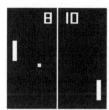

Released in 1980 by Atari, Centipede is one of the first games to rely on a trackball for user input. Centipede was quite popular in its day and still has some devoted fans. Centipede owns the distinction of being the first video game created by a woman, Dona Bailey, which is no small feat considering how few women worked in the video game industry in its early days.

Arcade Archive

From its inception, the joystick has been used chiefly as an input device for game systems. Admittedly, its name alone limits its usage to the entertainment industry, as I doubt too many accountants would purchase a "joystick" for crunching numbers in a spreadsheet. At any rate, joysticks and game pads both play an important role in modern video games of all kinds, including computer games. For this reason, it's important for you to have an understanding of how to interpret and respond to joystick input in your own games. This chapter introduces you to joysticks and what makes them tick, along with providing you with the knowledge and source code to handle joystick input in games.

In this chapter, you'll learn

- ▶ The basics of responding to joystick input in games
- ▶ How to properly calibrate a joystick in Windows XP
- ▶ How to add joystick support to the game engine
- ▶ How to use the new and improved game engine to create interesting programs that respond to a joystick

Understanding Joystick Basics

The concept of a joystick is straightforward, although you might be surprised by how loosely a joystick is defined in terms of Windows programming. In Windows, a *joystick* is a physical input device that allows variable movement along different axes with multiple pushbuttons. That's the geeky description of a joystick. What it means is that a joystick is an input device that can move in several different directions. Notice that I said *several* directions, not just two. Although a traditional joystick is thought of in terms of two axes (X and Y), a joystick in Windows can actually have up to six axes. Fortunately, we aren't going to worry about more than two joystick axes in this chapter, which helps simplify things considerably.

Construction Cue

> The six possible joystick axes supported by Windows can be arranged in many different ways. A traditional joystick has two axes that correspond to moving the joystick handle from side-to-side (one axis) and forward and back (another axis). A third axis of movement can be added by allowing the joystick handle to be pushed and pulled vertically. A fourth axis can be the twisting of the joystick handle. The fifth and sixth axes apply to more advanced input devices and are typically used for keeping track of moving the entire joystick in 3D space, such as with an input glove.

Because a traditional joystick has only two axes of motion, you can think of the joystick in much the same way as you think of the mouse. Although a mouse can be moved in any direction, its movement is limited to a single plane. In other words, you can always resolve mouse movement into an XY value. Joysticks are similar in this manner because you can identify their movement according to how far the handle is being pushed along each axis. If side-to-side movement is along the x axis and forward and back movement is along the y axis, a joystick can be tracked in a manner similar to the mouse by using an XY value.

Also similar to the mouse are the buttons on a joystick. Just as mouse devices are capable of supporting multiple buttons (typically three at most), joysticks are also capable of having several buttons. In fact, joysticks are much more flexible than mouse devices in terms of how many buttons they can have; joysticks in Windows are allowed to have up to 32 buttons. It would probably take super-human memory skills and hand/eye coordination to figure out how to use a joystick with that many buttons, but the option is there if someone wants to make a joystick for the truly gifted among us. A more realistic number for joystick buttons is six, which is still a lot to keep track of for the average game player. Similar to mouse button and keyboard key presses, handling joystick button presses is relatively straightforward, as you learn a little later in the chapter.

Calibrating Joysticks

Before getting into the details of how to handle joystick input from a programming perspective, it's worth addressing an important issue related to joysticks: calibration. *Calibration* is the process of fine-tuning the settings for a joystick so that the handle is properly centered. Joystick calibration is kind of like having your car aligned; when a joystick isn't properly calibrated, it has a tendency to pull to one side. Fortunately, joystick calibration is easy to perform and is readily available from the Windows Control Panel. To access joystick settings, just follow these steps in Windows XP:

1. Click the Start button and select Control Panel.

2. Double-click Game Controllers.

3. Select the joystick (game controller) to calibrate and then click the Properties button.

Even if you aren't using Windows XP, you'll still find some kind of joystick or controller icon in the Control Panel for calibrating and testing your game controllers. The specifics of calibrating your joystick might be a little different from the steps I've listed, but the general idea is the same.

Gamer's Garage

After following these steps, you'll be presented with a window that is specific to your particular joystick. In my case, I'm using a Microsoft SideWinder game pad, so the window I see is shown in Figure 7.1.

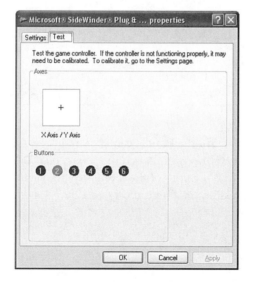

FIGURE 7.1
The Test window for your joystick should allow you to test the joystick.

After testing your joystick, you might find that it needs to be calibrated. To calibrate your joystick (game pad), first click the Settings tab, followed by the Calibrate button. This starts the Device Calibration Wizard, which is shown in Figure 7.2.

FIGURE 7.2
The Device Calibration Wizard provides a means of calibrating joysticks in Windows XP.

Click the Next button to get started calibrating the joystick (see Figure 7.3).

FIGURE 7.3
Calibrating a joystick first involves pressing a button on the joystick without touching the joystick handle (or control pad for game pads).

The first step in calibrating a joystick is to leave the handle centered and press a button, as shown in Figure 7.3. In the case of a game pad, you simply don't touch the *control pad* (D-Pad), and then press a button. You are then prompted to calibrate the axes of the joystick by moving the handle or control pad in all of its directions, followed by pressing another button (see Figure 7.4).

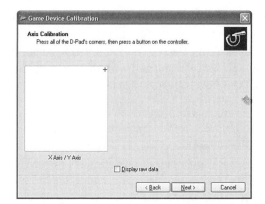

FIGURE 7.4
The Device
Calibration Wizard
determines the
range of each joy-
stick axis by asking
you to move the
handle or control
pad in each direc-
tion.

The final step is to leave the handle (control pad) alone once more and press a button. After performing these steps, you can click the Finish button to wrap up the calibration process. Although the steps to calibrating a joystick or game pad might seem trivial, the idea is that your computer is analyzing the range of movement along each axis and properly determining the center point of each. Once the center point and maximum extents are determined, the joystick can then be accurately centered. Again, it's very much like aligning a car so that it steers straight when you aren't touching the steering wheel.

It is important to calibrate your joystick any time it starts acting strange because it is possible for a joystick to lose calibration over a period of time as it begins to wear mechanically. Your joystick's Properties window usually provides a test option for testing the joystick after you've calibrated it; this helps to make sure that the calibration worked properly. Figure 7.1 shows the test window for the Microsoft SideWinder game pad.

The test window for a joystick or game pad is great because it quickly allows you to see if the device is working properly. If you get no response when testing a device, you know that something is wrong with the installation. You can also use the test window to see if a joystick or game pad is properly calibrated.

Tracking Joystick Movements

As you might have guessed, joysticks are a little more complicated to deal with than other input devices , such as the keyboard and mouse. This primarily has to do with the fact that joysticks aren't exactly considered standard devices, as well as the fact that there is a fair amount of variance when it comes to joystick features. The added complexity doesn't have so much to do with handling specific joystick events as it does with determining if a joystick is connected and available for use. You also have to concern yourself with the concept of *capturing* a joystick, which gives your program exclusive control over the joystick.

The first step in handling joystick input is checking to see if a joystick driver is installed and available on the computer system. Without the proper hardware driver in place, a physical joystick device is no good. Fortunately, Windows includes built-in drivers for most popular joysticks. However, it's good to perform the check anyway. This is made possible by a call to a Win32 API function called joyGetNumDevs(). The joyGetNumDevs() function tells you how many joysticks are capable of being used on the computer system. The following is an example of how you might call the joyGetNumDevs() function to determine the number of joysticks available for use on the system:

```
UINT uiNumJoysticks = joyGetNumDevs();
```

You now know how many joysticks can be used on the system, but that doesn't tell you much about how many joysticks are actually present. To see if a real joystick is actually plugged in and ready to use, you call the joyGetPos() function, which provides a lot of information about a joystick. You must pass this function an ID that identifies the joystick you're interested in; standard joystick IDs include JOYSTICKID1, JOYSTICKID2, and so on. So, to check for the presence of a single joystick, you can use code like this:

```
JOYINFO jiInfo;
if (joyGetPos(JOYSTICKID1, &jiInfo) != JOYERR_UNPLUGGED)
  // the joystick is plugged in and ready to go!
```

In this code, the joyGetPos() function is called to retrieve joystick information for a single joystick in the form of a JOYINFO structure. You learn how to use the JOYINFO structure to analyze the state of the joystick in just a moment. For now, you're simply providing it because the joyGetPos() function requires it. All you're looking for in this code is the return value of joyGetPos(), which indicates whether the joystick is plugged in and responding to user input. If the function doesn't return JOYERR_UNPLUGGED, you're in good shape.

When working with joysticks in the Win32 API, you always reference a joystick using a unique ID. This ID must be one of the built-in joystick IDs (JOYSTICKID1, JOYSTICKID2, and so on). In the case of the previous sample code, the JOYSTICKID1 ID checked out okay, so it's the ID you must use to continue interacting with the same joystick.

The joyGetPos() function is the function you call to check the status of the joy-stick, which is how you determine if the user has interacted with your game via the joystick. The status of the joystick is stored in the JOYINFO structure, which is defined as follows:

```
typedef struct {
  UINT wXpos;
  UINT wYpos;
  UINT wZpos;
  UINT wButtons;
} JOYINFO;
```

You'll notice that the JOYINFO structure is designed to accommodate joysticks with up to three axes of movement: x, y, and z. The first three members of the struc-ture (wXpos, wYpos, and wZpos) indicate the position of the joystick with respect to each of these axes. The final member, wButtons, indicates the state of the joystick buttons. The wButtons member supports up to four buttons, as indicated by the following constants: JOY_BUTTON1, JOY_BUTTON2, JOY_BUTTON3, and JOY_BUTTON4.

Earlier, I mentioned that Windows supports up to 6 axes and 32 buttons on joy-sticks, but the JOYINFO structure is obviously more limited than that. This disparity exists because the full range of joystick features is only available through the DirectX game API, which is significantly more complex to use than the built-in Win32 joystick support. If you're planning on supporting a gyroscopic nuclear-powered virtu-al reality game helmet in your games that takes advantage of all the axes and but-tons possible, you definitely need to get to work learning DirectX. Otherwise, I think you'll find the Win32 approach to joystick handling sufficient for most of your games.

Gamer's Garage

In order to examine a JOYINFO structure to see what's happened to a joystick, you must first obtain the joystick state using the joyGetPos() function, which is the same function you used to see if a joystick was plugged in. The following is a code example that examines a JOYINFO structure to see if the first joystick button is being pressed:

```
JOYINFO jiInfo;
if (joyGetPos(JOYSTICKID1, &jiInfo) == JOYERR_NOERROR)
  if (jiInfo.wButtons & JOY_BUTTON1)
    // Button 1 was pressed!
```

This code calls the joyGetPos()function to fill a JOYINFO structure with informa-tion about the current joystick state. If the return value of the function is JOYERR_NOERROR, there was no problem retrieving the information, and we can continue. The bitwise AND operator (&) is then used with the wButtons member of the JOYINFO structure and the JOY_BUTTON1 constant to see if button 1 on the joy-stick is being pressed. You can use the same approach to look at other joystick buttons.

You're probably wondering why I've avoided talking about the other members of the JOYINFO structure, and how they are used to determine the position of the joystick handle. The reason for this has to do with the fact that you need to understand the range of values possible for these members before you can make sense of them. More specifically, you need to find out the minimum and maximum values for each axis of movement that you're interested in checking. For example, if you want to see if the joystick has been moved left, you first need to find out the range of values for the x axis of the joystick. You can then use this range to see how far left the joystick handle is being pushed, if at all.

You can determine the ranges of joystick axes by calling the Win32 joyGetDevCaps() function. This function fills a JOYCAPS structure with more information about a joystick than you'll probably ever want to know. For that reason, I won't go into all the details of the JOYCAPS structure. Instead, I'd like to focus on how to use it to determine the range of the two primary joystick axes, x and y. The following is a code snippet that determines the center point of the x and y axis, which reveals the ranges of each:

```
JOYCAPS jcCaps;
joyGetDevCaps(JOYSTICKID1, &jcCaps, sizeof(JOYCAPS));
DWORD dwXCenter = ((DWORD)jcCaps.wXmin + jcCaps.wXmax) / 2;
DWORD dwYCenter = ((DWORD)jcCaps.wYmin + jcCaps.wYmax) / 2;
```

The minimum and maximum values for the x axis are wXmin and wXmax, whereas the y axis is bound by wYmin and wYmax. Adding these pairs of numbers and dividing by 2 gives you the center point of each axis, which is the point at which the joystick handle is at rest. With these values in hand, you can now determine a certain value that must be tripped in order to consider the joystick handle as having been moved in a given direction. This simplifies joystick movements into standard directions, such as up, down, left, right, and so on. If you want to provide for very fine joystick control in your game, you might consider taking advantage of the full range of movement along each axis.

Revamping the Game Engine for Joysticks

The discussion of joysticks has been leading to a task that you probably knew was coming: another enhancement to the game engine. The idea is to continue beefing up the game engine with features so that the unique code for each game remains as minimal as possible. Knowing this, it's important to place as much joystick handling code in the game engine as possible. Before showing you the code, however, it's important to clarify a compile-time issue related to the Win32 joystick functions and data structures.

Accessing Win32 Multimedia Features

Although joystick support is now a standard part of Win32, this wasn't always the case. A multimedia subsystem was later added separately to the Win32 API— of which joystick support is a part. For this reason, the joystick functions and data structures are not defined in the standard windows.h header file; instead, they are located in the mmsystem.h header file, which is provided as part of the Win32 API. The following is an example of how you include this file in your code (GameEngine.h):

```
#include <mmsystem.h>
```

Okay, there's nothing tricky there. However, just importing the header file into GameEngine.h isn't enough because the executable code for the joystick support is located in a separate library that you must link into your games. This library is called winmm.lib, and it is included with all Windows compilers. Before you attempt to compile a Windows program that takes advantage of joystick features of the Win32 API, make sure that you change the link settings for the program so that the winmm.lib library file is linked into the final executable. Refer to the documentation for your specific compiler for how this is done or follow these steps if you're using Microsoft Visual Studio:

1. Open the project in Visual Studio (Visual C++).

2. Right-click on the project's folder in Solution Explorer and click Properties in the pop-up menu.

3. Click the Linker folder in the left pane of the Properties window and then click Input.

4. Click next to Additional Dependencies in the right pane and type a space followed by `winmm.lib`. You should already have the msimg32.lib library entered here, which is why it is necessary to type a space before entering `winmm.lib`.

5. Click the OK button to accept the changes to the project.

Construction Cue

Of course, you don't have to worry about any of these steps if you just use one of the project files provided on the accompanying CD-ROM, which supports Visual Studio, C++Builder, and Dev-C++. For every example in the book, a project file exists with all the correct compiler and linker settings already made.

After completing these steps, you can safely compile a program and know that the winmm.lib library is being successfully linked into the executable program file.

Construction Cue

The source code for the examples in the book includes Visual Studio project files with the appropriate linker settings already made.

Developing the Joystick Code

As you now know, games interact with the game engine primarily through a series of functions that are called by the game engine at certain times throughout the game. In order to add joystick support to the game engine, it's important to add a new function that is going to receive joystick notifications. This function is called HandleJoystick(), and its prototype follows:

```
void HandleJoystick(JOYSTATE jsJoystickState);
```

The HandleJoystick() function accepts as its only argument a custom data type called JOYSTATE. The JOYSTATE data type is a custom type used to convey the state of a joystick at any given time. Listing 7.1 contains the code for the JOYSTATE data type.

LISTING 7.1   The JOYSTATE Data Type Includes Constant Flags that Describe the State of the Joystick

```
typedef WORD    JOYSTATE;
const JOYSTATE  JOY_NONE  = 0x0000L,
                JOY_LEFT  = 0x0001L,
                JOY_RIGHT = 0x0002L,
                JOY_UP    = 0x0004L,
                JOY_DOWN  = 0x0008L,
                JOY_FIRE1 = 0x0010L,
                JOY_FIRE2 = 0x0020L;
```

The JOYSTATE data type is a WORD value capable of containing one or more constant flags that indicate(s) the state of various aspects of a joystick. For example, if the joystick handle is currently in the left position, the JOY_LEFT flag will appear in a JOYSTATE value. Multiple flags can be combined in the JOY_STATE data type, which makes sense when you consider that a joystick could simultaneously be in several of the states listed in the code.

You learned earlier that a joystick is identified by a unique ID, which is basically a number. You also learned that a joystick movement can be simplified into a simple direction by analyzing the range of motion for the joystick handle. This is accomplished by establishing a *trip rectangle* for the joystick, which is an area that determines how far the joystick handle must move in order for it to count as a directional event (up, down, left, right, or a combination). The purpose of the trip rectangle is to only cause joystick movement events to be generated if the handle moves a certain minimum distance, as shown in Figure 7.5.

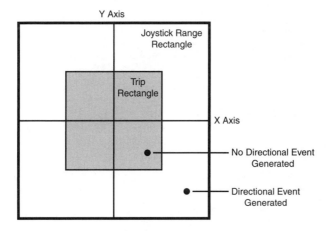

FIGURE 7.5
A trip rectangle for the joystick helps to ensure that a joystick movement event is only generated if the joystick handle moves a certain minimum distance.

You now know that the game engine needs to keep track of two pieces of information in order to support a joystick: the joystick's ID and a trip rectangle for interpreting joystick movement. The following are the two member variables added to the game engine that account for this information:

```
UINT m_uiJoystickID;
RECT m_rcJoystickTrip;
```

In addition to these member variables, the game engine also requires some support methods for managing joystick input. More specifically, it needs to properly initialize the Win32 joystick input system, which involves making sure that a joystick is connected and retrieving its ID, as well as calculating the trip rectangle. You also need methods to capture and release the joystick, which you learn about in a moment. Finally, you need a method to check the state of the joystick and convert numeric joystick movements into more meaningful directions. The following are the methods added to the game engine that accomplish all of these tasks:

```
BOOL InitJoystick();
void CaptureJoystick();
void ReleaseJoystick();
void CheckJoystick();
```

The InitJoystick() method must be called by a game in order to initialize the joystick, retrieve its ID, and determine the trip rectangle. Its code is shown in Listing 7.2.

LISTING 7.2   The GameEngine::InitJoystick() **Method Checks to Make Sure that a Joystick Is Present and Then Initializes It**

```
BOOL GameEngine::InitJoystick()
{
  // Make sure joystick driver is present
  UINT uiNumJoysticks;
  if ((uiNumJoysticks = joyGetNumDevs()) == 0)
    return FALSE;

  // Make sure the joystick is attached
  JOYINFO jiInfo;
  if (joyGetPos(JOYSTICKID1, &jiInfo) != JOYERR_UNPLUGGED)
    m_uiJoystickID = JOYSTICKID1;
  else
    return FALSE;

  // Calculate the trip values
  JOYCAPS jcCaps;
  joyGetDevCaps(m_uiJoystickID, &jcCaps, sizeof(JOYCAPS));
  DWORD dwXCenter = ((DWORD)jcCaps.wXmin + jcCaps.wXmax) / 2;
  DWORD dwYCenter = ((DWORD)jcCaps.wYmin + jcCaps.wYmax) / 2;
  m_rcJoystickTrip.left = (jcCaps.wXmin + (WORD)dwXCenter) / 2;
  m_rcJoystickTrip.right = (jcCaps.wXmax + (WORD)dwXCenter) / 2;
  m_rcJoystickTrip.top = (jcCaps.wYmin + (WORD)dwYCenter) / 2;
  m_rcJoystickTrip.bottom = (jcCaps.wYmax + (WORD)dwYCenter) / 2;

  return TRUE;
}
```

If there aren't any joysticks installed, you'll get a value of 0 here.

The joystick needs to be plugged in before moving forward.

Without setting a trip rectangle for the joystick, it would be too extremely sensitive to movements of the stick.

The code in this method should look reasonably familiar from the discussion earlier where you found out how to interact with joysticks. The joystick driver is first queried to make sure that it exists. A test is then performed to make sure that the joystick is plugged in and ready to go—after which, the ID of the joystick is stored in the m_uiJoystickID member variable. The trip rectangle is then calculated as a rectangle half the size of the joystick bounds in each direction. This size is somewhat arbitrary, so you could feasibly tweak it if you wanted, meaning that the user has to push the joystick handle half of its total possible distance in a given direction in order for it to register as a directional move.

Listing 7.3 contains the code for the `CaptureJoystick()` and `ReleaseJoystick()` methods, which are quite important. In order for a program to receive joystick input, it must first *capture* the joystick, which means that the joystick is only going to communicate with that program. When a program is deactivated, it's important to *release* the joystick so that it is no longer captured; this enables another program to capture the joystick, if necessary.

LISTING 7.3 The `GameEngine::CaptureJoystick()` and `GameEngine::ReleaseJoystick()` Methods Are Responsible for Capturing and Releasing the Joystick, Respectively

```
void GameEngine::CaptureJoystick()
{
  // Capture the joystick
  if (m_uiJoystickID == JOYSTICKID1)
    joySetCapture(m_hWindow, m_uiJoystickID, NULL, TRUE);
}

void GameEngine::ReleaseJoystick()
{
  // Release the joystick
  if (m_uiJoystickID == JOYSTICKID1)
    joyReleaseCapture(m_uiJoystickID);
}
```

Capturing and releasing a joystick are as simple as calling the `joySetCapture()` and `joyReleaseCapture()` Win32 functions. Keep in mind that it's up to a program to call these two methods at the appropriate times (upon activation and deactivation) in order for joystick input to work properly.

Listing 7.4 contains the last of the new game engine joystick methods, `CheckJoystick()`, which is the method that is repeatedly called by a program to analyze the current joystick state and see if anything interesting has happened.

LISTING 7.4 The `GameEngine::CheckJoystick()` Method Checks the State of the Joystick and Passes It Along to the `HandleJoystick()` Function

```
void GameEngine::CheckJoystick()
{
  if (m_uiJoystickID == JOYSTICKID1)
  {
    JOYINFO jiInfo;
    JOYSTATE jsJoystickState = 0;
```

LISTING 7.4   Continued

```
    if (joyGetPos(m_uiJoystickID, &jiInfo) == JOYERR_NOERROR)
    {
      // Check horizontal movement
      if (jiInfo.wXpos < (WORD)m_rcJoystickTrip.left)
        jsJoystickState |= JOY_LEFT;
      else if (jiInfo.wXpos > (WORD)m_rcJoystickTrip.right)
        jsJoystickState |= JOY_RIGHT;

      // Check vertical movement
      if (jiInfo.wYpos < (WORD)m_rcJoystickTrip.top)
        jsJoystickState |= JOY_UP;
      else if (jiInfo.wYpos > (WORD)m_rcJoystickTrip.bottom)
        jsJoystickState |= JOY_DOWN;

      // Check buttons
      if(jiInfo.wButtons & JOY_BUTTON1)
        jsJoystickState |= JOY_FIRE1;
      if(jiInfo.wButtons & JOY_BUTTON2)
        jsJoystickState |= JOY_FIRE2;
    }

      // Allow the game to handle the joystick
      HandleJoystick(jsJoystickState);
  }
}
```

This code is where a game gets a chance to respond to the joystick via its own HandleJoystick() function.

The CheckJoystick() method looks kind of complicated, but it's really not too bad. Understand that the idea behind this method is to quickly look at the state of the joystick, determine if enough movement has occurred to qualify as a directional movement (based on the trip rectangle), and then pass the results along to the HandleJoystick()function for game-specific joystick processing.

The standard JOYINFO structure is used to retrieve the joystick state via the joyGetPos() function. Different members of this structure are then compared against the trip rectangle to see if the joystick movement qualifies as a directional movement. If so, the appropriate directional flag is set on a JOYSTATE variable that is eventually passed to the HandleJoystick() function. The joystick buttons are also checked, and appropriate flags are set for those as well. The bottom line is that the HandleJoystick() function gets called with information that is easily analyzed by game-specific code to determine how to react to the joystick.

Supporting Two Joysticks in the Game Engine

The code you worked through in this section focused on adding support to the game engine for a single joystick. Likewise, the remainder of the book focuses on games that use a single joystick. However, it isn't too terribly difficult to modify the game engine to support multiple joysticks, and you might design a game that requires two joysticks. You just need to make a few changes throughout the joystick code in the game engine to support two joysticks. Here are some steps to put you on the right track in modifying the game engine:

▶ Change the m_uiJoystickID member variable in the game engine into an array with two values (one ID for each joystick).

▶ Everywhere you see the m_uiJoystickID variable in the game engine code, modify it to deal with two IDs instead of one—joystick 1 is JOYSTICKID1, and joystick 2 is JOYSTICKID2.

▶ Add a new parameter to the HandleJoystick() function to indicate which joystick it is being called for.

▶ Change the GameEngine::CheckJoystick() method to check both joysticks and call the HandleJoystick() function for each of them.

▶ In your game-specific code, use the new parameter in HandleJoystick() to distinguish between the two joysticks, like this:

```
void HandleJoystick(UINT uiJoystickID, JOYSTATE jsJoystickState)
{
  if (uiJoystickID == JOYSTICKID1)
  {
    // Handle joystick 1
  }
  else
  {
    // Handle joystick 2
  }
}
```

Although not exactly trivial, this enhancement to the game engine is definitely within your abilities as a maturing Windows game developer.

Building the UFO 2 Example

Chapter 5, "Controlling Games with the Keyboard and Mouse," guides you through the design and development of an interesting little program that allows you to control a flying saucer using the keyboard and mouse. The remainder of this chapter focuses on adding joystick support to the UFO example to create a new version of the program called UFO 2. In addition to providing joystick support, you also enhance the program a little by adding a thrust image to the flying saucer and a hyperspace feature. "Thrusting" in this case simply involves drawing a flying saucer with a flame shooting out of the bottom, whereas going into hyperspace involves repositioning the saucer at a random location on the game screen.

Writing the Program Code

The code for the UFO 2 program starts with the UFO.h header file, which includes a couple of changes from its previous version:

```
Bitmap*     g_pSaucer[2];
BOOL        g_bSaucerFlame;
```

The first change to this code from the previous version of the program is the modification of the g_pSaucer global variable to an array of two bitmaps, as opposed to one. This is necessary because the thrust bitmap has now been added to show the flying saucer with a flame shooting out. Figure 7.6 shows the new flying saucer image with the flame appearing out of the bottom; the original flying saucer image was also modified for this example so that its size matches the size of the saucer flame image. The other change to the code involves the addition of the g_bSaucerFlame variable, which keeps track of whether or not the saucer is to be displayed with a flame.

FIGURE 7.6
The UFO 2 example includes a new flying saucer image that has a flame shooting out of the bottom of the saucer to indicate thrust.

The GameInitialize() function is the first game function to revisit for the UFO 2 program. The only change to this code from the previous version is the addition of the call to the game engine's InitJoystick() method, which is necessary to get the joystick primed and ready for action:

```
g_pGame->InitJoystick();
```

The `GameStart()` function also has changed a little, as shown in Listing 7.5.

LISTING 7.5 The `GameStart()` Function Initializes the Background and Flying Saucer Bitmaps

```
void GameStart(HWND hWindow)
{
  // Seed the random number generator
  srand(GetTickCount());

  // Create and load the background and saucer bitmaps
  HDC hDC = GetDC(hWindow);
  g_pBackground = new Bitmap(hDC, IDB_BACKGROUND, g_hInstance);
  g_pSaucer[0] = new Bitmap(hDC, IDB_SAUCER, g_hInstance);
  g_pSaucer[1] = new Bitmap(hDC, IDB_SAUCERFLAME, g_hInstance);

  // Set the initial saucer position and speed
  g_iSaucerX = 250 - (g_pSaucer[0]->GetWidth() / 2);
  g_iSaucerY = 200 - (g_pSaucer[0]->GetHeight() / 2);
  g_iSpeedX = 0;
  g_iSpeedY = 0;
}
```

The new saucer flame image shows the flying saucer with a flame shooting out of the bottom.

Because the hyperspace feature of UFO 2 requires the calculation of a random location on the screen, it's necessary to seed the random number generator. This function also loads the new flaming saucer image.

As mentioned earlier, it's important for any program that supports joysticks to properly capture and release the joystick in response to the main program window being activated and deactivated. In the case of UFO 2, this takes place in the `GameActivate()` and `GameDeactivate()` functions, which are shown in Listing 7.6.

LISTING 7.6 The `GameActivate()` and `GameDeactivate()` Functions Capture and Release the Joystick in Response to the Main Program Window Being Activated and Deactivated

```
void GameActivate(HWND hWindow)
{
  // Capture the joystick
  g_pGame->CaptureJoystick();
}

void GameDeactivate(HWND hWindow)
{
  // Release the joystick
  g_pGame->ReleaseJoystick();
}
```

The GameActivate() function simply calls the CaptureJoystick() method of the game engine to capture the joystick. Similarly, the joystick is released in GameDeactivate() with a quick call to the ReleaseJoystick() method.

If you're curious as to how the thrusting flying saucer is drawn, well wonder no more! The GamePaint() function handles drawing the appropriate flying saucer depending on the value of the g_bSaucerFlame global variable, as shown in Listing 7.7.

LISTING 7.7 The GamePaint() Function Draws the Background and Flying Saucer Bitmaps, Making Sure to Determine Which Flying Saucer Bitmap to Draw

```
void GamePaint(HDC hDC)
{
  // Draw the background and saucer bitmaps
  g_pBackground->Draw(hDC, 0, 0);
  g_pSaucer[g_bSaucerFlame ? 1:0]->Draw(hDC, g_iSaucerX, g_iSaucerY, TRUE);
}
```

As the listing reveals, the g_bSaucerFlame variable directly determines which flying saucer is drawn. Of course, you're probably still curious as to how this variable gets modified in the first place; that's where the joystick enters the picture.

If you recall from earlier, a program that uses our super slick game engine to process joystick input must provide its own HandleJoystick() function to perform its own processing of joystick input. In this case, the HandleJoystick() function is responsible for altering the speed of the flying saucer in response to directional joystick movements, as well as controlling the thrust and hyperspace features of the flying saucer when the two joystick buttons are pressed. Listing 7.8 shows how the HandleJoystick() function carries out these tasks.

LISTING 7.8 The HandleJoystick() Function Takes Care of Processing Joystick Input and Altering the Flying Saucer Appropriately

```
void HandleJoystick(JOYSTATE jsJoystickState)
{
  // Check horizontal movement
  if (jsJoystickState & JOY_LEFT)
    g_iSpeedX = max(-g_iMAXSPEED, g_iSpeedX - 2);
  else if (jsJoystickState & JOY_RIGHT)
    g_iSpeedX = min(g_iMAXSPEED, g_iSpeedX + 2);

  // Check vertical movement
```

The flying saucer's horizontal speed is determined based on left-right joystick movements.

```
if (jsJoystickState & JOY_UP)
  g_iSpeedY = max(-g_iMAXSPEED, g_iSpeedY - 2);
else if (jsJoystickState & JOY_DOWN)
  g_iSpeedY = min(g_iMAXSPEED, g_iSpeedY + 2);

// Check primary joystick button
g_bSaucerFlame = (jsJoystickState & JOY_FIRE1);

// Check secondary joystick button
if (jsJoystickState & JOY_FIRE2)
{
  // Force the flying saucer into hyperspace
  g_iSaucerX = rand() % (500 - g_pSaucer[0]->GetWidth());
  g_iSaucerY = rand() % 320;
}
}
```

The flying saucer's vertical speed is determined based on up-down joystick movements.

The saucer flame Boolean is set and cleared based on the primary fire button being pressed.

Hyperspace is initiated by the secondary fire button being pressed.

Seeing how the HandleJoystick() function is your only real communication link to the joystick in the UFO 2 program, it's really quite simple. The first block of code in the function checks to see if a horizontal movement has occurred—in which case, the X component of the flying saucer's speed is modified. Similarly, the second block of code performs the same processing on vertical joystick movement. The g_bSaucerFlame global variable is then set using the state of the first joystick button. Finally, the hyperspace feature is carried out in response to the second joystick button being pressed.

Testing the Finished Product

If you haven't done so already, I encourage you to plug in your joystick and take the UFO 2 program for a test spin. You'll hopefully find that the joystick controls for the program have a surprisingly good feel, considering that the joystick handling code in the program is relatively simple. Try pressing the two primary buttons on the joystick to get a feel for the thrust and hyperspace features of the program. Figure 7.7 shows the flying saucer as it appears with the flaming thrust beneath it.

Gamer's Garage

If the flying saucer immediately starts moving without you touching the joystick, it's a pretty good sign that your joystick needs to be calibrated. Revisit the earlier section "Calibrating Joysticks," to find out how to calibrate your joystick and eliminate this problem.

FIGURE 7.7
The flying saucer in
the UFO 2 example
shows off its new
thrusting capabili-
ties.

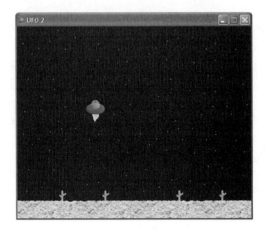

FIGURE 7.7
The flying saucer in the UFO 2 example shows off its new thrusting capabilities.

Granted, you might have a valid concern as to why the flying saucer visually thrusts but doesn't seem to have any additional lift when you press the thrust button. This is something I challenge you to solve as an exercise on your own; just kick up the vertical speed of the saucer a bit when the thrust button is pressed. You might also have noticed that hyperspace is quite sensitive. In fact, the hyperspace feature reveals how fast the game engine's joystick processing actually is.

Summary

Although joysticks don't quite share the widespread acceptance on PCs that keyboards and mouse devices do, they are the quintessential user input device for games. There aren't too many serious gamers who don't have a joystick or game pad. However, you don't have to be serious about games to enjoy the benefits of playing games with a joystick. For this reason and more, it's a good idea to try and support joysticks in games for which it makes sense to use a joystick for input. This chapter gave you the nuts and bolts of Windows joystick handling and even showed you how to build it into the ever-evolving game engine. You also saw how easy it is to add joystick support to an existing program.

Mark your calendar because Chapter 8, "Example Game: Light Cycles," represents a significant milestone in your game programming career—you develop your first complete action game. Even though the Brainiac game in the previous chapter was technically your first game, moving into the action realm is a huge step forward.

Field Trip

I realize that the people at your local computer store might be starting to get suspicious of your repeated trips, but a wealth of knowledge for learning about games can be found there. More specifically, I'd like you return yet again for a joystick reconnaissance mission. In case you haven't noticed, joystick technology has come a long way in recent years. As an aspiring game programming guru, it's important for you to have a solid base of knowledge about what's available in the way of modern joysticks. As you study the different joysticks on the shelves, pay particular attention to the number of buttons and their arrangement. If you already have a game in your mind that you're working on, see if you can figure out how to best make use of the joystick hardware available. Don't forget that it's possible to use only a few joystick buttons for basic game operations and then reserve additional buttons for more advanced features. Game players like to have options, and by intimately understanding the game controller marketplace, you'll be better prepared to provide them with those options.

CHAPTER 8

Example Game: Light Cycles

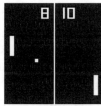

Another member of Atari's famous class of 1980, Missile Command, realized our fears of nuclear Armageddon by simulating a nuclear missile attack on a city. Like Centipede, Missile Command relies on a trackball as the primary means of user input. Missile Command has remained popular over the years, probably because of its nuclear war theme. In fact, the game appeared in the 1991 movie, *Terminator 2: Judgment Day*, which chronicles the days leading up to a global nuclear war. The Meteor Defense game that you create in Chapter 17, "Example Game: Meteor Defense," is loosely based on Missile Command.

In Chapter 14, "Example Game: Battle Office," you learn about the futuristic 1982 Disney movie called *Tron*, which is about a computer hacker who jacks into cyberspace to fight an evil computer program bent on world domination. More importantly, you find out about the Tron video game by Bally Midway, which coat-tailed the movie and became a huge arcade success. The Tron arcade game is unique in that it consists of four mini-games—each of which is really its own video game. One of the Tron mini-games involves two light cycles racing around the screen leaving a trail of light beams that cannot be crossed. In the movie, the characters race around chasing each other on light cycles, which are kind of like high-tech motorcycles. The light cycles game is actually very simple to play, but it presents some unique strategies for attempting to quickly outsmart the player controlling the other light cycle. This chapter leads you through the development of your own Light Cycles game that is very similar to the one popularized in the classic Tron arcade game. Unlike the Tron version of light cycles, which pits you against a computer opponent, in this chapter's Light Cycles game, you play against another person, so be thinking of a friend to play the game with you.

In this chapter, you'll learn

▶ How to avoid complex game programming problems whenever possible

▶ How to take a game idea and refine it into a game design

▶ How to turn a game design into actual game code

▶ That testing a game sometimes involves a helpful friend

How Does the Game Play?

The idea behind the Light Cycles game that you design and build in this chapter is to enable two light beam-powered motorcycles to race around the game screen until one of them runs out of space and collides with either the boundary of the game screen or a light beam trail that one of the cycles left behind. To help you understand what I'm talking about, imagine a motorcycle that leaves a trail of smoke behind it everywhere it goes. If you happen to ride the motorcycle around in a confined area, you'll eventually double back on yourself and ride through your own smoke trail. In Light Cycles, the cycles leave behind a trail of light that matches the color of each cycle. These light trails serve as impenetrable walls that will destroy either cycle if one collides with the trails. So, as you steer your light cycle around the game screen, you are also building walls that could destroy you or your opponent. The edges of the game screen serve as another border that will destroy a light cycle should it collide with them. Figure 8.1 shows a sketch of the light cycle game and how the cycles leave trails that act as walls.

Notice in the figure that the light cycles start at opposite sides of the screen (top and bottom) and begin the game heading toward each other in a game of futuristic "chicken." The goal is to cruise around the screen navigating a safe path for your cycle while simultaneously trying to box in your opponent and cause her to collide with a light trail or the edge of the game screen. The figure shows how a light cycle colliding with a light trail results in a crash.

Based on the game description thus far, you can probably guess what kind of user input controls the game needs. The light cycle speeds are fixed, so there is no way to speed up or slow down, which means that the controls are limited to steering the cycles in the direction you want to go. This can be accomplished via the arrow keys on the keyboard or a joystick. This brings up an important issue that I might as well address because we're talking about user controls: How do you make the game competitive? In other words, how do you make the game interesting from the perspective of playing against an opponent smart enough to dodge your cycle/trails and also cleverly try to box in your cycle? The answer is that there is no easy way to accomplish this task using a computer opponent. Although you learn about artificial intelligence (AI) in Part VI, "Adding Brains to Your Games," it is definitely beyond the scope of the Light Cycles game at this stage of the book. So what do you do? Read on because the next section reveals a brutally simple solution to this problem.

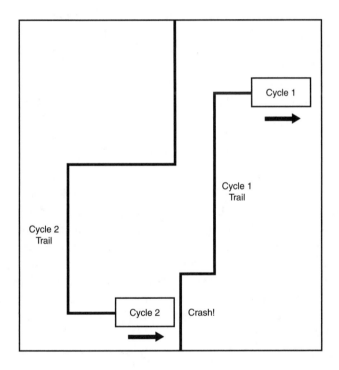

FIGURE 8.1
The Light Cycles game consists of two light cycles that leave light beam trails behind as they ride around the game screen.

Designing the Game

Although you're still only a third of the way through the book, the Light Cycles game hopefully doesn't sound too terribly complicated. Perhaps the biggest obstacle to creating the Light Cycles game is that you haven't been formally introduced to animation and how it works within the context of most games. While I'm certainly getting things out of order a bit by introducing the Light Cycles game prior to teaching you how animation works, I've done so deliberately to make the point that you will never be fully prepared for any game you create. The very nature of game programming is that it will present new and unusual challenges every step of the way, so you might as well get comfortable with the fact that you'll often be in over your head to some extent. This isn't to say that you should throw caution to the wind and ignore standard programming practices—I'm just trying to point out that you can never really know everything you need to know when first embarking on a game development project.

Getting back to the Light Cycles game, you've learned enough about animating an object on the game screen from the UFO examples to animate a couple of light cycles. So, I'm really not too worried about you understanding the animation side of the game. What I'm worried about is how you're going to understand the complex artificial intelligence code required to make a computer light cycle think intelligently enough to steer clear of a human player, yet play craftily enough to lure a human player into a trap. Hopefully, you have some experience with neural networks and fuzzy logic electronics design because it will come in handy as we develop thousands of lines of artificial intelligence code for the computer light cycle, or not. Maybe there's a simpler solution.

A better solution might be to rely on the most intelligent machine of all, the human brain! Instead of killing ourselves trying to develop a "smart" computer opponent, why not just design the game as a two-player game? Granted, you're limiting the game to only two players, but the idea is to create something fun without sidetracking the creative process with programming challenges that are literally beyond the scope of your current game development knowledge. This is a perfect example of how you can save yourself tons of trouble by simply altering the scope of a game. The difference between the Light Cycles game being designed for two players, as compared to designing it for one player with a computer opponent, is dramatic.

So, you've decided to save yourself a great deal of time and energy by designing the Light Cycles game as a two-player game. Now, the central design question becomes, "how do you retrieve user input from two players?" The ideal solution is to allow for networked game play across two computers, but this solution is akin to the artificially intelligent computer player in that it requires a considerable amount of complex code. Networked game programming is unfortunately beyond the scope of this book, although I encourage you to look into it for future learning. A more realistic solution is to consider two-player input options on a single computer. The most interesting approach to this solution is to allow one player to use the arrow keys on the keyboard while the other player uses the joystick. Because you already know how to handle input from the keyboard and joystick, this is all familiar territory.

I think it's safe to say that we've spent enough time pondering the user input side of the Light Cycles game, so let's move on to the design specifics of the cycles themselves. You know that the cycles are always moving, which means that their positions must somehow be updated with every passing game cycle. Additionally, the cycles must leave a visible trail capable of being redrawn when the game screen needs to be repainted. Not only do the light trails need to be redrawn, but they also need to be used as the basis for checking to see if one of the cycles has collided with them. One detail I neglected to mention earlier is that the light cycles can only turn at 90-degree angles, so you'll never have diagonal light trails. This is important because it simplifies collision detection between the cycles and the trails.

Before we get into detecting collisions, let's first address how to keep track of the trails. You know that a light cycle is constantly moving and that it can only make 90-degree turns. The simplest and most efficient way to keep up with the light trails is to store an array of points that represent each turn a light cycle makes. You can then reconstruct a light trail by "connecting the dots." Figure 8.2 shows a light cycle trail illustrated as a sequence of connected points.

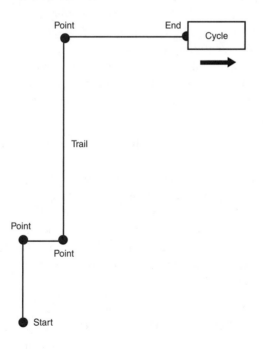

FIGURE 8.2
The most efficient way to keep track of a light trail is to store it as an array of interconnected points.

The light trail in the figure consists of a series of points with lines connecting them. In terms of game code, it isn't too difficult to store away these points in an array. At any given time, you can draw a light trail by simply looping through the points and drawing lines between them. The real trick is constructing the array of points as the light cycle cruises around the game screen. The end point must constantly be updated to reflect the cycle's current position. And each time the cycle makes a turn, you have to create a new end point. So, the process of recording points in the cycle's path goes like this:

1. Continually update the end point to match the cycle's current position.

2. When the cycle makes a turn, freeze the end point and create a new one.

3. Continue tracking the cycle's position with the new end point.

Just refer back to Figure 8.2 if this series of steps doesn't make immediate sense and visualize the cycle moving around the screen making 90-degree turns—at each turn, a new point must be created. You can think of each point in a light trail as representing a 90-degree bend in the trail.

Another big design issue in the Light Cycles game is tackling the problem of detecting collisions between the light cycles and the light trails. Although this could easily turn into a very challenging task, I found a relatively simple solution that makes the task much more straightforward. Keep in mind that my goal in this book isn't to create the most optimized code in terms of speed, but instead to create code that is as easy to understand as possible. You find out more about the light cycle collision detection solution in the next section when you dive into the code for the game.

Getting back to the light cycles themselves for a moment, I neglected to point out that the cycles are directional, which means that their images are always facing a certain direction, just like a real motorcycle. Knowing that the cycles in the game can turn and ride in any of four different directions (up, down, left, and right), it makes sense that each light cycle needs four different bitmap images to represent each direction. So in the game when you turn a cycle left, the cycle's image changes to an image of a cycle facing in a left direction. This design facet of the game is simple to implement, but goes a long way toward making the game look and play better.

To recap, the design of the Light Cycles game has led us to the following pieces of information that must be managed by the game:

- ▶ An array of light trail points for each cycle
- ▶ The number of trail points for each cycle
- ▶ The current position of each cycle
- ▶ A series of four directional bitmaps for each cycle

With this information in mind, you're now ready to move on and put the code together for the Light Cycles game.

Building the Game

Not to take anything away from the Brainiac game you created in Chapter 6, but you're about to take things to a whole new level with the Light Cycles game. Of course, the code for the Light Cycles game is also a bit more complex than that of the Brainiac game, but that's to be expected when you consider that Light Cycles involves animation and collision detection, not to mention some unique game elements, such as the light trails that are created on-the-fly as players steer their light cycles around the game screen. This section carefully guides you through the development of the code for the Light Cycles game. The complete source code and project files for the Light Cycles game, not to mention all of the examples throughout the book, are located on the accompanying CD-ROM.

The code for the Light Cycles game begins with the LightCycles.h header file, which is shown in Listing 8.1.

LISTING 8.1 The LightCycles.h Header File Declares Global Variables that Are Used to Manage the Game

```
#pragma once

//---------------------------------
// Include Files
//---------------------------------
#include <windows.h>
#include "Resource.h"
#include "GameEngine.h"
#include "Bitmap.h"

//---------------------------------
// Global Variables
//---------------------------------
HINSTANCE    g_hInstance;
GameEngine*  g_pGame;
Bitmap*      g_pBackground;
```

continues

There are two light cycles, and each one has four different directional images.

Each cycle is capable of having a light trail with a maximum of 100 connected lines; the assumption is that you'll never get near this maximum.

LISTING 8.1 Continued

```
Bitmap*        g_pCycle[2][4];
POINT          g_ptCyclePos[2];
POINT          g_ptCycleSpeed[2];

POINT          g_ptCycleTrail[2][100];

int            g_iTrailLen[2];
const int      g_iSPEED = 4;
BOOL           g_bGameOver;

//----------------------------------------
// Function Declarations
//----------------------------------------
void NewGame();
void UpdateCycles();
void SteerCycle(int iCycle, int iDirection);
void EndGame(int iCycle);
```

The first couple of things to notice in this code are the background and light cycle bitmaps. The background bitmap (see Figure 8.3) is a metallic futuristic image that serves as a good backdrop for the game, but otherwise serves no particular purpose in terms of game play. The light cycle bitmap images are stored in a two-dimensional array, which is necessary to accommodate the four directional animation frames for both cycles. Figure 8.4 shows the four animation frames for the first light cycle, which happens to be the blue cycle. You can see in the figure how each frame of animation corresponds to a different direction for the cycle.

FIGURE 8.3
The background bitmap for the Light Cycle game is a stylized metallic image the size of the game screen (500x400).

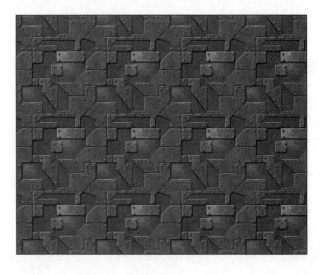

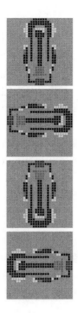

FIGURE 8.4
The four animation frames for each of the light cycles correspond to the directions in which the cycles can face.

Storing each animation frame for an animated graphical object as a separate bitmap isn't very efficient. However, it is simpler for the sake of this example. Later in the book, you learn how to place all the animation frames for an animated object in a single bitmap file so that the frames look sort of like a filmstrip.

Construction Cue

The next few global variables in the LightCycles.h header file are POINT structures used to store information related to the cycle positions, speeds, and light trails. If you recall from Windows programming, a POINT structure contains two integers that represent an XY coordinate. The g_ptCyclePos variable is an array that stores the current XY position of each cycle, whereas the g_ptCycleSpeed variable is also an array, but it stores the speed of each cycle. The speeds of the cycles don't change in the game as I've designed it, but I chose to store the speeds in a variable so that you could improve on the game by varying the cycle speeds over time if you want.

Another idea for incorporating varying cycle speeds into the Light Cycles game is to add "power-ups" to the game, which are objects that appear on the screen randomly to provide enhancements to the light cycles; running over a power-up gives your cycle an advantage of some sort. For example, a speed power-up would increase the speed of a cycle to make it quicker than the opponent. Of course, the specific strategy of Light Cycles might make a speed decrease power-up more useful because you could wall off a space and then take your time riding around inside it while your opponent runs out of space more quickly driving her faster cycle.

Construction Cue

The light cycle trail is stored in the g_ptCycleTrail global variable, which is a two-dimensional array of POINT structures. The two-dimensional array is necessary because there is an array of POINTs for each cycle. If you recall, each point in the array represents a point within a cycle's trail where the direction of the trail changes. I went ahead and made the arrays a fixed size of 100 elements based on the assumption that a cycle's trail will never get close to having 100 points. You could also design the code around a vector or linked list that grows dynamically, but for situations like this, it is actually more efficient to just use a fixed size array larger than you'll ever need. Even though the light cycle trail arrays are 100 elements in length, that certainly doesn't mean there are 100 points in a trail at any given time; in fact, you're banking on the array never being maxed out. The g_iTrailLen global variable keeps track of how many actual points are in each of the light trail arrays.

The remaining global variables are g_iSPEED and g_bGameOver. The default light cycle speed is stored in the g_iSPEED integer constant, whereas the g_bGameOver Boolean variable keeps track of whether a game is over (TRUE) or not (FALSE).

The remainder of the LightCycles.h header file consists of global function declarations. These functions serve important game-specific tasks within the Light Cycles game. The NewGame() function starts a new game, which primarily consists of setting the initial light cycle positions and speeds. The EndGame() function ends a game by displaying a message that indicates who won. The UpdateCycles() function handles the tricky task of updating the positions of the light cycles and checking to see if they have collided with the edges of the screen or their light trails. The SteerCycle() function takes care of steering a cycle in a given direction (up, down, left, or right). You see the specific code that makes these functions work a bit later in the chapter. However, before you get into that, let's take a look at the standard game-specific functions that must be supported for the game engine.

The GameInitialize() function for the Light Cycles game is similar to what you've seen in other examples, such as the UFO 2 example in the previous chapter, so we'll skip its details. The GameStart() and GameEnd() functions are of much more interest because they carry out tasks unique to the Light Cycles game. More specifically, they are responsible for initializing and cleaning up the game data, as shown in Listing 8.2.

LISTING 8.2   The `GameStart()` Function Creates and Loads the Background and Light Cycle Bitmaps, Whereas the `GameEnd()` Function Cleans Up the Bitmaps

```
void GameStart(HWND hWindow)
{
  // Create and load the background and light cycle bitmaps
  HDC hDC = GetDC(hWindow);
  g_pBackground = new Bitmap(hDC, IDB_BACKGROUND, g_hInstance);

  g_pCycle[0][0] = new Bitmap(hDC, IDB_CYCLEBLUE_0, g_hInstance);
  g_pCycle[0][1] = new Bitmap(hDC, IDB_CYCLEBLUE_90, g_hInstance);
  g_pCycle[0][2] = new Bitmap(hDC, IDB_CYCLEBLUE_180, g_hInstance);
  g_pCycle[0][3] = new Bitmap(hDC, IDB_CYCLEBLUE_270, g_hInstance);
  g_pCycle[1][0] = new Bitmap(hDC, IDB_CYCLEORANGE_0, g_hInstance);
  g_pCycle[1][1] = new Bitmap(hDC, IDB_CYCLEORANGE_90, g_hInstance);
  g_pCycle[1][2] = new Bitmap(hDC, IDB_CYCLEORANGE_180, g_hInstance);
  g_pCycle[1][3] = new Bitmap(hDC, IDB_CYCLEORANGE_270, g_hInstance);

  // Start a new game
  NewGame();
}

void GameEnd()
{
  // Cleanup the background and light cycle bitmaps
  delete g_pBackground;
  for (int i = 0; i < 4; i++)
  {
    delete g_pCycle[0][i];
    delete g_pCycle[1][i];
  }

  // Cleanup the game engine
  delete g_pGame;
}
```

The cycle bitmaps are named to indicate their direction in degrees, where 0 is north (up) and 180 is south (down).

The `GameStart()` function begins by loading the background and light cycle bitmaps. After loading the bitmaps, all that is left to do is call the `NewGame()` function to get the game started. The `GameEnd()` function plays a similar role as `GameStart()`, except that its job is to clean up the bitmaps that were created in `GameStart()`. The game engine is also cleaned up, as is standard in all games built on the game engine you develop throughout the book.

The Light Cycles game screen is painted in the `GamePaint()` function, which is shown in Listing 8.3.

LISTING 8.3   The GamePaint() Function Draws the Background, Light Cycle Trails, and Light Cycles

```
void GamePaint(HDC hDC)
{
  // Draw the background
  g_pBackground->Draw(hDC, 0, 0);

  // Draw the light cycle trails
  for (int i = 0; i < 2; i++)
  {
    // Create a blue/orange pen depending on which trail is being drawn
    HPEN hPen = CreatePen(PS_SOLID, 5, (i == 0) ?
    [ic:ccc]RGB(0, 0, 255):RGB(255, 146, 73));
    SelectObject(hDC, hPen);

    // Start at the first point in the trail
    MoveToEx(hDC, g_ptCycleTrail[i][0].x, g_ptCycleTrail[i][0].y, NULL);

    // Draw a line to each of the remaining points
    for (int j = 1; j < g_iTrailLen[i]; j++)
      LineTo(hDC, g_ptCycleTrail[i][j].x, g_ptCycleTrail[i][j].y);

    // Clean up the pen
    DeleteObject(hPen);
  }

  // Determine the directions of the light cycles

  int iDirection[2] = { 0, 0 };

  for (i = 0; i < 2; i++)

  {
    if (g_ptCycleSpeed[i].y < 0)
      iDirection[i] = 0;
    else if (g_ptCycleSpeed[i].x > 0)
      iDirection[i] = 1;
    else if (g_ptCycleSpeed[i].y > 0)
      iDirection[i] = 2;
    else if (g_ptCycleSpeed[i].x < 0)
      iDirection[i] = 3;
  }

  // Draw the light cycles
  g_pCycle[0][iDirection[0]]->Draw(hDC, g_ptCyclePos[0].x,
    g_ptCyclePos[0].y, TRUE);
  g_pCycle[1][iDirection[1]]->Draw(hDC, g_ptCyclePos[1].x,
    g_ptCyclePos[1].y, TRUE);
}
```

Remove the int *declaration in this line of code if your compiler gives you a multiple initialization error.*

The GamePaint() function is extremely important because it is solely responsible for drawing the graphics in the game. The function begins by drawing the background bitmap image, which involves a single line of code. It takes a little more effort to draw the light trails because you must create a colored pen for each trail and then step through the array of points for each light cycle. Notice that for each point in an array, a line is drawn to connect it to the next point; the pen used for each line is 5-pixels wide and is a color that matches the given light cycle. After drawing both light trails, the GamePaint() function moves on to determining the direction that each light cycle is facing, which is ascertained by examining the X and Y speeds of the cycles. Once the function figures out the direction for each light cycle, it uses the appropriate cycle bitmap to draw each light cycle at the end of their respective light trails.

Just to recap so that you understand what's going on in the GamePaint() function, here are the main drawing tasks taking place:

1. The background image is drawn.

2. Light trails as a series of interconnected lines are drawn.

3. Light cycles using images in the appropriate directions are drawn.

When you consider these tasks individually while studying the code for the GamePaint() function, it will hopefully make more sense. It really isn't a very complex function once you get a handle on what it is accomplishing.

Although GamePaint() is important in providing the visuals for the Light Cycles game, none of the animation for the game would take place without the help of the GameCycle() function, which is shown in Listing 8.4.

LISTING 8.4   The GameCycle() Function Updates the Light Cycles and Forces a Repaint of the Game Screen

```
void GameCycle()
{
  if (!g_bGameOver)
  {
    // Move the light cycles
    UpdateCycles();

    // Force a repaint to redraw the light cycles
    InvalidateRect(g_pGame->GetWindow(), NULL, FALSE);
  }
}
```

The GameCycle() function first checks to make sure that the game isn't over. If the game is indeed still in progress, this function updates the light cycles with a call to the UpdateCycles() function. An update of the game screen is then forced with a call to the InvalidateRect() Win32 API function. Keep in mind that the GameCycle() function is getting called 30 times every second because the frame rate is set to 30, which is what makes the animation in the game work smoothly.

Earlier in the chapter, I explained that the Light Cycles game is a two-player game with one player controlling her cycle via the keyboard, whereas the other player uses a joystick. Listing 8.5 contains the code for the HandleKeys() function, which is responsible for handling keyboard input for the player controlling the blue light cycle.

LISTING 8.5 The HandleKeys() Function Responds to the Arrow Keys to Move the Blue Light Cycle

```
void HandleKeys()
{
  if (!g_bGameOver)
  {
    // Steer the blue light cycle in response to arrow key presses

    if (GetAsyncKeyState(VK_UP) < 0)
      SteerCycle(0, 0);
    else if (GetAsyncKeyState(VK_RIGHT) < 0)
      SteerCycle(0, 1);
    else if (GetAsyncKeyState(VK_DOWN) < 0)
      SteerCycle(0, 2);
    else if (GetAsyncKeyState(VK_LEFT) < 0)
      SteerCycle(0, 3);
  }
  else if (GetAsyncKeyState(VK_RETURN) < 0)
    NewGame();
}
```

To control the orange light cycle with additional keys, just copy this code; change the key identifiers, and change the first parameter in SteerCycle() *to 1.*

The HandleKeys() function is very straightforward in that it simply looks for arrow key presses on the keyboard and calls the SteerCycle() function to steer the blue light cycle accordingly. As you learn in a moment, the first parameter of the SteerCycle() function is the number of the light cycle in which to steer, where 0 corresponds to the blue light cycle and 1 corresponds to the orange one. The second parameter is the new direction of the light cycle, where 0 is up, 1 is right, 2 is down, and 3 is left. Finally, the HandleKeys() function calls the NewGame() function to start a new game in response to the user pressing the Enter (Return) key.

The orange light cycle is controlled via the joystick, which means that the HandleJoystick() function is responsible for making it happen. Listing 8.6 contains the code for the HandleJoystick() function, which is surprisingly similar to the HandleKeys() function.

If you don't have a joystick or would otherwise prefer to play the Light Cycles game solely with a keyboard, you can easily support two players via the keyboard by adding additional code to the `HandleKeys()` function. Just decide which keys you want to use for the second player (W, A, D, or X, for example), and add code to steer the orange cycle in response to those key presses. Letter keys have similar virtual key code names such as VK_W, VK_A, VK_D, and VK_X.

LISTING 8.6   The `HandleJoystick()` Function Responds to Joystick Movements to Move the Orange Light Cycle

```
void HandleJoystick(JOYSTATE jsJoystickState)
{
  if (!g_bGameOver)
  {
    // Steer the orange light cycle in response to joystick moves
    if (jsJoystickState & JOY_UP)
      SteerCycle(1, 0);
    else if (jsJoystickState & JOY_RIGHT)
      SteerCycle(1, 1);
    else if (jsJoystickState & JOY_DOWN)
      SteerCycle(1, 2);
    else if (jsJoystickState & JOY_LEFT)
      SteerCycle(1, 3);
  }
  else if (jsJoystickState & JOY_FIRE1)
    NewGame();
}
```

As this code reveals, handling the joystick in the Light Cycles game is very much like handling the keyboard, at least in terms of game logic. The `HandleJoystick()` function begins by making sure that the game isn't over, and if the game is in progress, it moves the orange light cycle in response to joystick directional movements. If the game is over, and the user has pushed the primary fire button, the `NewGame()` function is called to start a new game.

Speaking of the `NewGame()` function, it's finally time to find out exactly how it works. Listing 8.7 shows the code for the `NewGame()` function, which is probably a little more involved than you might have imagined.

LISTING 8.7   The `NewGame()` Function Starts a New Game by Positioning the Light Cycles and Initializing Their Light Trails

```
void NewGame()
{
  // Set the initial blue light cycle position and speed
```

continues

The blue light cycle starts out centered along the bottom of the screen moving upward.

LISTING 8.7   Continued

```
g_ptCyclePos[0].x = 250 - (g_pCycle[0][0]->GetWidth() / 2);
g_ptCyclePos[0].y = 400 - g_pCycle[0][0]->GetHeight();
g_ptCycleSpeed[0].x = 0;
g_ptCycleSpeed[0].y = -g_iSPEED;

// Set the initial orange light cycle position and speed
g_ptCyclePos[1].x = 250 - (g_pCycle[1][0]->GetWidth() / 2);
g_ptCyclePos[1].y = 0;
g_ptCycleSpeed[1].x = 0;
g_ptCycleSpeed[1].y = g_iSPEED;

// Set the light cycle trail lengths and initial points
g_iTrailLen[0] = g_iTrailLen[1] = 2;
g_ptCycleTrail[0][0].x = g_ptCycleTrail[0][1].x = 250;
g_ptCycleTrail[0][0].y = g_ptCycleTrail[0][1].y = 400;
g_ptCycleTrail[1][0].x = g_ptCycleTrail[1][1].x = 250;
g_ptCycleTrail[1][0].y = g_ptCycleTrail[1][1].y = 0;

// Start the game
g_bGameOver = FALSE;
}
```

The orange light cycle starts out centered along the top of the screen moving downward.

Although there might be a little more code in the NewGame() function than you anticipated, none of it is particularly difficult to understand. The function starts off by setting the initial position of the blue light cycle so that it appears centered horizontally on the game screen and along the bottom edge. The speed of the blue light cycle is set so that it begins moving up the screen at the default speed stored in the g_iSPEED global constant. The initial settings for the orange light cycle are made in a similar fashion with the cycle being positioned in the center horizontally and along the top edge of the game screen. The orange cycle's speed is set so that it begins moving down the screen at the default speed.

With the light cycles themselves initialized, the NewGame() function turns its attention to the light cycle trails. Each trail begins with two points, the start and end points, and therefore, each has an initial length of two. The two points for each array are then initialized with coordinates on the game screen that match up with the initial cycle positions. The last step in the NewGame() function is to clear the g_bGameOver flag so that the game can officially get underway.

The workhorse function of the entire Light Cycles game is the UpdateCycles() function because it contains the most crucial game logic associated with moving the light cycles and detecting collisions associated with them. Listing 8.8 contains the code for the UpdateCycles() function, which I encourage you to take your time with.

LISTING 8.8 The `UpdateCycles()` Function Updates the Positions of the Light Cycles, Along with Performing Collision Detections for the Cycles

```
Begin new
  for (int i = 0; i < 2; i++)
  {
    // Update the light cycle position based on its speed
    g_ptCyclePos[i].x = g_ptCyclePos[i].x + g_ptCycleSpeed[i].x;
    g_ptCyclePos[i].y = g_ptCyclePos[i].y + g_ptCycleSpeed[i].y;

    // Update the light cycle trail based on its new position
    g_ptCycleTrail[i][g_iTrailLen[i] - 1].x =
      g_ptCyclePos[i].x + (g_pCycle[i][0]->GetWidth() / 2);
    g_ptCycleTrail[i][g_iTrailLen[i] - 1].y =
      g_ptCyclePos[i].y + (g_pCycle[i][0]->GetHeight() / 2);

    // See if the light cycle ran into the edge of the screen
    if (g_ptCyclePos[i].x < 0 ||
      g_ptCyclePos[i].x > (500 - g_pCycle[i][0]->GetWidth()) ||
      g_ptCyclePos[i].y < 0 ||
      g_ptCyclePos[i].y > (400 - g_pCycle[i][0]->GetHeight()))
    {
      // The game is over
      EndGame(1 - i);
      return;
    }

    // See if the light cycle collided with its own trail
    RECT rcTmpTrail;
    if (g_iTrailLen[i] > 2) // Must have steered at least once
    {
      for (int j = 0; j < g_iTrailLen[i] - 2; j++)
      {
        rcTmpTrail.left = min(g_ptCycleTrail[i][j].x,
          g_ptCycleTrail[i][j + 1].x) - 1;
        rcTmpTrail.right = max(g_ptCycleTrail[i][j].x,
          g_ptCycleTrail[i][j + 1].x) + 1;
        rcTmpTrail.top = min(g_ptCycleTrail[i][j].y,
          g_ptCycleTrail[i][j + 1].y) - 1;
        rcTmpTrail.bottom = max(g_ptCycleTrail[i][j].y,
          g_ptCycleTrail[i][j + 1].y) + 1;
        if (PtInRect(&rcTmpTrail, g_ptCycleTrail[i][g_iTrailLen[i] - 1]) != 0)
        {
          // The game is over
          EndGame(1 - i);
          return;
        }
      }
    }

    // See if the light cycle collided with the other cycle's trail
    for (int j = 0; j <= g_iTrailLen[1 - i] - 2; j++)
    {
      rcTmpTrail.left = min(g_ptCycleTrail[1 - i][j].x,
        g_ptCycleTrail[1 - i][j + 1].x) - 3;
      rcTmpTrail.right = max(g_ptCycleTrail[1 - i][j].x,
```

Because i *indicates the cycle that has collided,* 1 - i *indicates the winner.*

continues

LISTING 8.8   Continued

```
        g_ptCycleTrail[1 - i][j + 1].x) + 3;
      rcTmpTrail.top = min(g_ptCycleTrail[1 - i][j].y,
        g_ptCycleTrail[1 - i][j + 1].y) - 3;
      rcTmpTrail.bottom = max(g_ptCycleTrail[1 - i][j].y,
        g_ptCycleTrail[1 - i][j + 1].y) + 3;
      if (PtInRect(&rcTmpTrail, g_ptCycleTrail[i][g_iTrailLen[i] - 1]) != 0)
      {
        // The game is over
        EndGame(1 - i);
        return;
      }
    }
  }
}
```

The first step in the UpdateCycles() function is to update the positions of the
light cycles based on their speeds. Once the position of each light cycle is updated, it is necessary to carry over this updating to the last point in each of the light
trails. With those two updating tasks taken care of, the UpdateCycles() function
moves into the real task at hand, which is detecting collisions between the light
cycles and the game screen edges, not to mention the light trails. Detecting a collision between a light cycle and the edge of the game screen isn't too terribly difficult, but the light trails present a unique programming challenge.

You know that a light trail is really just a series of lines that are connected from
end to end. When trying to determine if a light cycle has collided with a trail,
what you're really doing is figuring out if a point (the cycle's position) lies within
a line (a section of trail). Although a variety of interesting algorithms exist for
determining how to carry out the mathematical function of detecting a point in a
line, there is an easier way that simplifies the code considerably. In fact, my
approach doesn't involve lines at all, but instead, is based on rectangles. It is easier to determine if a point lies inside a rectangle than if it lies on a line because
the Win32 API provides a convenient function called PtInRect(), which determines whether a point lies within a rectangle. Because I hate reinventing the
wheel unless absolutely necessary, I opted to use the PtInRect() function as the
basis for detecting collisions between light cycles and light trails. The question
then becomes how do you resolve a light cycle/light trail collision down to a
PtInRect() comparison?

If you recall, the light trails in the game actually have some width to them. To be
exact, the light trails are drawn 5-pixels wide, which means that a single section

of light trail is really a rectangle in terms of exact pixels. The idea behind my collision detection scheme is to handle each segment of a light trail as an individual rectangle and then see if the light cycle's position lies within that rectangle. If you carry out this check for every segment in each light trail, you can successfully determine if a light cycle has collided with it. So, the light trail collision detection code that you see in the UpdateCycles() function is just stepping through each line segment in a light trail and converting the line into a rectangle. The rectangle is then passed into the PtInRect() function to see if the light cycle's position lies within it. If so, a collision has occurred, and the game is over.

> You might be wondering why the EndGame() function is called with 1 - i to indicate the winning cycle, as opposed to just i. This is because i represents the cycle that has collided, which is the loser. To determine the winner, you subtract the loser from 1, which effectively flips the value; 0 becomes 1, or 1 becomes 0.

Construction Cue

It's important to note that all this collision detection code lies within a for loop that steps through the two light cycles. In other words, every bit of code is carried out equally for each light cycle, which means that both light trails are lethal to both light cycles if a collision occurs.

With the UpdateCycles() function under your belt, it's clear sailing through the rest of the Light Cycles game code. Listing 8.9 contains the code for the SteerCycle() function, which is used to steer a cycle in a given direction.

LISTING 8.9 The SteerCycle() Function Is a Helper Function used to Steer a Light Cycle in a Specified Direction

```
void SteerCycle(int iCycle, int iDirection)
{
  // Remember the old light cycle speed

  POINT ptOldSpeed;
  ptOldSpeed.x = g_ptCycleSpeed[iCycle].x;
  ptOldSpeed.y = g_ptCycleSpeed[iCycle].y;

  // Change the speed of the light cycle to steer it
  switch (iDirection)
  {
  case 0: // Up (0 degrees)
    if (g_ptCycleSpeed[iCycle].y == 0)
    {
      g_ptCycleSpeed[iCycle].x = 0;
      g_ptCycleSpeed[iCycle].y = -g_iSPEED;
    }
    break;
```

The old speed is necessary later in this function to see if the light cycle has actually changed direction.

LISTING 8.9 Continued

```
case 1: // Right (90 degrees)
  if (g_ptCycleSpeed[iCycle].x == 0)
  {
    g_ptCycleSpeed[iCycle].x = g_iSPEED;
    g_ptCycleSpeed[iCycle].y = 0;
  }
  break;

case 2: // Down (180 degrees)
  if (g_ptCycleSpeed[iCycle].y == 0)
  {
    g_ptCycleSpeed[iCycle].x = 0;
    g_ptCycleSpeed[iCycle].y = g_iSPEED;
  }
  break;

case 3: // Left (270 degrees)
  if (g_ptCycleSpeed[iCycle].x == 0)
  {
    g_ptCycleSpeed[iCycle].x = -g_iSPEED;
    g_ptCycleSpeed[iCycle].y = 0;
  }
  break;
}

// If the speed changed, move to a new point in the light cycle trail
if ((g_ptCycleSpeed[iCycle].x != ptOldSpeed.x) ||
  (g_ptCycleSpeed[iCycle].y != ptOldSpeed.y))
{
  // Increment the number of trail points
  g_iTrailLen[iCycle]++;

  // Set the initial position of the new trail point
  g_ptCycleTrail[iCycle][g_iTrailLen[iCycle] - 1].x =
    g_ptCyclePos[iCycle].x + (g_pCycle[iCycle][0]->GetWidth() / 2);
  g_ptCycleTrail[iCycle][g_iTrailLen[iCycle] - 1].y =
    g_ptCyclePos[iCycle].y + (g_pCycle[iCycle][0]->GetHeight() / 2);
}
}
```

The initial position of the new trail point is set to the current light cycle position.

Okay, so maybe "clear sailing" was a bit strong, given the length of the SteerCycle() function, but you'll find that this function is much simpler to understand than the UpdateCycles() function. The SteerCycle() function accepts two parameters that identify the cycle in which to steer, along with its new direction. You pass 0 into the iCycle parameter to indicate that you want to steer the blue cycle, and 1 for the orange cycle. The iDirection parameter accepts the new direction of the light cycle, with the following values indicating the direction:

- 0—Up (0 degrees)

- 1—Right (90 degrees)

- 2—Down (180 degrees)

- 3—Left (270 degrees)

A switch-case statement is used to set the appropriate direction based on the value of the iDirection parameter. Setting the direction is simply a matter of altering the cycle's speed so that it moves in the given direction. It isn't necessary to set the image of the cycle to the new direction because the correct image is determined automatically by the GamePaint() function when the cycle is drawn.

Earlier, you learned that each point in the light trail array represents a direction change for a cycle. Knowing this, it shouldn't come as a surprise that the SteerCycle() function is responsible for adding a point to the trail array in response to guiding the cycle in a new direction. After checking to make sure that the cycle is indeed heading in a new direction, the SteerCycle() function increments the number of trail points and then adds a new point with the current cycle position. This is all that is required to build a trail of points in response to changes in cycle direction.

The last function in the Light Cycles game is the EndGame() function, which takes care of ending the game when a light cycle collides with the edge of the game screen or one of the light trails. Listing 8.10 contains the code for the EndGame() function.

LISTING 8.10   The EndGame() Function Ends the Game and Displays the Winner

```
void EndGame(int iCycle)
{
  // Set the game over flag
  g_bGameOver = TRUE;

  // Display a message about the winner
  if (iCycle == 0)
    MessageBox(g_pGame->GetWindow(), TEXT("Blue wins!"), TEXT("Light Cycles"),
    ➥ MB_OK);
  else
    MessageBox(g_pGame->GetWindow(), TEXT("Orange wins!"), TEXT("Light Cycles"),
    ➥ MB_OK);
}
```

The EndGame() function begins by setting the g_bGameOver flag, which stops the game. Additionally, the Win32 MessageBox() function is called to display a message box identifying the winning player; the winning player is specified in the iCycle parameter (0 for the blue cycle, 1 for the orange cycle).

That wraps up the code for the Light Cycles game. Now it's time for you to find a buddy and start testing out the game!

Construction Cue

If you happen to get a "multiple initialization" compiler error while compiling the Light Cycles program, you can easily fix it by removing the int variable declaration in the second group of for loops in the GameStart() function where the tiles are randomly initialized. This error stems from the fact that some compilers don't fully support the standard C++ approach of declaring loop initializer variables local to the loop. So, the int variable i is mistakenly interpreted as being declared twice. Just remove the second int declaration, and everything will work fine.

Construction Cue

As with most of the examples in the book, the Light Cycles program relies on the standard msimg32.lib and winmm.lib libraries. These libraries are included with most Windows compilers, but they aren't automatically linked into programs when you create a new project. If you are using your own project or making files, as opposed to using the ones provided on the CD-ROM, make sure that you change the link settings so that these library files are properly linked into the final executable. Refer to the documentation for your specific compiler for how this is done.

Testing the Game

The Light Cycles game is the only two-player game tackled in the book, so it's important for you to find another human player to truly get the full effect of the game. If you find yourself friendless at the moment, however, don't despair because you can still tinker with the game by yourself and see how it works. When you first run the game, the game screen appears with the background showing and the light cycles visible along the top and bottom edges of the game screen. Because there is no splash screen or anything for this game, it immediately starts with the light cycles heading toward each other on a collision course (see Figure 8.5). This is why it is helpful to have another player.

FIGURE 8.5
The Light Cycles game begins with the cycles on a collision course headed straight at each other.

Some quick steering can avert immediate disaster in the game, and if you're testing the game alone, you'll need some serious two-handed skills to steer one cycle with the keyboard and the other one with a joystick. Remember that the goal of the game is to outlast the opposing cycle by not colliding with the edge of the game screen or one of the light trails. Figure 8.6 shows a game in progress after the cycles have successfully avoided each other for a few seconds.

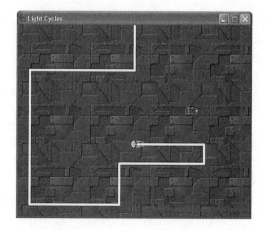

FIGURE 8.6
The light trails begin to build up as a game of Light Cycles wears on, making it increasingly difficult to avoid a collision.

Of course, sooner or later, one of the light cycles will make a mistake or be outfoxed by the other player—in which case, a collision will occur, and the game will end. Figure 8.7 shows a game ending with the winning player proudly displayed in a message box.

FIGURE 8.7
The winner of the
Light Cycles game
is displayed in a
message box when
the game ends.

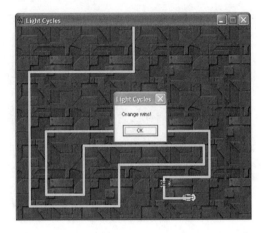

FIGURE 8.7
The winner of the
Light Cycles game
is displayed in a
message box when
the game ends.

You'll find that games of Light Cycles tend to finish rather quickly, which means that you'll likely find yourself starting new ones frequently. You can either press the Enter (Return) key on the keyboard or push the primary fire button on the joystick to start a new game.

Summary

This chapter guided you through the design and development of your first action game. I realize that the code in this chapter was a little more advanced than you might have been expecting so early in the book, but you might as well learn now that game programming is often "trial by fire" in terms of tackling challenges that are often just beyond your reach. That's ultimately what makes game programming such an exciting endeavor. The Light Cycles game definitely leaped ahead a few chapters by showing you how to use animation before you've been formally introduced to it. However, you saw how the game engine helped make the Light Cycles game code reasonably straightforward—with the most complex code involving the logic associated with detecting collisions between the cycles and light trails.

The next chapter provides the formal introduction to animation that I alluded to a moment ago. You learn all about sprite animation, including how to add support for sprite animation to the game engine. You find out how having support for sprite animation directly within the game engine makes the development of animated games much easier, especially as you start using more animated objects that interact with each other.

Extreme Game Makeover

The Light Cycles game is a good example of a game whose theme could be easily changed to resemble an entirely different game with very little work. As an example, let's say that you've been commissioned by John Deere to create a downloadable game to help advertise its tractors. You could take the existing Light Cycles game and replace the artwork to come up with a completely different game that plays exactly the same. Here's how you could turn Light Cycles into Tractor Assault:

1. Replace the light cycle images with tractor images.

2. Change the background image to a green image that looks like grass.

3. Change the tracks created by the tractors to a brown color to reflect newly tilled dirt. In this case, you would make the tracks of each tractor the same color, as opposed to the differing colors in the Light Cycles game.

4. You might also slow the speeds of the tractors down a bit to make the game play more realistic.

If dueling tractors isn't your idea of a fun game, feel free to dream up your own variation. The important point here is that you can completely make over a game without even touching a line of code.

PART III

Animating Games with Sprites

Making Things Move with Sprite Animation

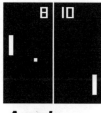

Released in 1981 by Namco, Galaga is widely regarded as one of the most popular video games of all time. It's also one of the first vertical shoot-em-ups to attain huge success following Space Invaders. Galaga introduced a unique game play feature in that you could allow an alien to steal your ship and then kill the alien, retrieve the ship, and control two ships at once for double the fire power. Galaga was re-released in a dual arcade cabinet with Ms. Pac-Man in 2001 to commemorate the 20th anniversary of both games.

The heart of graphics in almost all games is animation. Without animation, there would be no movement, and without movement, we'd all be stuck playing board games and card games. This chapter presents the fundamental concepts surrounding animation in games and, more specifically, sprite animation. As you'll soon learn, practically every game with animation employs some type of animation engine, typically involving sprites. Once the animation theory is out of the way, this chapter shows you how to design and build an all-purpose sprite class that will allow you to incorporate sprite animation into any program. You will end up reusing the sprite class in every example and game throughout the remainder of the book, so it's safe to say that it represents one of the most significant programming milestones in the book. Fortunately, the Sprite class is not very complex, and it serves as a great example of how sprite animation doesn't have to be complex.

In this chapter, you'll learn

- ▶ The basics of animation and how it works in games
- ▶ The difference between 2D and 3D animation

▶ The different types of 2D animation and when to use each one in games

▶ How sprites are used in games

▶ What it takes to design, develop, and use a sprite class

Understanding the Basics of Animation

Before getting into animation as it relates to games, it's important to understand the basics of what animation is and how it works. Let's begin by asking this fundamental question: What is animation? Put simply, *animation* is the illusion of movement. Could it be that all animation you've ever seen is really just an illusion? That's exactly right! Probably the most surprising animated illusion is one that captured attention long before computers—the television. When you watch television, you see a lot of things moving around, but what you perceive as movement is really just a trick being played on your eyes.

Animation and Frame Rate

In the case of television, the illusion of movement is created by displaying a rapid succession of images with slight changes in their appearance. The human eye perceives these changes as movement because of its low visual acuity, which means that your eyes are fairly easy to trick into believing the illusion of animation. More specifically, the human eye can be tricked into perceiving animated movement with as few as 12 frames of movement per second. It should come as no surprise that this animation speed is the minimum target speed for most computer games. Animation speed is measured in *frames per second (fps)*, which you've encountered a few times throughout the book already.

Although 12fps is technically enough to fool your eyes into seeing animation, animation at speeds this low often ends up looking somewhat jerky. Therefore, most professional animation uses a higher frame rate. Television, for example, uses 30fps. When you go to the movies, you see motion pictures at about 24fps. It's pretty apparent that these frame rates are more than enough to captivate your attention and successfully create the illusion of movement.

> ### Why the Difference in Film and Television Frame Rates?
>
> In case you're curious, the reason for the difference between film and television frame rates has to do more with technical necessity than careful design or planning. In its early days, film speeds were as low as 16fps, but were eventually standardized at 24fps, which turned out to be a good frame rate to accommodate sound reproduction. American television, also known as NTSC (National Television Standards Committee), came along later and relied on the power line frequency as a timing reference. This frequency was (and still is) 60Hz, which results in a frame rate of 30fps. The fact that film and television frame rates are different means that films have to be converted in order to be shown on television.

Unlike television and motion pictures, computer games are sometimes more limited when it comes to frame rate. Higher frame rates in games correspond to much higher processor overhead, so game developers are left to balance the frame rate against the system speed and resources. That is why some games provide different resolution and graphics quality options. By using a lower resolution and simpler graphics, a game can increase its frame rate and generate smoother animation. Of course, the trade-off is a lower resolution and simpler graphics.

When programming animation in Windows games, you typically have the ability to manipulate the frame rate a reasonable amount. The most obvious limitation on frame rate is the speed at which the computer can generate and display the animation frames. Actually, the same limitation must be dealt with by game developers, regardless of the programming language or platform. When determining the frame rate for a game, you usually have some give and take in establishing a low enough frame rate to yield smooth animation, while not bogging down the processor and slowing the system down for the vast majority of game players. However, don't worry too much about this right now. For now, just keep in mind that when programming animation for games, you are acting as a magician creating the illusion of movement.

Making the Move to Computer Animation

Most of the techniques used in computer animation have been borrowed or based on traditional animation techniques developed for animated films. The classic approach to handling traditional animation is to draw a background image separately from the animated objects that will be moving in the foreground. The animated objects are then drawn on clear celluloid sheets so that they can be overlaid on the background and moved independently. This type of animation is referred to as *cel animation*. Cel animation enables artists to save a great deal of time by only drawing the specific objects that change shape or position from one frame to the next. This explains why so many animated movies have detailed backgrounds with relatively simple animated characters. Computer game sprites, which you learn about a little later in the chapter, directly correspond to traditional cel animated objects.

As computer power improved over the past two decades, traditional animators saw the potential for automating many of their hands-on techniques. Computers enabled them to scan in drawings and overlay them with transparencies, for example. This is a similar approach to cel animation, but with one big difference: The computer imposes no limitations on the number of overlaid images. Cel animation is limited because only so many cel sheets can be overlaid. The technique of overlaying objects with transparencies is a fundamental form of computer game animation, as you soon find out.

Gamer's Garage

Modern animated movies have officially proven that computer animation is for more than just games. Popular movies such as *Toy Story*; *Ice Age*; *Monsters, Inc.*; *Finding Nemo*; and *The Incredibles* are great examples of how traditional animated movies are now being created solely on computers. Perhaps an even more advanced example of computer animation in movies is *Final Fantasy*, which is one of the first movies to use computer animation to simulate live action graphics.

Although computers have certainly improved upon traditional animation techniques, the animation potential available to the game programmer is far more flexible than traditional techniques. As a programmer, you have access to each individual pixel of each bitmap image, and you can manipulate each of them to your heart's content.

2D Versus 3D Animation

There are two fundamental types of animation that you might consider using when creating games: 2D and 3D. *2D animation* involves objects moving or being manipulated within two dimensions. Objects in 2D animation can still have a 3D look to them—they just can't physically move in three dimensions. Many 2D animation techniques simulate 3D animation by altering the look of objects to simulate depth, but they aren't truly 3D. As an example, animation of a car driving off into the distance would involve the car getting smaller as it gets farther away. However, this isn't necessarily 3D animation because you can achieve the 3D effect by making the car image get smaller as it moves away. Although the end result is three-dimensional, the car is very much a 2D object.

Unlike 2D animation, *3D animation* involves placing and manipulating objects in a three-dimensional, virtual world. A 3D object is defined by a model, rather than an image, because an image is inherently two-dimensional. A 3D model specifies the shape of an object with a series of points or vertices in 3D space. In other words, a 3D model is a mathematical representation of a physical object. For this reason, 3D graphics and animation can get extremely complicated because these things often rely on heavy-duty mathematical processing.

In reality, many games make use of a mixture of 2D and 3D graphics and animation. For example, the original Doom game uses 3D graphics for the building interiors. However, the monsters in the game are 2D graphics objects. The monsters have a 3D appearance, but they are represented by flat images on the screen. This mixture of 2D and 3D graphics works great in Doom because the 2D monsters look realistic enough when blending into 3D surroundings. Of course, things have evolved since the original Doom game. Quake and other more modern 3D first-person shooters (FPS) now use 3D objects throughout the game.

The remainder of this chapter and the book in general focus on 2D animation because it is the more straightforward and efficient technique of the two. The good news is that you can still do some pretty powerful things with 2D animation.

Understanding the Types of 2D Animation

Although the focus of this chapter is ultimately on sprite animation, it is important to understand the primary types of animation used in game programming. Actually, a lot of different types of animation exist—all of which are useful in different instances. However, for the purposes of implementing animation in games, I've broken animation down into two basic types: frame-based and cast-based. Technically speaking, there is also a third animation type known as *palette animation* that involves animating the colors in a graphic object, but I think of it as more of a graphics effect, rather than a fundamental type of animation.

Frame-Based Animation

The most simple animation technique is *frame-based animation*, which finds a lot of usage in non-gaming animations. Frame-based animation involves simulating movement by displaying a sequence of pre-generated, static frame images. A movie is a perfect example of frame-based animation; each frame of the film is a frame of animation, and when the frames are shown in rapid succession, they create the illusion of movement.

Frame-based animation has no concept of a graphical object distinguishable from the background; everything appearing in a frame is part of that frame as a whole. The result is that each frame image contains all the information necessary for that frame in a static form. This is an important point because it distinguishes frame-based animation from cast-based animation, which you learn about in the next section. Figure 9.1 shows a few frames of frame-based animation.

FIGURE 9.1
In frame-based ani-
mation, the entire
frame changes to
achieve the effect
of animation.

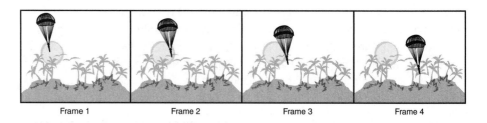

| Frame 1 | Frame 2 | Frame 3 | Frame 4 |

The figure shows how a paratrooper is drawn directly onto each frame of anima-tion, so there is no separation between the paratrooper object and the sky back-ground. This means that the paratrooper cannot be moved independently of the background. The illusion of movement is achieved by redrawing each frame with the paratrooper in a slightly different position. This type of animation is of limit-ed use in games because games typically require the ability to move objects around independently of the background.

Cast-Based Animation

A more powerful animation technique employed by many games is *cast-based animation*, which is also known as *sprite animation*. Cast-based animation involves graphical objects that move independently of a background. At this point, you might be a little confused by the usage of the term graphical object when refer-ring to parts of animation. In this case, a graphical object is something that logically can be thought of as a separate entity from the background of animation image. For example, in the animation of a space shoot-em-up game, the aliens are separate graphical objects that are logically independent of the star field background.

The Origins of Cast-Based Animation

You might be wondering where the term cast-based animation comes from. It comes from the fact that sprites can be thought of as cast members moving around on a stage. This analogy of relating computer animation to theatrical performance is very useful. By thinking of sprites as cast members and the background as a stage, you can take the next logical step and think of an animation as a theatrical performance. In fact, this isn't far from the mark because the goal of theatrical performances is to entertain the audience by telling a story through the interaction of the cast members. Likewise, cast-based animation uses the interaction of sprites to entertain the user, while often telling a story.

Each graphical object in cast-based animation is referred to as a *sprite* and can have a position that varies over time. In other words, sprites have a velocity associated with them that determines how their position changes over time. Almost every video game uses sprites to some degree. For example, every object in the classic Asteroids game is a sprite that moves independently of the background; even though Asteroids relies on vector graphics, the objects in the game are still sprites. Another good example of a rudimentary sprite is the flying saucer from the UFO example you've seen earlier in the book. Figure 9.2 shows an example of how cast-based animation simplifies the paratrooper example you saw in the previous section.

In this example, the paratrooper is now a sprite that can move independently of the background sky image. So, instead of having to draw every frame manually with the paratrooper in a slightly different position, you can just move the paratrooper image around on top of the background. This is the same approach you'll be using to inject animation into games throughout the remainder of the book.

Even though the fundamental principle behind sprite animation is the positional movement of a graphical object, there is no reason you can't incorporate frame-based animation into a sprite. This enables you to change the image of the sprite, as well as alter its position. This hybrid type of animation is actually what you will create later in the book as you add sprite support to the game engine.

FIGURE 9.2
In cast-based animation, a graphical object can move independently of the background to achieve the effect of animation.

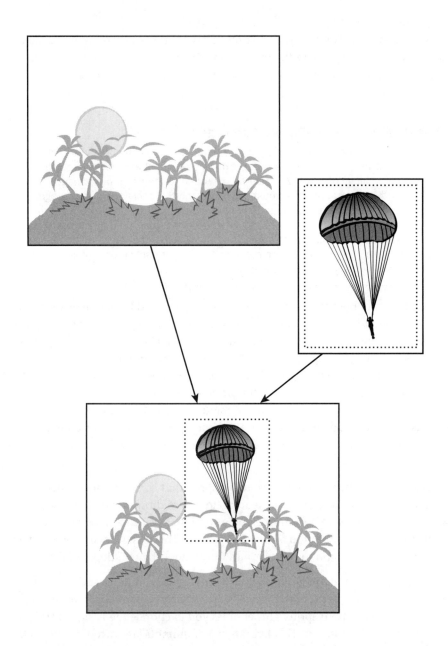

I mentioned in the frame-based animation discussion that television is a good example of frame-based animation. Can you think of something on television that is created in a manner similar to cast-based animation (other than animated movies and cartoons)? Have you ever wondered how weather people magically appear in front of a computer-generated map showing the weather? The news station uses a technique known as *blue-screening* or *green-screening*, which enables them to overlay the weatherperson on top of the weather map in real-time. It works like this: The person stands in front of a solid-color backdrop (blue or green), which serves as a transparent background. The image of the weatherperson is overlaid onto the weather map; the trick is that the colored background is filtered out when the image is overlaid so that it is effectively transparent. In this way, the weatherperson is acting exactly like a sprite!

Seeing Through Objects with Transparency

The weatherperson example brings up a very important point regarding sprites: transparency. Because bitmapped images are rectangular by nature, a problem arises when sprite images aren't rectangular in shape. In sprites that aren't rectangular in shape, which includes the majority of them, the pixels surrounding the sprite image are unused. In a graphics system without transparency, these unused pixels are drawn just like any others. The end results are sprites that have visible rectangular borders around them, which completely destroy the effectiveness of having sprites overlaid on a background image.

What's the solution? Well, one solution is to make all of your sprites rectangular. Because this solution isn't very practical, a more realistic solution is *transparency*, which allows you to define a certain color in an image as unused or transparent. When pixels of this color are encountered by drawing routines, they are simply skipped, leaving the original background intact. Transparent colors in images act exactly like the weatherperson's colored screen in the earlier example.

Fortunately, you've already learned how easy it is to support transparency when drawing bitmap images. In fact, you modified the `Bitmap` class to support transparency in Chapter 5, "Controlling Games with the Keyboard and Mouse."

Adding Depth with Z-Order

In many instances, you will want some sprites to appear on top of others. For example, in a war game, you might have planes flying over a battlefield dropping bombs on everything in sight. If a plane sprite happens to fly over a tank sprite, you obviously want the plane to appear above the tank and, therefore, hide the tank as it passes over. You handle this problem by assigning each sprite a screen depth, which is also referred to as *Z-order*.

Z-order is the relative depth of sprites on the screen. The depth of sprites is called Z-order because it works sort of like another dimension—like a Z axis. You can think of sprites moving around on the screen in the XY axis. Similarly, the Z axis can be thought of as another axis projected into the screen that determines how the sprites overlap each other. To put it another way, Z-order determines a sprite's depth within the screen. By making use of a Z axis, you might think that Z-ordered sprites are 3D. The truth is that Z-ordered sprites can't be considered 3D because the Z axis is a hypothetical axis only used to determine how sprite objects hide each other.

Just to make sure that you get a clear picture of how Z-order works, let's go back for a moment to the good old days of traditional animation. You learned earlier that traditional animators, such as those at Disney, used celluloid sheets to draw animated objects. They drew on celluloid sheets because the sheets could be overlaid on a background image and moved independently; cel animation is an early version of sprite animation. Each cel sheet corresponds to a unique Z-order value, determined by where in the pile of sheets the sheet is located. If a sprite near the top of the pile happens to be in the same location on the cel sheet as any lower sprites, it conceals them. The location of each sprite in the stack of cel sheets is its Z-order, which determines its visibility precedence. The same thing applies to sprites in cast-based animation, except that the Z-order is determined by the order in which the sprites are drawn, rather than the cel sheet location.

Detecting Collisions Between Objects

No discussion of animation as it applies to games would be complete without covering collision detection. *Collision detection* is the method of determining whether sprites have collided with each other. Although collision detection doesn't directly play a role in creating the illusion of movement, it is tightly linked to sprite animation and is extremely crucial in games.

Collision detection is used to determine when sprites physically interact with each other. In the Asteroids game, for example, if the ship sprite collides with an asteroid sprite, the ship is destroyed, and an explosion appears. Collision detection is the mechanism employed to find out whether the ship collided with the asteroid. This might not sound like a big deal—just compare their positions and see whether they overlap, right? Correct, but consider how many comparisons must take place when a lot of sprites are moving around; each sprite must be compared to every other sprite in the system. It's not hard to see how the processing overhead of effective collision detection can become difficult to manage.

Not surprisingly, there are many approaches to handling collision detection. The simplest approach is to compare the bounding rectangles of each sprite with the bounding rectangles of all the other sprites. This method is efficient, but if you have objects that are not rectangular, a certain degree of error occurs when the objects brush by each other. This is because the corners might overlap and indicate a collision, when really only the transparent areas are overlapping. The less rectangular the shape of the sprites, the larger the degree of error that typically occurs. Figure 9.3 shows how simple *rectangle collision* works.

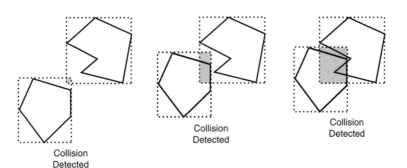

Collision
Detected

Collision
Detected

Collision
Detected

FIGURE 9.3
Collision detection using rectangle collision simply involves checking to see if the bounding rectangles of two objects overlap.

In the figure, the areas determining the collision detection are shaded. You can see how simple rectangle collision detection isn't very accurate unless you're dealing with sprites that are rectangular in shape. An improvement upon this technique is to shrink the collision rectangles a little, which reduces the error. This method improves things a little, but it has the potential to cause error in the reverse direction by allowing sprites to overlap in some cases without signaling a collision. Figure 9.4 shows how shrinking the collision rectangles can reduce the error on simple rectangle collision detection. *Shrunken rectangle collision* is just as efficient as simple rectangle collision because all you are doing is comparing rectangles for intersection.

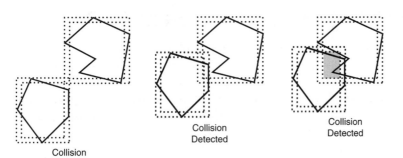

Collision
Not
Detected

Collision
Detected

Collision
Detected

FIGURE 9.4
Collision detection using shrunken rectangle collision involves checking to see if shrunken versions of the bounding rectangles of two objects overlap.

The most accurate collision detection technique is to detect collisions based on the sprite image data, which involves actually checking to see whether transparent parts of the sprites or the sprite images themselves are overlapping. In this case, you get a collision only if the actual sprite images are overlapping. This is the ideal technique for detecting collisions because it is exact, and it enables objects of any shape to move by each other without error. Figure 9.5 shows collision detection using the sprite image data.

FIGURE 9.5
Collision detection using image data involves checking the specific pixels of the images for two objects to see if they overlap.

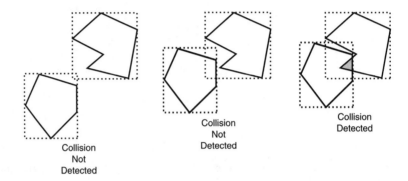

Collision
Not
Detected

Collision
Not
Detected

Collision
Detected

Unfortunately, the technique shown in Figure 9.5 requires far more processing overhead than rectangle collision detection and is often a major bottleneck in game performance. Furthermore, developing the code to carry out *image data collision detection* can get messy. Considering these facts, it's safe to say that you won't be worrying about image data collision detection in this book. It might be an avenue worth considering on your own at some point if you are willing to dig into the programming complexities involved in pulling it off.

Applying Sprite Animation to Games

Now that you have a basic understanding of the fundamental types of animation, you're probably wondering which is best for games. I've already alluded to the fact that cast-based animation is more efficient and often gives you more control over game graphics, but the truth is that most games use a combination of the two animation techniques. Each technique offers its own unique benefits, so combining the techniques gives you capabilities that would be hard to get by using one of them alone.

A good example of how games often require the use of more than one animation technique is the animation of a person walking. You obviously need to be able to alter the position of the person so that he appears to be moving across a landscape. This requires cast-based animation because you need to move the person independently of the background on which he appears. However, if we let it go at that, the person would appear to just be sliding across the screen because he isn't making any movements that simulate walking. To effectively simulate walking, the person needs to move his arms and legs as a real person does when walking. This requires frame-based animation because you need to show a series of frames of the leg and arm movements. The end result is an object that can both move and change its appearance, which is where the two animation techniques come together.

Sprites are incredibly important in virtually all two-dimensional games because they provide a simple, yet effective means of conveying movement while also enabling objects to interact with one another. By modeling the objects in a game as sprites, you can create some surprisingly interesting games in which the objects interact with each other in different ways. The simplest example of sprites used in a game is Pong, which involves a total of three sprites: the ball and the two paddles (vertical bars) along each side of the screen. All these objects must be modeled as sprites because they all move and interact with each other. The ball flies around on its own and bounces off the paddles, which are controlled by each of the two players.

As games get more complex, the role of sprites changes slightly, but their importance only increases. For example, a tank battle game would obviously use sprites to model the tanks and bullets that they shoot at each other. However, you could also use sprites to represent stationary objects, such as walls and buildings. Even though the stationary objects don't move, they benefit from being modeled as sprites because you can detect a collision between them and a tank and limit the tank's movement accordingly. Similarly, if a bullet strikes a building, you would want to destroy it or make it ricochet off the building at an angle; modeling the building as a sprite allows you to detect the bullet collision and respond accordingly.

It's important to point out that sprites are closely linked with bitmap images. Although it's certainly possible to create a sprite that is drawn out of graphics primitives, sprites are typically based on bitmap images. So, in the example of the tank game, each type of sprite corresponds to a bitmap image that is used to draw the sprite on the screen. The sprite's job is to keep track of the position, velocity, Z-order (depth), and visibility of a tank, whereas the bitmap keeps track of what the tank actually looks like. From a programming perspective, the `Bitmap` class is responsible for the appearance of a tank, whereas the `Sprite` class is responsible for how the tank moves and behaves with other objects.

Speaking of the `Sprite` class, there is no such existing class for us to borrow and use. Sprites represent a unique enough programming challenge that few standard programming libraries, such as Win32, support them directly. For this reason, you'll have to create your own `Sprite` class. The remainder of this chapter focuses on the design, development, and testing of this class.

Designing an All-Purpose Sprite

As you know by now, the primary purpose of a sprite is to model a graphical object in a game that is capable of moving over time. It takes several pieces of information to manage such an object. The following list reveals the specific properties of a sprite that must be accounted for in the `Sprite` class:

- ▶ Position
- ▶ Velocity
- ▶ Z-order
- ▶ Bounding rectangle
- ▶ Bounds action
- ▶ Hidden/visible

The most important property of a sprite is its position on the game screen, followed by its velocity. The idea is that the velocity of a sprite will be used in each cycle of the game to change the sprite's position. So, if a sprite has an X velocity of 1 and a Y velocity of -2, it will move 1 pixel to the right and 2 pixels down the game screen in every game cycle. Obviously, setting higher values for the velocity of a sprite makes it move faster.

Although it's logical to think of a sprite's position in terms of a single coordinate, typically the upper-left corner of the sprite, it's actually more useful from a programming perspective to keep track of a rectangular position for the sprite. In other words, the position of a sprite is a rectangle that basically outlines the sprite as it appears on the game screen. This allows you to factor in the width and height of a sprite when you work with its position.

In addition to position and velocity, it is also helpful to assign a Z-order to every sprite in a game. If you recall, Z-order is the depth of a sprite with respect to the screen. If two sprites are sharing the same space on the screen, the sprite with the higher Z-order will appear to be on top of the other sprite. The neat thing about Z-order is that it isn't as difficult to develop as you might think. When you think about it, sprites are naturally drawn on top of each other if you draw them in the proper order. So, establishing the Z-order for a system of sprites is all about ordering the drawing of the sprites so that sprites with a higher Z-order are drawn last. You don't actually learn how to write code to handle Z-order until Chapter 10, "Managing a World of Sprites," but you're going to go ahead and build Z-order into the Sprite class in this chapter so that it will be ready.

A less obvious sprite property that is very useful is a *bounding rectangle*, which is a rectangle that determines the area in which a sprite can travel. Generally speaking, the bounding rectangle would be assumed to be the entire game screen, but there are situations in which you might want to limit the movement of a sprite to a smaller area. For example, maybe you've created a bee sprite that you want to see buzzing around a flower. You could easily accomplish this by setting the bounding rectangle for the bee to be a rectangle that encompasses the flower. Taking the bounding rectangle concept a step further, you can also establish *bounds action*, which determines how a sprite acts when it encounters a boundary. More specifically, in a billiards game, you would probably want the balls to bounce when they hit the pool table boundary. On the other hand, in an Asteroids type game, you would probably want the asteroids to wrap around the edges of the game screen boundary. There are four primary bounds actions worth considering for any given sprite: Stop, Wrap, Bounce, and Die. You'll learn about these bounds actions in more detail in a moment, but for now, just understand that they determine what happens to a sprite when it encounters a boundary such as the edge of the game screen.

The last sprite property worth considering in the design of a sprite class is the sprite's visibility. Although you could certainly delete a sprite from memory in order to hide it from view, there are situations in which it is better to simply hide a sprite, rather than delete it. As an example, you might want to create a game along the lines of the traditional carnival Whack-A-Mole game in which plastic moles pop up out of holes, and you smash them with a mallet. In this type of game, you would only need to hide the mole sprites after they are hit (clicked with the mouse), as opposed to deleting them from memory and re-creating them each time. For this reason, it is helpful to have a property that determines whether a sprite is hidden.

Although you've learned about several different sprite properties, my goal isn't to explore every property a sprite might ever need; it's just a starting point. In fact, you'll be adding to the Sprite class over the course of the book, so you can think of this as version 1.0 of your sprite design. In fact, you will hopefully add to the Sprite class and make your own enhancements after you finish the book.

Creating the Sprite **Class**

The Sprite class is designed to model a single sprite that uses the familiar Bitmap class to represent its appearance. Listing 9.1 contains the code for the Sprite class definition, which shows the overall design of the Sprite class, including its member variables and methods.

LISTING 9.1   The Sprite Class Definition Shows How the Design of a Game Sprite Is Realized in Code

```
class Sprite
{
protected:
  // Member Variables
  Bitmap*      m_pBitmap;
  RECT         m_rcPosition;
  POINT        m_ptVelocity;
  int          m_iZOrder;
  RECT         m_rcBounds;
  BOUNDSACTION m_baBoundsAction;
  BOOL         m_bHidden;

public:
  // Constructor(s)/Destructor
  Sprite(Bitmap* pBitmap);
  Sprite(Bitmap* pBitmap, RECT& rcBounds,
    BOUNDSACTION baBoundsAction = BA_STOP);
  Sprite(Bitmap* pBitmap, POINT ptPosition, POINT ptVelocity, int iZOrder,
    RECT& rcBounds, BOUNDSACTION baBoundsAction = BA_STOP);
  virtual ~Sprite();

  // General Methods
  virtual void  Update();
  void          Draw(HDC hDC);
  BOOL          IsPointInside(int x, int y);

  // Accessor Methods
  RECT&   GetPosition()                 { return m_rcPosition; };
  void    SetPosition(int x, int y);
  void    SetPosition(POINT ptPosition);
  void    SetPosition(RECT& rcPosition)
    { CopyRect(&m_rcPosition, &rcPosition); };
  void    OffsetPosition(int x, int y);
  POINT   GetVelocity()                 { return m_ptVelocity; };
```

This method is handy for determining if a sprite has been clicked by the mouse, which is known as hit-testing.

```
void     SetVelocity(int x, int y);
void     SetVelocity(POINT ptVelocity);
BOOL     GetZOrder()              { return m_iZOrder; };
void     SetZOrder(int iZOrder)   { m_iZOrder = iZOrder; };
void     SetBounds(RECT& rcBounds) { CopyRect(&m_rcBounds, &rcBounds); };
void     SetBoundsAction(BOUNDSACTION ba) { m_baBoundsAction = ba; };
BOOL     IsHidden()               { return m_bHidden; };
void     SetHidden(BOOL bHidden)  { m_bHidden = bHidden; };
int      GetWidth()               { return m_pBitmap->GetWidth(); };
int      GetHeight()              { return m_pBitmap->GetHeight(); };
};
```

A hidden sprite isn't drawn on the game screen and doesn't collide with other sprites.

You might notice that the member variables for the Sprite class correspond one to one with the sprite properties you learned about in the previous section. The only real surprise in these variables is the use of the BOUNDSACTION data type, which is a custom data type that you'll learn about in a moment. This data type is used to describe the bounds action for the sprite.

The Sprite class offers several constructors that require differing amounts of information in order to create a sprite, as well as a destructor that you can use to clean up after the sprite. Three general methods in the Sprite class are extremely important when it comes to using the Sprite class. The first of these is Update(), which updates the sprite by applying its velocity to its position and carrying out any appropriate reactions to the sprite movement. Next, the Draw() method is responsible for drawing the sprite at its current position using the bitmap specified in one of the Sprite() constructors. Finally, the IsPointInside() method is used to see if a point is located within the sprite's position rectangle. This method basically performs a *hit test*, which is useful if you want to determine if the sprite has been clicked with the mouse.

The remaining methods in the Sprite class are accessor methods that get and set various properties of the sprite. Some of these methods come in multiple versions to make it more convenient to interact with sprites. For example, the SetPosition() methods allow you to set the position of a sprite using individual X and Y values, a point, or a rectangle. You might notice that most of the accessor methods include their code directly in the class definition. The accessor methods for which code isn't directly included next to the method definition are defined as *inline methods*, and their code appears in the Sprite.h header file below the Sprite class definition.

Earlier, I mentioned that a custom data type called BOUNDSACTION was used as the data type for the m_baBoundsAction member variable. This custom data type is defined in the Sprite.h header file as the following:

```
typedef WORD        BOUNDSACTION;
const BOUNDSACTION  BA_STOP   = 0,
                    BA_WRAP   = 1,
                    BA_BOUNCE = 2,
                    BA_DIE    = 3;
```

If you recall, the bounds actions described in the BOUNDSACTION data type correspond directly to those that were mentioned in the previous section when I first explained bounds actions and how they work. The idea here is that you use one of these constants to tell a sprite how it is to react when it runs into a boundary. If you were creating an Asteroids game, you'd want to use the BA_WRAP constant for the asteroids. On the other hand, games such as Pong or Breakout would rely on the BA_BOUNCE constant to enable the ball to bounce off the edges of the game screen. Regardless of which bounds action you choose for a sprite, it is entirely dependent on the bounding rectangle you set for the sprite. This rectangle can be as large as the game screen or as small as the sprite itself, although it wouldn't make much sense to bound a sprite with a rectangle the same size as the sprite.

Creating and Destroying the Sprite

You're probably ready to learn some more about how the Sprite class is actually put together. Listing 9.2 contains the code for the three Sprite() constructors, as well as the Sprite() destructor.

LISTING 9.2   The Sprite::Sprite() Constructors and Destructor Are Used to Create and Clean up After Sprites

```
Sprite::Sprite(Bitmap* pBitmap)
{
  // Initialize the member variables
  m_pBitmap = pBitmap;
  SetRect(&m_rcPosition, 0, 0, pBitmap->GetWidth(), pBitmap->GetHeight());
  m_ptVelocity.x = m_ptVelocity.y = 0;
  m_iZOrder = 0;
  SetRect(&m_rcBounds, 0, 0, 640, 480);
  m_baBoundsAction = BA_STOP;
  m_bHidden = FALSE;
}

Sprite::Sprite(Bitmap* pBitmap, RECT& rcBounds, BOUNDSACTION baBoundsAction)
{
  // Calculate a random position
```

The default bounding rectangle for a sprite is 640x480, which corresponds to the default game screen size.

```
  int iXPos = rand() % (rcBounds.right - rcBounds.left);
  int iYPos = rand() % (rcBounds.bottom - rcBounds.top);

  // Initialize the member variables
  m_pBitmap = pBitmap;
  SetRect(&m_rcPosition, iXPos, iYPos, iXPos + pBitmap->GetWidth(),
    iYPos + pBitmap->GetHeight());
  m_ptVelocity.x = m_ptVelocity.y = 0;
  m_iZOrder = 0;
  CopyRect(&m_rcBounds, &rcBounds);
  m_baBoundsAction = baBoundsAction;
  m_bHidden = FALSE;
}

Sprite::Sprite(Bitmap* pBitmap, POINT ptPosition, POINT ptVelocity, int iZOrder,
    RECT& rcBounds, BOUNDSACTION baBoundsAction)
{
  // Initialize the member variables
  m_pBitmap = pBitmap;
  SetRect(&m_rcPosition, ptPosition.x, ptPosition.y,
    ptPosition.x + pBitmap->GetWidth(), ptPosition.y + pBitmap->GetHeight());
  m_ptVelocity = ptVelocity;
  m_iZOrder = iZOrder;
  CopyRect(&m_rcBounds, &rcBounds);
  m_baBoundsAction = baBoundsAction;
  m_bHidden = FALSE;
}

Sprite::~Sprite()
{
}
```

With no position specified, the sprite is positioned randomly within its bounding rectangle.

The first Sprite() constructor accepts a single argument, a pointer to a Bitmap object, and uses default values for the remainder of the sprite properties. Although this constructor can work if you're in a hurry to create a sprite, you'll probably want to use a more detailed constructor to have more control over the sprite. The second Sprite() constructor adds a bounding rectangle and bounds action to the Bitmap pointer and uses them to help further define the sprite. The interesting thing about this constructor is that it randomly positions the sprite within the bounding rectangle, which is a handy little feature. The third constructor is the most useful because it gives you the most control over creating a new sprite. The Sprite() destructor doesn't do anything, but it's there to provide a means of adding cleanup code later, should you need it.

Updating the Sprite

There are only two methods in the Sprite class that you haven't seen the code for yet: Update() and Draw(). It turns out that these are the two most important methods in the class. Listing 9.3 contains the code for the Update() method, which is responsible for updating the sprite.

LISTING 9.3   The Sprite::Update() Method Updates a Sprite by Changing Its Position Based on Its Velocity and Taking Action in Response to the Movement

```
void Sprite::Update()
{
  // Update the position
  POINT ptNewPosition, ptSpriteSize, ptBoundsSize;
  ptNewPosition.x = m_rcPosition.left + m_ptVelocity.x;
  ptNewPosition.y = m_rcPosition.top + m_ptVelocity.y;
  ptSpriteSize.x = m_rcPosition.right - m_rcPosition.left;
  ptSpriteSize.y = m_rcPosition.bottom - m_rcPosition.top;
  ptBoundsSize.x = m_rcBounds.right - m_rcBounds.left;
  ptBoundsSize.y = m_rcBounds.bottom - m_rcBounds.top;

  // Check the bounds
  // Wrap?
  if (m_baBoundsAction == BA_WRAP)
  {
    if ((ptNewPosition.x + ptSpriteSize.x) < m_rcBounds.left)
      ptNewPosition.x = m_rcBounds.right;
    else if (ptNewPosition.x > m_rcBounds.right)
      ptNewPosition.x = m_rcBounds.left - ptSpriteSize.x;
    if ((ptNewPosition.y + ptSpriteSize.y) < m_rcBounds.top)
      ptNewPosition.y = m_rcBounds.bottom;
    else if (ptNewPosition.y > m_rcBounds.bottom)
      ptNewPosition.y = m_rcBounds.top - ptSpriteSize.y;
  }
  // Bounce?
  else if (m_baBoundsAction == BA_BOUNCE)
  {
    BOOL bBounce = FALSE;
    POINT ptNewVelocity = m_ptVelocity;
    if (ptNewPosition.x < m_rcBounds.left)
    {
      bBounce = TRUE;
      ptNewPosition.x = m_rcBounds.left;
      ptNewVelocity.x = -ptNewVelocity.x;
    }
    else if ((ptNewPosition.x + ptSpriteSize.x) > m_rcBounds.right)
    {
      bBounce = TRUE;
      ptNewPosition.x = m_rcBounds.right - ptSpriteSize.x;
      ptNewVelocity.x = -ptNewVelocity.x;
    }
    if (ptNewPosition.y < m_rcBounds.top)
    {
```

Alter the position of the sprite so that it wraps around the screen.

Alter the velocity of the sprite so that it reverses direction (bounces).

```
        bBounce = TRUE;
        ptNewPosition.y = m_rcBounds.top;
        ptNewVelocity.y = -ptNewVelocity.y;
      }
      else if ((ptNewPosition.y + ptSpriteSize.y) > m_rcBounds.bottom)
      {
        bBounce = TRUE;
        ptNewPosition.y = m_rcBounds.bottom - ptSpriteSize.y;
        ptNewVelocity.y = -ptNewVelocity.y;
      }
      if (bBounce)
        SetVelocity(ptNewVelocity);
    }
    // Stop (default)
    else
    {
      if (ptNewPosition.x  < m_rcBounds.left ||
        ptNewPosition.x > (m_rcBounds.right - ptSpriteSize.x))
      {
        ptNewPosition.x = max(m_rcBounds.left, min(ptNewPosition.x,
          m_rcBounds.right - ptSpriteSize.x));
        SetVelocity(0, 0);
      }
      if (ptNewPosition.y  < m_rcBounds.top ||
        ptNewPosition.y > (m_rcBounds.bottom - ptSpriteSize.y))
      {
        ptNewPosition.y = max(m_rcBounds.top, min(ptNewPosition.y,
          m_rcBounds.bottom - ptSpriteSize.y));
        SetVelocity(0, 0);
      }
    }
  SetPosition(ptNewPosition);
}
```

Alter the velocity to stop the sprite.

This method is probably considerably longer than you expected it to be, but on closer inspection, you'll realize that it is doing several important things. The primary purpose of the Update() method is to use the velocity of the sprite to alter its position, which has the effect of moving the sprite. However, simply changing the position of the sprite isn't good enough because you have to take into consideration what happens if the sprite runs into a boundary. If you recall, every sprite has a bounding rectangle that determines the area in which the sprite can move. A sprite also has a bounds action that determines what happens to the sprite when it runs into a boundary. The Update() method has to check for a boundary and then make the appropriate response based on the sprite's bounds action.

The Update() method begins by making some temporary calculations involving the new position, the size of the sprite, and the size of the boundary. The rest of the method handles each kind of bounds action, beginning with BA_WRAP. To handle the BA_WRAP bounds action, the sprite is simply moved to the opposite side of the bounding rectangle, which gives the effect of the sprite wrapping off one side and onto the other. The BA_BOUNCE action has to look a little closer at which boundary the sprite is crossing because it must correctly reverse the sprite's velocity in order to yield a bouncing effect. The final bounds action handled in the Update() method is BA_STOP, which is actually unnamed in this case because it is the default bounds action. This bounds action ensures that the sprite doesn't cross over the boundary, while setting the sprite's velocity to zero.

Throughout all the bounds action handling code, the new sprite position is calculated and stored in a temporary variable of type POINT, ptNewPosition. At the end of the Update() method, this variable is used to actually set the new position of the sprite.

Construction Cue

> If you're the overly observant type, you might recall that earlier in the chapter, the Sprite class was designed to support an additional bounds action, BA_DIE, which causes the sprite to be destroyed when it encounters a boundary. Although this bounds action is technically available for the Sprite class to use, it isn't possible to support the action without some additional code in the game engine to manage a system of sprites. You don't develop a sprite manager for the game engine until the next chapter, so you won't address the BA_DIE bounds action until then. Fortunately, there is plenty of fun to be had with the three other bounds actions, as you'll soon see.

Drawing the Sprite

The remaining method in the Sprite class is the Draw() method, which is shown in Listing 9.4.

LISTING 9.4   The Sprite::Draw() Method Draws a Sprite by Using the Sprite's Bitmap and Current Position

```
void Sprite::Draw(HDC hDC)
{
  // Draw the sprite if it isn't hidden
  if (m_pBitmap != NULL && !m_bHidden)
    m_pBitmap->Draw(hDC, m_rcPosition.left, m_rcPosition.top, TRUE);
}
```

If the Update() method surprised you by having too much code, hopefully the Draw() method surprises you by having so little. Because the Bitmap class includes its own Draw() method, there isn't much for the Sprite::Draw() method to do. It first checks to make sure that the Bitmap pointer is okay, along with making sure that the sprite isn't hidden. If all is well, the Draw() method calls on the Bitmap class with the `m_rcPosition` member variable used to convey the sprite's position for drawing the bitmap. The last argument to the `Bitmap::Draw()` method is a Boolean that determines whether the sprite's bitmap should be drawn with transparency, which in this case is `TRUE`. So, all sprites are assumed to use transparency.

Building the Planets Example Program

Although the `Sprite` class is certainly an engineering marvel, only so much gratification can be gained from staring at its code. For this reason, it's important to put together a demonstration program to put the `Sprite` class through its paces. In keeping with the space theme established earlier in the book with the UFO examples, a planetary sprite example might be good here. The Planets example uses a galaxy backdrop and several planet sprites to get your feet wet with sprite animation.

The idea behind the Planets program is to create several planet sprites and let them float around the game screen. Because it's not terribly important to factor in astronomy for this example, I opted to use the planets to demonstrate the three bounds actions supported by the `Sprite` class: Wrap, Bounce, and Stop. So, the program creates three planets with each of these bounds actions and then turns them loose on the game screen to see how they react. To make things a little more interesting, you can use the mouse to grab and drag any of the planets around the screen. Let's get started with the code because you're no doubt itching to see this program in action.

Writing the Program Code

As you know by now, every Windows program has a header file that includes other important header files, as well as declares global variables used by the program. Listing 9.5 contains the code for the Planets.h header file.

LISTING 9.5 The Planets.h Header File Imports Several Header Files and Declares Global Variables Required for the Planet Sprites

```
#pragma once

//- - - - - - - - - - - - - - - - - - - - - - - - - - - - - - - -.
// Include Files
//- - - - - - - - - - - - - - - - - - - - - - - - - - - - - - - -.
#include <windows.h>
#include "Resource.h"
#include "GameEngine.h"
```

continues

LISTING 9.5   Continued

```
#include "Bitmap.h"
#include "Sprite.h"

//—————————————————————————————————·
// Global Variables
//—————————————————————————————————·
HINSTANCE      g_hInstance;
GameEngine*    g_pGame;
Bitmap*        g_pGalaxyBitmap;
Bitmap*        g_pPlanetBitmap[3];
Sprite*        g_pPlanetSprite[3];
BOOL           g_bDragging;
int            g_iDragPlanet;
```

The three planets are represented by three sprites that make use of three bitmap images.

This variable keeps track of which planet (if any) is being dragged.

A quick look at this code reveals four bitmaps—one for the galaxy background and three more for the planets. Figure 9.6 shows one of the planet bitmap images, which uses the standard transparency color around the planet to indicate where the background should appear.

FIGURE 9.6
Each of the planet bitmap images is filled with a transparent color around the planet so that the background will show through.

Similar to their bitmaps, the planet sprites are stored in an array to make them easier to access. The last two member variables are used to allow you to drag a planet around with the mouse. The g_bDragging variable determines whether a planet is currently being dragged. If a planet is indeed being dragged, the g_iDragPlanet variable keeps track of which planet it is; this variable is actually an index into the g_pPlanetSprite array.

With the global variables for the Planets program in mind, you can now press on and examine the specific game functions for the program. The GameInitialize() function is virtually identical to the version of it that you've seen in other examples. The only point to make is that it sets the frame rate to 30 frames per second, which is relatively standard for the programs that use sprite animation throughout the book.

The GameStart() and GameEnd()functions are where the interesting things start taking place in the Planets program, as shown in Listing 9.6.

LISTING 9.6 The GameStart() Function Creates and Loads the Bitmaps and Sprites, Whereas the GameEnd() Function Cleans Them Up

```
void GameStart(HWND hWindow)
{
  // Seed the random number generator
  srand(GetTickCount());

  // Create and load the bitmaps
  HDC hDC = GetDC(hWindow);
  g_pGalaxyBitmap = new Bitmap(hDC, IDB_GALAXY, g_hInstance);
  g_pPlanetBitmap[0] = new Bitmap(hDC, IDB_PLANET1, g_hInstance);
  g_pPlanetBitmap[1] = new Bitmap(hDC, IDB_PLANET2, g_hInstance);
  g_pPlanetBitmap[2] = new Bitmap(hDC, IDB_PLANET3, g_hInstance);

  // Create the planet sprites
  RECT rcBounds = { 0, 0, 600, 400 };
  g_pPlanetSprite[0] = new Sprite(g_pPlanetBitmap[0], rcBounds);
  g_pPlanetSprite[1] = new Sprite(g_pPlanetBitmap[1], rcBounds, BA_WRAP);
  g_pPlanetSprite[2] = new Sprite(g_pPlanetBitmap[2], rcBounds, BA_BOUNCE);
  g_pPlanetSprite[0]->SetPosition(0, 0);
  g_pPlanetSprite[0]->SetVelocity(1, 1);
  g_pPlanetSprite[1]->SetVelocity(2, -1);
  g_pPlanetSprite[2]->SetVelocity(3, -2);

  // Set the initial drag info
  g_bDragging = FALSE;
  g_iDragPlanet = -1;
}

void GameEnd()
{
  // Cleanup the bitmaps
  delete g_pGalaxyBitmap;
  for (int i = 0; i < 3; i++)
    delete g_pPlanetBitmap[i];

  // Cleanup the sprites
  for (int i = 0; i < 3; i++)
    delete g_pPlanetSprite[i];

  // Cleanup the game engine
  delete g_pGame;
}
```

The first planet sprite stops when it encounters a boundary, whereas the second planet wraps, and the third planet bounces.

Similar to bitmap objects, sprite objects must be cleaned up. Remove the int declaration here if you get a multiple initialization error when compiling the example.

The GameStart() function does several important things, beginning with the loading of the galaxy and planet bitmaps. A bounding rectangle for the game screen is then created, which is important because it serves as the bounding rectangle for all the planet sprites. The three planet sprites are then created and stored in the g_pPlanetSprite array, and their velocities are set to differing values. The function ends by initializing the global variables that keep track of a sprite being dragged with the mouse. The GameEnd() function simply cleans up the bitmaps and sprites, as well as the game engine itself.

Construction
Cue

If you happen to get a "multiple initialization" compiler error while compiling the Planets program, you can easily fix it by removing the int variable declaration in the second group of for loops in the GameEnd() function where the tiles are randomly initialized. This error stems from the fact that some compilers don't fully support the standard C++ approach of declaring loop initializer variables local to the loop. So, the int variable i is mistakenly interpreted as being declared twice. Just remove the second int declaration, and everything will work fine.

The GamePaint() function is next on the agenda, and you might be surprised by its simplicity (see Listing 9.7).

LISTING 9.7   The GamePaint() Function Draws the Galaxy Background and the Planet Sprites

```
void GamePaint(HDC hDC)
{
  // Draw the background galaxy
  g_pGalaxyBitmap->Draw(hDC, 0, 0);

  // Draw the planet sprites
  for (int i = 0; i < 3; i++)
    g_pPlanetSprite[i]->Draw(hDC);
}
```

The GamePaint() function simply draws the galaxy bitmap followed by the three planet sprites. The Draw() method in the Sprite class makes drawing the sprites painfully easy.

Of course, the GamePaint() method alone wouldn't be too helpful in animating the planet sprites if the game screen wasn't told to repaint itself periodically. This is accomplished in the GameCycle() function (see Listing 9.8), which also updates the sprites.

LISTING 9.8 The `GameCycle()` Function Updates the Planet Sprites and then Repaints the Game Screen

```
void GameCycle()
{
  // Update the planet sprites
  for (int i = 0; i < 3; i++)
    g_pPlanetSprite[i]->Update();

  // Force a repaint to redraw the planets
  InvalidateRect(g_pGame->GetWindow(), NULL, FALSE);
}
```

This function begins by updating the planet sprites, which simply involves calling the `Update()` method on each sprite. After updating the sprites, the game screen is invalidated so that it gets repainted to show the new sprite positions. If you didn't invalidate the game screen, the `GamePaint()` method wouldn't get called, and you wouldn't see any changes on the screen, even though the sprites are being moved behind the scenes. In other words, in addition to changing the position of sprites, you must also make sure they get repainted so that the changes are visualized.

I mentioned earlier in the chapter that the Planets program allows you to click a planet sprite with the mouse and drag it around. This functionality is established in the `MouseButtonDown()`, `MouseButtonUp()`, and `MouseMove()` functions, which are shown in Listing 9.9.

LISTING 9.9 The `MouseButtonDown()`, `MouseButtonUp()`, and `MouseMove()` Functions Use the Left Mouse Button to Allow You to Click and Drag a Planet Sprite Around on the Game Screen

```
void MouseButtonDown(int x, int y, BOOL bLeft)
{
  // See if a planet was clicked with the left mouse button
  if (bLeft && !g_bDragging)
  {
    for (int i = 0; i < 3; i++)
      if (g_pPlanetSprite[i]->IsPointInside(x, y))
      {
        // Capture the mouse
        SetCapture(g_pGame->GetWindow());

        // Set the drag state and the drag planet
        g_bDragging = TRUE;
        g_iDragPlanet = i;

        // Simulate a mouse move to get started
```

continues

LISTING 9.9   Continued

By faking a mouse
move with the drag
flag set, you force
the planet to be
moved to the cur-
rent mouse posi-
tion.

```
        MouseMove(x, y);

        // Don't check for more planets
        break;
      }
   }
}

void MouseButtonUp(int x, int y, BOOL bLeft)
{
  // Release the mouse
  ReleaseCapture();

  // Stop dragging
  g_bDragging = FALSE;
}

void MouseMove(int x, int y)
{
  if (g_bDragging)
  {
    // Move the sprite to the mouse cursor position
    g_pPlanetSprite[g_iDragPlanet]->SetPosition(
      x - (g_pPlanetBitmap[g_iDragPlanet]->GetWidth() / 2),
      y - (g_pPlanetBitmap[g_iDragPlanet]->GetHeight() / 2));

    // Force a repaint to redraw the planets
    InvalidateRect(g_pGame->GetWindow(), NULL, FALSE);
  }
}
```

The planet is
centered on the
current mouse
position.

The MouseButtonDown() function starts the drag process by first checking to see if the left mouse button is being pressed, while making sure that a drag isn't some-how already in progress. The next check is to see if the mouse click actually occurred within a sprite. This involves looping through the sprites and seeing if the mouse coordinates lie within a sprite. If so, the mouse is captured so that its input is routed to the Planets program even if it strays outside the game window. The drag state and planet being dragged are then stored away because the other mouse functions need to know about them. The MouseMove() function is then called to simulate a mouse move so that the sprite is centered on the mouse cursor position. Finally, the sprite loop is broken out of because you don't want to check for more planets when one has been clicked with the mouse.

The MouseButtonUp() function ends a sprite drag by releasing the mouse capture and then clearing the g_bDragging global variable. This is sufficient to stop the sprite drag, while also allowing the user to initiate another drag by clicking a sprite and starting the process over.

The last of the mouse functions is MouseMove(), which moves a planet sprite so that it follows the location of the mouse cursor. The g_bDragging global variable is first checked to make sure that a drag is taking place. If so, the position of the appropriate planet sprite is set to correspond to the position of the mouse cursor. The program window is then invalidated so that the game screen is repainted, which is necessary so that the sprite is redrawn in the new position.

Construction Cue

As with most of the examples in the book, the Planets program relies on the standard msimg32.lib and winmm.lib libraries. These libraries are included with most Windows compilers, but they aren't automatically linked into programs when you create a new project. If you are using your own project or make files, as opposed to using the ones provided on the CD-ROM, make sure that you change the link settings so that these library files are properly linked into the final executable. Refer to the documentation for your specific compiler for how this is done.

Testing the Finished Product

Although it isn't a game, the Planets example is a quite interesting sample program in the sense that it demonstrates how powerful and straightforward sprite animation can be. After the Sprite class was created, it only took a few lines of code to create a few sprites and get them moving around the game screen. Figure 9.7 shows the planet sprites flying around on the galaxy background in the Planets example.

FIGURE 9.7
The planet sprites in the Planets program move around, thanks to the handy Sprite class that you created in this chapter.

If you watch the sprites carefully, you'll notice that each of them responds differently when encountering the edge of the game screen, which happens to serve as their bounding rectangle. One of the planets will wrap around to the other side of the screen, another will bounce off the side of the screen like a game of Pong, whereas the last planet will stop at the edge of the screen. The really neat thing about the program is that you can click and drag any of the planets on the screen, including the ones that are moving.

Construction Cue

> You will no doubt notice that the planets appear to flicker as they move around in the Planets example. This is a common problem associated with sprite animation, and you learn how to overcome it in the next chapter.

Granted, clicking and dragging a planet isn't exactly my idea of an exciting "game," but it does provide a good demonstration of the new Sprite class that you've now added to your game development toolkit.

Summary

This chapter introduced you to animation and how it applies to games. As you now know, animation is what makes many forms of modern entertainment work, including movies, television, and video games. Two primary types of animation are used in the development of computer games, and this chapter explored how they work and when you would want to use them. This chapter took a significantly closer look at sprite animation by guiding you through the development of a sprite class that can be used to inject sprite animation into your games. The Sprite class that you created supports standard sprite features, such as a bitmap, position, and velocity, as well as a handy bounding rectangle feature for controlling the area in which a sprite is allowed to travel. The chapter concluded by putting the Sprite class to work in an example that demonstrated how to create and use sprites.

The next chapter builds on your newly created sprite code by beefing up the game engine to support interactions between sprites. More specifically, you develop a sprite manager capable of detecting and responding to collisions between sprites. You also improve upon the paint mechanism you've been using so that your future games don't suffer from the annoying flicker that is inherent in sprite animation.

Field Trip

It's time for one of those field trips that you never get to take in school—a field trip to see a movie! Pick any traditional animated movie you want and go see it. By traditional animation, I mean a movie that isn't entirely computer generated—this eliminates Pixar movies, for example. It's not that I have anything against Pixar (quite the opposite, in fact), but traditional animation has more in common with sprite animation in games than does computer-generated animation. If you can't find a good traditional animated movie at the theater, rent one.

While you're watching the movie, pay particular attention to the movement of different objects on the screen. You will notice that there isn't as much going on as you might have first thought. Traditional animated movies tend to limit the animation to a few important characters while a lot of the background remains fixed. Granted, the background might pan and zoom, but the artwork itself doesn't usually change much. The goal of this field trip is to make the connection between traditional film animation and sprite animation in games, which are surprisingly similar. You might even learn some animation tricks that you can carry over into your game designs.

CHAPTER 10

Managing a World of Sprites

Arcade Archive

Released in 1981 by Nintendo, Donkey Kong represents a true milestone in video game history because it relies on such a unique story line. The challenge of creating Donkey Kong was given to a young Japanese artist named Shigeru Miyamoto, who had no game programming experience and was led solely by his imagination to dream up a game about a pet gorilla who kidnapped his owner's girlfriend. Donkey Kong established an entire genre of games with levels that involved climbing ladders and avoiding obstacles. The success of Donkey Kong eventually led to a lawsuit filed by Universal Studios, which claimed that Donkey Kong infringed on their copyright for the 1929 movie *King Kong*. Universal Studios lost the suit and ended up having to pay $1.8 million in penalties. Along with winning the lawsuit, Nintendo also won the hearts of gamers worldwide and collected more than enough quarters to fund its future console game endeavors.

When you think about it, the real world we live in is all about actions and reactions. If you kick a ball, the ball will respond to the impact by traveling a certain distance, where it might collide with another object or eventually come to rest, thanks to air and ground friction. The real world is therefore a system of objects that physically interact with one another. You can think of a system of sprites as a similar system of objects capable of interacting with each other in a variety of ways. The primary manner in which sprites can interact is through collisions, which involve objects running into each other. This chapter focuses on the design and development of a sprite manager that allows you to establish actions and reactions within a system of sprites.

In this chapter, you'll learn

- ▶ Why sprite management is important to games
- ▶ How to design a sprite manager
- ▶ How to modify the game engine to support the management of sprites
- ▶ How to eliminate animation flicker using a technique known as double-buffering
- ▶ How to build an example that takes advantage of new sprite features, such as collision detection

Assessing the Need for Sprite Management

In the previous chapter, you developed a sprite class that modeled the basic physical properties of a graphical object that can move. You then created an example called Planets that involved several planet sprites floating around in the same space. Although the sprites in the Planets program were visually sharing the same space, no actual connection existed between them. Unlike in the real world, the planet sprites were unable to collide with each other and respond accordingly. This limitation stems from the fact that the Sprite class alone can't account for the relationship between sprites. You need a sprite manager capable of overseeing a system of sprites and managing their interactions.

The idea behind a sprite manager is to group all the sprites in a system together so that they can be collectively updated and drawn. Additionally, a sprite manager must be capable of comparing the positions of sprites to each other and determining if any collisions have taken place. If so, the sprite manager must then somehow notify the program that the collision has occurred; in which case, the program can respond accordingly. This approach to sprite collision management is incredibly important in games, which makes the sprite manager an absolute necessity when building games that use sprite animation.

Another benefit of a sprite manager is that it provides a means of supporting an additional bounds action, Die. The Die bounds action causes a sprite to be destroyed if it encounters a boundary. This might be useful in a shoot-em-up game in which the bullet sprites need to be killed upon hitting the edge of the game screen. It's difficult to directly support the Die bounds action in the Sprite class because the premise of the action is killing the sprite; it's tough to convince a sprite to kill itself. This task is better left to an outside party whose job is to oversee all the sprites in a game—a sprite manager.

A moment ago, I mentioned that a sprite manager makes it possible to update and draw a system of sprites collectively. This is a significant feature as you move toward creating games that rely on several sprites. For example, it could quickly become a headache to try to update, draw, and generally keep tabs on dozens of sprites. The sprite manager dramatically simplifies this situation by allowing you to simply update and draw all the sprites being managed at once, regardless of how many there are.

Designing a Sprite Manager

You should now have a basic understanding of what is required of a sprite manager, so you can move on to the specific design for it. You might think that the sprite manager would be created as a class similar to the way that you created the `Sprite` class in the previous chapter. However, the sprite manager is closely linked with the game engine, which makes it more beneficial to integrate the sprite manager directly with the game engine. So, the sprite manager will actually be created as a set of methods within the `GameEngine` class.

Even though the sprite manager is created as a modification on the game engine, it does require some changes outside of the `GameEngine` class. More specifically, some changes are required in the `Sprite` class in order for sprites to work smoothly with the sprite manager. The first of these changes involves supporting *sprite actions*, which are used to inform the sprite manager that it should take action with regard to a particular sprite. Sprite actions are sort of like bounds actions, except that they are somewhat more flexible. As an example, the first sprite action supported is Kill, which is used to inform the sprite manager that a sprite is to be destroyed. The Kill sprite action is similar to the Die bounds action, except that Kill can be issued for a variety of different reasons. Sprite actions are typically invoked when a collision occurs, which enables a missile to destroy a tank upon impact, for example.

Beyond sprite actions, another major requirement of the `Sprite` class and the sprite manager code is that of collision detection. You learned in the previous chapter that collision detection involves checking to see if two sprites have collided with each other. You also found out that a technique known as *shrunken rectangle collision detection* involves using a rectangle slightly smaller than the sprite as the basis for detecting collisions. Because this form of collision detection requires its own rectangle, it only makes sense to add a collision rectangle as a member of the Sprite class, along with supporting methods to calculate the rectangle and test for a collision with another sprite.

That covers the changes required of the Sprite class in order to support the enhanced sprite animation features offered by the sprite manager. The sprite manager itself is integrated directly into the game engine, where it primarily involves adding a member variable to keep track of a list of sprites. This member variable could be an array with a fixed size representing the maximum number of sprites allowed, or it could be a more advanced data structure, such as a vector that can grow dynamically to hold additional sprites.

Regardless of the specifics of how the sprite list is established, the sprite manager must provide several methods that can be used to interact with the sprites being managed. The following is a list of the major tasks the sprite manager needs to make available using the following methods:

- Add a new sprite to the sprite list

- Draw all the sprites in the sprite list

- Update all the sprites in the sprite list

- Clean up all the sprites in the sprite list

- Test to see if a point lies within a sprite in the sprite list

In addition to these tasks that must be capable of being invoked on the game engine, it is important to provide a function for a game that is called whenever a sprite collision occurs. When you think about it, handling a sprite collision is a very game-specific task, so it makes sense to let game code handle it, as opposed to including it in the game engine. So, a sprite collision notification function must be provided by any game that uses the sprite manager so that it can respond to sprite collisions. Of course, the sprite manager must make sure that this function gets called whenever a collision actually takes place.

Adding the Sprite Manager to the Game Engine

Throughout the chapter thus far, I've drawn a distinction between the Sprite class and the game engine, as if they were two different things. In reality, the Sprite class is part of the game engine even though it is a self-contained class.

So, it's safe to say that you are upgrading the game engine even when you make changes to the Sprite class. The next couple of sections reveal the code changes required in both the Sprite class and the GameEngine class to add support for a sprite manager.

Improving the Sprite **Class**

The first piece of code required in the Sprite class is the addition of a collision rectangle, which is used to determine if one sprite has collided with another. This rectangle is added as a member variable of the Sprite class named m_rcCollision, as the following code reveals:

```
RECT m_rcCollision;
```

A single accessor method is required for the collision rectangle so that the sprite manager can access the rectangle for collision detections. This method is called GetCollision(), and it looks like the following:

```
RECT& GetCollision() { return m_rcCollision; };
```

Although there are no surprises with the GetCollision() method, you might find the CalcCollisionRect()method a little more interesting. This method is used internally by the Sprite class to calculate a collision rectangle based on the position rectangle. The CalcCollisionRect()method is defined as virtual in the Sprite class so that derived classes can override it and use their own specific collision rectangle calculation:

```
virtual void CalcCollisionRect();
```

Listing 10.1 shows the code for the CalcCollisionRect() method, which calculates the collision rectangle of a sprite by subtracting one-sixth of the sprite's size off the position rectangle.

LISTING 10.1   The Sprite::CalcCollisionRect() Method Calculates a Collision Rectangle for a Sprite Based on the Sprite's Position Rectangle

```
inline void Sprite::CalcCollisionRect()
{
  int iXShrink = (m_rcPosition.left - m_rcPosition.right) / 12;
  int iYShrink = (m_rcPosition.top - m_rcPosition.bottom) / 12;
  CopyRect(&m_rcCollision, &m_rcPosition);
  InflateRect(&m_rcCollision, iXShrink, iYShrink);
}
```

This code is a little misleading because a shrink value for the X and Y dimensions of the sprite are first calculated as one-twelfth the size of the sprite. These values are then passed into the Win32 InflateRect() function, which uses each value to shrink the sprite along each dimension. The end result is that the collision rectangle is one-sixth smaller than the position rectangle because the shrink values are applied to each side of the sprite.

Speaking of collisions, the Sprite class provides a method called TestCollision() to see if the sprite has collided with another sprite:

```
BOOL TestCollision(Sprite* pTestSprite);
```

Listing 10.2 contains the code for the TestCollision() method, which simply checks to see if any part of the sprite's collision rectangles overlap.

LISTING 10.2　The Sprite::TestCollision() Method Compares the Collision Rectangles of Two Sprites to See if They Overlap

```
inline BOOL Sprite::TestCollision(Sprite* pTestSprite)
{
  RECT& rcTest = pTestSprite->GetCollision();
  return m_rcCollision.left <= rcTest.right &&
         rcTest.left <= m_rcCollision.right &&
         m_rcCollision.top <= rcTest.bottom &&
         rcTest.top <= m_rcCollision.bottom;
}
```

If a collision has indeed occurred between the two sprites, the TestCollision() method returns TRUE; otherwise, it returns FALSE.

Getting back to the collision rectangle that was added to the Sprite class, it must be initialized in the Sprite() constructors. All three of these constructors include a call to CalcCollisionRect(), which sets the collision rectangle based on the position rectangle of the sprite. No other changes are required in the constructors to support collision detection in the Sprite class.

The other big change in the Sprite class involves the addition of sprite actions, which provide a means of enabling the sprite manager to manipulate sprites in response to events such as sprite collisions. A custom data type called SPRITEAC-TION is used to represent sprite actions, as follows:

```
typedef WORD       SPRITEACTION;
const SPRITEACTION SA_NONE   = 0x0000L,
                   SA_KILL   = 0x0001L;
```

As you can see, only two sprite actions are defined for the SPRITEACTION data type, although the idea is to add new actions as necessary to expand the role of the sprite manager later. The SA_NONE sprite action indicates that nothing is to be done to any sprites. On the other hand, the SA_KILL sprite action indicates that a sprite is to be removed from the sprite list and destroyed. These sprite actions are given real meaning in the Update() method, which is now defined to return a SPRITEACTION value to indicate any actions to take with respect to the sprite.

The big change to the Update() method is that it now supports the BA_DIE bounds action, which causes a sprite to be destroyed when it encounters a boundary. This bounds action is made possible by the SA_KILL sprite action, which is returned by the Update() method in response to the BA_DIE bounds action occurring. So, the Update() method responds to the BA_DIE bounds action by returning SA_KILL, which results in the sprite being destroyed and removed from the sprite list. The remaining bounds actions return SA_NONE, which results in nothing happening to the sprite in terms of sprite actions.

Enhancing the Game Engine

The Sprite class is now whipped into shape in preparation for the new sprite manager support in the GameEngine class. Fortunately, managing a system of sprites isn't really all that difficult of a proposition. This is largely possible, thanks to a suite of data collections known as the *Standard Template Library* or *STL*. The STL is a suite of data collection classes that can be used to store any kind of data, including sprites. Rather than using an array to store a list of sprites in the game engine, it is much more convenient and flexible to use the vector collection class from the STL. The STL vector class allows you to store away and manage a list of objects of any type and then manipulate them using a set of handy methods. The good news is that you don't have to know much about the vector class or the STL in order to put it to use in the game engine.

> The Standard Template Library is built into most C++ compilers and provides an extensive set of data collection classes that you can use in your programs. The STL is significant because it keeps you from having to spend time developing your own classes to perform common tasks. In other words, it saves you from having to reinvent the wheel.

Construction Cue

The first step in using any data collection class in the STL is to properly include the header for the class, as well as its namespace. If you've never heard of namespaces, don't worry because they don't really impact the code you're writing here.

The following two lines must be placed near the top of the header file for the GameEngine class, and they take care of including the vector class header file and establishing its namespace:

```
#include <vector>
using namespace std;
```

To use an STL collection class, such as the vector class, you simply declare a variable of type vector, but you also include the data type that you want stored in the vector inside angle brackets (<>). The following code shows how to create a vector of Sprite pointers:

```
vector<Sprite*> m_vSprites;
```

This code creates a vector containing Sprite pointers and is exactly what you need in the game engine to keep track of a list of sprites. You can now use the m_vSprites vector to manage a list of sprites and interact with them as necessary. It helps to set a property on the vector variable so that it operates a little more efficiently in games. I'm referring to the amount of memory reserved for the vector, which determines how many sprite pointers can be stored in the vector before it has to allocate more memory. This doesn't mean that you're setting a limit on the number of sprites that can be stored in the vector; you're just determining how often the vector class will have to allocate memory for new sprites. Because memory allocation takes time, it's beneficial to keep it at a minimum. Given the requirements of most games, it's safe to say that reserving room for 100 sprites before requiring additional memory allocation is sufficient. This memory reservation takes place in the GameEngine::GameEngine() constructor.

The sprite manager support in the game engine prompts you to add a new game function that must be provided by games as part of their game-specific code. This function is called SpriteCollision(), and its job is to respond to sprite collisions in a game-specific manner. The following is the function prototype for the SpriteCollision() function:

```
BOOL SpriteCollision(Sprite* pSpriteHitter, Sprite* pSpriteHittee);
```

Keep in mind that the SpriteCollision() function must be provided by each game that you create. The SpriteCollision() function is called by the CheckSpriteCollision() method within the game engine, which steps through the sprite list (vector) and checks to see if any sprites have collided:

```
BOOL CheckSpriteCollision(Sprite* pTestSprite);
```

The CheckSpriteCollision() method calls the SpriteCollision() function to handle individual sprite collisions. The CheckSpriteCollision() method steps through the entire list of sprites and checks for collisions between all of them. The first thing required to step through the sprite vector is an *iterator*, which is a special object used to move forward or backward through a vector. The good thing about iterators is that they are objects that provide functions for easily looping through a vector. For example, the begin() and end() iterator methods are used to establish a loop that steps through each sprite in the sprite vector. The code for the CheckSpriteCollision() method is included in the GameEngine.cpp source code file, which is available on the accompanying CD-ROM, along with all the source code for the examples in the book.

Within the loop, a check is first performed to make sure that you aren't comparing a sprite with itself. A collision test is then performed between the two sprites by calling the TestCollision() method. If a collision is detected, the SpriteCollision() function is called so that the game can respond appropriately to the collision. The return value of the SpriteCollision() function is also returned from the CheckSpriteCollision() method. This return value plays a vital role in determining how sprites react to collisions. More specifically, returning TRUE from CheckSpriteCollision() results in a sprite being restored to its original position prior to being updated, whereas a return value of FALSE allows the sprite to continue along its path. Without this mechanism for restoring the original position of a sprite, two sprites would tend to stick together, instead of bouncing off each other, when they collide. If there is no collision, FALSE is returned so that the sprite's new position isn't altered.

The CheckSpriteCollision() method is technically a helper method that is only used within the GameEngine class. It's also necessary to add a suite of public sprite management methods to the GameEngine class that are used to interact with the sprite manager. The following are the sprite manager methods that can be called on the game engine:

```
void    AddSprite(Sprite* pSprite);
void    DrawSprites(HDC hDC);
void    UpdateSprites();
void    CleanupSprites();
Sprite* IsPointInSprite(int x, int y);
```

The AddSprite() method is used to add a sprite to the sprite list, and it must be called in order for a sprite to be taken under management by the sprite manager. Before adding a sprite, the AddSprite() method checks to make sure that the pSprite argument is not set to NULL. If the sprite pointer is okay, the sprite vector is checked to see if any sprites are already in it. If sprites are in the vector, the AddSprite() method has to find a suitable spot to add the sprite because the sprite list is ordered so that the sprites are drawn in proper Z-order. In other words, the sprites are ordered in the list according to increasing Z-order. This allows you to simply draw the sprites as they appear in the sprite list, and they will properly overlap each other naturally.

Construction Cue

You might have noticed that I'm using the terms *list* and *vector* somewhat interchangeably. This is because the list of sprites in the game engine is technically stored in a vector, but conceptually, you can just think of it as a list. Therefore, I might use one term or the other, but they both refer to the same thing.

The DrawSprites() method is responsible for drawing all the sprites in the sprite list. The method does this by obtaining an iterator for the vector and then using the iterator to step through the vector and draw each sprite. The Draw() method in the Sprite class is used to draw each sprite, which makes the process of drawing the entire list of sprites relatively simple.

Rivaling the DrawSprites() method in terms of importance is the UpdateSprites() method, which updates the position of each sprite. The critical consideration in this method is that it must be careful to retain the old position of the sprite in case it needs to restore the sprite to that position. An iterator is created that enables the method to step through the sprite vector and update each sprite individually. The sprite is updated with a call to the Update() method, which returns a sprite action.

The sprite action returned from the Sprite::Update() method is checked to see if it corresponds to the SA_KILL action, which requires the sprite manager to kill the sprite being updated. In order to successfully destroy the sprite, it is first deleted from memory and then removed from the sprite vector. If the SA_KILL sprite action wasn't used on the sprite, the CheckSpriteCollision() method is called to see if the sprite has collided with any other sprites. The return value of this method determines whether the sprite's old position is restored; TRUE means that it should be restored, whereas FALSE means that the new position should stand.

Another sprite manager method is CleanupSprites(),which is responsible for freeing sprites from memory and emptying the sprite vector. The CleanupSprites() method steps through the sprite vector and deletes each sprite in the vector. It also makes sure to remove each sprite from the vector right after it frees the sprite memory. It is important for any game to call the CleanupSprites() method so that sprites aren't left hanging around in memory.

The last method in the GameEngine class pertaining to sprite management is the IsPointInSprite() method, which is used to see if a point lies within a sprite in the sprite list. This method is useful in situations in which you want to allow the user to click and somehow control a sprite. If the point lies within a sprite, the sprite is returned from the IsPointInSprite() method. Otherwise, NULL is returned, which indicates that the point doesn't lie within any sprites.

If this discussion of adding a sprite manager to the game engine was somewhat overwhelming, I apologize. In reality, you don't necessarily have to understand exactly how it works in order to create useful games with the game engine. However, should you ever need to tinker with the inner workings of the sprite manager, you can always come back to this discussion as a refresher on exactly how it works.

Eliminating Flicker with Double-Buffering

The sprite manager is now complete and ready to use within an example. However, one bit of unfinished business needs to be addressed before pressing onward. You might have noticed an annoying flicker in all the animated examples throughout the book thus far. This flicker is caused by the fact that the background image on the game screen is repainted before painting the animated graphics. In other words, animated graphics objects are erased and repainted each time they are moved. Because the erase and repaint process is taking place directly on the game screen, the image appears to flicker. To better understand the problem, imagine a movie in which a blank background is displayed quickly in between each frame containing actors that move. Although the film is cooking along at a fast enough pace to give the illusion of movement, you would still see a noticeable flicker because of the blank backgrounds.

The flicker problem associated with sprite animation can be solved using a technique known as *double-buffering*. In double-buffering, you perform all of your erasing and drawing on an offscreen drawing surface not visible to the user. After all the drawing is finished, the end result is painted straight to the game screen in one pass. Because no visible erasing is taking place, the end result is flicker-free animation. Figure 10.1 shows the difference between traditional single-buffer animation and double-buffer animation that eliminates flicker.

Gamer's Garage

A *buffer* is simply an area in memory to which you are drawing graphics. The buffer in traditional single-buffer animation is the game screen itself, whereas double-buffer animation adds an offscreen memory buffer to the equation.

FIGURE 10.1
Double-buffer animation eliminates the annoying flicker associated with drawing directly to the game screen with a single buffer.

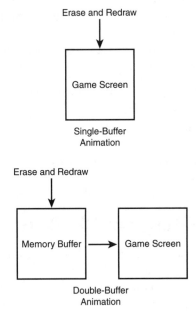

Figure 10.1 reveals how an offscreen memory buffer is used to perform all the incremental animation drawing, with only the finished image being drawn to the game screen. This might sound like a tricky programming problem, but double-buffering is really not very hard to incorporate into your games. The first step is to create two global variables to keep track of the offscreen device context and bitmap that serve as the offscreen buffer. The following is an example of how to create these global variables:

```
HDC     g_hOffscreenDC;
HBITMAP g_hOffscreenBitmap;
```

With these variables in place, you need to create the offscreen device context and then use it to create an offscreen bitmap the same size as the game screen. The offscreen bitmap then needs to be selected into the offscreen device context, and you're ready to go. The following code shows how these tasks are accomplished:

```
// Create the offscreen device context and bitmap
g_hOffscreenDC = CreateCompatibleDC(GetDC(hWindow));
g_hOffscreenBitmap = CreateCompatibleBitmap(GetDC(hWindow),
  g_pGame->GetWidth(), g_pGame->GetHeight());
SelectObject(g_hOffscreenDC, g_hOffscreenBitmap);
```

You now have an offscreen bitmap the same size as your game screen that is selected into an offscreen device context to which you can draw. The following code reveals how easy it is to use the offscreen device context and bitmap to add double-buffer support to the paint code in a game:

```
// Obtain a device context for repainting the game
HWND  hWindow = g_pGame->GetWindow();
HDC   hDC = GetDC(hWindow);

// Paint the game to the offscreen device context
GamePaint(g_hOffscreenDC);

// Blit the offscreen bitmap to the game screen
BitBlt(hDC, 0, 0, g_pGame->GetWidth(), g_pGame->GetHeight(),
  g_hOffscreenDC, 0, 0, SRCCOPY);

// Cleanup
ReleaseDC(hWindow, hDC);
```

This code would fit in perfectly in a GameCycle() function. The familiar GamePaint() function is passed the offscreen device context, which means that all the game painting takes place offscreen. The resulting image is then painted or *blitted* to the game screen's device context at once, which eliminates the possibility of flicker. Notice that this code is structured so that you don't have to do anything special in the GamePaint() function.

It's still important to clean up after yourself, and the following code shows how to clean up the offscreen bitmap and device context:

```
// Cleanup the offscreen device context and bitmap
DeleteObject(g_hOffscreenBitmap);
DeleteDC(g_hOffscreenDC);
```

Although the double-buffer code isn't technically part of the sprite manager, it is nonetheless an important improvement to sprite animation and is a technique you should definitely use in all of your future sprite animation programs. The next sections build on what you've learned thus far in this chapter to revamp the Planets example from the previous chapter to support the sprite manager and double-buffer animation.

Building the Planets 2 Example

The Planets example demonstrates how to use the Sprite class to create a few sprites and move them around on the game screen. You're now going to enhance that example a little by reworking it to support the new sprite management features built into the game engine, as well as double-buffer animation. The new version of the Planets program is called Planets 2, and it serves as a great test bed for exploring the sprite features you've now added to the game engine.

Writing the Program Code

As with most programs created using the game engine, the best place to start with the code is the GameStart() function, which is used to initialize global variables and get everything in place. Listing 10.3 shows the code for the GameStart() and GameEnd() functions in the Planets 2 program.

LISTING 10.3 The GameStart() Function Initializes the Offscreen Buffer, Whereas the GameEnd() Function Cleans Up the Offscreen Buffer

```
void GameStart(HWND hWindow)
{
  // Seed the random number generator
  srand(GetTickCount());

  // Create the offscreen device context and bitmap
  g_hOffscreenDC = CreateCompatibleDC(GetDC(hWindow));
  g_hOffscreenBitmap = CreateCompatibleBitmap(GetDC(hWindow),
    g_pGame->GetWidth(), g_pGame->GetHeight());
  SelectObject(g_hOffscreenDC, g_hOffscreenBitmap);

  // Create and load the bitmaps
  HDC hDC = GetDC(hWindow);
  g_pGalaxyBitmap = new Bitmap(hDC, IDB_GALAXY, g_hInstance);
  g_pPlanetBitmap[0] = new Bitmap(hDC, IDB_PLANET1, g_hInstance);
  g_pPlanetBitmap[1] = new Bitmap(hDC, IDB_PLANET2, g_hInstance);
  g_pPlanetBitmap[2] = new Bitmap(hDC, IDB_PLANET3, g_hInstance);

  // Create the planet sprites
  RECT    rcBounds = { 0, 0, 600, 400 };
  Sprite* pSprite;
  pSprite = new Sprite(g_pPlanetBitmap[0], rcBounds, BA_WRAP);
  pSprite->SetVelocity(3, 2);
  g_pGame->AddSprite(pSprite);
  pSprite = new Sprite(g_pPlanetBitmap[1], rcBounds, BA_WRAP);
  pSprite->SetVelocity(4, 1);
  g_pGame->AddSprite(pSprite);
```

The offscreen buffer is created based on the size of the game screen.

```
  rcBounds.right = 200; rcBounds.bottom = 160;
  pSprite = new Sprite(g_pPlanetBitmap[2], rcBounds, BA_BOUNCE);
  pSprite->SetVelocity(-4, 2);
  g_pGame->AddSprite(pSprite);
  rcBounds.left = 400; rcBounds.top = 240;
  rcBounds.right = 600; rcBounds.bottom = 400;
  pSprite = new Sprite(g_pPlanetBitmap[2], rcBounds, BA_BOUNCE);
  pSprite->SetVelocity(7, -3);
  g_pGame->AddSprite(pSprite);

  // Set the initial drag info
  g_pDragSprite = NULL;
}

void GameEnd()
{
  // Cleanup the offscreen device context and bitmap
  DeleteObject(g_hOffscreenBitmap);
  DeleteDC(g_hOffscreenDC);

  // Cleanup the bitmaps
  delete g_pGalaxyBitmap;
  for (int i = 0; i < 3; i++)
    delete g_pPlanetBitmap[i];

  // Cleanup the sprites
  g_pGame->CleanupSprites();

  // Cleanup the game engine
  delete g_pGame;
}
```

By using a bounding rectangle smaller than the game screen, the sprite is limited in its movement.

The first big change in the GameStart() function, as compared to its previous version, is the creation of the offscreen device context and bitmap. The other change has to do with how the planet sprites are created. Rather than using a global array of sprites to keep track of the sprites, they are now just created and added to the game engine via the AddSprite() method. Actually, there is an extra planet sprite in the Planets 2 example, which is helpful in demonstrating the collision detection features now built into the game engine.

You might notice that two of the sprites have their bounding rectangles set differently than the others. More specifically, the last two sprites have their bounding rectangles set so that they can only move in certain areas of the game screen; they are limited to movement in opposite ends of the galaxy.

The GameEnd() function is similar to the previous version, except that it now cleans up the offscreen bitmap and device context that are required for double-buffer animation.

One of the areas where the new sprite manager really simplifies things is in the
GamePaint() function, which is shown in Listing 10.4.

LISTING 10.4　The GamePaint() **Function Draws the Background and All
the Sprites in the Sprite List**

```
void GamePaint(HDC hDC)
{
  // Draw the background galaxy
  g_pGalaxyBitmap->Draw(hDC, 0, 0);

  // Draw the sprites
  g_pGame->DrawSprites(hDC);
}
```

Notice in this code that the entire list of sprites is drawn using a single call to the
DrawSprites() method in the game engine. This is a perfect example of how a
little work in the game engine can really help make your game code easier to
manage and understand.

Unlike the GamePaint() function, the GameCycle()function is a little more complex in the Planets 2 program than in its predecessor. However, as Listing 10.5
reveals, the new code consists solely of the familiar double-buffer code that you
saw in the previous section.

LISTING 10.5　The GameCycle() **Function Updates the Sprites in the
Sprite List and Then Draws Them to an Offscreen Memory Buffer Before
Updating the Game Screen**

```
void GameCycle()
{
  // Update the sprites
  g_pGame->UpdateSprites();

  // Obtain a device context for repainting the game
  HWND  hWindow = g_pGame->GetWindow();
  HDC   hDC = GetDC(hWindow);

  // Paint the game to the offscreen device context
  GamePaint(g_hOffscreenDC);

  // Blit the offscreen bitmap to the game screen
  BitBlt(hDC, 0, 0, g_pGame->GetWidth(), g_pGame->GetHeight(),
    g_hOffscreenDC, 0, 0, SRCCOPY);

  // Cleanup
  ReleaseDC(hWindow, hDC);
}
```

*The game graphics
are first painted to
the offscreen
buffer.*

*The offscreen
buffer is then
painted to the game
screen in one step
to eliminate flicker.*

The GameCycle() function first updates the sprites in the sprite list with a call to the game engine's UpdateSprites() method. The remainder of the code in the function should look familiar to you because it is identical to the code you saw earlier when you learned about double-buffer animation. The GamePaint() method is called to paint the game graphics to the offscreen device context. The offscreen image is then blitted to the game screen's device context to finish the painting.

If you recall from the previous chapter, the left mouse button can be used to click and drag a planet sprite around on the game screen. Listing 10.6 contains the code for the three mouse functions that make sprite dragging possible.

LISTING 10.6 The MouseButtonDown(), MouseButtonUp(), and MouseMove() Functions Simplify the Process of Dragging a Sprite Around the Game Screen

```
void MouseButtonDown(int x, int y, BOOL bLeft)
{
  // See if a planet was clicked with the left mouse button
  if (bLeft && (g_pDragSprite == NULL))
  {
    if ((g_pDragSprite = g_pGame->IsPointInSprite(x, y)) != NULL)
    {
      // Capture the mouse
      SetCapture(g_pGame->GetWindow());

      // Simulate a mouse move to get started
      MouseMove(x, y);
    }
  }
}

void MouseButtonUp(int x, int y, BOOL bLeft)
{
  // Release the mouse
  ReleaseCapture();

  // Stop dragging
  g_pDragSprite = NULL;
}

void MouseMove(int x, int y)
{
  if (g_pDragSprite != NULL)
  {
    // Move the sprite to the mouse cursor position
    g_pDragSprite->SetPosition(x - (g_pDragSprite->GetWidth() / 2),
      y - (g_pDragSprite->GetHeight() / 2));

    // Force a repaint to redraw the sprites
    InvalidateRect(g_pGame->GetWindow(), NULL, FALSE);
  }
}
```

The game engine's IsPointInSprite() method simplifies the task of performing hit tests on sprites.

The mouse functions in Planets 2 are simplified from their previous versions, thanks to the new and improved game engine. For example, the MouseButtonDown() function now relies on the IsPointInSprite() method in the game engine to check and see if the mouse position is located within a sprite. The other two mouse functions are very similar to their previous counterparts, except that they now rely on a sprite pointer to keep track of the drag sprite, as opposed to an index into an array of sprites. For example, notice that when the mouse button is released, the g_pDragSprite pointer is set to NULL. Similarly, the same pointer is used to set the position of the drag sprite in the MouseButtonUp() function.

The last function in the Planets 2 example is the SpriteCollision() function, which is called whenever two sprites collide with each other. Listing 10.7 contains the code for this function.

LISTING 10.7 The SpriteCollision() **Function Swaps the Velocities of Sprites that Collide, Which Makes Them Appear to Bounce Off Each Other**

```
BOOL SpriteCollision(Sprite* pSpriteHitter, Sprite* pSpriteHittee)
{
  // Swap the sprite velocities so that they appear to bounce
  POINT ptSwapVelocity = pSpriteHitter->GetVelocity();
  pSpriteHitter->SetVelocity(pSpriteHittee->GetVelocity());
  pSpriteHittee->SetVelocity(ptSwapVelocity);
  return TRUE;
}
```

The SpriteCollision() function receives the two sprites that collided as its only arguments. The function handles the collision by swapping the velocities of the sprites. This has the effect of making the sprites appear to bounce off each other and reverse directions. Notice that the SpriteCollision() function returns TRUE at the end to indicate that the sprites should be restored to their old positions prior to the collision.

Construction Cue

As with most of the examples in the book, the Planets 2 program relies on the standard msimg32.lib and winmm.lib libraries. These libraries are included with most Windows compilers, but they aren't automatically linked into programs when you create a new project. If you are using your own project or make files, as opposed to using the ones provided on the CD-ROM, make sure that you change the link settings so that these library files are properly linked into the final executable. Refer to the documentation for your specific compiler for how this is done.

Testing the Finished Product

The improvements you made in the Planets 2 example are somewhat subtle, but they are significant in terms of adding functionality to the game engine that is required to create real games. For example, it is critical that you be able to detect collisions between sprites and react accordingly. The collision detection support in the game engine now makes it very easy to tell when two sprites have collided and then take appropriate action. Although it's hard to show sprite collisions in a still image, Figure 10.2 shows the Planets 2 example in action.

FIGURE 10.2
The planet sprites in the Planets 2 program move around and bounce off each other, thanks to the new and improved sprite management features in the game engine.

If you pay close attention to the sprites, you'll notice that two of them are limited to movement in certain corners of the game screen. These two sprites are the ones whose bounding rectangles were reduced to limit their movement. You can see that bounding rectangles provide a simple, yet effective way to limit the movement of sprites. Keep in mind that you can still click and drag any of the sprites with the left mouse button. Now that the sprites are sensitive to collisions, dragging them around with the mouse is considerably more interesting.

Summary

Sprites are undoubtedly a critical part of two-dimensional game programming because they allow you to create graphical objects that can move around independently of a background image. Not only that, but sprites can be designed so that they reside together in a system in which they can interact with one another.

Most games represent a model of some kind of physical system, so a system of sprites becomes a good way of simulating a physical system in a game. This chapter built on the sprite code that you developed in the previous chapter by pulling sprites together into a system that is managed within the game engine. By actively managing the sprites in the game engine, you're able to ensure that they are layered properly according to Z-order, as well to handle collisions between them.

Moving into the next chapter, you'll quickly realize how important the new sprite features are to games. The next chapter guides you through the development of a complete game called Henway that is sort of a spinoff of the classic Frogger arcade game. You'll be using your newfound sprite knowledge to the maximum as you build Henway, so get ready!

Extreme Game Makeover

To illustrate the point that you can turn an existing code base for a game into something completely different with relatively little effort, I want you to change the Planets 2 example into an aquarium. That's right; you're going from outer space to underwater and only changing a few lines of code in the process. Here's how:

1. Change the planet images to underwater animals that don't have a direction. In other words, deliberately choose animals such as jellyfish and octopi over other kinds of fish because you don't currently have the ability to change the appearance of the sprites to indicate a change of direction.

2. Change the background image to an image of an empty aquarium. By empty, I simply mean that no fish are visible—it should still look as if it has water in it.

3. Assuming that the aquarium has walls that are visible on the screen, change the bounding rectangles of the sprites so that the sprites stay within the watery area of the aquarium. This is the critical step that makes the aquarium simulation work.

4. Slow down the speeds of the sprites a little so that they appear to float around more naturally.

By simply changing the graphics and tweaking the code slightly, you've changed an outer space example involving fast-moving planets into an aquarium simulator with gracefully moving jellyfish.

CHAPTER 11

Example Game: Henway

Released in 1981 by Midway, Frogger was originally developed by Konami as a twist on the famous question, "Why did the chicken cross the road?" In this case, the chicken was a frog, and the road was actually a busy highway followed by a river filled with floating logs and hungry alligators. Frogger had simple, yet addictive game play and was immediately a hit at arcades. As a testament to Frogger's impact on popular culture, it is the only game to serve as a major plot device in arguably the most popular television sitcom of all time, *Seinfeld*.

Arcade Archive

You've spent a great deal of time throughout the book thus far assembling a game engine and learning the ropes of what it takes to build games. You've even created a complete game, although it didn't involve any animation. In this chapter, you embark on your next complete game, which takes what you've learned about sprites and puts it to use. The Henway game developed in this chapter uses several sprites and most of the sprite features built into the game engine. The game is somewhat of a takeoff on the classic Frogger game, and it represents a significant milestone in your game programming quest because it is such an interesting little game. This is the kind of game that you can use as the basis for your own game development efforts.

In this chapter, you'll learn

- ▶ Why modeling a game on a classic arcade game is sometimes a good idea

- ▶ How to design a game called Henway that is somewhat of a takeoff on Frogger

- ▶ How to write the code for the Henway game

- ▶ Why testing a game of your own is often the most fun part of the development process

How Does the Game Play?

The original Frogger arcade game involved a frog whose goal was to make it safely across a highway and a river. Several obstacles appeared in the frog's path, including speeding cars, treacherous rushing water, and alligators, to name a few. Frogger played vertically, which means that you guided the frog from the bottom of the game screen to the top of the screen in order to reach safety. As you guided more and more frogs safely across, the game progressed to get more difficult by adding more cars and other obstacles to the mix. Although Frogger is certainly an incredibly simple game by modern gaming standards, it's a perfect example of a classic game with fun game play. This makes it a good candidate for creating a game of your own—just put a twist on the concept, and you can create your own Frogger-like masterpiece.

Gamer's Garage

In case you're wondering, I don't generally encourage basing all of your games on existing classics, but I have found that popular games of the past can provide good ideas for new games. These days, everyone is busy trying to model computer games after movies, but not everyone is interested in playing a heavily scripted drama. Sometimes it's fun to fire up a game and play for a few minutes as a light diversion; in which case, the classics are perfect.

The popularity of Frogger resulted in a variety of knockoff games being created to coattail Frogger's success. One of these games was called Freeway, and it involved a chicken trying to cross a busy highway. Freeway was made by Activision for the Atari 2600 game system, which was the first console system to really hit it big. As a proud owner and player of Freeway, I thought it would be fun to create a similar game in this chapter. However, the game you create is called Henway, which comes from an old joke. If you've never heard the joke, it goes like this: You mention the word "henway" a few times in a conversation with a friend, and eventually, he'll get up the nerve to say, "What's a henway?" to which you immediately respond, "Oh, about three pounds." I know, it's a very bad joke, but it makes for a fun name for a game involving a chicken and a highway.

Unlike Frogger, the hero in Henway is a chicken who desperately needs to get from one side of a busy highway to the other. Also unlike Frogger, Henway plays horizontally, which means that you guide the chicken from the left side of the screen to the right side. So, the game screen looks something like the drawing in Figure 11.1.

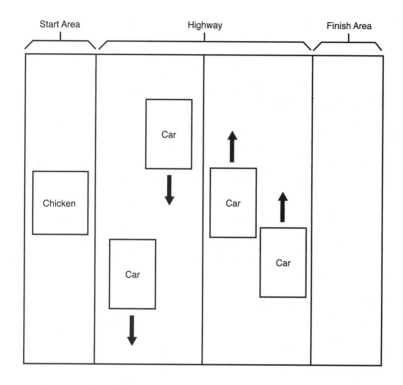

FIGURE 11.1
The Henway game consists of a Start Area, a Highway, and a Finish Area, along with chicken and car sprites.

As you can see, the obstacles working against the chicken are four cars cruising up and down four lanes of highway. The cars move at varying speeds, which makes it a little trickier to time the chicken's crossing. Unlike Frogger, which requires you to guide the frog into specific zones of the Finish Area, Henway just requires you to get the chicken across the road.

> You'll notice that a common thread throughout all of the game examples in the book is simplicity. Although there are all kinds of enticing ways to improve upon the games, I opted to leave it up to you to make the improvements. My goal is to provide you with a working game that is simple enough to understand. Then, you can jazz it up with extra features.

Gamer's Garage

You start the Henway game with a limited number of chickens: three. When all of your chickens get run over, the game is over. It's important to show somewhere on the screen how many chickens you have remaining. Additionally, some kind of notification should take place to inform you when you lose a chicken, as well as when you successfully make it across the highway. It also wouldn't hurt to have some kind of scoring system for rewarding good game play.

The Henway game is well suited for both keyboard and joystick input, although there isn't really a good way to use the mouse in the game. For this reason, you'll focus on supporting the keyboard and joystick, and you'll skip the mouse entirely.

Designing the Game

The overview of the Henway game has already given you a leg up on the game's design, even if you don't realize it. For example, you already know how many sprites are required for the game. Can you hazard a guess? There are five sprites in the game: one chicken sprite and four car sprites. There is certainly the opportunity to include additional car sprites, possibly as a way to increase the difficulty of the game over time, but the basic game only uses four.

Beyond the sprites, can you guess how many bitmap images the game needs? If you guessed six, you're very close. The following are the seven bitmap images required of the game:

- ▶ Background highway image
- ▶ Chicken image (see Figure 11.2)
- ▶ Four car images (see Figure 11.3)
- ▶ Small chicken head image (see Figure 11.4)

FIGURE 11.2
The chicken bitmap image shows a chicken facing to the right, ready for action.

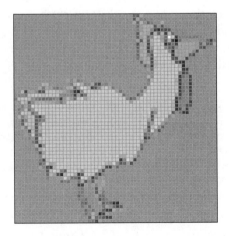

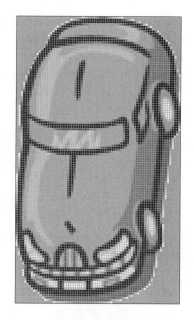

FIGURE 11.3
Each of the car bitmap images is oriented vertically so that the car appears to be traveling up or down.

FIGURE 11.4
The small chicken head bitmap image is sized to represent the number of lives remaining in the game.

You probably factored in all these images except the last one. The small chicken head image is used to convey to the player how many chickens are left. As an example, when the game starts, three small chicken heads are displayed in the lower-right edge of the screen. As you sacrifice your chickens to the highway, the chicken heads disappear until you have none left and the game is over.

Now that you have a feel for the graphical objects involved in the game, let's consider other data that must be maintained by the game. First, it's pretty obvious that you'll need to keep track of how many chicken lives are remaining. You'll also want to keep a running score that is added to each time a chicken makes it safely across the highway. A Boolean variable keeping track of whether the game is over is also required.

There is one last variable that would be hard for you to anticipate without actually developing the game and testing it out. I'm referring to an input delay variable, which helps to alter the keyboard and joystick input response to improve the playability of the game. If you directly responded to the keyboard and joystick in every game cycle, which is how you would logically support input in the game, the chicken would zip around the game screen too fast. Simply too many game cycles are taking place to give input devices that much attention. In order to slow down the input a little, you can use a delay variable and only check for keyboard and joystick input every third game cycle. Determining the appropriate delay is somewhat of a trial-and-error process, so you're free to tinker with it and see what you like best. The point is that the game benefits dramatically from putting a leash on the speed of the user input handling.

To recap, the design of the Henway game has led us to the following pieces of information that must be managed by the game:

- ▶ The number of chicken lives
- ▶ The score
- ▶ A Boolean game over variable
- ▶ An input delay variable

With this information in mind, you're now ready to move on and put the code together for the Henway game.

Building the Game

Hopefully by now, you're getting antsy to see how the Henway game is put together. The next couple of sections explore the code development for the Henway game, which is relatively simple when you consider that this is the first fully functioning game you've created that supports double-buffer sprite animation. The revamped game engine with sprite management really makes the Henway game a smooth game to develop.

Writing the Game Code

The code for the Henway game begins with the Henway.h header file, which is shown in Listing 11.1.

LISTING 11.1 The Henway.h Header File Declares Global Variables that Are Used to Manage the Game, as well as a Helper Function

```
#pragma once

//---------------------------------
// Include Files
//---------------------------------
#include <windows.h>
#include "Resource.h"
#include "GameEngine.h"
#include "Bitmap.h"
#include "Sprite.h"


//---------------------------------
// Global Variables
//---------------------------------
HINSTANCE    g_hInstance;
GameEngine*  g_pGame;
HDC          g_hOffscreenDC;
HBITMAP      g_hOffscreenBitmap;
Bitmap*      g_pHighwayBitmap;
Bitmap*      g_pChickenBitmap;
Bitmap*      g_pCarBitmaps[4];
Bitmap*      g_pChickenHeadBitmap;
Sprite*      g_pChickenSprite;
int          g_iInputDelay;
int          g_iNumLives;
int          g_iScore;
BOOL         g_bGameOver;


//---------------------------------
// Function Declarations
//---------------------------------
void MoveChicken(int iXDistance, int iYDistance);
```

The chicken sprite is the only sprite you need to keep up with in order to move it in response to user interactions.

The global variables for the Henway game consist largely of the different bitmaps used throughout the game. The offscreen device context and bitmap are declared, as well as the different bitmaps that compose the game's graphics. Even the sprite management features of the game engine are being used in this game; it's necessary to keep a pointer to the chicken sprite so that you can change its position in response to user input events. The g_pChickenSprite member variable is used to store the chicken sprite pointer. The input delay for the keyboard and joystick is declared next, along with the number of chicken lives remaining and the score. The last variable is the Boolean game over variable, which simply keeps track of whether or not the game is over.

You'll notice that a helper function named MoveChicken() is declared in the Henway.h file. This function is called by other game functions within the game to move the chicken sprite in response to user input events. The two arguments to the MoveChicken() function are the X and Y amounts to move the chicken.

The actual game functions appear in the Henway.cpp source code file, which is located on the accompanying CD-ROM. The first game function worth mentioning is the GameInitialize() function, which creates the game engine, establishes the frame rate, and initializes the joystick.

Construction Cue

> Keep in mind that I'm not listing every line of code used in the Henway game; it's much more useful to focus on the most important code. Refer to the CD-ROM for the complete source code for the game, along with project files for Microsoft Visual C++ and Borland C++Builder.

The GameStart() function is a little more interesting than GameInitialize(). This function is responsible for initializing the game data, as shown in Listing 11.2.

LISTING 11.2   The GameStart() Function Creates the Offscreen Buffer, Loads the Game Bitmaps, Creates the Game Sprites, and Initializes Game State Member Variables

```
void GameStart(HWND hWindow)
{
  // Seed the random number generator
  srand(GetTickCount());

  // Create the offscreen device context and bitmap
  g_hOffscreenDC = CreateCompatibleDC(GetDC(hWindow));
  g_hOffscreenBitmap = CreateCompatibleBitmap(GetDC(hWindow),
    g_pGame->GetWidth(), g_pGame->GetHeight());
  SelectObject(g_hOffscreenDC, g_hOffscreenBitmap);

  // Create and load the bitmaps
  HDC hDC = GetDC(hWindow);
  g_pHighwayBitmap = new Bitmap(hDC, IDB_HIGHWAY, g_hInstance);
  g_pChickenBitmap = new Bitmap(hDC, IDB_CHICKEN, g_hInstance);
  g_pCarBitmaps[0] = new Bitmap(hDC, IDB_CAR1, g_hInstance);
  g_pCarBitmaps[1] = new Bitmap(hDC, IDB_CAR2, g_hInstance);
  g_pCarBitmaps[2] = new Bitmap(hDC, IDB_CAR3, g_hInstance);
  g_pCarBitmaps[3] = new Bitmap(hDC, IDB_CAR4, g_hInstance);
  g_pChickenHeadBitmap = new Bitmap(hDC, IDB_CHICKENHEAD, g_hInstance);

  // Create the chicken and car sprites
  Sprite* pSprite;
  RECT    rcBounds = { 0, 0, 465, 400 };
  g_pChickenSprite = new Sprite(g_pChickenBitmap, rcBounds, BA_STOP);
  g_pChickenSprite->SetPosition(4, 175);
  g_pChickenSprite->SetVelocity(0, 0);
```

```
g_pChickenSprite->SetZOrder(1);
g_pGame->AddSprite(g_pChickenSprite);
pSprite = new Sprite(g_pCarBitmaps[0], rcBounds, BA_WRAP);
pSprite->SetPosition(70, 0);
pSprite->SetVelocity(0, 7);
pSprite->SetZOrder(2);
g_pGame->AddSprite(pSprite);
pSprite = new Sprite(g_pCarBitmaps[1], rcBounds, BA_WRAP);
pSprite->SetPosition(160, 0);
pSprite->SetVelocity(0, 3);
pSprite->SetZOrder(2);
g_pGame->AddSprite(pSprite);
pSprite = new Sprite(g_pCarBitmaps[2], rcBounds, BA_WRAP);
pSprite->SetPosition(239, 400);
pSprite->SetVelocity(0, -5);
pSprite->SetZOrder(2);
g_pGame->AddSprite(pSprite);
pSprite = new Sprite(g_pCarBitmaps[3], rcBounds, BA_WRAP);
pSprite->SetPosition(329, 400);
pSprite->SetVelocity(0, -10);
pSprite->SetZOrder(2);
g_pGame->AddSprite(pSprite);

// Initialize the remaining global variables
g_iInputDelay = 0;
g_iNumLives = 3;
g_iScore = 0;
g_bGameOver = FALSE;
}
```

Although subtle, the chicken's Z-order is set lower than the cars so that it appears to be under a car when it gets run over.

The GameStart() function contains a fair amount of code, which primarily has to do with the fact that creating each sprite requires a few lines of code. The function starts out by creating the offscreen device context and bitmap. All the bitmaps for the game are then loaded. Finally, the really interesting part of the function involves the creation of the sprites, which you should be able to follow without too much difficulty. The chicken sprite is first created at a position in the Start Area of the game screen and with 0 velocity. The car sprites are then created at different positions and with varying velocities. Notice that the bounds actions for the car sprites are set so that the cars wrap around the game screen, whereas the chicken sprite stops when it encounters a boundary. Also, the Z-order of the cars is set higher than the chicken so that the chicken will appear under the cars when it gets run over.

The remaining member variables in the Henway game are initialized in the GameStart() function after the sprites are created. The input delay is set to 0 (more on this in a moment), whereas the number of chicken lives is set to 3. The score is also set to 0, and the game over variable is set to FALSE to indicate that the game isn't over.

The Henway game relies on the keyboard and joystick for user input. In order to support joystick input, it's important to capture and release the joystick whenever the game window is activated and deactivated. Listing 11.3 shows the code for the GameActivate() and GameDeactivate() functions, which are responsible in this case for capturing and releasing the joystick.

LISTING 11.3   The GameActivate() and GameDeactivate() **Functions Capture and Release the Joystick, Respectively**

```
void GameActivate(HWND hWindow)
{
  // Capture the joystick
  g_pGame->CaptureJoystick();
}

void GameDeactivate(HWND hWindow)
{
  // Release the joystick
  g_pGame->ReleaseJoystick();
}
```

The GameActivate() function calls the CaptureJoystick() method on the game engine to capture the joystick, whereas the GameDeactivate() function calls ReleaseJoystick() to release the joystick.

As you know, the GamePaint() function is responsible for painting games. Listing 11.4 contains the code for the Henway game's GamePaint() function.

LISTING 11.4   The GamePaint()**Function Draws the Highway Background Image, the Game Sprites, and the Number of Remaining Chicken Lives**

```
void GamePaint(HDC hDC)
{
  // Draw the background highway
  g_pHighwayBitmap->Draw(hDC, 0, 0);

  // Draw the sprites
  g_pGame->DrawSprites(hDC);

  // Draw the number of remaining chicken lives
  for (int i = 0; i < g_iNumLives; i++)
    g_pChickenHeadBitmap->Draw(hDC,
      406 + (g_pChickenHeadBitmap->GetWidth() * i), 382, TRUE);
}
```

This GamePaint() function must draw all the game graphics for the Henway game, but this is accomplished in a relatively small amount of code. The function begins by drawing the background highway image, and then it draws the game sprites. The rest of the function draws the number of remaining chicken lives in the lower-right corner of the game screen using small chicken head bitmaps. A small chicken head is drawn for each chicken life remaining, which helps you to know how many times you can get run over before the game ends.

The GameCycle() function works hand in hand with GamePaint() to update the game's sprites and then reflect the changes onscreen. Listing 11.5 shows the code for the GameCycle() function.

LISTING 11.5 The GameCycle() Function Updates the Game Sprites and Repaints the Game Screen Using an Offscreen Buffer to Eliminate Flicker

```
void GameCycle()
{
  if (!g_bGameOver)
  {
    // Update the sprites
    g_pGame->UpdateSprites();

    // Obtain a device context for repainting the game
    HWND  hWindow = g_pGame->GetWindow();
    HDC   hDC = GetDC(hWindow);

    // Paint the game to the offscreen device context
    GamePaint(g_hOffscreenDC);

    // Blit the offscreen bitmap to the game screen
    BitBlt(hDC, 0, 0, g_pGame->GetWidth(), g_pGame->GetHeight(),
      g_hOffscreenDC, 0, 0, SRCCOPY);

    // Cleanup
    ReleaseDC(hWindow, hDC);
  }
}
```

The GameCycle() function first checks to make sure that the game isn't over; in which case, there would be no need to update anything. The function then updates the sprites and goes about redrawing the game graphics using double-buffer animation. This double-buffer code should be fairly familiar to you by now, so I won't go into the details. The main thing to notice is that the GamePaint() function is ultimately being used to draw the game graphics.

Construction Cue

> The usage of the GamePaint() function in the GameCycle() function is interesting because it highlights the flexibility of using device contexts. When the GamePaint() function is called automatically by Windows to repaint the game screen, it is given a device context to the actual game window. In the GameCycle() function, however, it is provided with an offscreen device context in order to support double-buffer animation. The point is that the GamePaint() function doesn't know or care anything about the device context onto which it is painting.

I mentioned earlier that the Henway game supports both keyboard and joystick input. Listing 11.6 contains the code for the HandleKeys() function, which takes care of processing and responding to keyboard input during the game.

LISTING 11.6   The HandleKeys() Function Responds to the Arrow Keys on the Keyboard by Moving the Chicken

The chicken's position changes 20 pixels for each directional movement.

```
void HandleKeys()
{
  if (!g_bGameOver && (++g_iInputDelay > 2))
  {
    // Move the chicken based upon key presses
    if (GetAsyncKeyState(VK_LEFT) < 0)
      MoveChicken(-20, 0);
    else if (GetAsyncKeyState(VK_RIGHT) < 0)
      MoveChicken(20, 0);
    if (GetAsyncKeyState(VK_UP) < 0)
      MoveChicken(0, -20);
    else if (GetAsyncKeyState(VK_DOWN) < 0)
      MoveChicken(0, 20);

    // Reset the input delay
    g_iInputDelay = 0;
  }
}
```

The HandleKeys() function begins by making sure that the game isn't over, as well as incrementing and testing the input delay. By testing the input delay before processing any keyboard input, the HandleKeys() function effectively slows down the input so that the chicken is easier to control. The chicken is actually controlled via the arrow keys, which are checked using the Win32 GetAsyncKeyState() function. Each arrow key is handled by calling the MoveChicken() function, which moves the chicken by a specified amount. After processing the keys, the input delay is reset so that the input process can be repeated.

If you find that the keyboard controls respond too sluggishly in the game, try lowering the value being tested against the g_iInputDelay variable from 2 to 1. This will speed up the controls by a third.

The joystick is handled in the Henway game in a similar manner as the mouse, as Listing 11.7 reveals.

LISTING 11.7   The `HandleJoystick()` Function Responds to Joystick Movements by Moving the Chicken and also Supports Using the Primary Joystick Button to Start a New Game

```
void HandleJoystick(JOYSTATE jsJoystickState)
{
  if (!g_bGameOver && (++g_iInputDelay > 2))
  {
    // Check horizontal movement
    if (jsJoystickState & JOY_LEFT)
      MoveChicken(-20, 0);
    else if (jsJoystickState & JOY_RIGHT)
      MoveChicken(20, 0);

    // Check vertical movement
    if (jsJoystickState & JOY_UP)
      MoveChicken(0, -20);
    else if (jsJoystickState & JOY_DOWN)
      MoveChicken(0, 20);

    // Reset the input delay
    g_iInputDelay = 0;
  }

  // Check the joystick button and start a new game, if necessary
  if (g_bGameOver && (jsJoystickState & JOY_FIRE1))
  {
    g_iNumLives = 3;
    g_iScore = 0;
    g_bGameOver = FALSE;
  }
}
```

The HandleJoystick() function performs the same check on the g_bGameOver and g_iInputDelay variables to make sure that it is time to check the joystick for input. If so, the joystick is first checked for horizontal movement by examining the jsJoystickState argument passed into the function. The chicken is then moved left or right, if necessary, by calling the MoveChicken() function. A similar process is then repeated for vertical joystick movement. After handling joystick movement, the HandleJoystick() function resets the g_iInputDelay variable. The function then concludes by checking to see if the primary joystick button was pressed; in which case, a new game is started.

Speaking of starting a new game, the mouse is used in the Henway game solely to start a new game if the current game has ended. Listing 11.8 shows the code for the MouseButtonDown() function, which starts a new game in response to a mouse button click.

LISTING 11.8 The MouseButtonDown() **Function Starts a New Game if the Current Game Is Over**

```
void MouseButtonDown(int x, int y, BOOL bLeft)
{
  // Start a new game, if necessary
  if (g_bGameOver)
  {
    g_iNumLives = 3;
    g_iScore = 0;
    g_bGameOver = FALSE;
  }
}
```

If a mouse button is clicked and the current game is over, the MouseButtonDown() function starts a new game by clearing the game state variables.

The game play of the Henway game is largely dictated by the sprites in the game. These sprites are capable of colliding, in which case, the SpriteCollision() function gets called. Of course, the car sprites are designed to only move vertically up and down the screen, so they'll never hit each other. This means that the SpriteCollision() function only gets called when a car hits the chicken or vice versa. Listing 11.9 shows how this collision is handled in the SpriteCollision() function.

LISTING 11.9 The SpriteCollision() **Function Checks to See if the Chicken Was Hit by a Car and Then Responds Accordingly**

```
BOOL SpriteCollision(Sprite* pSpriteHitter, Sprite* pSpriteHittee)
{
  // See if the chicken was hit
  if (pSpriteHittee == g_pChickenSprite)
  {
    // Move the chicken back to the start
    g_pChickenSprite->SetPosition(4, 175);

    // See if the game is over
    if (—g_iNumLives > 0)
      MessageBox(g_pGame->GetWindow(), TEXT("Ouch!"), TEXT("Henway"), MB_OK);
    else
    {
      // Display game over message
      TCHAR szText[64];
```

Moving the chicken sprite to its original position gives the illusion of starting with a new chicken.

```
      wsprintf(szText, "Game Over! You scored %d points.", g_iScore);
      MessageBox(g_pGame->GetWindow(), szText, TEXT("Henway"), MB_OK);
      g_bGameOver = TRUE;
    }

    return FALSE;
  }

  return TRUE;
}
```

Most of the game logic in the Henway game is located in the SpriteCollision() function. Keep in mind that this function is called any time a sprite collides with another sprite in the game. First, a check is made to ensure that the chicken was indeed involved in the collision. If so, you can safely assume that the chicken was hit by a car because cars are the only other sprites. Therefore, the chicken's position is restored to its starting position in the Start Area. The number of chicken lives is then decremented and checked to see if the game is over. If the game isn't over, a message is displayed indicating that you lost a chicken, and the game continues on. If the game is over, however, a special "Game Over" message is displayed, and the g_bGameOver variable is set to TRUE.

If you recall from the design of the sprite manager, the return value of the SpriteCollision() function determines whether the sprite's old position is restored; a value of TRUE restores the old position, whereas FALSE allows the sprite to keep its newly updated position. In this case, the chicken sprite keeps its new position when it collides with a car. Because the position was just set to the Start Area, the effect is that the chicken is allowed to move to the Start Area, which gives the appearance of a new chicken appearing.

The final function in the Henway game is the MoveChicken() function, which you've used several times throughout the game code. Listing 11.10 shows the code for the MoveChicken() function.

LISTING 11.10   The MoveChicken() **Function Moves the Chicken Sprite a Specified Distance While Checking to See if the Chicken Made It Across the Highway**

```
void MoveChicken(int iXDistance, int iYDistance)
{
  // Move the chicken to its new position
  g_pChickenSprite->OffsetPosition(iXDistance, iYDistance);

  // See if the chicken made it across
```

continues

LISTING 11.10   Continued

```
if (g_pChickenSprite->GetPosition().left > 400)
{
    // Move the chicken back to the start and add to the score
    g_pChickenSprite->SetPosition(4, 175);
    g_iScore += 150;
    MessageBox(g_pGame->GetWindow(), TEXT("You made it!"), TEXT("Henway"),
      MB_OK);
}
}
```

The MoveChicken() function is a helper function that simplifies the task of moving the chicken around on the game screen. The iXDistance and iYDistance arguments specify how many pixels to move the chicken in the X and Y directions. These arguments are used to move the chicken by calling the OffsetPosition() method on the Sprite class. If you didn't care what happened to the chicken, this is all the code you would need in the MoveChicken() function. However, you need to know when the chicken makes it across the highway, and this is a perfect place to perform the check. If the chicken made it safely across, its position is set back to the Start Area, and the score is increased. A message is also displayed that notifies the player of a successful highway crossing.

Construction Cue

As with most of the examples in the book, the Henway program relies on the standard msimg32.lib and winmm.lib libraries. These libraries are included with most Windows compilers, but they aren't automatically linked into programs when you create a new project. If you are using your own project or make files, as opposed to using the ones provided on the CD-ROM, make sure that you change the link settings so that these library files are properly linked into the final executable. Refer to the documentation for your specific compiler for how this is done.

Testing the Game

Unless you just happen to be a fan of memory games, you'll hopefully find the Henway game much more fun to test than the Brainiac game from Chapter 6, "Example Game: Brainiac." Henway is the first legitimate action game that you've created, which makes it considerably more interesting from a playability perspective. Keep in mind that action games often require a greater deal of testing because it's hard to predict how moving sprites will react in every little situation. You should play your games a great deal to make sure that nothing out of the ordinary ever happens or at least nothing detrimental that's out of the ordinary.

Figure 11.5 shows the Henway game at the start, with your lion-hearted chicken poised for a trip across the highway.

FIGURE 11.5
The Henway game begins with the chicken in the Start Area, ready to make an attempt at crossing the busy highway.

If the chicken immediately starts moving when you start the game, there's a good chance that your joystick needs calibrating. Refer back to the section titled "Calibrating Joysticks" in Chapter 7, "Improving Input with Joysticks," if you've forgotten how to calibrate your joystick.

Gamer's Garage

To get started with the game, just begin guiding your chicken through traffic using the keyboard or joystick. If you successfully navigate the chicken across the highway, the game will display a message and award you 150 points. Figure 11.6 shows the message that appears when you succeed in crossing the highway.

Of course, even the best Henway player will eventually get careless and steer the chicken into the path of an oncoming car. Figure 11.7 shows the message displayed after a chicken is hit by a car.

After you lose a chicken, the number of chicken lives in the lower right corner of the screen will reduce by one to show the remaining lives. When you eventually lose all three chickens, the game ends. Figure 11.8 shows the end of the game, which simply involves a message being displayed that notifies you of your final score.

FIGURE 11.6
Upon successfully making it across the highway, you are notified by the game and awarded 150 points.

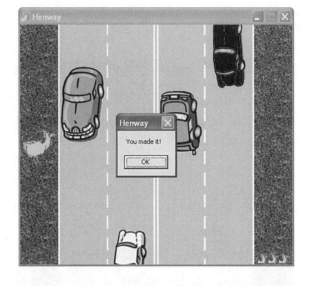

FIGURE 11.7
Getting hit by a car isn't as grisly as you might expect, but the game does display a message to let you know that you've lost a chicken.

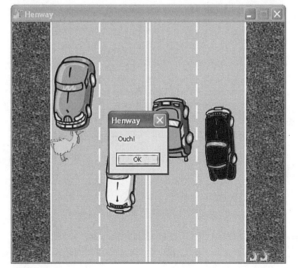

Although it might seem sad to steer three chickens to their demise on a highway full of busy traffic, it's all just a game. Despite its simplicity, hopefully, you can appreciate the Henway game in terms of it representing a culmination of much of what you've learned throughout the book thus far. Even so, there is much ahead as you continue to build more exciting games from here on.

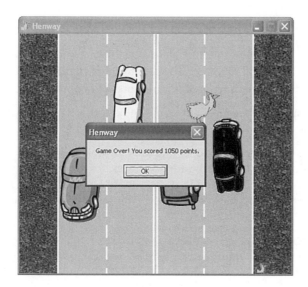

FIGURE 11.8
When you've depleted all of your chickens, the game ends.

Summary

It is a fact of life that book knowledge can only get you so far before you have to experience something for yourself. This chapter provided an example of how book knowledge was made real when you assembled a game that relied on what you've learned about game programming. The Henway game made use of the sprite animation code you developed in the previous two chapters, as well as a great deal of the user input code that you built into the game engine earlier in the book. Hopefully, you're feeling a sense of gratification that the work you've spent constructing the game engine is starting to pay off in the development of a complete game with a surprisingly small amount of code.

This chapter concludes the current part of the book. The next part, "Making Noise with Sound and Music," introduces you to digital sound effects and music, as well as the role they play in games. Not surprisingly, you learn how to add sound and music to games. In fact, you'll encounter the Henway game again in the next part when you add sound effects and music to it.

Extreme Game Makeover

I considered putting you through a complete game makeover of the Henway game, but quickly realized that this has already been done—the game is called Frogger. So instead of changing the theme of the Henway game, let's focus on improving the game. One change that would make the game more challenging is to add open manholes (sewage holes) in the streets that the chicken is capable of falling through. These manholes are created as sprites, and you use collision detection to see if the chicken has collided with them and fallen to its death. The following are the steps required to add manholes of doom to the Henway game:

1. Create a sprite image for the new manhole sprite, which is basically just a black hole.

2. In the `GameStart()` function, create the manhole sprites, making sure to provide the newly created bitmap as the sprites' bitmap. Make sure to set the position of the sprites so that they appear in the lanes of the road. Set their velocities to 0, and also set their Z-orders to 0 so that they appear below the cars and the chicken.

3. Add a check in the `SpriteCollision()` function to see if the chicken sprite has collided with a manhole sprite. If so, end the game as if the chicken had gotten run over by a car.

You'll find that this change to the Henway game makes the game considerably more challenging. It's even better if you add some randomness to the positioning of the manholes so that they appear in different locations with each new game.

PART IV

Making Noise with Sound and Music

CHAPTER 12

Playing Digital Sound Effects

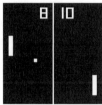

It's hard to argue the impact of compelling sound effects and music on video games of all types. Even the video game classics with their limited sound-making capabilities often incorporated music that you simply couldn't get out of your head, not to mention highly entertaining sound effects. Modern games now have the capability to use extremely realistic sound effects and intricate musical compositions. Even if you aren't musically inclined, you owe it to yourself to figure out a way to incorporate sound and music into your games. You might be thinking that if digital sounds are anything like bitmaps, this chapter will be fairly technical and will include a lot of messy code for loading and interacting with sound data. You'll be glad to know that sounds are actually quite easy to play, and adding sound effects to a game is simple to do.

In this chapter, you'll learn

- ▶ The basics of digital sound
- ▶ How digital sound in Windows is represented by waves
- ▶ How to create and edit your own sound effects for games
- ▶ How to play wave sounds using the Win32 API
- ▶ How to incorporate wave sounds into an existing game

Understanding Digital Sound

Although you could probably get away with playing sounds in games without understanding how digital sound works, I'm not going to let you off the hook that easily. It's important to at least have a basic understanding of digital sound and how it relates to physical sound that we hear in the real world. A physical sound is a wave that moves through the air, kind of like an air equivalent to an ocean wave. A *sound wave* is actually a result of the pressure of air expanding and contracting. In other words, a sound wave involves a series of traveling pressure changes in the air. You hear sound because the traveling sound wave eventually gets to your ears, where the pressure changes are processed and interpreted by your eardrums. If you think of your eardrums as rocky outcroppings on a beach, you hear sound when an ocean wave crashes against the rocks. The softness or loudness of a sound is determined by the amount of energy in the wave, which corresponds to the height and force of an ocean wave. Because sound waves lose energy as they travel, you hear sounds louder up close and softer from a distance. Eventually, sound waves travel far enough to be completely absorbed by the air or some other object, such as a wall in your house.

Sound Wave Energy and Rock Concerts

When I refer to the energy of a sound wave, I'm really talking about the amplitude of the wave. Amplitudes of sound waves are usually measured in decibels (dB). Decibels are logarithmic units of measurement, meaning that 80dB is 10 times louder than 79dB. This type of measurement is used because it reflects the hearing characteristics of the human ear. The threshold of human hearing is 0dB, which means that anything less is too soft to be heard by humans. Likewise, the threshold of pain is 120dB, which is the amplitude level at which humans experience physical pain. Prolonged exposure to sound this loud can cause permanent hearing damage.

Many rock concerts over the years have hit the 120dB sound level. In 1976, The Who made it into the Guinness Book of World Records with a 125dB concert that is now considered the loudest concert of all time.

When a microphone converts sound waves to voltage signals, the resulting signal is an *analog* (or continuous) signal. Because computers are *digital* machines, it is necessary to convert this analog signal to a digital signal for a computer to process. Analog to digital (A/D) converters handle the task of converting analog signals to digital signals, which is also referred to as *sampling*. The process of converting an analog signal to a digital signal doesn't always yield exact results. How closely a digital wave matches its analog counterpart is determined by the frequency at which it is sampled, as well as the amount of information stored in each sample.

To sample a sound, you just store the amplitude of the sound wave at regular intervals. Taking samples at more frequent intervals causes the digital signal to more closely approximate the analog signal and, therefore, sound more like the analog wave when played. So, when sampling sounds, the rate (*frequency*) at which the sound is sampled is very important, as is the amount of data stored for each sample. The unit of measurement for frequency is hertz (Hz), which specifies how many samples are taken per second. As an example, CD-quality audio is sampled at 44,000Hz (44KHz), which means that when you're listening to a music CD, you're actually hearing 44,000 digital sound samples every second.

In addition to the frequency of a sampled sound, the number of bits used to represent the amplitude of the sound impacts the sound quality, as well as whether the sound is a stereo or mono sound. Knowing this, it's possible to categorize the quality of a digital sound according to the following properties:

▶ Frequency

▶ Bits per sample

▶ Mono/stereo

The frequency of a sampled sound typically falls somewhere in the range of 8KHz to 44KHz, with 44KHz representing CD-quality sound. The bits-per-sample value of a sound is usually either 8bps (bits per sample) or 16bps, with 16bps representing CD-quality audio; this is also known as 16-bit audio. A sampled sound is then classified as being either mono or stereo—with mono meaning that there is only one channel of sound, whereas stereo has two channels. As you might expect, a stereo sound contains twice as much information as a mono sound. Not surprisingly, CD-quality audio is always stereo. Therefore, you now understand that a CD-quality sound is a 44KHz 16-bit stereo sound.

For you audiophiles out there, DVD-Audio has raised the ante for digital audio quality and is gaining in popularity. As a comparison to CD-quality sound, DVD-Audio supports sampling rates up to 192KHz, bits-per-sample values up to 24 bits, and up to six channels (as opposed to two channels for stereo CDs). The sheer amount of storage required for DVD-Audio will likely keep it from being useful in games in the near future, but don't count it out in the long run.

Gamer's Garage

Although it would be great to incorporate sounds that are CD-quality into all of your games, the reality is that high-quality sounds take up a lot of memory and can therefore be burdensome to play if your game already relies on a lot of images and other memory-intensive resources. Granted, most computers these days are capable of ripping through memory-intensive multimedia objects, such as MP3 songs, like they are nothing, but games must be designed for extreme efficiency. Therefore, it's important to consider ways to minimize the memory and processing burdens on games every chance you get. One way to minimize these burdens is to carefully choose a sound quality that sounds good without hogging too much memory.

Another issue you should consider with regard to using sound in games is that of copyrighted sounds—you can't use copyrighted sounds without written permission from the owner of the copyright. For example, sounds sampled from copyrighted movies or audio recordings can't be used without permission. It is technically no different than using copyrighted software without permission or a licensing agreement. So be careful when sampling sounds from copyrighted sources.

Gamer's Garage

> Some seemingly public domain sound collections are actually copyrighted and can get you into trouble. Most of these types of collections come in the form of an audio CD containing a variety of sound effects. Be sure to read the fine print on these CDs and make sure that you can legally reuse the sounds or get explicit permission from the publisher.

Getting to Know Windows Waves

Digital sounds in Windows are known as *waves*, which refer to the physical sound waves from which digital sounds originate. Windows waves are stored in files with a .WAV file extension and can be stored in a wide range of formats to accommodate different sound qualities. More specifically, you can save waves in frequencies from 8KHz to 44KHz with either 8 or 16 bits per sample as either mono or stereo. Just as with any other sampled digital audio, the size of a wave file is directly proportional to the quality of the wave sound. Therefore, higher-quality waves take up more memory than lower-quality waves.

You might be surprised to find out that waves are really just Windows resources such as bitmaps, icons, and cursors. This means that you can specify waves as resources in the resource script for your games and compile them directly into the executable program files. The benefit is that you don't have to worry about distributing a bunch of extra files when you make your game available to the public; all the wave files are included in the game's executable program file.

If you want to experiment a little with Windows waves and how they work, you'll be glad to know that Windows includes a built-in tool for working with waves. It's called Sound Recorder, and you'll find it by following these steps in Windows XP:

1. Click the Start button.

2. Select All Programs, followed by Accessories, and then Entertainment.

3. Select Sound Recorder to launch the program.

> If you aren't using Windows XP, don't worry because Sound Recorder is included with all versions of Windows. Just poke around within the Accessories folder, and you'll be able to find it.

The Sound Recorder program is shown in Figure 12.1.

FIGURE 12.1
The Sound Recorder program allows you to record sounds and then manipulate them to some degree.

You'll notice that the Sound Recorder tool includes a series of buttons that look like the buttons on a VCR. These buttons allow you to record new sounds using your computer's microphone or CD-ROM drive, as well as play, stop, rewind, and fast-forward sounds. Feel free to try your hand at recording a sound with the microphone and playing it back with Sound Recorder. You might also want to experiment with some of the effects that can be applied to the sound, such as reversing it and hearing the sound backwards. Remember all of the rumors about hidden messages in rock music when you play it backwards? Now, you can create your own!

Although Sound Recorder is a fairly primitive tool in terms of features, it does give you the capability to tinker with waves and even apply effects to them. Before you invest in a higher-powered sound tool, be sure to take some time to experiment with Sound Recorder. Later in this chapter in the section "Creating and Editing Sounds," you'll learn some interesting techniques used to create wave sound effects; you can certainly use Sound Recorder as the tool for creating these effects. If Sound Recorder ends up feeling too limited for you, read on because the next section introduces you to some high-powered alternatives.

Exploring Sound Tools

To be able to create and modify your own sounds, you need some type of software sound editing utility. Sound editing utilities usually provide a means of sampling sounds from a microphone, CD-ROM, or line input. From there, each utility varies as to what degree of editing it provides. Some sound editing utilities include very advanced signal processing features in addition to the relatively standard amplification and echoing features. Other sound utilities, such as the standard Windows Sound Recorder, are fairly bare bones tools for working with wave sounds.

The most important component of a good sound editor in regard to Windows games is the capability to save sounds in the wave audio format. It doesn't matter how cool the sounds are if you can't play them in your games. Fortunately, the wave audio standard is quite popular and is supported in most sound tools. Another key feature is the capability to zoom in and clip sounds down to exactly the portions you want to use. Because the length of sounds is of utmost importance in games, you should always clip sounds down to the absolute minimum length possible.

Construction Cue

> Clipping sounds down to exactly what you want is not only important for minimizing the storage of sounds, but it also makes sounds play more efficiently. If you perfectly clip a sound so that there is no silence at the beginning (and end), the sound will play very quickly in response to game actions. Otherwise, the silence will have the effect of causing a noticeable and annoying delay in the sound.

The next two sections focus on a couple of popular sound editors that you can use to edit sounds for games. They both support the wave sound format and provide a high degree of sound effects processing. You might also be able to find shareware sound utilities that are cheaper, possibly even free, but they likely won't compare with commercial sound editors in terms of features.

Sony Sound Forge

Sound Forge, by Sony Media Software, is one of the more expensive options available in terms of sound editors, but it is also one of the most powerful. In fact, Sound Forge is largely considered the standard for professional sound editing on PCs; it's most direct competitor is probably Adobe Audition, which you learn about in a moment. Of course, with power comes both price and complexity, which are two things that might be more than you're ready for at the moment. To learn more, visit the Sony Media Software Web site at http://mediasoftware.sonypictures.com/.

Adobe Audition

Audition, by Adobe Systems, is in many ways the Adobe Photoshop of sound editing. What this means is that Audition represents the high-end professional approach to sound editing, and it is one of the most powerful options if you want to become a master of sounds. Audition provides a wide variety of special effects for manipulating sounds, such as reverberation, noise reduction, echo and delay, flanging, filtering, and many others. Similar to Sound Forge, however, Audition might be a bit too expensive for many startup game developers. Owners of Cool Edit, the predecessor to Audition, are eligible for special upgrade pricing. You can get additional information and even download a trial version of Audition from the Adobe Systems Web site, which is located at http://www.adobe.com/.

Economical Sound Editors

If you're thinking more along the lines of an economical way to edit sounds, you might want to look into sound editors published by much smaller companies. A variety of different sound editors are available that will likely suit your needs in the $20–$50 range; most of which include a free trial you can download to make sure that you get your money's worth. The following is a list of some of the sound editors I found that are worth considering, along with Web sites for each:

- Audio Editor Pro—http://www.audioeditorpro.com/
- Ace of WAV—http://www.polyhedric.com/
- Fast Edit—http://www.minnetonkaaudio.com/
- Wave Creator—http://www.blazeaudio.com/
- Wave Flow—http://sagat.hypermart.net/

Creating and Editing Sounds

After you've decided on a sound editing tool, you're ready to start creating and editing sounds. The first decision to make is how you will create the sounds. For example, are you planning to record sounds yourself with a microphone or sample sounds from a stereo cassette deck or VCR? The microphone is probably the easiest route because many multimedia computers come equipped with one. It's also the most creative route. However, you might already have some sounds in mind from a prerecorded audio cassette, videocassette, or DVD, which means that you probably need to look into connecting an external sound source to your computer.

Regardless of where you sample sounds from, the process of getting a sampled sound cleaned up for use in a game is basically the same. After you've sampled a sound, play it back to make sure that it sounds okay. It's likely that the sound will either be too loud or too soft. You can judge whether the volume of the sound is acceptable by looking at the waveform displayed in the sound editor; the *waveform* of a sound is the graphical appearance of the sound when plotted over time. If the sound amplitude goes beyond the top or bottom of the waveform display, you know it's definitely too loud. If you can barely hear it, it's probably too soft. To remedy this problem, you can either adjust the input level for the sound device and resample the sound or try to use amplification effects provided by the sound editor.

The best way to fix the volume problem is to adjust the input level of the sound device and resample the sound. For example, in Windows XP, you can easily adjust the microphone or line input level from the Control Panel. After you have the volume of the sound at a level you like, you need to clip the sound to remove unwanted portions of it. *Clipping* a sound involves zooming in on the waveform in a sound editor and cutting out the silence that appears before and after the sound. This helps shorten the length of the sound and prevents unnecessary latency.

Construction Cue

Latency is the amount of time between when you queue a sound for playing and when the user actually hears it. Latency should be kept to a minimum so that sounds are heard when you want them to be heard without any delay. Unnecessary silence at the beginning of a sound is a common cause of latency problems.

Once you have a sound clipped, it should be ready for prime time. You might want to check out the kinds of effects that are available with the sound utility you are using. Some simple effects range from reverse to echo, with more advanced effects including fading and phase shifts. It's all up to your imagination and your discerning ears.

Finding Sounds and Music

If you've decided that you don't have what it takes to create your own sounds, you still have options. In this case, you need to seek an outside source for your sounds and probably for your music as well. The best source for finding prerecorded sounds and music is in sound archives on the Web. Many different archives are out there with a vast amount of sounds and music from which to choose.

Many are even available already in the wave and MIDI audio formats. Even if you get sounds and music from an online archive, be very careful about the copyright issues surrounding using them.

A good starting point for finding sounds and music is the World Wide Web Virtual Library, which maintains an Audio page with links to archives. This Audio Web site is located at http://archive.museophile.sbu.ac.uk/audio/.

Accessing Wave Sounds

If you record a wave using Sound Recorder or some other sound utility, the end result should be a file with a .WAV file extension. Hopefully, by now, you've already recorded a few sounds or maybe found a few on the Internet. Either way, you understand that a wave sound is stored in a file on disk, kind of like how bitmap images are stored. Similar to bitmaps, it's possible to load a wave directly from a file in a game. However, this isn't the most advantageous way to use waves in games.

If you recall from earlier in the book, I showed you how to include bitmaps as resources in your games. In fact, every example you've seen thus far that uses bitmaps, such as the Henway game in Chapter 11, "Example Game: Henway," has included them as resources that are stored directly in the executable program file. Waves are also resources, and they can therefore be included in the resource script of a program and compiled into the executable program file. Playing the wave sound is slightly different depending on whether the wave is stored in a file or placed directly within the program as a resource. It's ultimately up to you how you want to access waves, but organizationally, I think it's much better to use them as resources so that you don't have to worry about distributing separate wave files with your games.

Playing Wave Sounds

The Win32 API provides high-level support for playing wave sounds, which is extremely good news for you and me. When I say high-level support, I mean that you can play sounds using the Win32 API without getting into the ugly details of wave formats and working with raw sound data in memory. One drawback with the high-level wave support in the Win32 API is that it doesn't allow for *wave mixing*, which is the process of mixing wave sounds so that multiple sounds can be played at once. Unfortunately, this means that only one wave sound can be played at any given moment. You'll have to decide how you want this to impact your games because there are certainly going to be situations in which two or more sounds need to be played at once. You have the following options when it comes to resolving the problem of being able to play only one sound among several:

▶ Interrupt the currently playing sound to play the next sound.

▶ Allow every sound to play to completion and reject sounds that attempt to interrupt the currently playing sound.

Gamer's Garage

> Wave mixing is made possible by the DirectX game programming API, which I've mentioned a few times throughout the book. DirectX is incredibly powerful, especially when it comes to its digital sound capabilities, but it has a very steep learning curve. If you should decide to tackle DirectX after reading this book, by all means, go for it. However, for the purposes of creating your own games without spending a great deal of time and energy learning the inner workings of DirectX, the high-level Win32 API approach to playing wave sounds is sufficient.

Until you actually experiment with these two wave playing approaches, you might think that the first approach sounds appealing because it gives every sound a chance to play. However, in some situations, you'll find that sounds interrupting each other can be as annoying as a bunch of people interrupting each other in a heated debate. If you've ever seen the political television show, *Crossfire*, you know what I'm talking about. On the other hand, when you let sounds play to completion, you will inevitably be disallowing other sounds a chance at playing—some of which might be important to the game play. So, it ultimately depends on the kind of game whether it makes sense to interrupt sounds or allow them to play out.

Regardless of how you address the limitation of only being able to play one sound, the high-level Win32 API function that makes wave playing possible is called PlaySound(), and it looks like this:

```
BOOL PlaySound(LPCSTR szSound, HMODULE hModule, DWORD dwSound);
```

The three arguments to the PlaySound() function determine a variety of different things, such as whether the sound is being played from a wave file or from memory as a wave resource. Additionally, the function allows you to control whether a sound may be interrupted while playing, as well as whether it should be looped repeatedly. The next few sections examine the PlaySound() function in more detail and show you how to control the playback of wave sounds.

Playing a Wave from a File

The simplest way to use the PlaySound() function is to play a wave file directly from the local hard drive. When playing a wave from a file, the first argument to the PlaySound() function, szSound, identifies the name of the wave file. The second argument, hModule, applies only to playing wave resources, so you can pass NULL as the second argument when playing wave files. The third argument, dwSound, is used to determine the specific manner in which the wave is played.

The dwSound argument can contain one or more of several different flags that control various facets of the wave playback. For example, the SND_FILENAME flag indicates that you're playing the wave from a file. There are two other flags, SND_SYNC and SND_ASYNC, that determine whether a wave is played synchronously or asynchronously. A *synchronous* wave is a wave where the PlaySound() function doesn't allow a program to resume operation until it finishes playing, whereas an *asynchronous* wave is played while allowing a program to continue its business. As you might be guessing, synchronous waves are pretty much out of the question in games because you don't want the whole game to pause while a wave is playing. So, you'll need to use the SND_ASYNC flag when playing waves using the PlaySound() function.

The following is an example of playing a wave file using the PlaySound() function:

```
PlaySound("Explosion.wav", NULL, SND_ASYNC | SND_FILENAME);
```

As you can see, this is a pretty simple line of code when you think about everything it accomplishes. A wave file is being loaded from disk and played through the speakers on your computer while your program is allowed to continue operating.

Another PlaySound() flag worth mentioning is the SND_NOSTOP flag, which causes a sound to be more respectful of a sound that is already playing. More specifically, if you specify the SND_NOSTOP flag when playing a wave sound, the sound will not interrupt another wave if it is already playing. The downside to this flag is that the sound will end up never getting played. If you want to make sure that a sound is played no matter what, be sure not to specify the SND_NOSTOP flag. When you don't specify the SND_NOSTOP flag, the sound you're playing will interrupt the currently playing sound no matter what.

Playing a Wave as a Resource

Earlier in the chapter, I mentioned that playing a wave sound as a resource has advantages over playing a wave file because you can combine the wave resource into the main program file. This approach is also more efficient because you aren't opening a file and reading from it; resources are accessed directly from memory. The PlaySound() function includes a flag that allows you to specify that you're playing a wave resource, as opposed to a wave file. The SND_RESOURCE flag indicates that the wave is a resource and that the hInstance argument to PlaySound() is a resource identifier. Because a wave resource must be loaded from an executable program file, you must provide the module handle for the program in the second argument to PlaySound(). The games and examples you've seen throughout the book store away this handle in the g_hInstance global variable.

The following is an example of playing a wave sound as a resource using the PlaySound() function:

```
PlaySound((LPCSTR)IDW_EXPLOSION, g_hInstance, SND_ASYNC | SND_RESOURCE);
```

Construction Cue

> Wave resource IDs are typically named so that they begin with IDW_, which indicates that the ID is associated with a wave.

In this example, the resource ID of the wave sound is IDW_EXPLOSION, whereas the module handle of the program is the global variable g_hInstance. Also, the SND_RESOURCE flag is used to indicate that this is indeed a wave resource, as opposed to a wave file. One important thing to note about this code is that it assumes you've already declared the IDW_EXPLOSION resource ID and placed a reference to the wave resource in the resource script for the program. Just as when you add new bitmaps to a game, you'll need to create a resource ID and an entry in the resource script for each wave sound you use in a game.

Looping a Wave Sound

In some situations, you might want to play a sound repeatedly. For example, if you opt to use sampled music in a game, it probably will make sense to use a wave sound that can be *looped* over and over and sound like one continuous piece of music. The PlaySound() function supports a flag for playing a wave sound looped, which means that the sound is played repeatedly until you interrupt it with another sound or explicitly stop it using the PlaySound() function (more on stopping waves in a moment). The flag to which I'm referring is SND_LOOP, and specifying it results in a wave being repeated over and over.

I once used a looped wave sound to simulate the sound of a hovering helicopter in a game. The wave sound ended up being a very short sound clip, but when looped repeatedly, it sounded just like a helicopter.

The following is an example of playing a looped wave resource:

```
PlaySound((LPCSTR)IDW_BACKBEAT, _hInstance, SND_ASYNC ¦ SND_RESOURCE ¦
  SND_LOOP);
```

The SND_LOOP flag requires you to also use the SND_ASYNC flag because it wouldn't make sense to loop a sound synchronously. Keep in mind that a looped sound will continue to loop indefinitely unless you stop it by playing another wave or by stopping the looped wave with another call to PlaySound().

Because the high-level approach to playing sounds doesn't support sound mixing, when you loop a sound, it will be the only sound playing unless you stop it or allow another sound to interrupt it. In other words, a looped sound will steal the show in terms of your game's sound effects. For this reason, you're better off using MIDI music for background music, as opposed to sampled wave music. You learn how to play MIDI music in the next chapter.

Stopping a Wave Sound

If you ever use a looped wave, you will undoubtedly want to know how to stop it from playing at some point. Additionally, you might have a fairly lengthy wave sound that you'd like to be able to stop in case your game is deactivated or otherwise needs to slip into silent mode. You stop a wave from playing by using the SND_PURGE flag in the PlaySound() function. The SND_PURGE flag requires the first two arguments of PlaySound() to be used just as when you first played the sound. For example, if you provided a module handle as part of playing a wave resource, you'll still need to provide the handle when purging the wave.

It's always a good idea to provide an option for disabling sound in your games. It could be as simple as responding to the S key on the keyboard and toggling sound on and off, but there will undoubtedly be situations in which the player wants to turn off the sound.

The following is an example of stopping the looped sound played in the previous section:

```
PlaySound((LPCSTR)IDW_BACKBEAT, _hInstance, SND_PURGE ¦ SND_RESOURCE);
```

This example reveals how to stop a single wave from playing. It's also possible to stop any waves from playing so that you don't have to be so specific about what you're doing. This is accomplished by passing NULL as the first argument to PlaySound(), like this:

```
PlaySound(NULL, NULL, SND_PURGE);
```

This line of code results in the currently playing sound being stopped, regardless of what it is and how it was played.

Building the Brainiac 2 Example Program

You now have enough wave playing skills to see how waves are played in the context of a real game. In fact, instead of embarking on an entirely new game project, it makes sense to revisit a game you've already created and examine how to spiff it up with wave sounds. I'm referring to the Brainiac game from Chapter 6, "Example Game: Brainiac," which is a simple tile matching memory game, if you recall.

The Brainiac game isn't necessarily suffering from a lack of sound support, but it could definitely be made more interesting with some carefully injected waves. Think about how the game plays and how playing a wave sound here and there might improve its playability. After playing the game a few times and thinking about what would make it more fun, I came up with the following list of game events that could benefit from having sound effects associated with them:

- ▶ Selecting a tile
- ▶ Matching a pair of tiles
- ▶ Mismatching a pair of tiles
- ▶ Winning the game by matching all the tiles

If you play the game again and pay attention to each of these game events, you can start to see how a brief sound could add some interest to the game and make it a little more fun. The next few sections explore how to create a new version of the Brainiac game called Brainiac 2 that plays wave sounds in response to each of these game events.

Writing the Program Code

If you recall, the bulk of the code for the game logic in the Brainiac game resides in the MouseButtonDown() function. This function is called whenever the player clicks the mouse on the game screen and is therefore where all of the tile matching takes place. Not surprisingly, this function is where you'll find all the game events for the Brainiac game, such as tile selections, matches, and mismatches. Listing 12.1 shows the new MouseButtonDown() function, which includes several calls to the PlaySound() function to play sounds in response to game events.

LISTING 12.1 The MouseButtonDown() **Function Plays Wave Sounds in Response to Several Important Game Events**

```
void MouseButtonDown(int x, int y, BOOL bLeft)
{
  // Determine which tile was clicked
  int iTileX = x / g_pTiles[0]->GetWidth();
  int iTileY = y / g_pTiles[0]->GetHeight();

  // Make sure the tile hasn't already been matched
  if (!g_bTileStates[iTileX][iTileY])
  {
    // See if this is the first tile selected
    if (g_ptTile1.x == -1)
    {
      // Play a sound for the tile selection
      PlaySound((LPCSTR)IDW_SELECT, g_hInstance, SND_ASYNC | SND_RESOURCE);

      // Set the first tile selection
      g_ptTile1.x = iTileX;
      g_ptTile1.y = iTileY;
    }
    else if ((iTileX != g_ptTile1.x) || (iTileY != g_ptTile1.y))
    {
      if (g_ptTile2.x == -1)
      {
        // Play a sound for the tile selection
        PlaySound((LPCSTR)IDW_SELECT, g_hInstance, SND_ASYNC | SND_RESOURCE);

        // Increase the number of tries
        g_iTries++;

        // Set the second tile selection
        g_ptTile2.x = iTileX;
        g_ptTile2.y = iTileY;

        // See if it's a match
        if (g_iTiles[g_ptTile1.x][g_ptTile1.y] ==
          g_iTiles[g_ptTile2.x][g_ptTile2.y])
        {
          // Play a sound for the tile match
          PlaySound((LPCSTR)IDW_MATCH, g_hInstance, SND_ASYNC | SND_RESOURCE);
```

The standard PlaySound() function makes it very easy to play a sound upon selecting a tile.

continues

LISTING 12.1 Continued

```
                  // Set the tile state to indicate the match
                  g_bTileStates[g_ptTile1.x][g_ptTile1.y] = TRUE;
                  g_bTileStates[g_ptTile2.x][g_ptTile2.y] = TRUE;

                  // Clear the tile selections
                  g_ptTile1.x = g_ptTile1.y = g_ptTile2.x = g_ptTile2.y = -1;

                  // Update the match count and check for winner
                  if (++g_iMatches == 8)
                  {
                    // Play a victory sound
                    PlaySound((LPCSTR)IDW_WIN, g_hInstance, SND_ASYNC | SND_RESOURCE);
                    TCHAR szText[64];
                    wsprintf(szText, "You won in %d tries.", g_iTries);
                    MessageBox(g_pGame->GetWindow(), szText, TEXT("Brainiac"), MB_OK);
                  }
                }
                else
                  // Play a sound for the tile mismatch
                  PlaySound((LPCSTR)IDW_MISMATCH, g_hInstance, SND_ASYNC |
                    SND_RESOURCE);
              }
              else
              {
                // Clear the tile selections
                g_ptTile1.x = g_ptTile1.y = g_ptTile2.x = g_ptTile2.y = -1;
              }
            }

            // Force a repaint to update the tile
            InvalidateRect(g_pGame->GetWindow(), NULL, FALSE);
          }
}
```

Like the other PlaySound() calls in this example, this code plays a sound asynchronously, which means that the PlaySound() function returns immediately, instead of waiting for the sound to finish playing.

The first two calls to the PlaySound() function occur in response to tile selections. If you recall, two tiles must be selected in each turn of the game, so the IDW_SELECT sound is played in response to each of the two tile selections. The IDW_MATCH sound is played whenever a pair of tiles is successfully matched. Similarly, the IDW_MISMATCH sound is played whenever two mismatched tiles are selected. Finally, the IDW_WIN wave is played whenever all the tiles have been matched.

Assembling the Resources

Because waves are resources similar to bitmaps and icons, you must declare resource IDs for them, as well as include them in the resource script for your games. In the case of the Brainiac 2 game, the wave resource IDs are declared in the Resource.h header file, which is shown in Listing 12.2.

LISTING 12.2 The Resource.h Header File Defines New Resource IDs for the Wave Sounds

```
//----------------------------------.
// Icons                 Range : 1000 - 1999
//----------------------------------.
#define IDI_BRAINIAC       1000
#define IDI_BRAINIAC_SM    1001


//----------------------------------.
// Bitmaps               Range : 2000 - 2999
//----------------------------------.
#define IDB_TILEBLANK      2000
#define IDB_TILE1          2001
#define IDB_TILE2          2002
#define IDB_TILE3          2003
#define IDB_TILE4          2004
#define IDB_TILE5          2005
#define IDB_TILE6          2006
#define IDB_TILE7          2007
#define IDB_TILE8          2008


//----------------------------------.
// Wave Sounds           Range : 3000 - 3999
//----------------------------------.
#define IDW_SELECT         3000
#define IDW_MATCH          3001
#define IDW_MISMATCH       3002
#define IDW_WIN            3003
```

The wave resources all begin with the IDW_ prefix.

The in Listing 12.2 four wave resource IDs are declared in the Resource.h header file, which means that you can now place them in the Brainiac.rc resource script. This script is shown in Listing 12.3.

LISTING 12.3 The Brainiac.rc Resource Script Includes Four New Wave Resources

```
//----------------------------------.
// Include Files
//----------------------------------.
#include "Resource.h"


//----------------------------------.
// Icons
//----------------------------------.
IDI_BRAINIAC      ICON        "Res\\Brainiac.ico"
IDI_BRAINIAC_SM   ICON        "Res\\Brainiac_sm.ico"


//----------------------------------.
// Bitmaps
//----------------------------------.
IDB_TILEBLANK     BITMAP      "Res\\TileBlank.bmp"
IDB_TILE1         BITMAP      "Res\\Tile1.bmp"
IDB_TILE2         BITMAP      "Res\\Tile2.bmp"
```

continues

LISTING 12.3   Continued

```
IDB_TILE3        BITMAP        "Res\\Tile3.bmp"
IDB_TILE4        BITMAP        "Res\\Tile4.bmp"
IDB_TILE5        BITMAP        "Res\\Tile5.bmp"
IDB_TILE6        BITMAP        "Res\\Tile6.bmp"
IDB_TILE7        BITMAP        "Res\\Tile7.bmp"
IDB_TILE8        BITMAP        "Res\\Tile8.bmp"

//———————————————————————————————·
// Wave Sounds
//———————————————————————————————·
IDW_SELECT       WAVE          "Res\\Select.wav"
IDW_MATCH        WAVE          "Res\\Match.wav"
IDW_MISMATCH     WAVE          "Res\\Mismatch.wav"
IDW_WIN          WAVE          "Res\\Win.wav"
```

The WAVE *resource type is used to identify wave resources in the RC file.*

The resource script for the Brainiac 2 game is very similar to the original Brainiac resource script, except that it now includes wave resources. Notice that the resource type WAVE is used when listing each of the wave resources in the script. This script successfully maps the wave sounds to resource identifiers that can then be used with the PlaySound() function, as you saw in the previous section.

Construction Cue

If you happen to get a "multiple initialization" compiler error while compiling the Brainiac 2 program, you can easily fix it by removing the int variable declaration in the second group of for loops in the GameStart() function where the tiles are randomly initialized. This error stems from the fact that some compilers don't fully support the standard C++ approach of declaring loop initializer variables local to the loop. So, the int variable i is mistakenly interpreted as being declared twice. Just remove the second int declaration, and everything will work fine.

Construction Cue

As with most of the examples in the book, the Brainiac 2 program relies on the standard msimg32.lib and winmm.lib libraries. These libraries are included with most Windows compilers, but they aren't automatically linked into programs when you create a new project. If you are using your own project or make files, as opposed to using the ones provided on the CD-ROM, make sure that you change the link settings so that these library files are properly linked into the final executable. Refer to the documentation for your specific compiler for how this is done.

Testing the Finished Product

You already have a pretty good idea how to play the Brainiac game, so testing out the new wave sounds is very straightforward. Just take the game for a spin and pay attention to how sounds are played in response to different game events, such as selecting and matching tiles. Figure 12.2 shows the game in action.

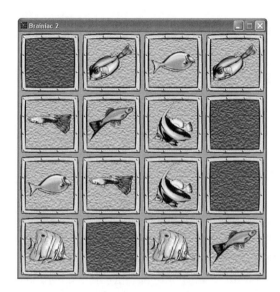

FIGURE 12.2
The Brainiac 2 game is made more interesting than its predecessor by playing wave sounds in response to game events.

Believe it or not, a sound is being played in this figure. Because I couldn't convince the publisher to include an audio tape with the book, you'll just have to imagine the sound as you look at the figure, or just fire up the game yourself and experience the sounds on your own!

Summary

Just as tiny colored squares called pixels allow you to represent images digitally, it is possible to represent a physical sound digitally by sampling it several thousand times a second. Sampled digital audio can be recorded in a variety of different sound qualities, which dramatically impact the size and memory requirements of the digital sounds. Digital sounds in Windows are known as waves and are stored in files with a .WAV file extension. This chapter showed you how to play wave sounds using a high-level Win32 API function called `PlaySound()`. Although this function certainly has its limitations, you can't beat it when it comes to sheer simplicity; a single line of code is all it takes to play a wave sound. You found out how to play wave sounds from a file or as a resource, as well as how to play looped wave sounds and how to stop a sound once it has started playing.

You might be wondering about the fact that this chapter focused solely on sampled digital audio, as opposed to MIDI music. The playback of wave sounds is, in fact, dramatically different than the playback of MIDI music at the programming level, which is why this chapter dodged the topic of playing MIDI music. However, the next chapter digs right into the playback of MIDI music, as well as how to add music to games.

Field Trip

For this field trip, you're going to need an electronic device capable of recording sounds. If you have one of those slick little digital audio recorders (some MP3 players have a record feature), you're in perfect shape; if not, you can also use a tape recorder. The goal of this field trip is to go record real world sounds for use in your games. So if you have a particular game in mind, you might already have some sound needs. You'll probably find that recording sounds is surprisingly fun, and it conveniently dodges copyright issues because they are your own sounds that you have exclusive rights to use.

To get started, walk around your house or office and experiment with making different noises using everyday items. It's interesting how you can turn a clack or clang sound into gunfire in the context of a game. If you live near a busy street, try recording some automobile sounds; the Henway game from the previous chapter is a good example of a game in which these sounds would be useful. If you have a game in mind with a nature theme, try going to a park and recording natural sounds—animals moving, water rushing, leaves rustling, and so on. Even the snap of a twig can be made into an interesting sound effect in some games. The process of recording sounds in the real world is limited only by your creativity.

CHAPTER 13

Playing MIDI Music

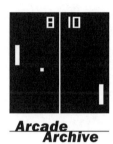

Arcade Archive

Having undoubtedly one of the strangest story lines in video game history, Dig Dug has endeared itself to quite a few gamers over the years. Dig Dug was released by Atari in 1982 as a game involving a robot guy named Dig Dug who digs tunnels below the ground while being chased by two enemies, Pooka and Fyger. The Dig Dug character can destroy enemies by inflating them with a pump until they explode. Dig Dug also involves some neat game play tricks, such as tunneling under rocks so that they fall and crush enemies. Although it doesn't rank quite as high as other classic games released during the same era, Dig Dug still has earned an important place in video game history.

Jaws is probably my favorite movie of all time, and few people who have seen the movie will ever forget the nerve-racking music used to communicate that the shark is about to strike. This is just one example of how simple music is capable of establishing a very specific mood. Video games are capable of using music in the same way. In fact, seeing as how movies are generally capable of being more expressive visually, it becomes even more important for games to take advantage of music as a means of reinforcing a mood or enhancing the reality of a virtual environment. MIDI music is one of the best ways to incorporate music into games, and this chapter shows you exactly how to play MIDI music with a relatively small amount of code.

In this chapter, you'll learn

▶ What MIDI means and how it relates to computer music

▶ About the Media Control Interface (MCI) and how it relates to MIDI music

▶ How to use the MCI to play MIDI music

▶ How to add MIDI music to a game

Feeling the Music with MIDI

Musical Instrument Digital Interface or *MIDI* started out in the early '80s as an attempt to establish a standard interface between musical instruments. The main use for MIDI back then was to enable a dedicated keyboard to control a synthesizer. Keyboard synthesizers consist of two main components: the keyboard and the synthesizer. The keyboard is responsible for keeping up with input information, such as which musical note is being generated and how hard the key is being pressed on the keyboard. The synthesizer, on the other hand, is responsible for generating sounds based on the input information provided by the keyboard. So, the original goal of MIDI was to provide a standardized approach to controlling a synthesizer with a keyboard. MIDI eventually expanded to support an incredibly wide range of musical instruments and devices, but the keyboard/synthesizer relationship is significant to MIDI as it applies to computers.

One way to view a MIDI device is as a note generator in the input sense and as a sound generator in the output sense. It isn't important how a MIDI device works internally as long as it adheres to a MIDI interface for generating or outputting notes. You might be thinking that the design of MIDI sounds somewhat reminiscent of the device-independent design of Windows, and in many ways, this comparison is accurate. Just as Windows makes it possible to mix and match different kinds of hardware and have them work together, MIDI makes it possible to connect different kinds of musical devices and have them work together. Most electronic musical equipment now comes standard with MIDI interface ports. In fact, most sound cards on modern computers have a MIDI-compatible interface through which a MIDI device can communicate with your computer.

Gamer's Garage

Computer MIDI ports are often also used as joystick ports. They are fairly easy to spot on the back of a sound card—look for a 15-pin connector, which will look noticeably different from the individual RCA jacks that make up most of a sound card's external interface.

Similar to wave sounds, MIDI music is digital. However, unlike waves, which are just approximations of analog sound waves, MIDI music consists of musical notes. In other words, a MIDI song consists of a series of carefully timed musical notes. This means that you can create a MIDI song much like you might write out a musical composition on paper. This task requires special software, but it is possible if you have the knowledge and skill to write music. Because MIDI music is composed of notes, rather than wave data, the resulting output sound quality is entirely dependent on the MIDI output device used to play the music. In the case of your computer, your sound card likely includes a MIDI synthesizer that can be used to play MIDI music. It's up to the synthesizer and Windows multimedia features to decide how the specific MIDI musical notes sound when played.

The main benefit of MIDI is that it allows you to use one MIDI device to control others. You can use a MIDI keyboard to play notes through another MIDI device, such as a MIDI sequencer. Even though you're generating notes by playing them on the keyboard, the actual instrument sounds are processed and output by the sequencer. In other words, you are *triggering* the sequencer with the keyboard. A similar situation occurs when you play MIDI music on your computer. The notes contained within the music are sent to the sound card where they trigger the synthesizer to play the actual sound.

I've mentioned MIDI music several times throughout this discussion, but I haven't really clarified how it is stored or how you work with it. Similar to waves, MIDI music is stored in files, but MIDI files have the file extension .MID. Unlike waves, MIDI music files are typically fairly small because musical notes simply don't take up a whole lot of space. Like waves, you can play MIDI files using Windows Media Player (see Figure 13.1). There is no built-in Windows tool for creating or editing MIDI files because creating MIDI music is more difficult than recording waves, and it involves a fair amount of music knowledge.

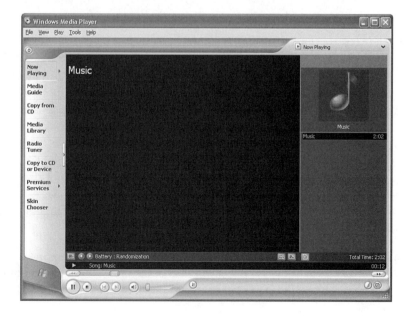

FIGURE 13.1
Windows Media Player can be used to play MIDI files, as well as wave files.

Playing a MIDI file in Windows Media Player is as simple as double-clicking the file in Windows Explorer. This works because MIDI files are automatically associated with Windows Media Player. You will likely use Windows Media Player to screen MIDI files for use in your games. On the other hand, if you're ambitious enough to create your own game music, you'll likely use Windows Media Player as a final means of testing a MIDI file before incorporating it into a game.

Understanding the Windows Media Control Interface

In the previous chapter, you found out that the Win32 API provides a single function, PlaySound(), that makes it possible to play wave sounds with very little effort. Unfortunately, there is no such function available for playing MIDI music. The Win32 API groups MIDI music with other kinds of multimedia objects, such as video clips, which require a different programming approach for playback. In order to play a MIDI song in a Windows program, you have to work with a special multimedia API known as the *Media Control Interface* or *MCI*. The Media Control Interface is a high-level API that allows you to control multimedia devices, such as a MIDI synthesizer or a video player. Because the MCI is so versatile in supporting a lot of different multimedia objects and devices, the MCI API is somewhat complex. The good news is that I'm going to carefully steer you through the MCI API and highlight only the portions you need in order to play MIDI music in games.

The idea behind the MCI is that you communicate with a multimedia device by sending it commands. A *command* is simply an instruction to carry out a particular action, such as playing, pausing, or stopping a song or video clip. Two kinds of commands are actually supported by the MCI: command messages and command strings. Both approaches work equally well, but for the sake of simplicity, I opted to use command messages to communicate with the MIDI synthesizer device throughout this chapter. A *command message* basically allows you to have a conversation with a multimedia device by sending it a message that tells it what to do. So, if you want to play a song, you send a command message that includes the name of the song file along with the *play* command. I'm simplifying things a little here, but hopefully, you get the idea.

Keep in mind that the Win32 API also supports a low-level programming interface that allows you to dig really deep into the details of multimedia programming. For example, you could use low-level multimedia functions to develop your own music editing software. However, the low-level multimedia API is extremely complex, so I don't recommend working with it until you have considerable experience with multimedia programming. Fortunately, you can accomplish everything you need for games without having to resort to low-level multimedia programming. Just use the MCI.

Using the MCI to Play MIDI Music

The device used to play MIDI music in a game is called the MIDI synthesizer, and its job is to take notes of music and play them aloud. The MIDI synthesizer isn't a physical device that you plug into your computer—it's built into your sound card. Just about every sound card these days includes a MIDI synthesizer, so you shouldn't have any trouble playing MIDI music. A big part of using the MCI to play MIDI music is establishing a line of communication with the MIDI synthesizer device. For example, you must first open the device before you can issue a command, such as playing a MIDI song. The next section shows you how to open the MIDI sequencer device for playing MIDI music, and subsequent sections reveal how to play MIDI songs.

Opening the MIDI Device

When working with MIDI devices using the MCI, it's important to understand that a device is referenced using a unique device identifier. So, when you open a MIDI device to play MIDI music, you'll want to keep track of the device ID that is returned when you first open the device. This ID is your ticket for communicating with the device from then on. You can think of the device ID as the phone number you need in order to call the device and tell it what you want it to do; the trick is to remember the ID when it is given to you after opening a MIDI device.

To perform any MIDI tasks with the MCI, you must get comfortable with the mciSendCommand() function, which sends a command string to a MIDI device. This function is described in the Win32 API as follows:

```
MCIERROR mciSendCommand(MCIDEVICEID IDDevice, UINT uiMsg, DWORD dwCommand,
  DWORD_PTR pdwParam);
```

The mciSendCommand() function is used to send command messages to a MIDI device. The arguments to this function vary depending on what kind of message you're sending, so we'll analyze them on a message-by-message basis. Before you can send a message to play a MIDI song, you must first open a MIDI device by sending an *open* message using the mciSendCommand() function. The *open* message

is called MCI_OPEN, and it requires the use of a special data structure called
MCI_OPEN_PARMS, which is defined as follows:

```
typedef struct {
  DWORD_PTR    dwCallback;
  MCIDEVICEID  wDeviceID;
  LPCSTR       lpstrDeviceType;
  LPCSTR       lpstrElementName;
  LPCSTR       lpstrAlias;
} MCI_OPEN_PARMS;
```

The only members of this structure that we're interested in are the middle three:
wDeviceID, lpstrDeviceType, and lpstrElementName. The wDeviceID member
stores the device ID for the MIDI sequencer and in our case will be used to retrieve
this ID. In other words, the wDeviceID member gets filled in with the device ID
when you open the device. The other two fields have to be specified when you
open the device. The lpstrDeviceType field must be set to the string "sequencer"
to indicate that you want to open the MIDI sequencer. The lpstrElementName
field must contain the name of the MIDI file that you want to play. This reveals
an interesting aspect of the MCI—you must specify a multimedia object when you
open a device. In other words, you don't just open a device and then decide what
multimedia file you want to play.

Although I could go on and on about how interesting the mciSendCommand() function is, I'd rather just show you the code for opening the MIDI sequencer device,
so here goes:

```
UINT uiMIDIPlayerID;
MCI_OPEN_PARMS mciOpenParms;
mciOpenParms.lpstrDeviceType = "sequencer";
mciOpenParms.lpstrElementName = "Music.mid";
if (mciSendCommand(NULL, MCI_OPEN, MCI_OPEN_TYPE | MCI_OPEN_ELEMENT,
  (DWORD_PTR)&mciOpenParms) == 0)
  // Get the ID for the MIDI player
  uiMIDIPlayerID = mciOpenParms.wDeviceID;
```

Hopefully, this code isn't too terribly shocking, considering that I just primed you
with a brief explanation of the MCI_OPEN_PARMS data structure. This code initializes the two important fields of this structure, lpstrDeviceType and
lpstrElementName, and then passes the entire structure as the last argument to
the mciSendCommand() function. Notice that the MIDI music file in this example is
named Music.mid. The first argument to the mciSendCommand() function is set to
zero because you don't yet know the ID of the device. The second argument,
MCI_OPEN, is the message you're sending to the MIDI sequencer. Finally, the third
argument identifies the fields of the MCI_OPEN_PARMS data structure that are to be
taken into consideration for the message.

> You might have noticed that the MCI approach to playing MIDI songs involves opening and playing a MIDI file, as opposed to using MIDI songs as resources. Unfortunately, there is no good workaround for this problem, so you won't be able to compile .MID music files into your executable game files as you've done with bitmaps and wave sounds. This means that you'll have to provide separate .MID files with your games when you distribute the games.

Construction Cue

If all goes well, the mciSendCommand() function returns 0 to indicate that the MIDI sequencer was successfully opened. You can then store away the device ID since it is now available in the wDeviceID field of the MCI_OPEN_PARMS data structure.

Playing a MIDI Song

Now that you have the MIDI sequencer opened for a specific MIDI song, you're ready to issue a play command and start playing the song. This is accomplished with the same mciSendCommand() function, but this time, you provide a different command. In this case, the command is MCI_PLAY, and its required arguments are somewhat simpler than those for the MCI_OPEN command. However, the MCI_PLAY command does involve another data structure, MCI_PLAY_PARMS, although you can leave it uninitialized when you're just playing a song from start to finish.

> The MCI_PLAY_PARMS data structure comes into play whenever you want a finer degree of control over how a MIDI song is played, such as selecting a different starting and ending point for the song.

Construction Cue

Unlike the MCI_OPEN command, which doesn't require a device ID, the MCI_PLAY command requires a device ID in order to successfully play a MIDI song. The following is code to play a song based on the previous code that opened the MIDI sequencer for the Music.mid song:

```
MCI_PLAY_PARMS mciPlayParms;
mciSendCommand(uiMIDIPlayerID, MCI_PLAY, 0, (DWORD_PTR)&mciPlayParms);
```

You're probably thinking that there must be a catch because this code looks way too simple. Unless you're wanting to do something tricky, such as skip the first three seconds of a MIDI song, this is all that's required to play a song from start to finish using the MCI. Notice that the device ID is provided in the first argument to mciSendCommand(), while the MCI_PLAY command is provided as the second argument. The third argument isn't applicable to the MCI_PLAY command, so you simply pass 0. Finally, the fourth argument isn't meaningful in this case either, but you must still pass a legitimate structure, even if it's just left uninitialized.

Pausing a MIDI Song

There are situations in which you will definitely want to pause a MIDI song while it's being played. For example, you don't want the music to continue playing when the main game window is deactivated. So, you need a way to pause a MIDI song. This is accomplished with the MCI_PAUSE command, which is surprisingly simple to use. The following is an example of pausing a MIDI song using the MCI_PAUSE command and the mciSendCommand() function:

```
mciSendCommand(uiMIDIPlayerID, MCI_PAUSE, 0, NULL);
```

Notice that the only two arguments of significance in this code are the device ID (the first argument) and the *pause* message (the second argument). The remaining two arguments have no bearing on the MCI_PAUSE command, so you can pass empty values for them. In order to play a MIDI song that has been paused, you just issue another *play* command.

Closing the MIDI Device

Of course, all good things must come to an end, and eventually, you'll want to close the MIDI sequencer device because you're finished with it or because you want to stop playing a song. The MCI_CLOSE command is used to close a MIDI device with the mciSendCommand() function. The following is an example of closing the MIDI sequencer by issuing an MCI_CLOSE command:

```
mciSendCommand(uiMIDIPlayerID, MCI_CLOSE, 0, NULL);
```

Similar to the MCI_PAUSE command, the only two arguments of significance in this code are the device ID (the first argument) and the *close* message (the second argument).

One point I haven't clarified with regard to playing and closing devices is that it's possible to encounter a problem when you attempt to play a MIDI song—in which case, the mciSendCommand() function will return a value other than 0 when you issue the MCI_PLAY command. In the earlier play example, I didn't bother looking at the return value of the mciSendCommand() function. However, it's a good idea to check and see if the song was successfully played because you should close the device if a problem occurred while playing the song. The following is revised play code that shows how to close the MIDI sequencer device if an error took place while playing the song:

```
MCI_PLAY_PARMS mciPlayParms;
if (mciSendCommand(uiMIDIPlayerID, MCI_PLAY, 0, (DWORD_PTR)&mciPlayParms) != 0)
{
```

```
  mciSendCommand(uiMIDIPlayerID, MCI_CLOSE, 0, NULL);
  uiMIDIPlayerID = 0;
}
```

This code checks the return value of the `mciSendCommand()` function for the *play* command and then closes the device if an error occurred. Notice that the device ID is also cleared after closing the device. This helps to make sure that you don't try to send any more commands to the device since the ID is no longer valid.

Adding MIDI Music Support to the Game Engine

Now that you're an MCI programming expert, you're no doubt ready to find out how to incorporate MIDI music capabilities into the game engine. You might not realize it, but you've already seen the majority of the MIDI code required to add music support to the game engine. It's mainly just a matter of creating a clean user interface for opening and closing the MIDI sequencer device, as well as playing MIDI songs.

> Don't forget that the entire source code for the game engine and all examples is included on the accompanying CD-ROM. I've deliberately avoided listing all the code for the game engine's MIDI functions here so that you can better spend your time focusing on the game-specific code.

Construction Cue

The first step required for adding MIDI support to the game engine is to keep track of the MIDI sequencer device ID. This is easily accomplished with a new member variable, which looks like this:

```
UINT m_uiMIDIPlayerID;
```

The `m_uiMIDIPlayerID` member variable contains the device ID for the MIDI sequencer. Any time the ID is not 0, you will know that you have the device open and ready for playing music. If this member variable is set to 0, the device is closed. This means that you need to initialize the `m_uiMIDIPlayerID` member variable to 0 in the `GameEngine()` constructor, like this:

```
m_uiMIDIPlayerID = 0;
```

This is the only change required in the `GameEngine()` constructor to support MIDI music, and it simply involves setting the `m_uiMIDIPlayerID` member variable to 0.

A moment ago, I mentioned that the most important requirement for the game engine with respect to MIDI music is to establish an interface for carrying out MIDI music tasks. The following are three new methods in the game engine that carry out important MIDI music playback tasks:

```
void PlayMIDISong(LPTSTR szMIDIFileName = TEXT(""), BOOL bRestart = TRUE);
void PauseMIDISong();
void CloseMIDIPlayer();
```

The roles of these methods hopefully are somewhat self-explanatory in that they are used to play a MIDI song, pause a MIDI song, and close the MIDI player (sequencer). You might be wondering why there isn't a method for opening the MIDI player. The opening of the player is actually handled within the PlayMIDISong() method. In fact, you'll notice that the PlayMIDISong() method has a string parameter that is the filename of the MIDI file to be played. This filename is used as the basis for opening the MIDI player. It might seem strange that the MIDI filename has a default value, meaning that you don't have to provide it if you don't want to. Calling the PlayMIDISong() method with no filename only works if you've already begun playing a song and it is now paused; it will resume playing the song.

The purpose for allowing you to pass an empty filename to the PlayMIDISong() method is to allow you to restart or resume the playback of a song that has already started playing. In this case, the second parameter to the method, bRestart, is used to determine how the song is played. Resuming playback would be useful if you had simply paused the music in a game, whereas restarting the playback would be useful if you were starting a new game and wanted to start the music over.

The PlayMIDISong() method is responsible for opening the MIDI player if it isn't already open. The method first checks to see if the player isn't yet open, and if it isn't, an *open* command is issued to open the MIDI sequencer device. The device ID for the MIDI sequencer is stored in the m_uiMIDIPlayerID variable. The PlayMIDISong() method continues by restarting the song if the bRestart argument is TRUE. The MIDI song is then played by issuing a play command via MCI. If the play command fails, the MIDI sequencer device is closed.

At some point, it's likely that you might want to pause a MIDI song once it has started playing. You can do this using the PauseMIDISong() method, which simply issues a *pause* command to the MIDI player, provided the device ID isn't set to 0.

The `CloseMIDIPlayer()` method is used to close the MIDI device and clear the device ID. This method first checks to make sure that the device is indeed open by checking to see if the device ID is not equal to 0. If the device is open, the `CloseMIDIPlayer()` method proceeds to close the device by issuing a *close* command and then clearing the device ID member variable.

> If you're using Visual C++ 6.0, you might need to change the type casts from (DWORD_PTR) to (DWORD) in GameEngine.cpp in order for the MIDI code to compile properly.

Construction Cue

Building the Henway 2 Example Program

You spent the previous section learning how to incorporate MIDI features into the game engine. By adding the code to the game engine, you've made it possible to play music in games with only a small amount of game code. In other words, the new and improved game engine now makes it painfully easy to add MIDI music support to any game. The remainder of this chapter proves my point by showing you how to add MIDI music to the Henway game that you developed back in Chapter 11, "Example Game: Henway." In fact, the Henway 2 game that you're about to develop not only includes MIDI music, but it also uses wave sounds to incorporate sound effects into the game. The MIDI music added to the game simply serves as background music to make the game a little more interesting. No doubt, you'll find the game to be a major improvement over its earlier version.

Writing the Program Code

The code for the audio supercharged Henway 2 game begins with the `GameStart()` function, which now includes a single line of code near the end that plays the MIDI song stored in the file Music.mid:

```
g_pGame->PlayMIDISong(TEXT("Music.mid"));
```

There isn't too much to say about this code because it simply passes the name of the MIDI song file to the `PlayMIDISong()` method in the game engine. This line of code shows how painfully easy the game engine makes it to play a MIDI song in a game.

Just as the `GameStart()` function opens the MIDI player by starting the playback of a MIDI song, the `GameEnd()` function is responsible for cleaning up by closing the MIDI player. The following line of code appears near the beginning of the `GameEnd()` function:

```
g_pGame->CloseMIDIPlayer();
```

The GameEnd() function performs the necessary MIDI music cleanup by calling the CloseMIDIPlayer() method to close the MIDI player.

Earlier in the chapter, I mentioned how it wouldn't be good for a MIDI song to continue playing if the game window is deactivated. In order to keep this from happening, it's important to pause the MIDI song when a window deactivation occurs and then play it again when the window regains activation. Listing 13.1 contains the code for the GameActivate() and GameDeactivate() functions, which are responsible for carrying out these tasks.

LISTING 13.1   The GameActivate() and GameDeactivate() Functions Are Used to Pause and Play the MIDI Song Based on the State of the Game Window

```
void GameActivate(HWND hWindow)
{
  // Capture the joystick
  g_pGame->CaptureJoystick();

  // Resume the background music
  g_pGame->PlayMIDISong(TEXT(""), FALSE);
}

void GameDeactivate(HWND hWindow)
{
  // Release the joystick
  g_pGame->ReleaseJoystick();

  // Pause the background music
  g_pGame->PauseMIDISong();
}
```

Calling PlayMIDISong() with an empty string and a value of FALSE results in the current MIDI song resuming play.

The GameActivate() function is responsible for continuing the playback of a paused MIDI song, and it does so by calling the PlayMIDISong() method and specifying FALSE as the second argument. If you recall from earlier in the chapter, the second argument determines whether the MIDI song is rewound before it is played. So, passing FALSE indicates that the song shouldn't be rewound, which has the effect of continuing playback from the previously paused position. The GameDeactivate() function performs an opposite task by pausing the MIDI song with a call to the PauseMIDISong() method.

The GameCycle() function doesn't have any MIDI-related code, but it does include some new sound effects code. More specifically, the GameCycle() function now plays car horn sounds at random intervals to help add some realism to the game (see Listing 13.2).

LISTING 13.2   The `GameCycle()` Function Randomly Plays Car Horn
Sounds

```
void GameCycle()
{
  if (!g_bGameOver)
  {
    // Play a random car sound randomly
    if (rand() % 100 == 0)
      if (rand() % 2 == 0)
        PlaySound((LPCSTR)IDW_CARHORN1, g_hInstance, SND_ASYNC | SND_RESOURCE);
      else
        PlaySound((LPCSTR)IDW_CARHORN2, g_hInstance, SND_ASYNC | SND_RESOURCE);

    // Update the sprites
    g_pGame->UpdateSprites();

    // Obtain a device context for repainting the game
    HWND  hWindow = g_pGame->GetWindow();
    HDC   hDC = GetDC(hWindow);

    // Paint the game to the offscreen device context
    GamePaint(g_hOffscreenDC);

    // Blit the offscreen bitmap to the game screen
    BitBlt(hDC, 0, 0, g_pGame->GetWidth(), g_pGame->GetHeight(),
      g_hOffscreenDC, 0, 0, SRCCOPY);

    // Cleanup
    ReleaseDC(hWindow, hDC);
  }
}
```

By randomly choosing between two different car horns, the traffic sounds more realistic.

The modified `GameCycle()` function establishes a 1 in 100 chance of playing a car
horn in every game cycle. Because the game cycles are flying by at 30 per second,
these really aren't as bad of odds as they sound. Whenever the odds do work out
and a car horn is played (on average about once every three seconds), another
random number is selected to see which car horn is played. You could have just
as easily played a single car horn, but having two horns with different sounds
makes the game much more interesting. The little touches like this make a game
more intriguing to players.

If you recall from the earlier design of the Henway game, you can start a new
game by clicking the mouse anywhere on the game screen after the game is over.
Listing 13.3 contains code for a new `MouseButtonDown()` function that restarts the
MIDI song as part of starting a new game.

LISTING 13.3 The `MouseButtonDown()` Function Restarts the MIDI Song to Coincide with a New Game

```
void MouseButtonDown(int x, int y, BOOL bLeft)
{
  // Start a new game, if necessary
  if (g_bGameOver)
  {
    // Restart the background music
    g_pGame->PlayMIDISong();

    // Initialize the game variables
    g_iNumLives = 3;
    g_iScore = 0;
    g_bGameOver = FALSE;
  }
}
```

Calling `PlayMIDISong()` with no parameters results in the current song restarting.

It makes sense to start the background music over when a new game starts. Because the default action of the `PlayMIDISong()` method is to rewind a song before playing it, it isn't necessary to pass any arguments to the method in this particular case.

Speaking of restarting the MIDI song, Listing 13.4 contains the code for the `HandleJoystick()` function, which also restarts the song as part of starting a new game.

LISTING 13.4 The `HandleJoystick()` Function Also Restarts the MIDI Song to Signal a New Game

```
void HandleJoystick(JOYSTATE jsJoystickState)
{
  if (!g_bGameOver && (++g_iInputDelay > 2))
  {
    // Check horizontal movement
    if (jsJoystickState & JOY_LEFT)
      MoveChicken(-20, 0);
    else if (jsJoystickState & JOY_RIGHT)
      MoveChicken(20, 0);

    // Check vertical movement
    if (jsJoystickState & JOY_UP)
      MoveChicken(0, -20);
    else if (jsJoystickState & JOY_DOWN)
      MoveChicken(0, 20);

    // Reset the input delay
    g_iInputDelay = 0;
  }

  // Check the joystick button and start a new game, if necessary
  if (g_bGameOver && (jsJoystickState & JOY_FIRE1))
```

```
  {
    // Restart the background music
    g_pGame->PlayMIDISong();
```

Restarting the background music is now part of starting a new game.

```
    // Initialize the game variables
    g_iNumLives = 3;
    g_iScore = 0;
    g_bGameOver = FALSE;
  }
}
```

The call to the PlayMIDISong() method again occurs with no arguments, which results in the MIDI song being started over at the beginning.

You've now seen all the MIDI music-related code in the Henway 2 game, but there are still some wave sound effects left to be played. Two of these sound effects are played in the SpriteCollision() function, which is shown in Listing 13.5.

LISTING 13.5 The SpriteCollision() Function Plays Sound Effects in Response to the Chicken Getting Run Over and the Game Ending

```
BOOL SpriteCollision(Sprite* pSpriteHitter, Sprite* pSpriteHittee)
{
  // See if the chicken was hit
  if (pSpriteHittee == g_pChickenSprite)
  {
    // Move the chicken back to the start
    g_pChickenSprite->SetPosition(4, 175);

    // See if the game is over
    if (--g_iNumLives > 0)
      // Play a sound for the chicken getting hit
      PlaySound((LPCSTR)IDW_SQUISH, g_hInstance, SND_ASYNC | SND_RESOURCE);
    else
    {
      // Play a sound for the game ending
      PlaySound((LPCSTR)IDW_GAMEOVER, g_hInstance, SND_ASYNC | SND_RESOURCE);

      // Display game over message
      TCHAR szText[64];
      wsprintf(szText, "Game Over! You scored %d points.", g_iScore);
      MessageBox(g_pGame->GetWindow(), szText, TEXT("Henway 2"), MB_OK);
      g_bGameOver = TRUE;

      // Pause the background music
      g_pGame->PauseMIDISong();
    }

    return FALSE;
  }

  return TRUE;
}
```

The squish sound adds a bit of tragic humor to the game.

If you remember, the SpriteCollision() function is where you detect a collision between the chicken and a car. This makes it an ideal place to play a squish sound when the chicken is run over. Similarly, the SpriteCollision() function also knows when the game ends, so it only makes sense to play a sound whenever the player runs out of chickens.

The final sound effects in the Henway 2 game occur in the MoveChicken() function, which is where the chicken is moved and is also where the game determines when the chicken has made it across the road. Listing 13.6 shows how a movement sound is made with each chicken move, along with a celebration sound that is played each time the chicken makes it safely across the road.

LISTING 13.6   The MoveChicken() **Helper Function Plays a Celebration Sound Whenever the Chicken Makes It Safely Across the Road**

```
void MoveChicken(int iXDistance, int iYDistance)
{
  // Play the "bok" chicken sound
  PlaySound((LPCSTR)IDW_BOK, g_hInstance, SND_ASYNC | SND_NOSTOP | SND_RESOURCE);

  // Move the chicken to its new position
  g_pChickenSprite->OffsetPosition(iXDistance, iYDistance);

  // See if the chicken made it across
  if (g_pChickenSprite->GetPosition().left > 400)
  {
    // Play a sound for the chicken making it safely across
    PlaySound((LPCSTR)IDW_CELEBRATE, g_hInstance, SND_ASYNC | SND_RESOURCE);

    // Move the chicken back to the start and add to the score
    g_pChickenSprite->SetPosition(4, 175);
    g_iScore += 150;
  }
}
```

The "bok" chicken sound is played with the SND_NOSTOP option so that it doesn't interrupt any other sounds that are playing.

Whenever the chicken moves, this function first plays a "bok" sound that's similar to the noise a chicken makes in real life. It's very important to note a subtle trick in this code that keeps the sound effects in the game rolling along smoothly. The "bok" sound is played with the SND_NOSTOP flag in the PlaySound() function, which means that it isn't allowed to interrupt any other sound already playing. This is necessary because the chicken is constantly being moved during the game, and the "bok" sound would interrupt the car horn sounds and dominate the sound effects in the game. The result of this code is that no "bok" sound is allowed to play during a car honk, but otherwise, you hear the chicken moving around—this is a very good trade-off in terms of sacrificing a little on one sound effect to allow another to be heard.

The MoveChicken() function also makes sure that a celebration wave sound is played whenever the chicken successfully crosses the road. This might be a small concession for working so hard to get the chicken across, but keep in mind that the previous version of the game offered no audible reward at all!

Construction Cue

Testing the Finished Product

You'll find that testing sounds and music in games is initially one of the most exciting test phases of a game, but eventually, it becomes quite monotonous. The music in the Henway 2 game (see Figure 13.2) will no doubt haunt me for years considering that I had to listen to it over and over as I developed and debugged the game. You will likely experience the same joy and frustration when developing and testing your own games that take advantage of wave sounds and music.

FIGURE 13.2
Although the Henway 2 example game looks harmless enough here in print, listening to game music for hours on end while developing and debugging a game can drive you crazy.

To test the Henway 2 game, just launch the game and listen. The music will immediately start playing, and you'll quickly begin hearing random car horns that help create the atmosphere of busy traffic buzzing by the chicken. You will notice the new sound effects as you safely navigate the chicken across the road, as well as when you get run over. More important from the perspective of the MIDI music is to test the game as it is deactivated and then reactivated. Just minimize the game or activate a different program to see how the game responds. The music should immediately stop playing. Reactivating the game results in the music continuing to play from where it left off.

Summary

Just as sound effects add interest and excitement to specific events that take place in a game, music can be extremely effective in establishing a mood or simply making a game more fun. This chapter explored MIDI music and how to work with it at the programming level. You learned about the Media Control Interface or MCI, which is used to play MIDI songs without having to get into a bunch of messy low-level code. You then took your new MCI programming knowledge and used it to add MIDI music support to the game engine. Finally, you revisited the Henway game from Chapter 11 and added both MIDI music and wave sound effects to it.

The next chapter pulls together everything you've learned throughout the book thus far in the creation of another complete game. The game is called Battle Office, and I think you'll find it to be a pretty neat little game.

Field Trip

Try watching a scary movie with the sound turned off, and you'll get a feel for how music (or the lack thereof) dramatically impacts the suspense of a movie. This same scenario applies to games, and simply changing the music in a game can make the game "feel" completely different. To experiment with how this works, try changing the MIDI music for the Henway 2 game to a different tune. Keep in mind that the MIDI music file isn't stored as a resource in the compiled executable, so all you really have to do is copy a different music file over the Music.mid file included in the Henway 2 code. You might want to save or rename the original Music.mid file so that you still have it, or you might find that your new music is a dramatic improvement to the game.

CHAPTER 14

Example Game: Battle Office

Arcade Archive

Quick, what futuristic 1982 Disney movie starred Jeff Bridges and served as the first major motion picture to use computer-generated special effects? Give up? It's the movie *Tron*, which is about a computer hacker who is beamed into cyberspace to do battle with an evil computer program with the intent of taking over the world. *Tron*, the movie, spawned Tron, the video game, which was released in 1982 by Bally Midway. Tron, the video game, was incredibly popular, primarily because it divided game play into four mini-games. Tron is still very popular today among arcade game collectors, largely because it has a visually appealing case with an illuminated joystick. Tron is perhaps the only arcade game to name its levels after programming languages. What's not to like about that?

Well, here you are, ready to embark on your fourth complete game. At this point in the book, you've successfully added wave sound effects and MIDI music programming to your repertoire of game development skills. What better way to celebrate than to design and develop another game to put the skills to good use? This chapter leads you through the construction of a game called Battle Office that chronicles an interoffice war between co-workers. Don't worry: It's not as violent as it sounds. The job of the player in the game is to use the mouse to fire at co-workers as they appear in various places on the game screen. The game makes interesting use of the sprite classes, as well as wave sound effects and music.

In this chapter, you'll learn

▶ How to design a game called Battle Office that simulates a battle between co-workers within an office

▶ How to write the code for the Battle Office game

▶ About the joys of testing a completely new game

How Does the Game Play?

I once worked at a software company where it was fairly common for balls and other objects to be thrown around for fun while taking a break from the seriousness of programming. On some rare occasions, the speed of the throws would increase to the point where an all-out game of dodge ball erupted. Sometimes the games were friendly, and sometimes they progressed to being almost dangerous. In fact, prior to me joining the company, there was a story of a guy being knocked out because someone threw a small bag of change that caught him in the head—not a good idea! In case you're thinking about starting your own interoffice dodge ball game, I encourage you to use soft balls and to make sure that everyone is up for it before firing the first shot.

My experience hurling balls and other objects at people in my former job serves as the inspiration for the Battle Office game, which involves firing at co-workers in an office environment. The game screen in Battle Office consists of an office space with several desks and a doorway in the back. Co-workers will periodically pop up from behind their desks, as well as run by in the background through the doorway. Your job is simple: Bean every co-worker who appears onscreen.

Gamer's Garage

Although the Battle Office game does simulate a battle, it's safe to say that it's a friendly battle. In fact, the specifics of what is being fired at the co-workers are deliberately left vague so that the player can imagine what is being fired. These could be paper wads, Koosh balls, rubber bands, or dinner rolls—it's up to the player's imagination to fill in the blanks here.

If the object of the game is to shoot every person who appears on the screen, you might be wondering how you lose. Since the Battle Office game is all about efficiency and perfection, you are only allowed so many misses. In other words, each time a person on the screen escapes, it is considered a miss because he got away. When you run out of misses, the game ends. On the other hand, the game keeps track of how many people you successfully hit, so there is a score to gauge how well you're playing.

Construction Cue

An interesting enhancement to the Battle Office game would be to add an innocent co-worker who pops up or runs by from time to time. Firing and hitting the innocent co-worker would take away points; the resulting effect would be that the player would be forced to look and decide whether a target is legitimate before firing, as opposed to shooting at everything that moves. I encourage you to consider adding this enhancement to the game after you finish the chapter and have some time to tinker with it.

Designing the Game

The design of the Battle Office game flows fairly smoothly from the overview of the game that you just went through. You know that there is a background image required to show the office inhabited by the people at whom you're shooting. You also know that the people themselves can probably be represented by sprites. Granted, not all the people are moving, but keep in mind that sprites can be used in a variety of different ways. For example, you can use a sprite to simply show and hide an image of a person, as well as perform *hit testing* on the sprite to see if it has been clicked with the mouse. This approach works well for the people hiding behind desks. Similarly, sprites can be used to represent the people running in the back of the office.

To help you get a feel for how the Battle Office game is laid out, take a look at Figure 14.1.

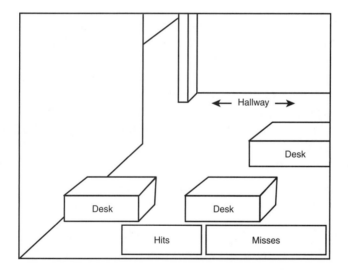

FIGURE 14.1
The Battle Office game consists of an office with desks behind which people can hide, as well as a hallway through which people can run back and forth.

Notice that the office in the figure includes three desks that are suitable for people to hide behind, along with a hallway. The hallway provides a way for people to run back and forth, which supplies you with moving targets at which to shoot. Again, the main premise of the game is to shoot at the office workers as they pop up from behind desks and run back and forth down the hallway. In the lower-right corner of the game screen, you'll notice that there are boxes to display the number of hits and misses in the game.

As I mentioned earlier, your weapon is up to your imagination; all you use to shoot people is a special bull's-eye sprite designed to follow the mouse pointer. It's probably a little healthier to think in terms of using a "friendly" weapon, such as a wad of paper, but this is ultimately up to each individual player. Rather than focus on a weapon, the game instead displays a red bull's-eye that you control with the mouse and use to shoot the people in the office. When you score a hit, a "pow" image is displayed to indicate that you hit the target.

Now that you understand the basics of the game and how it is played, it's time to examine what kinds of sprites need to be used. The following is a list of the sprites that go into the Battle Office game:

- Five office worker sprites
- Target sprite
- Pow sprite (as in "Pow!")

The five office worker sprites represent the people in the office at whom you are shooting when you play the game. Three of these people sprites are stationary behind desks and simply appear and disappear, whereas the two others run across the hallway near the back of the office. The target sprite is the bull's-eye that you use to aim with the mouse. Finally, the pow sprite is used to indicate that you've scored a hit, and it is placed directly over the person you've hit. Although you can certainly score multiple hits throughout the game, a single pow sprite is sufficient to represent each hit; the sprite is simply moved to the new hit location when a new hit occurs.

Beyond the sprites, the Battle Office game also requires several bitmaps. The following are the ten bitmap images required of the game:

- Background office image
- Bull's-eye target image (see Figure 14.2)
- Pow image (see Figure 14.3)
- Five office worker images (see Figure 14.4)
- Small office worker image (see Figure 14.5)
- Game over image (see Figure 14.9)

FIGURE 14.2
The bull's-eye target bitmap image shows a bull's-eye with transparent areas around the red circles.

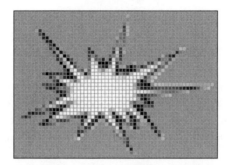

FIGURE 14.3
The pow bitmap image shows a comic book style "explosion" to indicate a hit in the game.

FIGURE 14.4
There are a variety of different worker bitmap images—some of which are cut off to appear as if they are standing behind a desk.

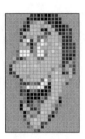

The background and game over images should be pretty obvious, given the game design thus far, and the others are shown in the figures. Even so, you're probably curious about the small office worker image, which is used to indicate how many people you've missed. When the game begins, there are no misses, so none of the small worker images are displayed. As the game progresses and some of the people get away, the small worker image is drawn repeatedly to indicate each miss. Five misses result in the game ending; in which case, the game over image is displayed.

Now that you have a feel for the graphical objects involved in the game, let's consider other data that must be maintained by the game. First, it's pretty obvious that you'll need to keep track of how many misses you've had because it determines when the game ends. It's also important to keep track of the number of hits so that you'll have a means of keeping score—the number of hits is the score in the Battle Office game. A Boolean variable to keep track of whether or not the game is over is also required.

A couple of other pieces of information that aren't immediately obvious involve the manner in which the office workers are displayed. By the way, when you see the bitmaps, you'll realize that all the workers are men, so I've opted to refer to them as "guys" in the game code. So, I might as well start using the same terminology in this discussion. The game displays the five different guys at random time intervals, which gives the game a more spontaneous feel. In order to establish these intervals, you need to keep track of each guy's time delay. Additionally, the game is much better if it gradually gets harder the longer you play. So, a master delay is used to provide a means of slowly reducing the length of time the stationary guys appear on screen. In other words, the guys behind the desks slowly begin appearing for shorter periods of time, which makes it harder to shoot them.

> Feel free to change the bitmaps in the game to anything you want, including you and your real friends or co-workers. I didn't deliberately leave women and children out of the game graphics; it just worked out that the artwork I found was all of men.

Construction Cue

To recap the data requirements of the Battle Office game, the game design has led us to the following pieces of information that must be managed by the game:

- ▶ The number of guys missed
- ▶ The number of guys hit
- ▶ A Boolean game over variable
- ▶ A delay variable for each guy
- ▶ A master delay variable for controlling the game's difficulty level

With this information in mind, you're now ready to move on and assemble the code for the Battle Office game.

Building the Game

The construction of the Battle Office game follows the same pattern you've grown accustomed to in other examples and games. The next few sections guide you through the development of the game's code and resources.

Writing the Program Code

The code for the Battle Office game begins in the BattleOffice.h header file, which is responsible for declaring the global variables used throughout the game. Listing 14.1 contains the code for this file.

LISTING 14.1   The BattleOffice.h Header File Declares Global Variables that Are Used to Manage the Game

```
#pragma once

//---------------------------------------------.
// Include Files
//---------------------------------------------.
#include <windows.h>
#include "Resource.h"
#include "GameEngine.h"
#include "Bitmap.h"
#include "Sprite.h"
```

continues

LISTING 14.1   Continued

```
//----------------------------------------.
// Global Variables
//----------------------------------------.
HINSTANCE    g_hInstance;
GameEngine*  g_pGame;
HDC          g_hOffscreenDC;
HBITMAP      g_hOffscreenBitmap;
Bitmap*      g_pOfficeBitmap;
Bitmap*      g_pTargetBitmap;
Bitmap*      g_pPowBitmap;
Bitmap*      g_pGuyBitmaps[5];
Bitmap*      g_pSmallGuyBitmap;
Bitmap*      g_pGameOverBitmap;
Sprite*      g_pTargetSprite;
Sprite*      g_pPowSprite;
Sprite*      g_pGuySprites[5];
int          g_iGuyDelay[5];
int          g_iGuyMasterDelay;
int          g_iHits;
int          g_iMisses;
BOOL         g_bGameOver;
```

The target sprite is visible in the game all the time, whereas the pow sprite is only shown when a hit occurs.

The guy master delay controls the difficulty level of the game by specifying the minimum amount of time between displaying new guys; as this value goes down, the game gets harder.

As the listing reveals, the global variables for the Battle Office game largely consist of the different bitmaps used throughout the game. The offscreen device context and bitmap are declared first, as well as the different bitmaps that make up the game's graphics. The sprite variables for the game are declared after the bitmaps, and they include the target sprite, the pow sprite, and the five guy sprites. The delays for each of the five guys are then declared, along with the master delay that controls the game's difficulty level. Finally, the number of hits and misses are declared, as well as the familiar game over Boolean variable.

The initialization of the game variables primarily takes place in the GameStart() function, which is shown in Listing 14.2.

LISTING 14.2   The GameStart() Function Initializes the Bitmaps, Sprites, and Game State Variables

```
void GameStart(HWND hWindow)
{
  // Seed the random number generator
  srand(GetTickCount());

  // Create the offscreen device context and bitmap
  g_hOffscreenDC = CreateCompatibleDC(GetDC(hWindow));
  g_hOffscreenBitmap = CreateCompatibleBitmap(GetDC(hWindow),
    g_pGame->GetWidth(), g_pGame->GetHeight());
  SelectObject(g_hOffscreenDC, g_hOffscreenBitmap);

  // Create and load the bitmaps
```

```
HDC hDC = GetDC(hWindow);
g_pOfficeBitmap = new Bitmap(hDC, IDB_OFFICE, g_hInstance);
g_pTargetBitmap = new Bitmap(hDC, IDB_TARGET, g_hInstance);
g_pPowBitmap = new Bitmap(hDC, IDB_POW, g_hInstance);
g_pGuyBitmaps[0] = new Bitmap(hDC, IDB_GUY1, g_hInstance);
g_pGuyBitmaps[1] = new Bitmap(hDC, IDB_GUY2, g_hInstance);
g_pGuyBitmaps[2] = new Bitmap(hDC, IDB_GUY3, g_hInstance);
g_pGuyBitmaps[3] = new Bitmap(hDC, IDB_GUY4, g_hInstance);
g_pGuyBitmaps[4] = new Bitmap(hDC, IDB_GUY5, g_hInstance);
g_pSmallGuyBitmap = new Bitmap(hDC, IDB_SMALLGUY, g_hInstance);
g_pGameOverBitmap = new Bitmap(hDC, IDB_GAMEOVER, g_hInstance);

// Create the target, pow, and guy sprites
RECT    rcBounds = { 0, 0, 500, 400 };
g_pTargetSprite = new Sprite(g_pTargetBitmap, rcBounds, BA_STOP);
g_pTargetSprite->SetZOrder(4);
g_pGame->AddSprite(g_pTargetSprite);
g_pPowSprite = new Sprite(g_pPowBitmap, rcBounds, BA_STOP);
g_pPowSprite->SetZOrder(3);
g_pPowSprite->SetHidden(TRUE);
g_pGame->AddSprite(g_pPowSprite);
g_pGuySprites[0] = new Sprite(g_pGuyBitmaps[0], rcBounds);
g_pGuySprites[0]->SetPosition(92, 175);
g_pGuySprites[0]->SetZOrder(2);
g_pGuySprites[0]->SetHidden(TRUE);
g_pGame->AddSprite(g_pGuySprites[0]);
g_pGuySprites[1] = new Sprite(g_pGuyBitmaps[1], rcBounds);
g_pGuySprites[1]->SetPosition(301, 184);
g_pGuySprites[1]->SetZOrder(2);
g_pGuySprites[1]->SetHidden(TRUE);
g_pGame->AddSprite(g_pGuySprites[1]);
g_pGuySprites[2] = new Sprite(g_pGuyBitmaps[2], rcBounds);
g_pGuySprites[2]->SetPosition(394, 61);
g_pGuySprites[2]->SetZOrder(2);
g_pGuySprites[2]->SetHidden(TRUE);
g_pGame->AddSprite(g_pGuySprites[2]);
rcBounds.left = 340;
g_pGuySprites[3] = new Sprite(g_pGuyBitmaps[3], rcBounds, BA_WRAP);
g_pGuySprites[3]->SetPosition(500, 10);
g_pGuySprites[3]->SetVelocity(-3, 0);
g_pGuySprites[3]->SetZOrder(1);
g_pGuySprites[3]->SetHidden(TRUE);
g_pGame->AddSprite(g_pGuySprites[3]);
rcBounds.left = 385;
g_pGuySprites[4] = new Sprite(g_pGuyBitmaps[4], rcBounds, BA_WRAP);
g_pGuySprites[4]->SetPosition(260, 60);
g_pGuySprites[4]->SetVelocity(5, 0);
g_pGuySprites[4]->SetZOrder(1);
g_pGuySprites[4]->SetHidden(TRUE);
g_pGame->AddSprite(g_pGuySprites[4]);

// Initialize the remaining global variables
```

The target sprite's Z-order is highest, followed by the pow sprite and then the guy sprites.

continues

LISTING 14.2 Continued

The initial value of the guy master delay was arrived at primarily through trial and error and provides a good example of how you have to test a game to find suitable default values for game play variables.

```
g_iGuyMasterDelay = 50;
g_iHits = 0;
g_iMisses = 0;
g_bGameOver = FALSE;

// Play the background music
g_pGame->PlayMIDISong(TEXT("Music.mid"));
}
```

I know that's a heck of a lot of code for a function whose only job is to get the game started. However, you have to consider what it takes to start a game like this. The bitmaps must be loaded and the sprites must be created—not to mention initializing the other global variables in the game and starting the background music. Of course, a few specific parts of this function are worth closer attention.

First, notice that the target sprite is set so that it stops when it reaches the boundary of the game screen. This ensures that the bull's-eye target is always visible on the screen, no matter where you drag the mouse. Similarly, the pow sprite is also given the stop bounds action, as well as being hidden when the game first starts. This sprite is only displayed when a successful hit is made, which is why it begins the game hidden. At this point, it's worth pointing out that the Z-order of the target sprite is set higher than that of the pow sprite, whereas the pow sprite's Z-order is set higher than those of the guy sprites. This results in the target sprite always appearing on top of the other sprites, whereas the pow sprite appears on top of the guys.

The first three guy sprites are created at fixed positions on the screen and are also hidden. The fixed positions are already calculated to display each guy so that he appears to be standing behind a desk in the background office image. The remaining two guy sprites are designed to move across the hallway section of the office background so that they appear to be running. For this reason, the sprites are given velocities that cause them to move horizontally across the screen. These sprites are also hidden, which enables the game to start with no guys in the office.

The other global variables in the Battle Office game are initialized with values suitable for the game's start. For example, the master delay for the guys is set to 50, which is a value that you'll get a better understanding of a little later in the chapter. The hits and misses are then zeroed out, and the game over variable is set to FALSE. Finally, the PlayMIDISong() method of the game engine is used to start playing the background music for the game.

Although it is longer than what you've seen in most of the examples throughout the book thus far, the GameEnd() function is still much smaller than the GameStart() function you just saw. Listing 14.3 contains the code for the GameEnd() function.

LISTING 14.3   The GameEnd() Function Cleans Up After the Game

```
void GameEnd()
{
  // Close the MIDI player for the background music
  g_pGame->CloseMIDIPlayer();

  // Cleanup the offscreen device context and bitmap
  DeleteObject(g_hOffscreenBitmap);
  DeleteDC(g_hOffscreenDC);

  // Cleanup the bitmaps
  delete g_pOfficeBitmap;
  delete g_pTargetBitmap;
  delete g_pPowBitmap;
  for (int i = 0; i < 5; i++)
    delete g_pGuyBitmaps[i];
  delete g_pSmallGuyBitmap;
  delete g_pGameOverBitmap;

  // Cleanup the sprites
  g_pGame->CleanupSprites();

  // Cleanup the game engine
  delete g_pGame;
}
```

As you can see, this function is responsible for performing a variety of different cleanup tasks for the Battle Office game. The first step is to close the MIDI player. The bitmaps and sprites are then wiped away, and the game engine is deleted.

Because the Battle Office game plays MIDI music, you know that it's important to pause and resume the music appropriately when the game is deactivated and reactivated. These actions take place in the familiar GameActivate() and GameDeactivate() functions, which you've already seen performing these tasks in other examples.

The game screen in the Battle Office game is painted entirely by the GamePaint() function, which is shown in Listing 14.4.

LISTING 14.4 The GamePaint() Function Draws the Office Background Bitmap, the Sprites, and the Number of Hits and Misses

```
void GamePaint(HDC hDC)
{
  // Draw the background office
  g_pOfficeBitmap->Draw(hDC, 0, 0);

  // Draw the sprites
  g_pGame->DrawSprites(hDC);

  // Draw the number of guys who were hit
  TCHAR szText[64];
  RECT  rect = { 237, 360, 301, 390 };
  wsprintf(szText, "%d", g_iHits);
  DrawText(hDC, szText, -1, &rect, DT_SINGLELINE | DT_CENTER | DT_VCENTER);

  // Draw the number of guys who were missed (got away)
  for (int i = 0; i < g_iMisses; i++)
    g_pSmallGuyBitmap->Draw(hDC, 389 + (g_pSmallGuyBitmap->GetWidth() * i),
      359, TRUE);

  // Draw the game over message, if necessary
  if (g_bGameOver)
    g_pGameOverBitmap->Draw(hDC, 120, 110, TRUE);
}
```

The standard DrawText() function requires you to draw text within a specified rectangle.

This GamePaint() function is responsible for drawing all the game graphics for the game. The function begins by drawing the background office image, and then it draws the game sprites. The remainder of the function primarily draws the number of hits and misses in the lower-right corner of the game screen. The hits are drawn as a number using the Win32 DrawText() function. The misses, on the other hand, are drawn using small guy bitmaps. A small guy is drawn for each guy who was missed, which helps you know how many additional guys can escape before the game ends.

The GameCycle() function controls most of the game play in the Battle Office game and also works closely with GamePaint() to update the game's sprites and reflect the changes onscreen. Listing 14.5 shows the code for the GameCycle() function.

LISTING 14.5 The GameCycle() Function Randomly Controls the Guys in the Office and Determines if the Game Has Ended

```
void GameCycle()
{
  if (!g_bGameOver)
  {
    // Randomly show and hide the guys
    for (int i = 0; i < 5; i++)
```

```
    if (g_pGuySprites[i]->IsHidden())
    {
      if (rand() % 60 == 0)
      {
        // Show the guy
        g_pGuySprites[i]->SetHidden(FALSE);

        // Start the countdown delay
        if (i == 3)
        {
          // Start the guy running left
          g_iGuyDelay[i] = 80;
          g_pGuySprites[i]->SetPosition(500, 10);
        }
        else if (i == 4)
        {
          // Start the guy running right
          g_iGuyDelay[i] = 45;
          g_pGuySprites[i]->SetPosition(260, 60);
        }
        else
          // Start the stationary guys
          g_iGuyDelay[i] = 20 + (rand() % g_iGuyMasterDelay);
      }
    }
    else
    {
      if (—g_iGuyDelay[i] == 0)
      {
        // Play a sound for the guy getting away
        PlaySound((LPCSTR)IDW_TAUNT, g_hInstance, SND_ASYNC | SND_RESOURCE);

        // Hide the guy
        g_pGuySprites[i]->SetHidden(TRUE);

        // Increment the misses
        if (++g_iMisses == 5)
        {
          // Play a sound for the game ending
          PlaySound((LPCSTR)IDW_BOO, g_hInstance, SND_ASYNC | SND_RESOURCE);

          // End the game
          for (int i = 0; i < 5; i++)
            g_pGuySprites[i]->SetHidden(TRUE);
          g_bGameOver = TRUE;

          // Pause the background music
          g_pGame->PauseMIDISong();
        }
      }
    }

// Update the sprites
g_pGame->UpdateSprites();

// Obtain a device context for repainting the game
```

This code positions and sets the velocity for the guy running to the left.

This code positions and sets the velocity for the guy moving to the right.

The stationary guys are simply shown (not hidden) for a specified amount of time.

If five guys have gotten away, end the game.

continues

LISTING 14.5   Continued

```
    HWND   hWindow = g_pGame->GetWindow();
    HDC    hDC = GetDC(hWindow);

    // Paint the game to the offscreen device context
    GamePaint(g_hOffscreenDC);

    // Blit the offscreen bitmap to the game screen
    BitBlt(hDC, 0, 0, g_pGame->GetWidth(), g_pGame->GetHeight(),
      g_hOffscreenDC, 0, 0, SRCCOPY);

    // Cleanup
    ReleaseDC(hWindow, hDC);
  }
}
```

The GameCycle() function is one of the heftiest functions you've seen thus far in the book, and there's a good reason for it. This function is carrying out a great deal of the Battle Office game logic by determining when and how the office guys appear. The function first loops through the five guy sprites, checking to make sure that each one is hidden before attempting to show it. If the guy is hidden, he is first made visible. Then some interesting things take place, depending upon which guy is being shown. If one of the moving guys is being shown, which is indicated by an array index value of 3 or 4, a countdown delay is started, and the sprite position is set. The position makes sure that the guy starts moving from the edge of the game screen, whereas the delay gives him just enough time to run across the hallway before being hidden again. If the guy sprite is not one of the moving guys, a delay is set based on the master delay, which gets shorter as the game progresses. The idea is that the stationary guys will be displayed for shorter and shorter periods of time as the game continues.

If the first sprite check inside the loop shows that the guy sprite is already being displayed, the delay is decreased and checked to see if the guy has been shown long enough to hide him again. In other words, this is the part of the game logic that counts down the delay and results in each guy only being on the screen for a limited amount of time before being hidden again. If the delay gets to 0 before the guy is shot, he gets away. If the guy gets away, the first step is to play a sound effect to let the player know. The guy sprite is then hidden, and the number of misses is increased by one.

Because the number of misses is being increased, this is a good spot to check and see if the game is over. If there have been five misses, the game is over. A sound effect is then played to let the player know that the game is over, and the guy sprites are all hidden. Ending the game also involves setting the g_bGameOver variable, as well as stopping the MIDI music. In this case, the music is only paused—there is no reason to close the MIDI device yet because the player might decide to start another game.

The remaining code in the GameCycle() function should be familiar to you because it is fairly generic game code. More specifically, it updates the sprites and then draws the game graphics using double-buffer animation.

You survived the GameCycle() function, which was about as messy as the code in this book gets. Listing 14.6 contains another important function in the Battle Office game, MouseButtonDown().

LISTING 14.6   The MouseButtonDown() **Function Checks to See if a Guy Was Clicked with the Mouse**

```
void MouseButtonDown(int x, int y, BOOL bLeft)
{
  // Only check the left mouse button
  if (!g_bGameOver && bLeft)
  {
    // Temporarily hide the target and pow sprites
    g_pTargetSprite->SetHidden(TRUE);
    g_pPowSprite->SetHidden(TRUE);

    // See if a guy sprite was clicked
    Sprite* pSprite;
    if ((pSprite = g_pGame->IsPointInSprite(x, y)) != NULL)
    {
      // Play a sound for hitting the guy
      PlaySound((LPCSTR)IDW_WHACK, g_hInstance, SND_ASYNC | SND_RESOURCE);

      // Position and show the pow sprite
      g_pPowSprite->SetPosition(x - (g_pPowSprite->GetWidth() / 2),
        y - (g_pPowSprite->GetHeight() / 2));
      g_pPowSprite->SetHidden(FALSE);

      // Hide the guy that was clicked
      pSprite->SetHidden(TRUE);

      // Increment the hits and make the game harder, if necessary
      if ((++g_iHits % 5) == 0)
        if (-g_iGuyMasterDelay == 0)
          g_iGuyMasterDelay = 1;
    }

    // Show the target sprite again
```

You don't want the target and pow sprites included in the hit-testing, so temporarily hide them.

Position and show the pow sprite to signify a hit.

A guy master delay of 1 represents the maximum difficulty level.

continues

LISTING 14.6 Continued

Because the target
sprite is hidden and
shown before this
function exits, you
never see it happen
in the game.

```
    g_pTargetSprite->SetHidden(FALSE);
  }
  else if (g_bGameOver && !bLeft)
  {
    // Start a new game
    g_bGameOver = FALSE;
    g_iHits = 0;
    g_iMisses = 0;

    // Restart the background music
    g_pGame->PlayMIDISong();
  }
}
```

The MouseButtonDown() function responds to mouse clicks in the game and serves as a means of determining if the player scored a hit on one of the office guys. The function first checks to make sure that the game isn't over and that the player clicked the left mouse button. If so, the target and pow sprites are temporarily hidden so that they don't interfere with performing a hit test on the mouse position. This is necessary because the next task in the function is to see if the mouse position lies within any of the guy sprites. Because the target and pow sprites have higher Z-orders than the guys, they will always supercede the guys. In other words, the hit test will always return either the target or pow sprites and will never detect any of the guys; avoiding this problem is one of those little tricks that is sometimes necessary to make a game work the way you want.

The MouseButtonDown()function checks to see if one of the guy sprites was clicked by calling the IsPointInSprite() method on the game engine and passing in the mouse coordinates. If one of the guys was hit, a sound effect is played and the pow sprite is positioned and displayed to indicate the successful hit. The guy sprite who was hit is then hidden, which makes sense, considering that he's been shot. The number of hits is then increased and checked to see if the difficulty level of the game needs to increase. The difficulty level is raised by decreasing the master delay for the guys, which determines how long the stationary guys appear on the screen. Regardless of whether a hit was detected on a guy sprite, the target sprite is made visible after performing the test.

The last block of code in the function allows you to right-click to start a new game. A new game is started by resetting the game state variables and restarting the background MIDI music.

Another mouse-related function used in the Battle Office game is `MouseMove()`, which is used to move the target sprite so that it tracks the mouse pointer. This is necessary so that you are always in control of the target sprite with the mouse. Listing 14.7 shows the code for the `MouseMove()` function.

LISTING 14.7   The `MouseMove()` **Function Tracks the Mouse Cursor with the Target Sprite**

```
void MouseMove(int x, int y)
{
  // Track the mouse with the target sprite
  g_pTargetSprite->SetPosition(x - (g_pTargetSprite->GetWidth() / 2),
    y - (g_pTargetSprite->GetHeight() / 2));
}
```

The target sprite is made to follow the mouse pointer by simply calling the `SetPosition()` method on the sprite and passing in the mouse coordinates. The position of the target sprite is actually calculated so that the mouse pointer points at the center of the sprite.

The last function of interest in the Battle Office game is the `SpriteCollision()` function, which is called in response to sprites colliding. Listing 14.8 shows how uneventful the `SpriteCollision()` function is in this game.

LISTING 14.8   The `SpriteCollision()` **Function Does Nothing Because There is No Need to Respond to Sprite Collisions**

```
BOOL SpriteCollision(Sprite* pSpriteHitter, Sprite* pSpriteHittee)
{
  return FALSE;
}
```

When you think about how the Battle Office game works, there is no reason to respond to any sprite collisions. Therefore, the `SpriteCollision()` function simply returns `FALSE` to indicate that nothing special is to take place in response to a collision.

> If you're using Visual C++ 6.0, you might need to change the type casts from `(DWORD_PTR)` to `(DWORD)` in GameEngine.cpp in order for the Battle Office code to compile properly.

Construction Cue

Construction Cue

As with most of the examples in the book, the Battle Office program relies on the standard msimg32.lib and winmm.lib libraries. These libraries are included with most Windows compilers, but they aren't automatically linked into programs when you create a new project. If you are using your own project or make files, as opposed to using the ones provided on the CD-ROM, make sure that you change the link settings so that these library files are properly linked into the final executable. Refer to the documentation for your specific compiler for how this is done.

Testing the Game

You've finally arrived at the most fun step in the construction of a game: testing! Testing the Battle Office game is quite interesting because a fair numnber of things are going on in the game. Figure 14.6 shows the game at the start with one guy jumping from behind his desk to give you a quick scare. Notice that your bull's-eye target is near the guy, ready for you to click and fire at him.

FIGURE 14.6
The Battle Office game gets started quickly with a guy jumping from behind an office desk.

Clicking the mouse with the target over the guy results in a hit, which causes the pow sprite to be displayed on the screen, as shown in Figure 14.7.

It won't take long for one of the moving guys to appear in the hallway near the top of the game screen. These guys are a little tougher to hit because they are moving, but it's still not too hard. Of course, the game doesn't really get tough until all the guys start appearing at the same time. Figure 14.8 shows an example of how the guys can start getting overwhelming.

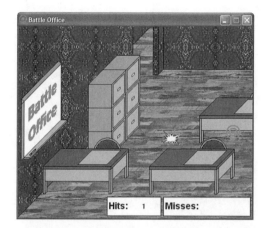

FIGURE 14.7
The pow sprite is displayed whenever you score a hit.

FIGURE 14.8
As the game progresses, the guys will start overwhelming you, which makes it harder to hit them all.

Once five guys get away, the game ends. Figure 14.9 shows the end of the game, which involves displaying the game over image on the screen on top of the other game graphics.

I really don't encourage you to think of office co-workers as targets, but hopefully, you can see the humor in the Battle Office game. If not, at least you can appreciate the game development techniques that went into making the game a reality.

Summary

Any time you're learning a new skill, it's helpful to put it into practice as much as possible to reinforce what you've learned. This chapter helped to reinforce the game programming knowledge you've learned thus far throughout the book by guiding you through the design and development of the Battle Office game. The game made interesting use of the sprite features in the game engine—not to mention wave sound effects and MIDI music. Hopefully, you're starting to get some confidence that you're capable of constructing a complete game of your own creation.

This chapter concludes this part of the book. The next part revisits animation and explores some ways to enhance the animation features in the game engine so that you can create even more interesting games than those you've seen thus far.

Field Trip

Unless you happen to work by yourself in a home office, this field trip doesn't require much travel at all. In fact, all you need are a few co-workers and a willingness to cause mayhem. Without putting your job at serious risk, organize a game of real-world Battle Office. You might have to make a quick trip to a toy store to find suitable projectiles that won't cause injury, but convince your co-workers that this is a good "team-building" exercise. Just make sure that your team is the one with all of the ex-minor league baseball pitchers. There aren't really any rules to the game, other than trying to bean as many people as possible while attempting to destroy as little of the office as possible. Oh, and you have to be able to quickly stop and resume the game on short notice when a supervisor strolls by. Feel free to use my favorite technique: Lob an object high into the air, and while everyone is mesmerized watching its graceful arc, unleash a direct attack. Hey, it's good, clean office fun!

PART V

Taking Animation to the Next Level

CHAPTER 15

Animating the Appearance of Sprites

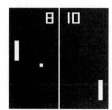

Arcade Archive

Joust is, without a doubt, one of my favorite video games of all time. Joust was released in 1982 by Williams Electronics, and it had the distinction of being one of the first games to merge both competitive and cooperative two-player game play into a single game. Joust is a great example of a game that is extremely simple to learn, yet very difficult to master. Joust actually didn't fare as well in arcades as other games because it was considered too difficult to play by some. However, many serious game players still regard it as one of the best games ever. Better still, a sequel to Joust was later released called Joust 2: Survival of the Fittest, which was an even better game. However, for some reason, it was limited to an extremely small production run. If you ever run across a deal on a Joust 2 game, be sure to drop me an email!

You're hopefully fairly comfortable with using sprites to create graphical objects that can move around the game screen and interact with each other. You've seen sprites in action in several examples and a couple of complete games. One thing you might have found missing in the sprites you've worked with is that they don't have any capability to change their appearances. Granted, being able to move around is certainly a huge benefit, but it would also be nice for some sprites to change their appearances every so often. For example, the guys moving across the screen in the Battle Office game would look much better if their legs were moving to give a more realistic impression that they were running. This chapter takes a look at how to add frame animation features to your sprites so that their appearances can change.

In this chapter, you'll learn

- ▶ How frame animation can be incorporated into sprite animation
- ▶ How to design and integrate frame animation support into the existing game engine
- ▶ How to modify an existing game to take advantage of frame-animated spritesv

Frame Animation Revisited

Back in Chapter 9, "Making Things Move with Sprite Animation," you learned all about animation, including the two fundamental types of animation: frame-based animation and cast-based (sprite) animation. Although you learned that both types of animation are equally useful, you've focused solely on sprite animation since Chapter 9 because it is more immediately useful in terms of allowing you to move objects around on the game screen. However, frame-based animation (*frame animation* for short) is still very important to games. In fact, you'll find that the ideal usage of frame animation in games is when you combine it with sprite animation.

To better understand how frame animation fits in with sprite animation, consider a simple maze game, such as Pac-Man. In Pac-Man, the main character moves around the game screen eating dots. To convey the effect of the main character eating, his mouth opens and closes as he moves around. The simple movement of the character around the maze is made possible with sprite animation, but the change in his appearance brought on by his mouth moving is made possible by frame animation. In other words, frame animation makes it possible to change the appearance of a sprite, independent of whether the sprite is moving around the game screen.

Okay, so frame animation makes it possible to change the appearance of a sprite, but how does it work? If you recall, a basic sprite without frame animation uses a single bitmap image to reflect its appearance; when you draw the sprite, you are just drawing the bitmap image. A frame-animated sprite relies on a series of bitmap images to represent more than one appearance for the sprite. You can think of this series of images as a reel of film on a traditional film projector. The illusion of frame animation is made possible by cycling through the images on the reel of film. Figure 15.1 shows how this concept applies to adding animation to the Pac-Man character.

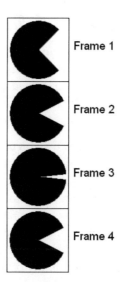

Frame 1

Frame 2

Frame 3

Frame 4

FIGURE 15.1
A series of images
shows how frame
animation can
make Pac-Man
appear to be eating
something.

In the figure, the Pac-Man character consists of a series of four images. When this
image series is incorporated into a game and played in sequence, the effect will
be that Pac-Man is moving his mouth and eating something. If you look carefully, you'll notice that frame 4 is the same as frame 2. This is necessary because the
animation sequence cycles back to frame 1 when it finishes, so duplicating frame
2 provides a smooth transition back to the first frame. Just visualize the frames
being displayed in succession to see what I'm talking about.

> You could eliminate the last frame of animation in the Pac-Man example by cycling
> back and forth through the frames, instead of looping in one direction. This is more
> than likely how the Pac-Man sprite was animated in the real arcade game.

Construction
Cue

One problem associated with frame animation is that of controlling how fast the
frame images are cycled through. For example, a frame-animated Pac-Man sprite
might need to change its appearance slower than an animated sprite of an explosion. For this reason, there needs to be a way to establish a timing delay that controls how fast the frames change. Increasing the delay would slow down the
frame animation, which, in some cases, would be a desirable effect. You will definitely take a frame delay into consideration as you design and develop frame
animation support for the game engine throughout the remainder of this chapter.

Designing an Animated Sprite

Even though sprites are already animated in the sense that they can move around on the game screen, for the purposes of this discussion, I'm going to refer to a frame-animated sprite as simply an *animated sprite*. The animation, in this case, means that the sprite's appearance is being animated. The first place to start designing an animated sprite is in its bitmap image.

In the previous section, you learned how a series of images is used to represent an animated sprite because the images can be cycled through to give the effect of animation. There are a variety of different ways to store a series of images for an animated sprite, but the easiest I've found is to store the frame images vertically in a single image. For example, the series of Pac-Man images you saw in Figure 15.1 shows several frame images appearing next to each other vertically. These four frame images could be stored together as a single image just as they appear in the figure. It then becomes the responsibility of the animated sprite code to draw only the frame image representing the current frame. You can think of the sprite image at any given moment as being a little window that moves from one frame image to the next to reveal only one frame image at a time. Figure 15.2 shows what I'm talking about.

FIGURE 15.2
The current sprite image is drawn from within the series of frame images.

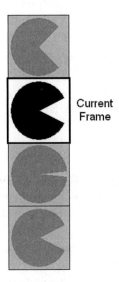

Current
Frame

Construction Cue

You could just as easily arrange the frame images for an animated sprite horizontally, but because of how images are stored in memory, it is more efficient to arrange the frames vertically.

This figure shows how the second frame of the Pac-Man sprite is currently being displayed. The figure also reveals how the bitmap image for an animated sprite is put together. The image is the same width as a normal unanimated sprite image, but its height is determined by the number of frames. So, if a single frame is 25 pixels high, and there are a total of 4 frames of animation, the entire image is 100 pixels high. To create an image such as this, you just place the frame images immediately next to each other with no space in between them.

With the animated sprite image in place, you can now turn your attention to the actual data for the sprite used to manage frame animation. First of all, you know that the sprite needs to understand how many frame images there are because this is crucial information in determining how to cycle through the frames of the sprite's bitmap image. In addition to knowing the total number of animation frames, it's also necessary to keep track of the currently selected frame—this is the frame image currently being displayed.

Earlier in the chapter, I talked about how it's important to be able to control the speed at which an animated sprite cycles through its frame images. This speed is controlled by a piece of information known as a *frame delay*. The frame delay for a sprite basically determines how many game cycles must elapse before the frame image is changed. In order to carry out the frame delay feature for an animated sprite, you must keep up with a trigger (counter) that counts down the delay and indicates when it's time to move to the next frame. So, when an animated sprite first starts out, the trigger is set to the frame delay, and it begins counting down with each game cycle. When the trigger reaches zero, the sprite moves to the next frame and resets the trigger to the frame delay again.

To recap, the following pieces of information are required of the new animated sprite, in addition to the bitmap image that contains the vertically-oriented frame images:

▶ Total number of frames

▶ Current frame

▶ Frame delay

▶ Frame trigger

The next section puts code behind this sprite data as you add animated sprite support to the game engine.

Adding Animated Sprite Support to the Game Engine

In order to add animated sprite support to the game engine, a few changes have to be made to existing code. These changes impact the Bitmap and Sprite classes, but strangely enough, they don't directly impact the GameEngine class at all. The next couple of sections show you exactly what changes need to be made to the Bitmap and Sprite classes to integrate frame-animated sprites into the game engine.

Drawing Only Part of a Bitmap

The first change is related to the Bitmap class, which represents a bitmap image. As you know, the Sprite class already relies on the Bitmap class to handle the details of storing and drawing a sprite's visual appearance. However, the Bitmap class is currently only designed to draw a complete image. This presents a problem for animated sprites because the frame images are all stored in a single bitmap image. It is therefore necessary to modify the Bitmap class so that it supports drawing only a part of the bitmap.

If you recall, the Bitmap class includes a Draw() method that accepts a device context and an XY coordinate to indicate where the bitmap is to be drawn. The new method you now need is called DrawPart(), and it accepts the familiar device context and XY coordinate, as well as the XY position and width and height of the frame image within the overall sprite bitmap. So, the new DrawPart() method basically allows you to select and draw a rectangular subsection of a bitmap image. Listing 15.1 contains the code for the Bitmap::DrawPart() method.

LISTING 15.1   The Bitmap::DrawPart() Method Supports Frame Animation by Allowing You to Draw Only a Part of a Sprite's Bitmap Image

```
void Bitmap::DrawPart(HDC hDC, int x, int y, int xPart, int yPart,
  int wPart, int hPart, BOOL bTrans, COLORREF crTransColor)
{
  if (m_hBitmap != NULL)
  {
    // Create a memory device context for the bitmap
    HDC hMemDC = CreateCompatibleDC(hDC);

    // Select the bitmap into the device context
```

```
  HBITMAP hOldBitmap = (HBITMAP)SelectObject(hMemDC, m_hBitmap);

  // Draw the bitmap to the destination device context
  if (bTrans)
    TransparentBlt(hDC, x, y, wPart, hPart, hMemDC, xPart, yPart,
      wPart, hPart, crTransColor);
  else
    BitBlt(hDC, x, y, wPart, hPart, hMemDC, xPart, yPart, SRCCOPY);

  // Restore and delete the memory device context
  SelectObject(hMemDC, hOldBitmap);
  DeleteDC(hMemDC);
  }
}
```

The specified transparency color is used as the basis for drawing a bitmap with transparent areas.

This code is very similar to the original `Draw()` method in the `Bitmap` class, except that it doesn't take for granted the parameters of the source bitmap image. More specifically, the `DrawPart()` method uses the new arguments xPart, yPart, wPart, and hPart to single out a frame image within the bitmap image to draw. These arguments are passed in to the `TransparentBlt()` function to draw a frame image with transparency and the `BitBlt()` function to draw a frame image without transparency.

It's important to note that the `Draw()` method still works fine for drawing sprites that don't involve frame animation. In fact, the `Draw()` method has now been modified to use the `DrawPart()` method, which helps to conserve code because the methods are very similar. Listing 15.2 shows the code for the new `Bitmap::Draw()` method, which is surprisingly simple.

LISTING 15.2   The New `Bitmap::Draw()` Method Simply Calls the DrawPart() Method to Draw a Bitmap Image in Its Entirety

```
void Bitmap::Draw(HDC hDC, int x, int y, BOOL bTrans, COLORREF crTransColor)
{
  DrawPart(hDC, x, y, 0, 0, GetWidth(), GetHeight(), bTrans, crTransColor);
}
```

Notice that the new `Draw()` method just calls the `DrawPart()` method and passes in arguments that result in the entire bitmap image being drawn. You could've kept the original `Draw()` method without modifying it, but it's wasteful to duplicate code without a good reason. More importantly, if you ever need to change the manner in which a bitmap is drawn, you only have to modify one section of code, the `DrawPart()` method.

Animating the Sprite Class

Now that you've altered the Bitmap class to support the drawing of only part of a bitmap image, you're ready to make changes to the Sprite class to support frame animation. Earlier in the chapter, you worked through the design of a frame-animated sprite that involved adding several important pieces of information to a traditional unanimated sprite. The following new member variables of the Sprite class represent these pieces of information:

```
int m_iNumFrames, m_iCurFrame;
int m_iFrameDelay, m_iFrameTrigger;
```

These member variables correspond one to one with the pieces of animated sprite information mentioned earlier in the chapter. They are all initialized in the Sprite() constructors, as the following code reveals:

```
m_iNumFrames = 1;
m_iCurFrame = m_iFrameDelay = m_iFrameTrigger = 0;
```

The default value of the m_iNumFrames variable is 1 because a normal sprite that doesn't use frame animation includes only one bitmap image or one frame. The other three variables are initialized with values of 0, which is suitable for a sprite without frame animation.

In order to create a sprite that takes advantage of frame animation, you must call the SetNumFrames() method and possibly even the SetFrameDelay() method. Listing 15.3 contains the code for the SetNumFrames() method.

LISTING 15.3 The Sprite::SetNumFrames() Method Turns a Normal Sprite into an Animated Sprite by Setting Its Number of Frames

```
inline void Sprite::SetNumFrames(int iNumFrames)
{
  // Set the number of frames
  m_iNumFrames = iNumFrames;

  // Recalculate the position
  RECT rect = GetPosition();
  rect.bottom = rect.top + ((rect.bottom - rect.top) / iNumFrames);
  SetPosition(rect);
}
```

The listing shows how the number of frames is set by assigning the specified argument to the m_iNumFrames member variable. It's also important to recalculate the sprite's position because it is no longer based on the entire image size, since the image now includes multiple frames.

The SetFrameDelay() method goes hand in hand with the SetNumFrames() method, and it's even easier to follow:

```
void SetFrameDelay(int iFrameDelay) { m_iFrameDelay = iFrameDelay; };
```

As you can see, the SetFrameDelay() method is a simple accessor method that sets the m_iFrameDelay member variable. Setting the number of frames and the frame delay are all that are required to turn an ordinary sprite into a frame-animated sprite. Of course, you also need to make sure that you've laid out the frame images for the sprite in the sprite's single bitmap image.

Although the SetNumFrames() and SetFrameDelay() methods are all you need to worry about from the perspective of game code, work still needs to be done to get the Sprite class ready to use its new member variables. For example, the GetHeight() method needs to take into consideration the number of frames when calculating the height of the sprite image. This height is either the entire sprite image (for an unanimated sprite) or the height of a single frame image (for an animated sprite). The following is the code for the new GetHeight() method:

```
Int GetHeight() { return (m_pBitmap->GetHeight() / m_iNumFrames); };
```

Notice that this code simply divides the height of the sprite image by the number of frames. For an unanimated sprite, the number of frames is one, which means that the normal bitmap height is returned. For animated sprites, the height returned reflects the height of an individual frame image.

A new helper method is included in the Sprite class to handle the details of updating the current animation frame. This method is called UpdateFrame()and it is shown in Listing 15.4.

LISTING 15.4   The Sprite::UpdateFrame() Method Updates the Sprite's Current Animation Frame

```
inline void Sprite::UpdateFrame()
{
  if ((m_iFrameDelay >= 0) && (-m_iFrameTrigger <= 0))
  {
    // Reset the frame trigger;
    m_iFrameTrigger = m_iFrameDelay;

    // Increment the frame
    if (++m_iCurFrame >= m_iNumFrames)
        m_iCurFrame = 0;
  }
}
```

The UpdateFrame() method is called by the Update() method to update the frame image of the sprite, if necessary. The method starts off by making sure that the frame indeed needs to be updated. This check involves seeing if the frame delay is greater than or equal to 0, as well as if the frame trigger is less than or equal to 0. If both of these conditions are met, the frame trigger is reset to the frame delay, and the current frame is moved to the next frame.

The Update() method is responsible for calling the UpdateFrame() method to make sure that the frame is updated. Listing 15.5 shows how the UpdateFrame() method is now called in the Update() method.

LISTING 15.5 The `Sprite::Update()` Method Now Calls the UpdateFrame() Method to Update the Sprite's Animation Frame

```
SPRITEACTION Sprite::Update()
{
  // Update the frame
  UpdateFrame();

  ...

}
```

The update of the frame is now taken care of first thing in the Update() method. I deliberately left out the remainder of the Update() code because none of it changed, and it's quite lengthy; the only code of importance to this discussion is the new call to UpdateFrame().

The last Sprite method impacted by the addition of animation support is the Draw() method, which must now take into account the current frame when drawing a sprite. Listing 15.6 shows the new and improved Draw() method—complete with frame animation support.

LISTING 15.6 The `Sprite::Draw()` Method Draws the Sprite Differently Depending on Whether or Not It Is an Animated Sprite

```
void Sprite::Draw(HDC hDC)
{
  // Draw the sprite if it isn't hidden
  if (m_pBitmap != NULL && !m_bHidden)
  {
    // Draw the appropriate frame, if necessary
    if (m_iNumFrames == 1)
      m_pBitmap->Draw(hDC, m_rcPosition.left, m_rcPosition.top, TRUE);
    else
      m_pBitmap->DrawPart(hDC, m_rcPosition.left, m_rcPosition.top,
        0, m_iCurFrame * GetHeight(), GetWidth(), GetHeight(), TRUE);
  }
}
```

If there is only one frame, the sprite is drawn as a single bitmap image; otherwise, only part of the image is drawn (the current frame).

This version of the Draw() method now takes a look at the number of frames before deciding how to draw the sprite. If there is only one frame, the familiar Bitmap::Draw() method is called to draw the single bitmap image as you've been accustomed to doing. However, if there is more than one frame, the new Bitmap::DrawPart() method is used to draw only the current frame image within the sprite bitmap. This is a critical piece of code that reveals why you needed to make the changes to the Bitmap class earlier in the chapter.

Building the Battle Office 2 Example Program

You're now sitting there with a perfectly good game engine with a shiny new feature, so you're no doubt anxious to see how it works in a practical game. Fortunately, it's not too difficult to find a good application for animated sprites. Earlier in the chapter, I mentioned that the Battle Office game has a deficiency in that the guys moving across the hallway near the top of the game screen appear to slide, as opposed to run. It would look as if they were running if their legs were moving as they traveled across the game screen. This kind of visual effect is only possible through frame animation, which you now have the capability of carrying out within the game engine you've grown to love. Okay, love might be too strong a word, but hopefully, you've at least grown to appreciate what it can do.

The next couple of sections focus on what it takes to animate the two moving guys in the Battle Office game using frame-animated sprites. Because you've already built the animation logic into the game engine, modifying the Battle Office game takes very little effort. You'll call the new version of the game with the animated guys Battle Office 2.

Writing the Program Code

Earlier in this chapter, I mentioned that the only things required to add animated sprites to a game from a programming perspective are setting the number of frames and the frame delay for each sprite. Of course, you'll also need to create a suitable bitmap image containing the frames for the sprite, but that doesn't directly impact the programming side of things. In the case of the Battle Office 2 game, the only two sprites being altered for frame animation are the two moving guy sprites. Both sprites use four frame images, which means that they each need to be set to use four frames. Figures 15.3 and 15.4 show the two new guy bitmap images—each of which contains four frames of animation.

FIGURE 15.3
The first animated guy requires four images to simulate him running.

FIGURE 15.4
The second animated guy also requires four images to simulate him running.

Getting back to the sprite code for the Battle Office 2 game, Listing 15.7 contains the sprite creation code for the first moving guy sprite.

> If you set the number of frames for a sprite to a number greater than one, but you don't change the sprite's bitmap image, you definitely will get strange results. This has to do with the fact that the sprite automatically assumes that the individual frame images are arranged vertically down the sprite image.

Construction Cue

LISTING 15.7   The Sprite Creation Code for the First Moving Guy Establishes the Number of Frames for the Animated Sprite

```
g_pGuySprites[3] = new Sprite(g_pGuyBitmaps[3], rcBounds, BA_WRAP);
g_pGuySprites[3]->SetNumFrames(4);
g_pGuySprites[3]->SetPosition(500, 10);
g_pGuySprites[3]->SetVelocity(-3, 0);
g_pGuySprites[3]->SetZOrder(1);
g_pGuySprites[3]->SetHidden(TRUE);
g_pGame->AddSprite(g_pGuySprites[3]);
```

Indicates that this is an animated sprite with four animation frames.

This code shows how easy it is to change a normal sprite into an animated sprite. A single call to the `SetNumFrames()` method is all it takes to inform the sprite that it is to use four frames of animation. It's important to note that the frame delay is not being set for this sprite, which means that it is cycling through the frames at maximum speed.

The second moving guy sprite is a little different in that it opts for a frame delay, as shown in Listing 15.8.

LISTING 15.8   The Sprite Creation Code for the Second Moving Guy Establishes the Number of Frames and the Frame Delay for the Animated Sprite

```
g_pGuySprites[4] = new Sprite(g_pGuyBitmaps[4], rcBounds, BA_WRAP);
g_pGuySprites[4]->SetNumFrames(4);
g_pGuySprites[4]->SetFrameDelay(5);
g_pGuySprites[4]->SetPosition(260, 60);
g_pGuySprites[4]->SetVelocity(5, 0);
g_pGuySprites[4]->SetZOrder(1);
g_pGuySprites[4]->SetHidden(TRUE);
g_pGame->AddSprite(g_pGuySprites[4]);
```

This code not only sets the number of frames for the sprite, but it also sets the frame delay for the sprite. Setting the frame delay to 5, as in this code, means that the sprite's animation frame will be updated in every fifth game cycle. In other words, the second moving guy sprite is animating at one-fifth the speed of the first moving guy sprite.

Construction Cue

> As with most of the examples in the book, the Battle Office 2 program relies on the standard msimg32.lib and winmm.lib libraries. These libraries are included with most Windows compilers, but they aren't automatically linked into programs when you create a new project. If you are using your own project or make files, as opposed to using the ones provided on the CD-ROM, make sure that you change the link settings so that these library files are properly linked into the final executable. Refer to the documentation for your specific compiler for how this is done.

Testing the Finished Product

Testing the animated sprites in the Battle Office 2 game is not a very involved process, as you might imagine. Figure 15.5 shows the two guys moving across the hallway, and although it's difficult to see on the static page of a book, I promise you that they're kicking their legs like crazy! Admittedly, the animation images used to make the guys appear to be running could be improved a bit.

FIGURE 15.5
The Battle Office 2 game shows off the new animated sprite features in the game engine.

The new animated sprites in the Battle Office 2 game don't really impact the play of the game very much. However, it's still hard to argue that a little more playful realism can never hurt a game. In fact, anything you can do to make a game more interesting will add to the satisfaction of game players and, ultimately, the success of the game.

Summary

This chapter built upon your knowledge of sprite animation by expanding the sprite support in the game engine to support frame-animated sprites. Frame animation allows you to change the appearance of a sprite, which can be used to achieve a variety of different effects. This chapter demonstrated how to use animated sprites to make the moving guys in the Battle Office game appear to run across the game screen. You could also make similar modifications to the Henway game so that the chicken appears to be running, or maybe you could change the car images so that their brake lights come on or a driver shakes his fist out of the window every once in a while. Regardless of how you use them, animated sprites can add significantly to the allure of games.

The next chapter continues along the same path of improving games with better graphics effects by showing you how to create interesting backgrounds. You've grown accustomed to seeing backgrounds that are just fixed images, but how about a space background complete with twinkling stars? Read on to find out how it's done.

Extreme Game Makeover

If you're like most people, the thought of bugs crawling all over the place isn't too appealing. I'm not talking about programming bugs in your code—I mean real bugs, like people eat in those gross-out reality shows. What do bugs have to do with this chapter's extreme game makeover, you ask? Bugs make up the new theme you're going to use in revamping the Battle Office 2 game. More specifically, the modification of the Battle Office 2 game involves a kitchen with a really bad bug problem. Bugs run across the floor, as well as the kitchen table you're going to create. Of course, the floor and table artwork are really part of the background, but you're going to code the game so that it looks as if the table is a separate object. Here are the steps required to turn Battle Office 2 into Bugs Be Gone:

1. Change the cross-hair graphic for aiming to a shoe instead of a cross-hair. A shoe is undoubtedly the most common weapon to use in defending against pesky bugs.

2. Change the background image to that of a kitchen with a kitchen table that is visible.

3. Change the office co-worker (guy) images to bug images. Feel free to get creative here in terms of your bug selection. The only suggestion I have is to make all the bugs animated so that their legs appear to be moving.

4. Change the small guy image to a small bug image to show how many bugs have escaped.

5. Change the code for the co-worker sprites so that they all are moving when they appear; there are no stationary bugs in this game. Choose one of the bugs to only appear on the kitchen table; use the bounding rectangle for the bug sprite to limit its area to the table top.

6. Change the sound effects so that hitting a bug results in a squishing sound.

The real trick to pulling off this game makeover is changing the code for the bug sprites so that they all appear to scramble across the kitchen floor and table. If you animate the bug images correctly, the effects should work quite well.

CHAPTER 16

Creating Backgrounds for Your Sprites

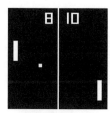

Arcade Archive

If your idea of a good time playing video games is sensory overload, look no further than Robotron: 2084. Released in 1982 by Williams Electronics, Robotron: 2084 is one of the fastest-paced games ever created. The premise of the game is simple: Rescue the last human family on Earth from hordes of enemies, which are called Robotrons. The game controls consist of two joysticks—one for moving your character and the other for firing in different directions. Part of the reason for the two-joystick design was because the designer of the game, Eugene Jarvis, had a broken right hand from an automobile accident and wanted to be able to play the game without pressing buttons. The sheer number of Robotrons that are unleashed on your character can be astounding at times, which is why the game's pace is so hectic. Nevertheless, it's a lot of fun to play.

If you've ever watched a cartoon or an animated movie that isn't entirely computer generated, you are familiar with the importance of backgrounds. If you pay careful attention the next time you watch an animated movie, notice how the characters move on top of a background that doesn't tend to change much. This is because the characters are overlaid on the background, very much like sprites. Although you've already seen how to use an image as a background, this chapter shows you how to create a general background class that you can use in your games. Not only that, but you learn how to create animated backgrounds that can be used to display a starry night complete with twinkling stars.

In this chapter, you'll learn

- ▶ Why backgrounds are so important in games
- ▶ About the four main types of backgrounds

▶ How to add support for backgrounds to the game engine

▶ How to use an animated background with animated sprites to simulate an asteroid field

Assessing the Significance of Game Backgrounds

It's hard to argue the significance of backgrounds in games, especially when you consider the example games you've seen thus far. For example, picture the Henway game without the highway background or the Battle Office game without the office background. Both of these backgrounds are critical in supporting the sprites in these games and in giving them context. Without the backgrounds, neither of the games would be as entertaining, and they certainly wouldn't make as much sense from a game play perspective.

In the two examples I mentioned, both backgrounds were created directly from bitmap images. The background image was drawn just before drawing the sprites, which gave the effect that the sprites appeared on top of the background. Although a stationary image was perfectly acceptable for these games, there are situations in which an animated background makes more sense. For example, consider a driving game where a sense of movement needs to be associated with objects passing by as you're driving. These objects could certainly be represented by sprites, which might even make more sense than using an animated background, but there would still be aspects of the background that would need to be animated. For example, the lines painted on the road would need to move to some degree to give the illusion of movement.

Another good example of an animated background is the background of a space game, which might consist of a solid black region with stars drawn on it. The animation comes into play when you make the stars twinkle, which is a subtle, but compelling enhancement to the background. A space background with twinkling stars adds considerably to the realism of a space game and helps to immerse the player in the setting.

I could go through countless examples of how important backgrounds are in improving the visual feel of a game, but hopefully, you're starting to get the idea. Most of the more interesting background effects involve animation of some sort.

However, this animation usually isn't as simple as frame-based sprite animation; you typically must write custom animation code to handle each specific background. For example, a frame-based animation approach is overkill in the twinkling star background. For that background, it makes more sense to write custom code that varies the color of the stars over time. This is not only more efficient, but it also yields a more realistic effect than cycling through the same series of frame images over and over.

Understanding the Types of Game Backgrounds

Now that you have a basic understanding of how backgrounds fit into games, as well as why they are important, I'd like to spend a moment exploring the basic kinds of backgrounds that you'll encounter in game programming. The following are the four primary types of backgrounds:

▶ Solid backgrounds

▶ Image backgrounds

▶ Animated backgrounds

▶ Scrolling backgrounds

The next few sections explore these different types of backgrounds in more detail.

Solid Backgrounds

A *solid background* is a background consisting only of a solid color. This is by far the simplest of all backgrounds, and requires very little code to pull off. Not surprisingly, solid backgrounds are also the dullest of all backgrounds, and they aren't used very often in games. Generally speaking, any time you could use a solid background, you could also use an image background and get a much better result. For example, if you were developing a football game, it might make sense to create a solid green background to represent the grass on the field. However, a grassy-textured image would look much better in the same context, without a whole lot more development effort. So, although it's important to have the option of using a solid background, it's usually not your best option.

Gamer's Garage

One situation in which you might find a solid background useful is in testing a game. For example, if you have a game that has a complex background image in which the sprites tend to blend in well, you might find it easier to fine-tune the sprites while viewing them against a stark background. By temporarily replacing a background image with a solid background of a contrasting color, you can easily make out what the sprites are doing and fix any problems with them.

Image Backgrounds

Image backgrounds are a step beyond solid backgrounds in that they use a bitmap image to represent the backdrop for a game, as opposed to a solid color. You've already used image backgrounds in the games you've developed throughout the book, so hopefully, you can appreciate their usefulness. The primary work involved in using an image background is creating the image itself; from a programming perspective, the `Bitmap` class in the game engine already handles most of the details of using an image background.

The problem with image bitmaps is that they are static, which means they don't move or do anything interesting to convey that they are real. For example, the galaxy image background used in the Planets example in Chapter 9, "Making Things Move with Sprite Animation," would have been infinitely more interesting if the galaxy would have swirled a little and maybe spun off a shooting star every now and then. Of course, such subtleties aren't always easy to add to a game, and you have to carefully weigh adding complexity for the sake of including small details in a game—sometimes they're worth it, sometimes they're not. One way to improve upon the basic image background is to use an animated background.

Animated Backgrounds

An *animated background* is a background that somehow changes its appearance over time, which is similar in some ways to an animated sprite. However, an animated background doesn't necessarily have to involve a series of frame images. It's entirely possible to create an animated background in which the animation is derived from custom code. The key to making an animated background work is providing some kind of mechanism for updating and drawing the background. Again, this is similar to sprites in that they, too, must be updated periodically to convey a sense of motion.

Another reason why I hesitate to draw too close of a comparison between an animated background and an animated sprite is because backgrounds are usually much larger than sprites. Therefore, using a series of frame images for a background could hog a lot of memory, especially, when you consider that backgrounds are typically hundreds of pixels in width and height. It is much more efficient to focus on coming up with interesting and more effective ways of animating backgrounds. For example, the starry background I mentioned earlier could be created by changing the color of individual pixels in a background image.

Another approach to creating an animated background involves using several smaller images capable of moving around on the background. For example, if you wanted to enhance the starry background, you could feasibly add a few distant planets that are animated on the background by slightly changing their appearance every so often. It's debatable whether you should create these planets as sprites, as opposed to creating them as part of the background, but these are the kinds of decisions you have to make when creating a game.

Scrolling Backgrounds

The final type of background is the *scrolling background*, which involves an image or set of graphical objects capable of being shifted or scrolled around on the screen. The best way to understand a scrolling background is to picture a background that is much larger than the game screen, which means that the game screen provides a view onto part of the background. To see other parts of the background, you have to scroll the view to another part. Figure 16.1 shows what I mean by a "view on a background."

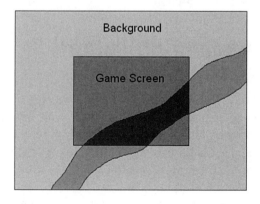

FIGURE 16.1
When you use a scrolling background, the game screen provides a view on a portion of the background.

The figure illustrates how the game screen shows only a portion of a larger background. This type of background is used a lot in adventure games in which you control a character around a large virtual world. As you might have guessed, scrolling backgrounds are considerably more complex to develop than the other types of backgrounds because they involve a lot more game logic. For example, the background must respond to you moving the character, not to mention the fact that sprites have to be moved so that they appear to scroll with the background. Not only that, but scrolling backgrounds often must be capable of wrapping so that you don't encounter a boundary.

An interesting type of scrolling background commonly used in 2D games is a parallax scrolling background, which is a background that scrolls at differing rates. *Parallax scrolling* involves the use of multiple layered background images, such as buildings in the foreground, trees in the mid-ground, and mountains in the background. The idea is to provide the illusion of depth by moving each image at a different speed. So, the mountains move slowest because they are farthest away, the trees move a little faster, and the buildings move the fastest. This simulates the effect of movement we perceive in the real world when passing by objects that are at different distances.

Creating a scrolling background isn't too terribly difficult, but it is a formidable challenge when you approach it from the perspective of still learning the ropes of game development. Therefore, you won't be tackling scrolling backgrounds in this chapter. However, you will revisit the topic later and will learn how to create a side-scrolling background for a motorcycle jumping game in Chapter 24, "Example Game : Stunt Jumper." In the meantime, you're going to focus on learning how to create animated backgrounds, which I think you'll find useful for adding some pizzazz to your games.

Adding Background Support to the Game Engine

Because you're not going to worry about creating scrolling backgrounds just yet, that leaves three types of backgrounds you're going to incorporate into the game engine: solid backgrounds, image backgrounds, and animated backgrounds. The first two background types can easily coexist in a single class, whereas the third requires a custom class of its own. So, you're going to be creating two new classes that will become part of the game engine. The first class is a basic background class that encompasses solid backgrounds and image backgrounds, whereas the second class contains a specific type of animated background that displays a starry night sky with twinkling stars. The starry background will serve as a good enough demonstration of how to create an animated background that you should be able to create your own custom animated backgrounds without any trouble.

Creating a Basic Background Class

The basic background class that supports both solid and image backgrounds is contained within the Background class. The Background class is flexible in that the same class can be used to create both kinds of backgrounds—the decision regarding which kind of background you're creating is decided by which constructor you use. Listing 16.1 shows the code for the Background class, which reveals its overall design.

LISTING 16.1   The Background Class Is Used to Create Both Solid and Image Backgrounds

```
class Background
{
protected:
  // Member Variables
  int       m_iWidth, m_iHeight;
  COLORREF  m_crColor;
  Bitmap*   m_pBitmap;

public:
  // Constructor(s)/Destructor
          Background(int iWidth, int iHeight, COLORREF crColor);
          Background(Bitmap* pBitmap);
  virtual ~Background();

  // General Methods
  virtual void  Update();
  virtual void  Draw(HDC hDC);

  // Accessor Methods
  int GetWidth()  { return m_iWidth; };
  int GetHeight() { return m_iHeight; };
};
```

Every background has a width and height that usually match the size of the game screen.

The Background class contains several member variables that support both solid and image backgrounds. The m_iWidth and m_iHeight member variables keep track of the width and height of the background, which apply to any kind of background. The m_crColor variable stores the color of the background and only applies to solid backgrounds. Similarly, the m_pBitmap variable stores a pointer to a Bitmap object, which is used to draw the bitmap image for an image background.

The Background class includes two constructors—each of which corresponds to one of the two basic background types. The first constructor accepts a width and height, along with a color, for the solid background. The second constructor accepts a bitmap image, which it uses as the basis for calculating the width and height of the image background.

Two familiar methods are included in the Background class for updating and drawing the background. The Update() method is called to update the appearance of the background, and in the case of solid and image backgrounds, it does nothing. The purpose for having the Update() method is to enable derived animated background classes to use it to update themselves. The Draw() method applies to all kinds of backgrounds and simply accepts a device context on which to draw the background. The last two methods in the Background class are the GetWidth() and GetHeight() accessor methods, which simply return the width and height of the background.

Now that you have an understanding of how the Background class is assembled, you can take a look at the specific code that makes it work. Listing 16.2 shows the code for the Background() constructors.

LISTING 16.2 The Background::Background() Constructors Are Used to Create and Clean Up After a Background

```
Background::Background(int iWidth, int iHeight, COLORREF crColor)
{
  // Initialize the member variables
  m_iWidth = iWidth;
  m_iHeight = iHeight;
  m_crColor = crColor;
  m_pBitmap = NULL;
}

Background::Background(Bitmap* pBitmap)
{
  // Initialize the member variables
  m_crColor = 0;
  m_pBitmap = pBitmap;
  m_iWidth = pBitmap->GetWidth();
  m_iHeight = pBitmap->GetHeight();
}
```

Solid-colored back-grounds don't require the bitmap member variable.

Bitmap back-grounds don't require the color member variable.

The constructors for the Background class are pretty straightforward in that they simply initialize the member variables for the class based on the arguments provided. It is important to note that the bitmap pointer is set to NULL in the first constructor, which indicates that the background is a solid background, as opposed to an image background. Similarly, the background color is set to 0 in the second constructor because an image background doesn't have a background color.

The Update() and Draw()methods in the Background class are responsible for updating and drawing the background. However, because neither a solid nor an image background is animated, the Update() method serves as more of a place-holder for future derived background classes. Listing 16.3 shows the code for these two methods.

LISTING 16.3 The Background::Update() and Background::Draw() Methods Handle the Updating and Drawing of a Background

```
void Background::Update()
{
  // Do nothing since the basic background is not animated
}

void Background::Draw(HDC hDC)
{
  // Draw the background
  if (m_pBitmap != NULL)
    m_pBitmap->Draw(hDC, 0, 0);
  else
  {
    RECT    rect = { 0, 0, m_iWidth, m_iHeight };
    HBRUSH  hBrush = CreateSolidBrush(m_crColor);
    FillRect(hDC, &rect, hBrush);
    DeleteObject(hBrush);
  }
}
```

To draw a solid-colored background, you simply draw a rectangle using a brush in the appropriate color.

As I mentioned earlier, the Update() method is designed to be overridden with animation code in derived background classes, so it makes sense to leave it blank in this class. However, the Draw() method makes up for this lack of action by drawing a solid background or image background, depending on the state of the bitmap pointer. If the bitmap pointer is not NULL, you know that this is an image bitmap, so the Draw() method is called on the Bitmap object. Otherwise, you know that this is a solid bitmap, so a solid rectangle is drawn in the color of the background. The code in the Draw() method reveals how two types of back-grounds are supported in a single class.

Creating an Animated Background Class

If the Background class didn't get you too excited, hopefully, you'll be intrigued by the StarryBackground class, which represents an animated background of a starry sky. The starry sky could also be interpreted as a starry view of outer space, which makes the background more flexible in terms of how you use it in games.

The StarryBackground class is derived from the Background class, which means that it inherits member variables and methods from the Background class. However, the StarryBackground class requires its own constructor, as well as its own version of the Update() and Draw() methods. The StarryBackground class also adds some new member variables to the equation, which are used to manage the twinkling stars in the background. Listing 16.4 contains the code for the StarryBackground class.

Construction Cue

> The StarryBackground class is included with the code for the Background class in the Background.h and Background.cpp source code files on the accompanying CD-ROM. Although the StarryBackground class could've been broken out into its own source code files, it's useful enough that I thought it made sense to place it with the code for the core Background class.

LISTING 16.4   The StarryBackground Class Is Used to Create an Animated Background of a Starry Sky

```
class StarryBackground : Background
{
protected:
  // Member Variables
  int        m_iNumStars;
  int        m_iTwinkleDelay;
  POINT      m_ptStars[100];
  COLORREF   m_crStarColors[100];

public:
  // Constructor(s)/Destructor
        StarryBackground(int iWidth, int iHeight, int iNumStars = 100,
            int iTwinkleDelay = 50);
  virtual ~StarryBackground();

  // General Methods
  virtual void  Update();
  virtual void  Draw(HDC hDC);
};
```

If you want your starry backgrounds to be capable of having more stars, increase these two arrays higher than 100; however, make sure that you use the same number for both.

The most important member variable in the StarryBackground class is m_iNumStars, which keeps track of how many stars appear on the background. This number is stored as a variable, as opposed to a constant, because you might want to vary the number of stars in different games. The m_iTwinkleDelay member variable is used to control how fast the stars twinkle—the longer the delay, the slower they twinkle. So, setting a small value for the twinkle delay causes the stars to twinkle rapidly, which isn't very realistic. You'll find out in a moment that there is a default twinkle delay that I've found to be reasonably realistic in most situations.

The stars themselves are stored in two different member variables, m_ptStars and m_crStarColors. The m_ptStars variable is an array of points that stores the location of each individual star. You still need to keep track of the color of each star, which is a shade of gray that can vary between black and bright white. The m_crStarColors array stores the color of each star and corresponds directly to the stars stored in the m_ptStars array. Notice that both arrays are created with 100 elements, which means that you can't have more than 100 stars in the starry background; feel free to change this number if you feel strongly about having more stars in your own starry backgrounds.

Moving right along, the constructor for the StarryBackground class accepts several arguments to describe the starry background. More specifically, it allows you to provide the width, height, number of stars, and twinkle delay for the background. It's important to note that the number of stars and twinkle delay arguments have default values, which you might find suitable for your games. You can also use your own trial and error approach to deciding exactly how many stars you like, as well as what kind of twinkle delay results in a good look for the twinkling stars.

The constructor for the StarryBackground class is shown in Listing 16.5 and reveals how the stars are created.

LISTING 16.5 The StarryBackground::StarryBackground() Constructor Is Used to Create a Starry Background

```
StarryBackground::StarryBackground(int iWidth, int iHeight, int iNumStars,
  int iTwinkleDelay) : Background(iWidth, iHeight, 0)
{
  // Initialize the member variables
  m_iNumStars = min(iNumStars, 100)
  m_iTwinkleDelay = iTwinkleDelay;

  // Create the stars
  for (int i = 0; i < iNumStars; i++)
  {
    m_ptStars[i].x = rand() % iWidth;
    m_ptStars[i].y = rand() % iHeight;
    m_crStarColors[i] = RGB(128, 128, 128);
  }
}
```

To support more stars, raise the 100 in this code to match the larger arrays from the member variable declarations.

The StarryBackground() constructor first initializes the m_iNumStars member variable, making sure not to allow it to be set any higher than 100. The twinkle delay is then set, and the star creation process begins. The creation of the stars involves looping through the number of stars and then setting the position of each star to a random value, as well as setting the color of each star to a neutral color. By neutral color, I mean a shade of gray that isn't too bright or too dark.

Once the stars are created in the constructor, you can turn your attention to the Update() and Draw() methods, which are really the most important parts of the StarryBackground class. Listing 16.6 contains the code for these methods.

LISTING 16.6 The StarryBackground::Update() and StarryBackground::Draw() Methods Handle the Updating and Drawing of a Starry Background

```
void StarryBackground::Update()
{
  // Randomly change the shade of the stars so that they twinkle
  int iRGB;
  for (int i = 0; i < m_iNumStars; i++)
    if ((rand() % m_iTwinkleDelay) == 0)
    {
      iRGB = rand() % 256;
      m_crStarColors[i] = RGB(iRGB, iRGB, iRGB);
    }
}

void StarryBackground::Draw(HDC hDC)
{
  // Draw the solid black background
  RECT    rect = { 0, 0, m_iWidth, m_iHeight };
  HBRUSH  hBrush = CreateSolidBrush(RGB(0, 0, 0));
  FillRect(hDC, &rect, hBrush);
  DeleteObject(hBrush);

  // Draw the stars
  for (int i = 0; i < m_iNumStars; i++)
    SetPixel(hDC, m_ptStars[i].x, m_ptStars[i].y, m_crStarColors[i]);
}
```

As long as the red, blue, and green color components are always equal, the star will be a shade of gray.

The standard SetPixel() function allows you to set the color of a single pixel on the game screen.

The Update() method in this code is responsible for causing the stars to twinkle. This is accomplished by randomly changing the color of each star to a different shade of gray. The stars are looped through, and the twinkle delay is used as the basis for determining if the color of a star should be changed. If so, a random number is selected between 0 and 255, and this color is used for each of the three color components to establish a new color for the star.

The Draw() method for the StarryBackground class is used to draw the background, and it involves first drawing a solid black rectangle, followed by drawing the individual stars. The black rectangle is drawn with a call to FillRect(), which you saw earlier in the book. The more interesting code occurs near the end of the method and consists of a loop that draws each individual star with a call to SetPixel(). The SetPixel() function is a Win32 function that sets an individual pixel to a specified color.

Building the Roids Example

As with every new improvement to the game engine, new concepts only fully make sense when you see them in action. The remainder of the chapter shows you how to put the new background classes to use in an example called Roids. The Roids program simulates an asteroid field by displaying several animated asteroid sprites over an animated starry background. Not surprisingly, the StarryBackground class is used as the basis for the background in the Roids program.

Writing the Program Code

The Roids program begins with the Roids.h header file, which declares global variables that are important to the program. Take a look at Listing 16.7 to see these variables.

LISTING 16.7 The Roids.h Header File Imports Several Header Files and Declares Global Variables Required for the Background and Asteroid Sprites

```
#pragma once

//----------------------------------
// Include Files
//----------------------------------
#include <windows.h>
#include "Resource.h"
#include "GameEngine.h"
#include "Bitmap.h"
```

LISTING 16.7   Continued

```
#include "Sprite.h"
#include "Background.h"

//---------------------------------.
// Global Variables
//---------------------------------.
HINSTANCE           g_hInstance;
GameEngine*         g_pGame;
HDC                 g_hOffscreenDC;
HBITMAP             g_hOffscreenBitmap;
Bitmap*             g_pAsteroidBitmap;
StarryBackground*   g_pBackground;
```

The asteroid bitmap contains 14 animation frames to simulate an asteroid tumbling through space.

The first variable unique to the Roids program is g_pAsteroidBitmap, which is a bitmap for an asteroid image. This image is actually a series of frame images for an asteroid that appears to be tumbling when it is animated. In total, there are 14 frames in the asteroid image (see Figure 16.2), as you find out in a moment when you create the asteroid sprites. The other important global variable in the Roids program is the g_pBackground variable, which stores a pointer to a StarryBackground object. This object serves as the background for the program.

FIGURE 16.2
Although only the first 7 frames are shown here, the animated asteroid sprite consists of 14 animation frames to provide a smooth tumbling effect.

The GameStart() function is where the Roids program really gets rolling because it is responsible for creating bitmaps and sprites, not to mention the starry background. Listing 16.8 shows the code for this function.

LISTING 16.8 The GameStart() Function Creates and Loads the Asteroid Bitmap, the Starry Background, and the Asteroid Sprites

```
void GameStart(HWND hWindow)
{
  // Seed the random number generator
  srand(GetTickCount());

  // Create the offscreen device context and bitmap
  g_hOffscreenDC = CreateCompatibleDC(GetDC(hWindow));
  g_hOffscreenBitmap = CreateCompatibleBitmap(GetDC(hWindow),
    g_pGame->GetWidth(), g_pGame->GetHeight());
  SelectObject(g_hOffscreenDC, g_hOffscreenBitmap);

  // Create and load the asteroid bitmap
  HDC hDC = GetDC(hWindow);
  g_pAsteroidBitmap = new Bitmap(hDC, IDB_ASTEROID, g_hInstance);

  // Create the starry background
  g_pBackground = new StarryBackground(500, 400);

  // Create the asteroid sprites
  RECT    rcBounds = { 0, 0, 500, 400 };
  Sprite* pSprite;
  pSprite = new Sprite(g_pAsteroidBitmap, rcBounds, BA_WRAP);
  pSprite->SetNumFrames(14);
  pSprite->SetFrameDelay(1);
  pSprite->SetPosition(250, 200);
  pSprite->SetVelocity(-3, 1);
  g_pGame->AddSprite(pSprite);
  pSprite = new Sprite(g_pAsteroidBitmap, rcBounds, BA_WRAP);
  pSprite->SetNumFrames(14);
  pSprite->SetFrameDelay(2);
  pSprite->SetPosition(250, 200);
  pSprite->SetVelocity(3, -2);
  g_pGame->AddSprite(pSprite);
  pSprite = new Sprite(g_pAsteroidBitmap, rcBounds, BA_WRAP);
  pSprite->SetNumFrames(14);
  pSprite->SetFrameDelay(3);
  pSprite->SetPosition(250, 200);
  pSprite->SetVelocity(-2, -4);
  g_pGame->AddSprite(pSprite);
}
```

The starry background is created to be the same size as the game screen.

Each asteroid is animated with 14 animation frames, but their frame delays are different so that they appear to tumble at varying speeds.

The first few sections of code in the GameStart() function should be familiar to you from other examples, so I'll spare you a recap. Instead, let's jump straight to the line of code that creates the StarryBackground object. As you can see, the starry background is set to a size of 500x400, which is the same size as the game screen. Because no other arguments are provided for the new object, the default values of 100 for the number of stars and 50 for the twinkle delay are assumed.

The remainder of the GameStart() function focuses on the creation of the asteroid sprites. Notice that the number of frames for each of these sprites is set to 14, which indicates that 14 frame images are stored in the image for the asteroid. Also, the frame delay of each sprite is set differently so that the asteroids appear to tumble at various speeds. Beyond those settings, nothing is tricky or otherwise noteworthy regarding the asteroid sprites.

The GamePaint()function is responsible for drawing the graphics in the Roids program, as shown in Listing 16.9.

LISTING 16.9   The GamePaint() **Function Draws the Starry Background and the Asteroid Sprites**

```
void GamePaint(HDC hDC)
{
  // Draw the background
  g_pBackground->Draw(hDC);

  // Draw the sprites
  g_pGame->DrawSprites(hDC);
}
```

The important line of code worth paying attention to here is the line that calls the Draw() method on the StarryBackground object. As long as the background is drawn before the sprites, everything works great.

The final function on the Roids agenda is GameCycle(),which takes care of updating the animated graphics in the program. Because the background is animated, it also must be updated in the GameCycle() function, as shown in Listing 16.10.

LISTING 16.10   The GameCycle() **Function Updates the Starry Background and Asteroid Sprites and then Repaints the Game Screen**

```
void GameCycle()
{
  // Update the background
  g_pBackground->Update();

  // Update the sprites
  g_pGame->UpdateSprites();

  // Obtain a device context for repainting the game
  HWND  hWindow = g_pGame->GetWindow();
```

```
HDC   hDC = GetDC(hWindow);

// Paint the game to the offscreen device context
GamePaint(g_hOffscreenDC);

// Blit the offscreen bitmap to the game screen
BitBlt(hDC, 0, 0, g_pGame->GetWidth(), g_pGame->GetHeight(),
  g_hOffscreenDC, 0, 0, SRCCOPY);

// Cleanup
ReleaseDC(hWindow, hDC);
}
```

The background is the first thing updated in the GameCycle() function, and this simply involves a call to the Update() method on the StarryBackground class (the g_pBackground global variable). This call is sufficient enough to cause the entire background to come alive with twinkling stars. If you don't believe me, try commenting out this line of code and see what happens to the background—no animation and, therefore, not much excitement!

Construction Cue

If you're using Visual C++ 6.0, you might need to change the type casts from (DWORD_PTR) to (DWORD) in GameEngine.cpp in order for the Roids code to compile properly.

Construction Cue

As with most of the examples in the book, the Roids program relies on the standard msimg32.lib and winmm.lib libraries. These libraries are included with most Windows compilers, but they aren't automatically linked into programs when you create a new project. If you are using your own project or make files, as opposed to using the ones provided on the CD-ROM, make sure that you change the link settings so that these library files are properly linked into the final executable. Refer to the documentation for your specific compiler for how this is done.

Testing the Finished Product

Granted, the Roids example isn't quite up to par with the classic Asteroids game. In fact, Roids isn't a game at all. This is because I wanted to focus on the specific task of using an animated background without the distraction of trying to assemble a complete game. If you're dying to build another complete game, your wishes will be answered in the next chapter. But for now, take a look at Figure 16.3 to see the Roids program in action.

FIGURE 16.3
The asteroid sprites in the Roids program float and tumble over an animated starry background, thanks to the new background classes in the game engine.

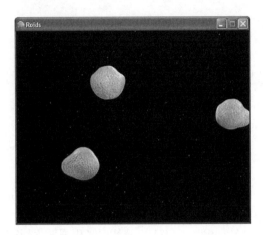

In addition to noticing how effective the twinkling stars are at presenting an interesting space background, hopefully, you're now appreciating the power of animated sprites. This has to do with the fact that the animated asteroids in the Roids program are considerably smoother and more detailed than the animated guys in the Battle Office 2 game through which you first learned about animated sprites. It's starting to become clear that you can get some surprisingly powerful visual effects out of the game engine when you combine an animated background with high-quality sprite graphics.

Summary

Although you've certainly included backgrounds in several of the examples and games you've developed throughout the book thus far, this chapter took a closer look at the role of backgrounds and why they are so important to games. You also found out about the main types of backgrounds and what kinds of games demand each of them. The remainder of the chapter focused on adding background support to the game engine in the form of two new classes, Background and StarryBackground. You now have a few classes you can reuse in your own games, as well as the knowledge to create custom animated backgrounds of your own.

The next chapter incorporates much of what you've learned throughout the book in an example game called Meteor Defense. If you're familiar at all with the classic Missile Command game, you'll no doubt appreciate the Meteor Defense game.

Field Trip

Find a local theatrical performance that sounds interesting and go see it. Although I'll admit to being part of the generation that grew up on motion pictures, instead of live theater, viewing a live theatrical production in person can teach you a thing or two about set design as it applies to games. If you happen to be in Las Vegas, I highly recommend Penn and Teller's show. If not, I'm sure that you can find something worthwhile in your area. If you're the kind of person who frowns on theater in contrast to a good action movie, allow me to share with you that I had a friend in college who got a job at LucasArts as a game developer primarily because of his experience in local theater. So if you've ever thought that working on a Star Wars video game might be cool, give theater a chance. While you're there, pay close attention to how the background is manipulated to help visually enhance each scene.

CHAPTER 17

Example Game: Meteor Defense

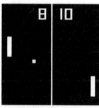

Widely regarded as one of the most comical arcade games of all time, BurgerTime was released in 1982 by Bally Midway. The game follows a chef named Peter Pepper, who is busy making several rather large hamburgers. The heroic chef must walk over the different parts of the hamburgers to make them fall and stack up at the bottom of the screen. His enemies are Mr. Hotdog, Mr. Egg, and Mr. Pickle—all of whom chase him around and can only be defended against with pepper. If this premise sounds like a strange nightmare, you'll be glad to know that the game is actually fun to play. In case you're wondering, the name of the hamburger restaurant in the game is unnamed, although rumors claim it is named BurgerTime after the game.

This chapter guides you through the design and development of another complete game. You've spent the past couple of chapters learning how to animate the appearance of sprites and spruce up the background of games, and it's now time to put this knowledge to work in an entirely new game. The game is called Meteor Defense, and it is loosely based on the classic Missile Command arcade game. Seeing as how there have been several news reports and major motion pictures in the past few years about the potential of a significant meteor collision with the Earth, I thought it might make a neat premise for a game. It wouldn't necessarily be a bad idea to have a missile-based system for stopping incoming meteors, which is the premise behind the game Meteor Defense.

In this chapter, you'll learn

- ▶ About the conceptual overview of the Meteor Defense game
- ▶ How to design the Meteor Defense game

- ▶ How to add a few new sprite features to the game engine
- ▶ What it takes to build the Meteor Defense game
- ▶ How much fun it can be testing a new game

How Does the Game Play?

One of the classic arcade games that many people remember is Missile Command, which involves the defense of a group of cities against a nuclear attack. The nuclear attack is made up of missiles that travel down from the top of the screen toward the cities at the bottom. Your job is to fire upon the missiles and destroy them before they reach the cities. Although Missile Command made for an interesting game in the era of the hit movie *War Games*, the threat of a global thermonuclear war is somewhat diminished these days—at least in terms of what most of us perceive as a realistic threat. However, there has been increasing talk in the past few years about the possibility of a meteor striking the Earth and causing major damage.

The premise of the game you develop in this chapter is similar to Missile Command in that you're defending helpless cities against an incoming threat. In this case, however, the threat is comprised of giant meteors, not nuclear warheads. The Meteor Defense game employs a game play strategy similar to Missile Command in that you fire missiles at the incoming meteors to stop them from destroying the cities below. As you'll find out, the critical skills to becoming a good player at Meteor Defense (and Missile Command as well) are learning how to target a meteor and to give a missile time to get there. In other words, you often have to lead a meteor by a certain distance in order to give the missile time to get there and make contact.

The object of Meteor Defense is to simply protect the cities against the incoming meteors for as long as possible. One interesting aspect of the game is that you lose points whenever you fire a missile, which makes it important to be efficient when you fire on the meteors. In other words, if you unleash missiles indiscriminately, you will no doubt protect the cities, but your score will suffer. This is a subtle way to discourage sloppy game play. Small touches, such as this, can often make a game much more appealing to serious game players.

Designing the Game

The design of the Meteor Defense game flows directly from the overview of the game that you just went through. The game is well suited for the starry background that you created and used in the previous chapter. It's also fairly obvious that the meteors should be represented by animated sprites similar to those found in the Roids example from the previous chapter. Because you must be able to detect a collision between a meteor and a city, the cities also need to be modeled as sprites, even though they don't move. Representing cities as sprites also gives you the freedom to hide them whenever they are destroyed by a meteor.

Gamer's Garage

In case you were wondering, the terms meteor, meteorite, and meteoroid are all closely related. A *meteoroid* is a chunk of rock in space that ranges in size from a speck of dust to 100 meters across. A *meteor* is the bright flash of light generated by a meteoroid when it travels through Earth's atmosphere. Finally, a *meteorite* is a meteor that has survived the transition through Earth's atmosphere and comes to rest on the Earth's surface.

The missiles in the game are ideal candidates for sprites because they move and collide with meteors. This is generally a good rule of thumb when it comes to deciding which graphical objects should be represented as sprites and which ones can simply be placed in the background: If the object needs to move, animate, and/or collide with other objects, it should be a sprite. A good application of this test involves the guns used to fire missiles in the Meteor Defense game. The guns don't move or animate, and it isn't important to detect a collision between them and anything else. Therefore, you can simply include the guns in the background image for the game.

Wait a minute—I just mentioned using a background image, but I already said that the background is the starry background from earlier in the book. The Meteor Defense game actually uses a hybrid background in that it displays an image of the ground over the starry background. This allows you to get the benefits of the animated starry sky, while also showing the ground where the cities are located—not to mention the guns that fire the missiles. To help you get a feel for how the Meteor Defense game is laid out, take a look at Figure 17.1.

FIGURE 17.1
The Meteor Defense game consists of a starry background, a ground image with guns, several cities, incoming meteors, and missiles.

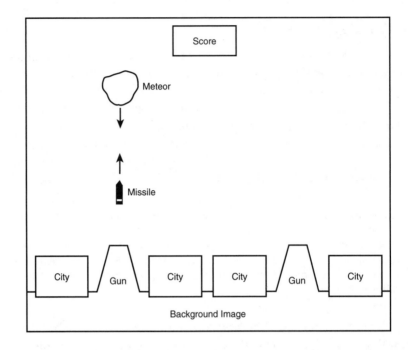

The figure reveals how the guns make up part of the background image that appears along the bottom edge of the game screen. Keep in mind that a starry background still appears in the majority of the screen—the background image just shows the ground where the cities are located. The city sprites are laid on top of the edge of the ground so that they blend into the ground image. The missile and meteor sprites move around on top of the starry background, while the score is displayed centered near the top of the game screen. One last piece of the game not shown in the figure is the target sprite that you guide with the mouse, much like the target sprite you saw in the Battle Office game earlier in the book.

Now that you understand the basics of the game and how it is laid out, it's time to examine what kinds of sprites need to be used. The following is a list of the sprites that go into the Meteor Defense game:

▶ City sprites

▶ Meteor sprites

- ▶ Missile sprites
- ▶ Explosion sprites
- ▶ Target sprite

The city sprites appear along the bottom of the screen, as shown in Figure 17.1. The meteor sprites are created at random and fall from the top of the screen toward the cities at the bottom. The missile sprites are fired from the gun locations on the screen up toward the meteors. I haven't mentioned the explosion sprites yet because there aren't a whole lot to them. An explosion sprite appears whenever a meteor is blown up or a city is destroyed and involves displaying animation of a fiery explosion. Finally, the target sprite appears as a crosshair that you guide with the mouse to aim missiles that you launch via the left mouse button.

To go along with the sprites, the Meteor Defense game requires several bitmap images. The following are the seven bitmap images required of the game:

- ▶ Background ground image
- ▶ City image (see Figure 17.2)
- ▶ Animated meteor image (see Figure 17.3)
- ▶ Missile image (see Figure 17.4)
- ▶ Animated explosion image (see Figure 17.5)
- ▶ Crosshair target image (see Figure 17.6)
- ▶ Game over image

FIGURE 17.2
The city bitmap image shows the skyline of a city waiting to be defended.

FIGURE 17.3
The first seven frames of the animated meteor bitmap image reveal how the meteor sprite will appear to tumble in the game.

FIGURE 17.4
The missile bitmap image consists of a missile aimed up with a visible propulsion from the bottom.

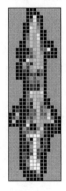

These images should make sense based on the description of the game and the sprites you've learned about.

With the graphical objects squared away, you need to turn your attention to the other information that must be maintained by the game. For example, the score needs to be maintained throughout the game, as does the number of remaining cities; the game ends when all four cities are destroyed by meteors. This is a game in which it is important to increase the difficulty level as the game progresses. So, it's important to store the difficulty level of the game and gradually increase it as the player continues to keep his cities protected. The last critical piece of information to maintain is a Boolean variable to keep track of whether or not the game is over.

FIGURE 17.5
The first eight frames of the animated explosion bitmap image reveal how the explosion sprite will appear to flame outward and then dissipate.

FIGURE 17.6
The crosshair target bitmap image is used to provide a means of aiming missiles in the game.

To recap, the design of the Meteor Defense game has led us to the following pieces of information that must be managed by the game:

▶ The number of cities remaining

▶ The score

▶ The difficulty level

▶ A Boolean game over variable

With this information in mind, you're now almost ready to take the big step of assembling the code for the Meteor Defense game. However, there is a modification you need to make to the game engine to support a critical feature of the game and, ultimately, improve the game engine for future games.

Enhancing Sprites in the Game Engine

If you're a particularly inquisitive person, you might have wondered how exactly the explosion sprites will work in the game. The animation part is simple enough because the Sprite class in the game engine now allows you to flip through a series of animation images. However, an explosion sprite must cycle through its animation frames and then immediately go away, which sounds simple but presents a problem for the game engine. The problem is that there currently is no mechanism for a sprite to hide or kill itself automatically when it is no longer needed. Granted, you can kill a sprite from within the game code, but how would you keep track of when the frame animation for an explosion is finished?

The real problem I'm talking about here is that of allowing a sprite to animate through one cycle and then go away. The game engine doesn't currently support this feature, but it's not too difficult to add. Without this feature, there is no straightforward way to use a sprite, such as an explosion that must cycle through its animation once and then exit the game. The key to adding this feature to the game engine is to include a couple of new variables to the Sprite class:

```
BOOL m_bDying;
BOOL m_bOneCycle;
```

The m_bDying member variable determines whether a sprite has been flagged as dying. In other words, normal sprites have their m_bDying variables set to FALSE, whereas a sprite on the way to the sprite graveyard has it set to TRUE. The cool thing about this variable is that it allows you to kill a sprite at any time by simply setting the variable to TRUE. Of course, this requires some additional code in both the Sprite and GameEngine classes to make it actually work.

The second member variable, m_bOneCycle, indicates whether a sprite should animate once through its frames and then kill itself. Because this variable only makes sense within the context of a frame-animated sprite, it is set when you call the SetNumFrames() method. You'll see how the SetNumFrames() method is modified to account for the m_bOneCycle variable in a moment.

For now, let's take a look at how the two new Sprite member variables are initialized in the Sprite() constructors:

```
m_bDying = FALSE;
m_bOneCycle = FALSE;
```

As you might expect, the default value of each variable is FALSE, which makes sprites behave normally.

The m_bDying member variable can be set to TRUE through the Kill() method, which is really just an accessor method because all it does is set the variable:

```
void Kill()  { m_bDying = TRUE; };
```

This method now gives you a clean and efficient means of killing any sprite— with the security of knowing that it will be properly removed from the sprite list maintained by the game engine. This is a crucial aspect of destroying a sprite because the sprite list in the game engine would go haywire if you were to simply delete a sprite from memory and not remove it from the list. The Kill() method provides a clean interface for carrying out this task.

Although the Kill() method provides an immediate way to kill a sprite that can be useful in some situations, the more elegant approach is to allow a sprite to kill itself when it finishes cycling through its frame animations. The UpdateFrame() method now supports this feature by examining the m_bOneCycle variable and then setting the m_bDying variable accordingly. The original version of this method simply set the m_iCurFrame variable to 0 so that the animation started over, which this method still does if the m_bOneCycle variable is FALSE. However, if the m_bOneCycle variable is TRUE, the m_bDying variable is set to TRUE, which starts the sprite on a path to destruction.

The m_bOneCycle variable is set in the SetNumFrames() method, which now looks like this:

```
void SetNumFrames(int iNumFrames, BOOL bOneCycle = FALSE);
```

As you can see, the SetNumFrames() method now includes a second argument for setting the m_bOneCycle member variable. To help make the transition to using the new version of the method easier, the m_bOneCycle argument is given a default value of FALSE. This allows you to use the method just as you've already grown accustomed. However, if you want to create a sprite that cycles through its animation once and then goes away, just pass TRUE as the second argument to SetNumFrames().

Getting back to the killing of a sprite via the m_bDying member variable, the place where the murder plot unfolds is in the Update() method, which is shown in Listing 17.1.

LISTING 17.1   The `Sprite::Update()` Method Kills a Sprite if It Is Flagged as Dying

```
SPRITEACTION Sprite::Update()
{
  // See if the sprite needs to be killed
  if (m_bDying)
    return SA_KILL;

  // Update the frame
  UpdateFrame();

  ...
}
```

If you recall, the `Sprite::Update()` method is actually a large method, so I'm only showing you the beginning of it here because this part of the code is all that has changed. The method now checks the value of the `m_bDying` member variable and then returns `SA_KILL` if it is set to `TRUE`. If you recall from earlier in the book, `SA_KILL` is a sprite action you created that notifies the game engine when a sprite needs to be killed. Prior to now, it was only used to kill a sprite when it encountered a boundary.

Simply killing a sprite isn't quite sufficient when it comes to improving the game engine for future games. You'll find out later in the chapter that it can be incredibly useful to know when a sprite is being destroyed—regardless of why it is being destroyed. For example, when a meteor sprite is destroyed, you can create an explosion sprite to show the destruction of the meteor. The notification of a sprite being killed is made possible through the `SpriteDying()` function, which is called whenever a sprite is dying:

```
void SpriteDying(Sprite* pSprite);
```

Understand that the `SpriteDying()` function is a function that you must provide as part of a game. In other words, it is designed to house game-specific code that responds to particular types of sprites dying within a game.

The final change to the game engine to support the new sprite-killing features appears within the `GameEngine` class in the `UpdateSprites()` method, which now includes a call to `SpriteDying()` that notifies a game of a sprite being destroyed and removed from the sprite list. This gives the game a chance to respond to the sprite's demise and carry out any appropriate actions.

Building the Game

You can breathe a sigh of relief because you're finished making changes to the game engine for a little while. However, the real challenge of putting together the Meteor Defense game now awaits you. Fortunately, the game isn't too difficult to understand because you've already worked through a reasonably detailed game design. The next few sections guide you through the development of the game's code and resources.

Writing the Game Code

The code for the Meteor Defense game begins in the MeteorDefense.h header file, which is responsible for declaring the global variables used throughout the game, as well as a couple of useful functions. Listing 17.2 contains the code for this file.

LISTING 17.2   The MeteorDefense.h Header File Declares Global Variables and Game-Specific Functions for the Meteor Defense Game

```
#pragma once

//----------------------------------------------.
// Include Files
//----------------------------------------------.
#include <windows.h>
#include "Resource.h"
#include "GameEngine.h"
#include "Bitmap.h"
#include "Sprite.h"
#include "Background.h"


//----------------------------------------------.
// Global Variables
//----------------------------------------------.
HINSTANCE           g_hInstance;
GameEngine*         g_pGame;
HDC                 g_hOffscreenDC;
HBITMAP             g_hOffscreenBitmap;
Bitmap*             g_pGroundBitmap;
Bitmap*             g_pTargetBitmap;
Bitmap*             g_pCityBitmap;
Bitmap*             g_pMeteorBitmap;
Bitmap*             g_pMissileBitmap;
Bitmap*             g_pExplosionBitmap;
Bitmap*             g_pGameOverBitmap;
StarryBackground*   g_pBackground;
Sprite*             g_pTargetSprite;
int                 g_iNumCities, g_iScore, g_iDifficulty;
BOOL                g_bGameOver;
```

continues

LISTING 17.2   Continued

```
// ------------------------------------------------.
// Function Declarations
// ------------------------------------------------.
void NewGame();
void AddMeteor();
```

As the listing reveals, the global variables for the Meteor Defense game largely consist of the different bitmaps that are used throughout the game. The starry background for the game is declared after the bitmaps, followed by the crosshair target sprite. Member variables storing the number of remaining cities, the score, and the difficulty level are then declared, along with the familiar game over Boolean variable.

The NewGame() function declared in the MeteorDefense.h file is important because it is used to set up and start a new game. Unlike the GameStart() function, which performs critical initialization tasks such as loading bitmaps, the NewGame() function deals with actually starting a new game once everything else is in place. The AddMeteor() function is a support function used to simplify the task of adding meteor sprites to the game. You'll find out more about how these functions work later in the chapter.

The initialization of the game variables primarily takes place in the GameStart() function, which is shown in Listing 17.3.

LISTING 17.3   The GameStart() Function Initializes the Bitmaps and Background for the Game and Calls the NewGame() Function

```
void GameStart(HWND hWindow)
{
  // Seed the random number generator
  srand(GetTickCount());

  // Create the offscreen device context and bitmap
  g_hOffscreenDC = CreateCompatibleDC(GetDC(hWindow));
  g_hOffscreenBitmap = CreateCompatibleBitmap(GetDC(hWindow),
    g_pGame->GetWidth(), g_pGame->GetHeight());
  SelectObject(g_hOffscreenDC, g_hOffscreenBitmap);

  // Create and load the bitmaps
  HDC hDC = GetDC(hWindow);
  g_pGroundBitmap = new Bitmap(hDC, IDB_GROUND, g_hInstance);
  g_pTargetBitmap = new Bitmap(hDC, IDB_TARGET, g_hInstance);
  g_pCityBitmap = new Bitmap(hDC, IDB_CITY, g_hInstance);
  g_pMeteorBitmap = new Bitmap(hDC, IDB_METEOR, g_hInstance);
  g_pMissileBitmap = new Bitmap(hDC, IDB_MISSILE, g_hInstance);
```

```
g_pExplosionBitmap = new Bitmap(hDC, IDB_EXPLOSION, g_hInstance);
g_pGameOverBitmap = new Bitmap(hDC, IDB_GAMEOVER, g_hInstance);

// Create the starry background
g_pBackground = new StarryBackground(600, 450);

// Play the background music
g_pGame->PlayMIDISong(TEXT("Music.mid"));

// Start the game
NewGame();
}
```

Notice that this starry background is a different size from the one used in the Roids example in the previous chapter.

After loading the bitmaps for the game and creating the starry background, the GameStart() function starts playing the background music. The function then finishes by calling the NewGame() function to start a new game.

The GameEnd() function plays a complementary role to the GameStart() function and cleans up after the game. Listing 17.4 contains the code for the GameEnd() function.

LISTING 17.4   The GameEnd() Function Cleans Up After the Game

```
void GameEnd()
{
  // Close the MIDI player for the background music
  g_pGame->CloseMIDIPlayer();

  // Cleanup the offscreen device context and bitmap
  DeleteObject(g_hOffscreenBitmap);
  DeleteDC(g_hOffscreenDC);

  // Cleanup the bitmaps
  delete g_pGroundBitmap;
  delete g_pTargetBitmap;
  delete g_pCityBitmap;
  delete g_pMeteorBitmap;
  delete g_pMissileBitmap;
  delete g_pExplosionBitmap;
  delete g_pGameOverBitmap;

  // Cleanup the background
  delete g_pBackground;

  // Cleanup the sprites
  g_pGame->CleanupSprites();

  // Cleanup the game engine
  delete g_pGame;
}
```

The first step in the GameEnd() function is to close the MIDI music player. The bitmaps and sprites are then wiped away, as is the background. Finally, the sprites are cleaned up, and the game engine is destroyed.

The game screen in the Meteor Defense game is painted by the GamePaint() function, which is shown in Listing 17.5.

LISTING 17.5   The GamePaint() Function Draws the Background, the Ground Bitmap, the Sprites, the Score, and the Game Over Message

```
void GamePaint(HDC hDC)
{
  // Draw the background
  g_pBackground->Draw(hDC);

  // Draw the ground bitmap
  g_pGroundBitmap->Draw(hDC, 0, 398, TRUE);

  // Draw the sprites
  g_pGame->DrawSprites(hDC);

  // Draw the score
  TCHAR szText[64];
  RECT  rect = { 275, 0, 325, 50 };
  wsprintf(szText, "%d", g_iScore);
  SetBkMode(hDC, TRANSPARENT);
  SetTextColor(hDC, RGB(255, 255, 255));
  DrawText(hDC, szText, -1, &rect, DT_SINGLELINE ¦ DT_CENTER ¦ DT_VCENTER);

  // Draw the game over message, if necessary
  if (g_bGameOver)
    g_pGameOverBitmap->Draw(hDC, 170, 150, TRUE);
}
```

The background is drawn first to ensure that it does indeed appear in the background of the game.

As you know by now, the GamePaint() function is responsible for drawing all the graphics for the game. The function begins by drawing the starry background, followed by the ground image. The sprites are drawn next, followed by the score. Notice that the score text is set to white, whereas the background for drawing the score is set to transparent so that the starry sky shows through the numbers in the score. The GamePaint() function finishes up by drawing the game over image, if necessary.

The GameCycle() function works closely with GamePaint() to update the game's sprites and reflect the changes onscreen. Listing 17.6 shows the code for the GameCycle()function.

LISTING 17.6   The `GameCycle()` Function Randomly Adds Meteors to the Game Based on the Difficulty Level

```
void GameCycle()
{
  if (!g_bGameOver)
  {
    // Randomly add meteors
    if ((rand() % g_iDifficulty) == 0)        ⎤
      AddMeteor();                            ⎦

    // Update the background
    g_pBackground->Update();

    // Update the sprites
    g_pGame->UpdateSprites();

    // Obtain a device context for repainting the game
    HWND   hWindow = g_pGame->GetWindow();
    HDC    hDC = GetDC(hWindow);

    // Paint the game to the offscreen device context
    GamePaint(g_hOffscreenDC);

    // Blit the offscreen bitmap to the game screen
    BitBlt(hDC, 0, 0, g_pGame->GetWidth(), g_pGame->GetHeight(),
      g_hOffscreenDC, 0, 0, SRCCOPY);

    // Cleanup
    ReleaseDC(hWindow, hDC);
  }
}
```

Meteors are randomly added at a rate determined by the difficulty level.

Aside from the standard `GameCycle()` code that you've grown accustomed to seeing, this function doesn't contain a whole lot of additional code. The new code involves randomly adding new meteors, which is accomplished by calling the `AddMeteor()` function after using the difficulty level to randomly determine if a meteor should be added.

The `MouseButtonDown()`function is where most of the game logic for the Meteor Defense game is located, as shown in Listing 17.7.

LISTING 17.7   The `MouseButtonDown()` Function Launches a Missile Sprite Toward the Location of the Mouse Pointer

```
void MouseButtonDown(int x, int y, BOOL bLeft)
{
  if (!g_bGameOver && bLeft)
  {
    // Create a new missile sprite and set its position
    RECT    rcBounds = { 0, 0, 600, 450 };
```

continues

LISTING 17.7   Continued

It is important for the missile sprite to start its trajectory from one of the two cannons.

The velocity of the missile is calculated so that it flies toward the target.

```
int      iXPos = (x < 300) ? 144 : 449;
Sprite* pSprite = new Sprite(g_pMissileBitmap, rcBounds, BA_DIE);
pSprite->SetPosition(iXPos, 365);

// Calculate the velocity so that it is aimed at the target
int iXVel, iYVel = -6;
y = min(y, 300);
iXVel = (iYVel * ((iXPos + 8) - x)) / (365 - y);
pSprite->SetVelocity(iXVel, iYVel);

// Add the missile sprite
g_pGame->AddSprite(pSprite);

// Play the fire sound
PlaySound((LPCSTR)IDW_FIRE, g_hInstance, SND_ASYNC ¦
  SND_RESOURCE ¦ SND_NOSTOP);
```

The score is decreased slightly with each missile fired, which rewards accuracy in the game.

```
// Update the score
g_iScore = max(-g_iScore, 0);
}
else if (g_bGameOver && !bLeft)
// Start a new game
NewGame();
}
```

The MouseButtonDown() function handles firing a missile toward the target. The function first checks to make sure that the game isn't over and that the player clicked the left mouse button. If so, a missile sprite is created based on the position of the mouse pointer. The position is important first because it determines which gun is used to fire the missile—the left gun fires missiles toward targets on the left side of the game screen, whereas the right gun takes care of the right side of the screen. The target position is also important because it determines the trajectory and, therefore, the XY velocity of the missile.

After the missile sprite is created, the MouseButtonDown() function adds it to the game engine. A sound effect is then played to indicate that the missile has been fired. Earlier in the chapter during the design of the game, I mentioned how the score would be decreased slightly with each missile firing, which discourages inaccuracy in firing missiles because you can only build up your score by efficiently destroying meteors with the missiles. The score is decreased upon firing a missile near the end of the function. The last code in the MouseButtonDown() function takes care of starting a new game via the right mouse button if the game is over.

Another mouse-related function used in the Meteor Defense game is MouseMove(), which is used to move the crosshair target sprite so that it tracks the mouse pointer. This is necessary so that you are always in control of the target sprite with the mouse. Listing 17.8 shows the code for the MouseMove() function.

LISTING 17.8 The `MouseMove()` Function Tracks the Mouse Cursor with the Target Sprite

```
void MouseMove(int x, int y)
{
  // Track the mouse with the target sprite
  g_pTargetSprite->SetPosition(x - (g_pTargetSprite->GetWidth() / 2),
    y - (g_pTargetSprite->GetHeight() / 2));
}
```

The target sprite is made to follow the mouse pointer by simply calling the `SetPosition()` method on the sprite and passing in the mouse coordinates. The position of the target sprite is calculated so that the target sprite always appears centered on the mouse pointer.

The `SpriteCollision()` function is called in response to sprites colliding and is extremely important in the Meteor Defense game, as shown in Listing 17.9.

LISTING 17.9 The `SpriteCollision()` Function Detects and Responds to Collisions Between Missiles, Meteors, and Cities

```
BOOL SpriteCollision(Sprite* pSpriteHitter, Sprite* pSpriteHittee)
{
  // See if a missile and a meteor have collided
  if ((pSpriteHitter->GetBitmap() == g_pMissileBitmap &&
    pSpriteHittee->GetBitmap() == g_pMeteorBitmap) ||
    (pSpriteHitter->GetBitmap() == g_pMeteorBitmap &&
    pSpriteHittee->GetBitmap() == g_pMissileBitmap))
  {
    // Kill both sprites
    pSpriteHitter->Kill();                          ──── If a missile and a
    pSpriteHittee->Kill();                               meteor have collid-
                                                         ed, kill them both.
    // Update the score
    g_iScore += 6;
    g_iDifficulty = max(50 - (g_iScore / 10), 5);
  }

  // See if a meteor has collided with a city
  if (pSpriteHitter->GetBitmap() == g_pMeteorBitmap &&
    pSpriteHittee->GetBitmap() == g_pCityBitmap)
  {
    // Play the big explosion sound
    PlaySound((LPCSTR)IDW_BIGEXPLODE, g_hInstance, SND_ASYNC |
      SND_RESOURCE);

    // Kill both sprites
    pSpriteHitter->Kill();                          ──── If a meteor and a
    pSpriteHittee->Kill();                               city have collided,
                                                         kill them both.
    // See if the game is over
```

continues

LISTING 17.9   Continued

End the game if no [
more cities are left.

```
    if (--g_iNumCities == 0)
      g_bGameOver = TRUE;
  }

  return FALSE;
}
```

The first collision detected in the SpriteCollision() function is the collision between a missile and a meteor. You might be a little surprised by how the code is determining what kinds of sprites are colliding. In order to distinguish between sprites, you need a piece of information that uniquely identifies each type of sprite in the game. The bitmap pointer turns out to be a handy and efficient way to identify and distinguish between sprites because you already have the bitmap pointers for the sprites stored in global variables. Getting back to the collision between a missile and a meteor, the SpriteCollision() function kills both sprites and increases the score because a meteor has been successfully hit with a missile. You might be wondering why an explosion isn't displayed at this point. This task is handled in the SpriteDying() function, which you'll learn about in a moment.

The difficulty level is also modified in the SpriteCollision() function so that it gradually increases along with the score. It's worth pointing out that the game gets harder as the difficulty level increases, with the maximum difficulty being reached at a value of 5 for the g_iDifficulty global variable; the game is pretty much raining meteors at this level, which corresponds to reaching a score of 450. You can obviously tweak these values to suit your own tastes if you decide that the game gets difficult too fast or if you want to stretch out the time it takes for the difficulty level to increase.

The second collision detected in the SpriteCollision() function is between a meteor and a city. If this collision takes place, a big explosion sound is played, and both sprites are killed. The number of cities is then checked to see if the game is over.

Earlier in the chapter, you added a new SpriteDying()function to the game engine that allows you to respond to a sprite being destroyed. This function comes in quite handy in the Meteor Defense game because it allows you to conveniently create an explosion sprite any time a meteor sprite is destroyed. Listing 17.10 shows how this is made possible by the SpriteDying() function.

LISTING 17.10 The SpriteDying() Function Creates an Explosion Whenever a Meteor Sprite Is Destroyed

```
void SpriteDying(Sprite* pSpriteDying)
{
  // See if a meteor sprite is dying
  if (pSpriteDying->GetBitmap() == g_pMeteorBitmap)
  {
    // Play the explosion sound
    PlaySound((LPCSTR)IDW_EXPLODE, g_hInstance, SND_ASYNC |
      SND_RESOURCE | SND_NOSTOP);

    // Create an explosion sprite at the meteor's position
    RECT rcBounds = { 0, 0, 600, 450 };
    RECT rcPos = pSpriteDying->GetPosition();
    Sprite* pSprite = new Sprite(g_pExplosionBitmap, rcBounds);
    pSprite->SetNumFrames(12, TRUE);
    pSprite->SetPosition(rcPos.left, rcPos.top);
    g_pGame->AddSprite(pSprite);
  }
}
```

To show a meteor's destruction, an explosion sprite is created and displayed at the final position of the meteor.

The bitmap pointer of the sprite is used again to determine if the dying sprite is indeed a meteor sprite. If so, an explosion sound effect is played, and an explosion sprite is created. Notice that the SetNumFrames() method is called to set the number of animation frames for the explosion sprite, as well as to indicate that the sprite should be destroyed after finishing its animation cycle. If you recall, this is one of the other important sprite-related features you added to the game engine earlier in the chapter.

The remaining two functions in the Meteor Defense game are support functions that are completely unique to the game. The first one is NewGame(), which performs the steps necessary to start a new game (see Listing 17.11).

LISTING 17.11 The NewGame() Function Gets Everything Ready for a New Game

```
void NewGame()
{
  // Clear the sprites
  g_pGame->CleanupSprites();

  // Create the target sprite
  RECT rcBounds = { 0, 0, 600, 450 };
  g_pTargetSprite = new Sprite(g_pTargetBitmap, rcBounds, BA_STOP);
  g_pTargetSprite->SetZOrder(10);
  g_pGame->AddSprite(g_pTargetSprite);

  // Create the city sprites
  Sprite* pSprite = new Sprite(g_pCityBitmap, rcBounds);
  pSprite->SetPosition(2, 370);
```

The target sprite has the highest Z-order in the game so that it is always visible.

LISTING 17.11   Continued

```
g_pGame->AddSprite(pSprite);
pSprite = new Sprite(g_pCityBitmap, rcBounds);
pSprite->SetPosition(186, 370);
g_pGame->AddSprite(pSprite);
pSprite = new Sprite(g_pCityBitmap, rcBounds);
pSprite->SetPosition(302, 370);
g_pGame->AddSprite(pSprite);
pSprite = new Sprite(g_pCityBitmap, rcBounds);
pSprite->SetPosition(490, 370);
g_pGame->AddSprite(pSprite);

// Initialize the game variables
g_iScore = 0;
g_iNumCities = 4;
g_iDifficulty = 50;
g_bGameOver = FALSE;

// Play the background music
g_pGame->PlayMIDISong();
}
```

The NewGame() function starts off by clearing the sprite list, which is important because you don't really know what might have been left over from the previous game. The crosshair target sprite is then created, as are the city sprites. The global game variables are then initialized, and the background music is started up.

To help keep from duplicating code throughout the game, it's handy to break out the code for creating a new meteor into its own function. The AddMeteor() function is shown in Listing 17.12, and its job is to add a new meteor to the game in a random position, aimed at a random city.

LISTING 17.12   The AddMeteor() Function Adds a New Meteor in a Random Position aimed at a Random City

```
void AddMeteor()
{
  // Create a new meteor sprite and set its position
  RECT    rcBounds = { 0, 0, 600, 390 };
  int     iXPos = rand() % 600;
  Sprite* pSprite = new Sprite(g_pMeteorBitmap, rcBounds, BA_DIE);
  pSprite->SetNumFrames(14);
  pSprite->SetPosition(iXPos, 0);

  // Calculate the velocity so that it is aimed at one of the cities
```

```
int iXVel, iYVel = (rand() % 4) + 3;
switch(rand() % 4)
{
case 0:
  iXVel = (iYVel * (56 - (iXPos + 50))) / 400;
  break;
case 1:
  iXVel = (iYVel * (240 - (iXPos + 50))) / 400;
  break;
case 2:
  iXVel = (iYVel * (360 - (iXPos + 50))) / 400;
  break;
case 3:
  iXVel = (iYVel * (546 - (iXPos + 50))) / 400;
  break;
}
pSprite->SetVelocity(iXVel, iYVel);

// Add the meteor sprite
g_pGame->AddSprite(pSprite);
}
```

Every meteor targets one of the cities, although the city might or might not still exist.

The AddMeteor() function adds a new meteor to the game. Its code is probably a little longer than you expected, simply because it tries to add meteors so that they are aimed at cities, as opposed to just zinging around the game screen aimlessly. Granted, a real meteor wouldn't target a city; but this is a game, and the idea is to challenge the player by forcing him to save cities from incoming meteors. So, in the world of Meteor Defense, the meteors act more like incoming nuclear warheads in that they tend to target cities.

The function begins by creating a meteor sprite and setting it to a random position along the top edge of the game screen. The big section of code in the middle of the function takes care of setting the meteor's velocity so that it targets one of the four cities positioned along the bottom of the screen. I realize that this code looks a little tricky, but all that's going on is some basic trigonometry to figure out what velocity is required to get the meteor from point A to point B, where point A is the meteor's random position and point B is the position of the city. The AddMeteor() function ends by adding the new meteor sprite to the game engine.

That wraps up the code for the Meteor Defense game, which hopefully, doesn't have your head spinning too much. Now, you just need to put the resources together, and you can start playing. Don't forget that the complete source code and resources for all the examples and games throughout the book, including Meteor Defense, are located on the accompanying CD-ROM, as are the project files for popular compilers.

Construction Cue

If you're using Visual C++ 6.0, you might need to change the type casts from (DWORD_PTR) to (DWORD) in GameEngine.cpp in order for the Meteor Defense code to compile properly.

Construction Cue

As with most of the examples in the book, the Meteor Defense program relies on the standard msimg32.lib and winmm.lib libraries. These libraries are included with most Windows compilers, but they aren't automatically linked into programs when you create a new project. If you are using your own project or make files, as opposed to using the ones provided on the CD-ROM, make sure that you change the link settings so that these library files are properly linked into the final executable. Refer to the documentation for your specific compiler for how this is done.

Testing the Game

It's safe to congratulate yourself at this point because you've worked through the design and development of the Meteor Defense game, and you can bask in the glory of playing the game. Granted, playing a game for the first time is certainly more of a test than it is a true playing experience, but in this case, I can vouch that the game works pretty well. Figure 17.7 shows the game at the start, with a couple of meteors hurtling toward the cities.

FIGURE 17.7
The Meteor Defense game gets started with a couple of meteors hurtling at the cities.

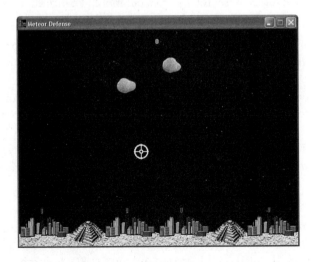

Saving the cities from the meteors involves targeting the meteors and blasting them with missiles. When you successfully blast a meteor, you'll see an explosion as the missile and meteor both are destroyed (see Figure 17.8)

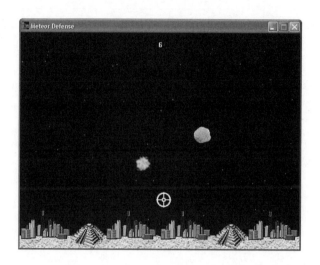

FIGURE 17.8
Successfully destroying a meteor results in an explosion being displayed.

As the game progresses and more meteors fall, you'll eventually start losing cities to the meteors. Figure 17.9 shows an example of how the meteors can begin to overwhelm you late in the game.

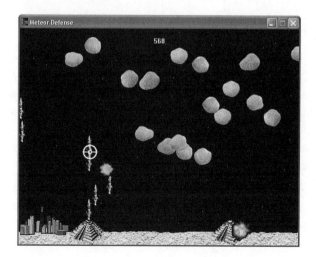

FIGURE 17.9
As the game progresses, you tend to lose cities as the meteors start to overwhelm you.

When you finally lose all four cities to the meteors, the game ends. Figure 17.10 shows the end of the game, which involves displaying the game over image on the screen on top of the other game graphics.

FIGURE 17.10
When all four cities are destroyed, the game ends, and the game over image is displayed.

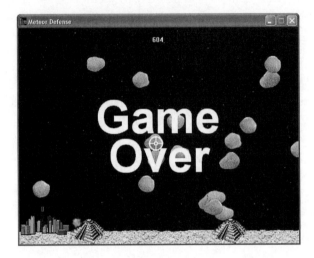

Although it's a little sad to think that you've ultimately failed to save the cities in the Meteor Defense game, you can sleep well knowing that you can always right-click the mouse to start over and take another stab at it.

Summary

This chapter carried you through the design and construction of another complete game, Meteor Defense. The Meteor Defense game took advantage of the new game engine features you developed in the previous two chapters and also took a leap forward in terms of showing you how to create engaging action games. The game makes heavy use of sprites, including frame animation—not to mention a great deal of collision detection. Perhaps most important is the fact that the Meteor Defense game can serve as a great starting point for creating an action game of your own that takes full advantage of the game engine.

This chapter concludes this part of the book. The next part of the book tackles artificial intelligence or AI, which allows you to make your games more intelligent.

Extreme Game Makeover

Although I like the theme of the Meteor Defense game, there are always ways to make games more interesting by changing their themes. In this case, an interesting and somewhat unusual theme switch for Meteor Defense involves changing the game to a seafaring survival game. You are the captain of a fleet of ships attempting to journey across the ocean, and you are being continually attacked by pirates in submarines. Yes, these are unorthodox pirates who use hidden subs instead of ships! The game is basically the Meteor Defense game inverted so that the threat comes from below, and you fire down, instead of up. The following are the steps required to turn Meteor Defense into Pirates from the Deep:

1. Change the background image to a side sea view in which you see a small area above the surface for the ships and a large area underwater for the game action.

2. Change the cannon image to a battleship image, and change the city image to a normal ship with no firing capability.

3. Invert the missile image so that it is aiming downward, instead of upward.

4. Change the meteor image to a torpedo image aiming upward; this image can be similar to the missile image, but larger and more threatening.

5. Set the vertical positions of the ships so that they appear to be floating on the surface of the water; their horizontal positions can be the same as those of the cannons and cities in Meteor Defense.

6. Change the firing code for the missiles so that they originate from the battle ships and fire down toward the incoming torpedoes.

You could take the game a step further by adding pirate submarines as sprites and having the torpedoes originate from them, instead of just appearing from off-screen. I simply didn't want to burden you with too much with the makeover.

PART VI

Adding Brains to Your Games

CHAPTER 18

Teaching Games to Think

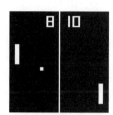

Arcade Archive

Undoubtedly, one of the strangest game themes to ever grace arcades belongs to Q*bert, a quirky game released in 1982 by Gottlieb. Q*bert is the name of the main game character, which is a strange-looking orange creature with two legs and a big nose. Q*bert's task is to jump around on a pyramid and change the colors of the blocks upon which he lands. Q*bert's enemies include a snake named Coily, a pig named Ugg, and a toothy creature named Wrong-Way. There are also a couple of friendly creatures known as Slick and Sam. Q*bert is a very simple game, but it has an endearing cast of characters and unique enough game play to make it a classic. In recent years, a rumor was started that the original designer and programmer of Q*bert, Warren Davis, also invented the popular Furby toy, but this is not the case.

Creating truly engaging games is often a matter of effectively mimicking human thought within the confines of a computer. Because you no doubt want your games to be engaging, you need at least a basic understanding of how to give games some degree of brain power. This chapter focuses on understanding the fundamental theories of artificial intelligence and how they can be applied to games. Hopefully this chapter will arm you with the basic knowledge required to begin implementing artificial intelligence strategies in your own games. More importantly, you will leave this chapter with a practical sample of how to incorporate simple AI into an example.

In this chapter, you'll learn

- ▶ About the basics of artificial intelligence (AI)
- ▶ About the different types of AI used in games
- ▶ How to develop an AI strategy of your own
- ▶ How to put AI to work in a practical example involving sprites that interact with each other "intelligently"

Understanding Artificial Intelligence

Artificial intelligence (AI) is defined as the techniques used to emulate the human thought process in a computer. This is admittedly a fairly general definition for AI, as it should be; AI is a very broad research area—with game-related AI being a relatively small subset of the whole of AI knowledge. The goal in this chapter is not to explore every facet of AI because that would easily fill more than one book, but rather to explore the fundamental concepts behind AI as it applies to games.

As you might have already guessed, human thought is no simple process to emulate, which explains why AI is such a broad area of research. Even though there are many different approaches to AI, all of them basically boil down to attempting to make human decisions within the confines of a computer "brain." Most traditional AI systems use a variety of information-based algorithms to make decisions, just as people use a variety of previous experiences and mental rules to make decisions. In the past, the information-based AI algorithms were completely *deterministic*, meaning that every decision could be traced back to a predictable flow of logic. Figure 18.1 shows an example of a purely logical human thought process. Obviously, human thinking doesn't work this way at all; if we were all this predictable, it would be quite a boring planet!

FIGURE 18.1
A completely logical human thought process involves nothing more than strict reason.

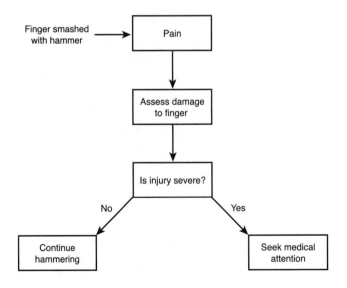

Eventually, AI researchers realized that the deterministic approach to AI wasn't sufficient to accurately model human thought. Their focus shifted from deterministic AI models to more realistic AI models that attempted to factor in the subtle complexities of human thought, such as best-guess decisions. In people, these types of decisions can result from a combination of past experience, personal bias, and/or the current state of emotion—in addition to the completely logical decision-making process. Figure 18.2 shows an example of this type of thought process. The point is that people don't always make scientifically predictable decisions based on analyzing their surroundings and arriving at a logical conclusion. The world would probably be a better place if we did act like this, but again, it would be awfully boring!

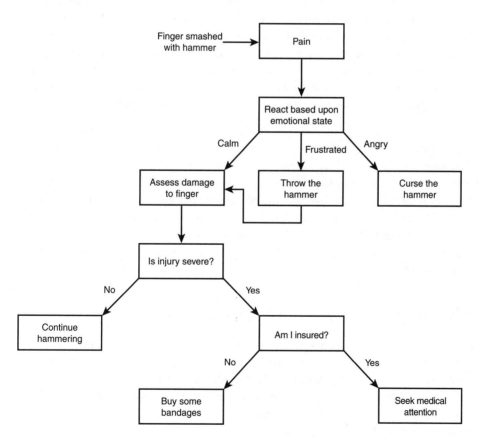

FIGURE 18.2
A more realistic human thought process adds emotion and a dash of irrationality with reason.

The logic flow in Figure 18.1 is an ideal scenario in which each decision is made based on a totally objective, logical evaluation of the situation. Figure 18.2 shows a more realistic scenario, which factors in the emotional state of the person, as well as a financial angle (the question of whether the person has insurance). Examining the second scenario from a completely logical angle, it makes no sense for the person to throw the hammer because that only slows down the task at hand. However, this is a completely plausible and fairly common human response to pain and frustration. For an AI carpentry system to effectively model this situation, there would definitely have to be some hammer-throwing code somewhere!

This hypothetical thought example is meant to give you a tiny clue as to how many seemingly unrelated things go into forming a human thought. Likewise, it only makes sense that it should take an extremely complex AI system to effectively model human thought. Most of the time, this statement is true. However, the word "effectively" allows for a certain degree of interpretation, based on the context of the application requiring AI. For your purposes, effective AI simply means AI that makes computer game objects more realistic and engaging.

AI research in recent years has been focused on tackling problems similar to the ones illustrated by the hypothetical carpentry example. One particularly interesting area is *fuzzy logic*, which attempts to make "best-guess" decisions rather than the concrete decisions of traditional AI systems. Another interesting AI research area in relation to games involves *genetic algorithms*, which try to model evolved thought similar to how scientists believe nature evolves through genetics. A game using genetic algorithms would theoretically have computer opponents that learn as the game progresses, providing the human player with a seemingly never ending series of challenges.

Exploring Types of Game AI

There are many different types of AI systems and even more algorithms that carry out those systems. Even when you limit AI to the world of games, there is still a wide range of information and options from which to choose when it comes to adding AI to a game of your own. Many different AI solutions are geared toward particular types of games—with a plethora of different possibilities that can be applied in different situations.

What I'm getting at is that there is no way to just present a bunch of AI algorithms and tell you which one goes with which particular type of game. Instead, it makes more sense to give you the theoretical background on a few of the most important types of AI and then let you figure out how they might apply to your particular gaming needs. Having said all that, I've broken down game-related AI into three fundamental types:

- ▶ Roaming AI
- ▶ Behavioral AI
- ▶ Strategic AI

Please understand that these three types of AI are in no way meant to encompass all the AI approaches used in games; they are simply the most common types to recognize and use. Feel free to do your own research and expand upon these if you find AI to be an interesting topic worthy of further study.

Roaming AI

Roaming AI refers to AI that models the movement of game objects—that is, the decisions game objects make that determine how they roam around a virtual game world. A good example of roaming AI is in shoot-em-up space games, such as the classic arcade game Galaga, where aliens often tend to track and go after the player. Similarly, aliens that fly around in a predetermined pattern are also implemented using roaming AI. Basically, roaming AI is used whenever a computer-controlled object must make a decision to alter its current path—either to achieve a desired result in the game or simply to conform to a particular movement pattern. In the Galaga example, the desired result is following a pattern while also attempting to collide with and damage the player's ship. In other games, the desired result might be to dodge the bullets being fired at a computer opponent from a human player.

Implementing roaming AI is usually fairly simple; it typically involves altering an object's velocity or position (the alien) based on the position of another object (the player's ship). The roaming movement of the object can also be influenced by random or predetermined patterns. Three different types of roaming AI exist: chasing, evading, and patterned. The next few sections explore these types of roaming AI in more detail.

Chasing

Chasing is a type of roaming AI in which a game object tracks and goes after another game object or objects. Chasing is the approach used in many shoot-em-up games where an alien chases after the player's ship. It is implemented by altering the alien's velocity or position based on the current position of the player's ship. The following is an example of a simple chasing algorithm involving an alien and a ship:

```
if (iXAlien > iXShip)
  iXAlien--;
else if (iXAlien < iXShip)
  iXAlien++;
if (iYAlien > iYShip)
  iYAlien--;
else if (iYAlien < iYShip)
  iYAlien++;
```

As you can see, the XY position (iXAlien and iYAlien) of the alien is altered based on where the ship is located (iXShip and iYShip). The only potential problem with this code is that it can work too well; the alien will hone in on the player with no hesitation, basically giving the player no chance to dodge it. This might be what you want, but more than likely, you want the alien to fly around a little while it chases the player. You probably also want the chasing to be a little imperfect, giving the player at least some chance of outmaneuvering the alien. In other words, you want the alien to have a *tendency* to chase the player without going in for an all-out blitz.

One method of smoothing out the chasing algorithm is to throw a little randomness into the equation, like this:

```
if ((rand() % 3) == 0) {
  if (iXAlien > iXShip)
    iXAlien-;
  else if (iXAlien < iXShip)
    iXAlien++;
}
if ((rand() % 3) == 0) {
  if (iYAlien > iYShip)
    iYAlien-;
  else if (iYAlien < iYShip)
    iYAlien++;
}
```

In this code, the alien has a one in three chance of tracking the player in each direction. Even with only a one in three chance, the alien will still tend to chase the player aggressively, while still allowing the player a fighting chance at getting out of the way. You might think that a one in three chance doesn't sound all that effective, but keep in mind that the alien only alters its path to chase the player. A smart player will probably figure this out and change directions frequently.

If you aren't too fired up about the random approach to leveling off the chase, you probably need to look into patterned movement. However, you're getting a little ahead of yourself. Let's take a look at evading first.

Evading

Evading is the logical counterpart to chasing; it is another type of roaming AI in which a game object specifically tries to get away from another object or objects. Evading is implemented in a similar manner to chasing, as the following code shows:

```
if (iXAlien > iXShip)
  iXAlien++;
else if (iXAlien < iXShip)
  iXAlien--;
if (iYAlien > iYShip)
  iYAlien++;
else if (iYAlien < iYShip)
  iYAlien--;
```

This code basically does the opposite of the code used by the chasing algorithm— with the only differences being the unary operators (++, --) used to change the alien's position so that it runs away, as opposed to chasing. Similar to chasing, evading can be softened using randomness or patterned movement. A good example of evading involves the ghosts in the classic arcade game Pac-Man, who run away from you (the player) when you eat a power pellet. Of course, the Pac-Man ghosts also take advantage of chasing when you don't have the ability to eat them, which is most of the time.

Another good example of using the evading algorithm would be a computer-controlled version of the player's ship in a space game with a computer player. If you think about it, the player is using the evading algorithm to dodge the aliens; it's just implemented by pressing keys, rather than in a piece of computer-controlled code. If you want to provide a demo mode in a game like this where the computer plays itself, you would use an evading algorithm to control the player's ship. Chapter 21, "Showing Off Your Game with Demo Mode," shows you exactly how to create a demo mode for your games.

Patterned Roaming

Patterned movement refers to a type of roaming AI that uses a predefined set of movements for a game object. Good examples of patterned movement are the aliens in the classic Galaga arcade game, which perform all kinds of neat aerobatics on their way down the screen. Patterns can include circles, figure eights, zigzags, or even more complex movements. An even simpler example of patterned movement is the Space Invaders game, in which a herd of aliens slowly and methodically inches across and down the screen.

Gamer's Garage

In truth, the aliens in Galaga use a combined approach of both patterned and chasing movement; although they certainly follow specific patterns, the aliens still make sure to come after the player whenever possible. Additionally, as the player moves into higher levels, the roaming AI starts favoring chasing over patterned movement in order to make the game harder. This is a great use of combined roaming AI that touches on the concept of behavioral AI, which you learn about in the next section.

Patterns are usually stored as an array of velocity or position offsets (or multipliers) that are applied to an object whenever patterned movement is required of it, like this:

```
int iZigZag[2][2] = { {3, 2}, {-3, 2} };
iXAlien += iZigZag[iPatternStep][0];
iYAlien += iZigZag[iPatternStep][1];
```

This code shows how to implement a very simple vertical zigzag pattern. The integer array iZigZag contains pairs of XY offsets used to apply the pattern to the alien. The iPatternStep variable is an integer representing the current step in the pattern. When this pattern is applied, the alien moves in a vertical direction at a speed of 2 pixels per game cycle, while zigzagging back and forth horizontally at a speed of 3 pixels per game cycle.

Behavioral AI

Although the types of roaming AI strategies are pretty useful in their own rights, a practical gaming scenario often requires a mixture of all three. *Behavioral AI* is another fundamental type of gaming AI that often uses a mixture of roaming AI algorithms to give game objects specific behaviors. Using the trusted alien example again, what if you want the alien to chase sometimes, evade other times, follow a pattern still other times, and maybe even act totally randomly every once in a while? Another good reason for using behavioral AI is to alter the difficulty of a game. For example, you could favor a chasing algorithm more than random or patterned movement to make aliens more aggressive in higher levels of a space game.

To implement behavioral AI, you would need to establish a set of behaviors for the alien. Giving game objects behaviors isn't too difficult; it usually involves establishing a ranking system for each type of behavior present in the system and then applying it to each object. For example, in the alien system, you would have the following behaviors: chase, evade, fly in a pattern, and fly randomly. For each different type of alien, you would assign different percentages to the different behaviors, thereby giving them each different personalities. For example, an aggressive alien might have the following behavioral breakdown: chase 50% of the time, evade 10% of the time, fly in a pattern 30% of the time, and fly randomly 10% of the time. On the other hand, a more passive alien might act like this: chase 10% of the time, evade 50% of the time, fly in a pattern 20% of the time, and fly randomly 20% of the time.

This behavioral approach works amazingly well and yields surprising results, considering how simple it is to implement. A typical implementation simply involves a `switch` statement or nested `if-else` statements to select a particular behavior. A sample implementation for the behaviorally aggressive alien would look like this:

```
int iBehavior = abs(rand() % 100);
if (iBehavior < 50)
  // chase
else if (iBehavior < 60)
  // evade
else if (iBehavior < 90)
  // fly in a pattern
else
  // fly randomly
```

As you can see, creating and assigning behaviors is open to a wide range of creativity. One of the best sources of ideas for creating game object behaviors involves the primal responses common in the animal world (and, unfortunately, all too often in the human world, too). As a matter of fact, a simple fight or flight behavioral system can work wonders when applied intelligently to a variety of game objects. Basically, just use your imagination as a guide and create as many unique behaviors as you can dream up.

Strategic AI

The final fundamental type of game AI I want to mention is *strategic AI*, which is basically any AI designed to play a game with a fixed set of well-defined rules. For example, a computer-controlled chess player would use strategic AI to determine each move based on trying to improve the chances of winning the game. Strategic AI tends to vary more based on the nature of the game, simply because it is so tightly linked to the rules of the game. Even so, there are established and successful approaches to applying strategic AI to many general types of games, such as games played on a rectangular board with pieces. Checkers and chess immediately come to mind as fitting into this group and, likewise, have a rich history of AI research devoted to them.

Strategic AI, especially for board games, typically involves some form of *look-ahead* approach to determining the best move to make. The look-ahead approach is usually used in conjunction with a fixed table of predetermined moves. For a look-ahead approach to make sense, however, there must be a method of looking at the board in any state and calculating a score. This is known as *weighting*, and it is often the most difficult part of implementing strategic AI in a board game. As an example of how difficult weighting can be, watch a game of chess or checkers and try to figure out who is winning after every single move, even very early in the game. Then, go a step farther and think about trying to calculate a numeric score for each player at each point in the game. Obviously, near the end of the game, it gets easier, but early on, it is very difficult to tell who is winning, simply because so many different things can happen. Attempting to quantify the state of the game in a numeric score is even more difficult.

Nevertheless, there are ways to successfully calculate a weighted score for strategic games. Using a look-head approach with scoring, a strategic AI algorithm can test, for every possible move for each player, multiple moves into the future and determine which move is the best. This move is often referred to as the "least worst" move, rather than the best, because the goal typically is to make the move that helps the other player the least, rather than the other way around. Of course, the end result is basically the same, but it is an interesting way to look at a game nevertheless. Even though look-ahead approaches to implementing strategic AI are useful in many cases, they can require a fair amount of processing if very much depth is required (in other words, if the computer player needs to be very smart).

To better understand strategic AI, consider the case of a computer backgammon player. The computer player has to choose two or four moves from possibly several dozen, as well as decide whether to double or resign. A practical backgammon program might assign weights to different combinations of positions and calculate the value of each position reachable from the current position and dice roll. A scoring system would then be used to evaluate the worth of each potential position, which gets back to the often difficult proposition of scoring, even in a game (such as backgammon) with simple rules. Now, apply this scenario to a hundred-unit war game—with every unit having unique characteristics, and the terrain and random factors complicating the issue even further. The optimal system of scoring simply cannot be determined in a reasonable amount of time, especially with the limited computing power of a workstation or PC.

The solution in these cases is to settle for a "good enough" move, rather than the "best" move. One of the best ways to develop the algorithm for finding the "good enough" move is to set up the computer to play both sides in a game, using a lot of variation between the algorithms and weights playing each side. Then sit back and let the two computer players battle it out and see which one wins the most. This approach typically involves a lot of tinkering and trial and error with the AI code, but it can result in very good computer players, and it can be a lot of fun to watch.

Developing an AI Strategy

Now that you understand the basic concepts behind AI in games, you can start thinking about an AI strategy for your own specific games. When deciding how to implement AI in a game, you need to do some preliminary work to assess exactly what type and level of AI you think are warranted. You need to determine what level of computer response suits your needs, abilities, resources, and project time frame.

If your main concern is developing a game that keeps human players entertained and challenged, go with the simplest AI possible. Actually, try to go with the simplest AI regardless of your goals because you can always enhance it in phases. If you think your game needs a type of AI that doesn't quite fit into any I've described, do some research and see whether something out there is closer to what you need. Most importantly, budget plenty of time for implementing AI because 90% of the time, it will take longer than you ever anticipated to get it all working at a level with which you are happy.

What is the best way to get started? Start in small steps, of course. Many programmers like to write code as they design, and although that approach might work in some cases, I recommend at least some degree of preliminary design on paper. Furthermore, try to keep this design limited to a subset of the game's AI, such as a single computer opponent. Start with a small, simple map or grid and simple movement rules. Write the code to get a single opponent from point A to point B. Then, add complications piece by piece, building onto a complete algorithm at each step. If you are careful to make each piece of the AI general and open enough to connect to other pieces, your final algorithms should be general enough to handle any conditions your game might encounter.

Getting back to more basic terms, a good way to gain AI experience is to write a computer opponent for a simple board game, such as tic-tac-toe or checkers.

Detailed AI solutions exist for many popular games, so you should be able to find them if you search around a little on the Web. Another good way to get some experience with AI is to modify an existing game in an attempt to make its computer-controlled characters a little smarter. For example, you could modify the Henway game so that the cars speed up and slow down deliberately to make it tougher on the chicken as she gets near each car. You could also change the speed of the moving guys in the Battle Office game so that they speed up when you get close to shooting them. Finally, you could add an entirely new element to the Meteor Defense game, such as attacking alien sprites that have the capability to dodge your missiles, at least from a certain distance.

Building the Roids 2 Example Program

Rather than modify an existing game to demonstrate AI programming, I decided that it would be better to demonstrate AI within the context of an example that doesn't involve an objective. In other words, I wanted to create a program that you could tinker with without worrying about messing up the outcome of a game. The program I'm talking about is called Roids 2, and it's a revamped version of the Roids program from Chapter 16, "Creating Backgrounds for Your Sprites." If you recall, the original Roids program displays an animated asteroid field. You're now going to add a flying saucer to the program that is intelligent enough to dodge the asteroids or, at least, do its best to dodge the asteroids.

The Roids 2 example is very similar to the original Roids program, except for the addition of the flying saucer sprite. The remainder of the chapter focuses on the development of this program and how AI influences the flying saucer sprite.

Writing the Program Code

The Roids 2 program begins with the Roids.h header file, which declares global variables that are important to the program. More specifically, a flying saucer bitmap has been declared, along with sprites for the asteroids and the flying saucer:

```
Bitmap*        g_pSaucerBitmap;
Sprite*        g_pAsteroids[3];
Sprite*        g_pSaucer;
```

The g_pSaucerBitmap is a bitmap for the flying saucer image. The g_pAsteroids and g_pSaucer variables both store sprite pointers. These pointers are necessary so that you can compare the positions of the saucer and asteroids and alter the saucer's velocity; this is how you add "intelligence" to the flying saucer.

The Roids 2 program also includes a new helper function named UpdateSaucer(), which is responsible for updating the saucer sprite. Of course, the saucer sprite is already being updated in terms of its position and velocity in the game engine. However, in this case, an additional update is taking place that alters the saucer's velocity based on its proximity to nearby asteroids. You'll learn exactly how this facet of the program works in a moment.

The GameStart() function is similar to the previous version, except that it now contains code to initialize the flying saucer. Listing 18.1 shows the code for this function.

LISTING 18.1 The GameStart() Function Initializes the Flying Saucer Bitmap and Sprite

```
void GameStart(HWND hWindow)
{
  // Seed the random number generator
  srand(GetTickCount());

  // Create the offscreen device context and bitmap
  g_hOffscreenDC = CreateCompatibleDC(GetDC(hWindow));
  g_hOffscreenBitmap = CreateCompatibleBitmap(GetDC(hWindow),
    g_pGame->GetWidth(), g_pGame->GetHeight());
  SelectObject(g_hOffscreenDC, g_hOffscreenBitmap);

  // Create and load the asteroid and saucer bitmaps
  HDC hDC = GetDC(hWindow);
  g_pAsteroidBitmap = new Bitmap(hDC, IDB_ASTEROID, g_hInstance);
  g_pSaucerBitmap = new Bitmap(hDC, IDB_SAUCER, g_hInstance);

  // Create the starry background
  g_pBackground = new StarryBackground(500, 400);

  // Create the asteroid sprites
  RECT    rcBounds = { 0, 0, 500, 400 };
  g_pAsteroids[0] = new Sprite(g_pAsteroidBitmap, rcBounds, BA_WRAP);
  g_pAsteroids[0]->SetNumFrames(14);
  g_pAsteroids[0]->SetFrameDelay(1);
  g_pAsteroids[0]->SetPosition(250, 200);
  g_pAsteroids[0]->SetVelocity(-3, 1);
  g_pGame->AddSprite(g_pAsteroids[0]);
  g_pAsteroids[1] = new Sprite(g_pAsteroidBitmap, rcBounds, BA_WRAP);
  g_pAsteroids[1]->SetNumFrames(14);
  g_pAsteroids[1]->SetFrameDelay(2);
  g_pAsteroids[1]->SetPosition(250, 200);
  g_pAsteroids[1]->SetVelocity(3, -2);
  g_pGame->AddSprite(g_pAsteroids[1]);
  g_pAsteroids[2] = new Sprite(g_pAsteroidBitmap, rcBounds, BA_WRAP);
  g_pAsteroids[2]->SetNumFrames(14);
  g_pAsteroids[2]->SetFrameDelay(3);
  g_pAsteroids[2]->SetPosition(250, 200);
  g_pAsteroids[2]->SetVelocity(-2, -4);
```

continues

LISTING 18.1 Continued

```
g_pGame->AddSprite(g_pAsteroids[2]);

// Create the saucer sprite
g_pSaucer = new Sprite(g_pSaucerBitmap, rcBounds, BA_WRAP);
g_pSaucer->SetPosition(0, 0);
g_pSaucer->SetVelocity(3, 1);
g_pGame->AddSprite(g_pSaucer);
}
```

Unlike in the earlier UFO examples, the flying saucer now wraps around the screen with more freedom.

The changes to the GameStart() function primarily involve the addition of the flying saucer sprite. The saucer bitmap is first loaded, and then the saucer sprite is created and added to the game engine. It's also worth pointing out that the asteroid sprite pointers are now being stored in the g_pAsteroids array because you need to reference them later when helping the saucer avoid hitting the asteroids.

The GameCycle() function in Roids 2 requires a slight modification to ensure that the flying saucer sprite is updated properly. This change involves the addition of a call to the UpdateSaucer() function, which is responsible for updating the velocity of the flying saucer sprite to help it dodge the asteroids. Listing 18.2 shows the new and improved GameCycle() function.

LISTING 18.2 The GameCycle() Function Now Calls the UpdateSaucer() Function to Enable the Flying Saucer to "Think"

```
void GameCycle()
{
  // Update the background
  g_pBackground->Update();

  // Update the sprites
  g_pGame->UpdateSprites();

  // Update the saucer to help it dodge the asteroids
  UpdateSaucer();

  // Obtain a device context for repainting the game
  HWND  hWindow = g_pGame->GetWindow();
  HDC   hDC = GetDC(hWindow);

  // Paint the game to the offscreen device context
  GamePaint(g_hOffscreenDC);

  // Blit the offscreen bitmap to the game screen
  BitBlt(hDC, 0, 0, g_pGame->GetWidth(), g_pGame->GetHeight(),
    g_hOffscreenDC, 0, 0, SRCCOPY);
```

The UpdateSaucer() function takes care of figuring out how to move the saucer based on the locations of the asteroids.

```
  // Cleanup
  ReleaseDC(hWindow, hDC);
}
```

The call to the UpdateSaucer() function is the only change to the GameCycle()
function from its original version. Speaking of the UpdateSaucer() function, its
code is shown in Listing 18.3.

LISTING 18.3 The UpdateSaucer() Function Updates the Flying
Saucer's Velocity to Help It Dodge Asteroids

```
void UpdateSaucer()
{
  // Obtain the saucer's position
  RECT rcSaucer, rcRoid;
  rcSaucer = g_pSaucer->GetPosition();

  // Find out which asteroid is closest to the saucer
  int iXCollision = 500, iYCollision = 400, iXYCollision = 900;
  for (int i = 0; i < 3; i++)
  {
    // Get the asteroid position
    rcRoid = g_pAsteroids[i]->GetPosition();

    // Calculate the minimum XY collision distance
    int iXCollisionDist = (rcSaucer.left +
      (rcSaucer.right - rcSaucer.left) / 2) -
      (rcRoid.left +
      (rcRoid.right - rcRoid.left) / 2);
    int iYCollisionDist = (rcSaucer.top +
      (rcSaucer.bottom - rcSaucer.top) / 2) -
      (rcRoid.top +
      (rcRoid.bottom - rcRoid.top) / 2);
    if ((abs(iXCollisionDist) < abs(iXCollision)) ||
      (abs(iYCollisionDist) < abs(iYCollision)))
      if ((abs(iXCollisionDist) + abs(iYCollisionDist)) < iXYCollision)
      {
        iXYCollision = abs(iXCollision) + abs(iYCollision);
        iXCollision = iXCollisionDist;
        iYCollision = iYCollisionDist;
      }
  }

  // Move to dodge the asteroids, if necessary
  POINT ptVelocity;
  ptVelocity = g_pSaucer->GetVelocity();
  if (abs(iXCollision) < 60)
  {
    // Adjust the X velocity
    if (iXCollision < 0)
      ptVelocity.x = max(ptVelocity.x - 1, -8);
    else
      ptVelocity.x = min(ptVelocity.x + 1, 8);
  }
```

The end result of this code is to determine if there is an imminent threat of collision with an asteroid in the X direction, the Y direction, or both directions.

See if the saucer needs to make an evasive move in the X direction.

continues

LISTING 18.3 Continued

See if the saucer needs to make an evasive move in the Y direction.

```
if (abs(iYCollision) < 60)
{
  // Adjust the Y velocity
  if (iYCollision < 0)
    ptVelocity.y = max(ptVelocity.y - 1, -8);
  else
    ptVelocity.y = min(ptVelocity.y + 1, 8);
}

// Update the saucer to the new position
g_pSaucer->SetVelocity(ptVelocity);
}
```

I realize that this function contains a lot of code, but if you take it a section at a time, it's really not too complex. First of all, let's understand how the UpdateSaucer() function is helping the flying saucer dodge the asteroids. The idea is to check for the closest asteroid in relation to the saucer and then alter the saucer's velocity so that it has a tendency to move in the opposite direction of the asteroid. I say "tendency" because you don't want the saucer to jerk and immediately start moving away from the asteroid. Instead, you want to gradually alter its velocity so that it appears to steer away from the asteroid. This is a subtle difference, but the effect is dramatic because it looks as if the saucer is truly steering through the asteroid field, as opposed to jumping around instantaneously.

The first step in the UpdateSaucer() function is to obtain the position of the flying saucer. You can then loop through the asteroids and find out the minimum XY collision distance, which is the closest distance between an asteroid and the saucer. Inside the loop, the asteroid position is first obtained, which is critical for determining the collision distance. The minimum XY collision distance is then calculated and used as the basis for determining if this asteroid is currently the closest one to the saucer. This is where the function gets a little tricky because you must add the X and Y components of the collision distance to see which asteroid is closer to the saucer. This technique isn't flawless, but it helps to eliminate "false alarm" situations in which an asteroid is close to the saucer horizontally, but far away vertically.

When the asteroid loop is exited, you have two pieces of important information to work with: the X collision distance and the Y collision distance. It's now possible to check and see if these distances are below a certain minimum distance that is required in order for the saucer to be in danger of colliding with an asteroid. My own trial-and-error testing led to a value of 60, but you might decide on a slightly different value based on your own testing. In order to steer the saucer to safety horizontally, the X collision distance is checked to see if it is below the minimum distance of 60; in which case, the saucer's velocity is adjusted. The same process is then repeated for the saucer's Y collision distance. Finally, the new velocity of the saucer is set by calling the SetVelocity() method on the saucer sprite.

If you're using Visual C++ 6.0, you might need to change the type casts from (DWORD_PTR) to (DWORD) in GameEngine.cpp in order for the Roids 2 code to compile properly.

Construction Cue

As with most of the examples in the book, the Roids 2 program relies on the standard msimg32.lib and winmm.lib libraries. These libraries are included with most Windows compilers, but they aren't automatically linked into programs when you create a new project. If you are using your own project or make files, as opposed to using the ones provided on the CD-ROM, make sure that you change the link settings so that these library files are properly linked into the final executable. Refer to the documentation for your specific compiler for how this is done.

Construction Cue

Testing the Finished Product

The premise behind the Roids 2 program is to show how a certain degree of simple AI can be injected into a sprite object so that it can avoid other sprite objects. In this context, the evading sprite object is a flying saucer desperately trying to keep from colliding with asteroids in an asteroid field. Although you have to actually run the program yourself to see the flying saucer evade the asteroids, Figure 18.3 shows the saucer in the process of steering away from a close call.

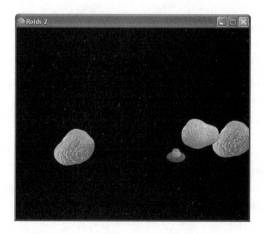

FIGURE 18.3
The flying saucer in the Roids 2 program does its best to dodge the asteroids that are floating around the game screen.

This is one of those rare examples that is actually fun to just sit back and watch because the program appears to have a mind of its own. In other words, you've created the logic for the flying saucer, and now you get to see how it responds in different situations. This is the part of the process of developing AI in games that is often frustrating because objects can do strange things that are quite unexpected at times. Even so, the flying saucer does a pretty good job of avoiding asteroids in the Roids 2 program.

Summary

If you find artificial intelligence to be a fascinating area of computer research, you hopefully enjoyed this chapter. You learned about the three fundamental types of game AI (roaming, behavioral, and strategic), along with how they are used in typical gaming scenarios. As a game programmer with at least a passing interest in AI, your AI knowledge will likely grow a great deal as you encounter situations in which you can apply AI techniques. After you get comfortable with implementing the basics, you can move on to more advanced AI solutions based on prior experience and research on the Web. I hope this chapter at least provided you with a roadmap to begin your journey into the world of the computer mind.

The next chapter applies your newfound AI knowledge to the most ambitious game in the book. The game is called Space Out, and it's a space shoot-em-up with a quirky cast of characters.

Field Trip

As if reading a book on game programming isn't fun enough, I want you to really take a step into the realm of childish fun by hosting your own game of tag. That's right; gather together some friends or family members in your yard or a park and start a wild game of tag. What you are hosting is actually not a game at all, but a psychological experiment—just don't tell anyone that you have ulterior motives! The experiment involves observing the "roaming patterns" of the tag participants. You'll probably find that each person has a unique strategy that suits his particular personality and fitness level. We played a similar game at a Halloween party once, and it was too funny watching one of my fitter friends do laps around the outer perimeter of the yard while everyone else stood around watching. The behavior patterns of your friends and family members in a game of tag can be translated into patterns for objects in your games, which is the true basis for this field trip.

CHAPTER 19

Example Game: Space Out

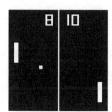

Arcade Archive

Nowadays, it's common for a video game to ride on the coattails of a popular movie's success. However, this wasn't necessarily always the case. One of the first video games to successfully take advantage of a popular movie was *Star Wars*, which was released in 1983 by Atari. Although the game certainly had merits on its own, it would have been difficult to fail with a video game based on such a cultural phenomenon as *Star Wars*. Even so, the game had a few interesting technical features that still make it an enduring classic. For one, Star Wars was one of the earliest games to use sampled audio clips. If you've ever played the game, you can't forget hearing, "Use the force, Luke." The game also made use of color vector graphics, which were a neat twist on the original black and white vector games that were popular at the time.

This chapter embarks on the development of yet another complete game. The game is called Space Out, and it represents a culmination of everything you've learned about game programming throughout the book. The Space Out game is a vertical space shoot-em-up that takes advantage of just about every feature you've built into the game engine. The closest arcade comparison I can make to Space Out is Galaga, but the aliens in Space Out don't move with patterns as intricate as those in Galaga. Nevertheless, I think you'll find Space Out to be a fun and entertaining game, from both programming and playability perspectives.

In this chapter, you'll learn

- ▶ About the basic premise behind the Space Out game
- ▶ How to design the Space Out game
- ▶ About the nuts and bolts of programming the Space Out game
- ▶ Why testing is still the most fun part of developing a new game

How Does the Game Play?

One of the most classic genres of video games has always been the vertical space shoot-em-up. Space Invaders started it all back in 1978, but many games followed and added their own unique contributions to the genre. One of the most enduring vertical space shooters is Galaga, which you learned about in the introduction to Chapter 9, "Making Things Move with Sprite Animation." In Galaga, a relentless sequence of invading aliens fly down from the top of the game screen and attack your ship, which is free to move horizontally across the bottom of the screen. The Space Out game that you develop in this chapter is similar in some ways to Galaga, although the theme for the game is a little more whimsical.

In Space Out, you are the driver of a small green car on a trek across the desert. Whether or not you believe in UFOs, it's hard to argue that quite a few sightings seem to have occurred in remote desert settings such as Roswell, New Mexico. For this reason, your traveler in the game can't seem to get away from a constant onslaught of alien visitors from above. Unfortunately, the aliens in Space Out are bent on putting an end to our traveler's trip. The cast of alien characters in the Space Out game are somewhat comical and add a degree of whimsy to the game. The following are the three kinds of aliens that appear throughout the game:

▶ Blobbo the Galactic Ooze

▶ Jellybiafra (Jelly for short)

▶ Timmy the Space Worm

Granted, these probably aren't very realistic aliens when it comes to what you might imagine truly encountering in an extraterrestrial sighting, but this game isn't about reality. Each of the aliens has its own movement pattern and style of attack, and each fires different missiles. The idea here isn't to simulate a realistic alien invasion, but to have some fun with outlandish characters in the context of a vertical shoot-em-up. To keep the comical theme going, your ill-fated desert traveler fires Twinkies snack cakes up at the aliens as bullets. (Like I said, this game isn't about realism.)

Gamer's Garage

The characters and concept for the Space Out game were created by Rebecca Rose, a computer artist and game designer.

Designing the Game

Now that you understand the basic idea behind the game, let's focus on a few details regarding the design of the game. The player's car can move horizontally across the game screen, which means that its position is confined to the x axis. The player can shoot up vertically—with his Twinkies missiles terminating at the top of the screen, similar to the missiles in the Meteor Defense game from Chapter 17, "Example Game: Meteor Defense."

The aliens in Space Out can move around in any direction and at different velocities. The Blobbo and Jelly aliens bounce off the edges of the screen, whereas Timmy is allowed to wrap around and appear on the other side. This is because Timmy has a tendency to fly horizontally across the screen, whereas the others move around a little more randomly. All the aliens fire missiles down toward the player's car—with the missiles terminating when they strike the car or the ground. The aliens are immune from their own missiles, so they can't hit each other. This is a good thing for the aliens because they aren't very careful in terms of how they aim.

Space Out has no discrete levels and no real goal other than surviving. However, the difficulty level of the game does gradually increase as the player progresses through the game. The difficulty of the game increases by adding new aliens at a faster pace. Eventually the player will have his hands full trying to contend with a never ending army of aliens. That's the whole fun of shoot-em-ups!

To help you get a feel for how the Space Out game is laid out, take a look at Figure 19.1.

The figure shows the background image of the desert, which serves as a backdrop for the car to drive around on. The starry background still appears in the majority of the screen, whereas the background image shows the desert where the car drives around. The background image actually includes a horizontal band of sky that helps blend the desert landscape into the starry background. The car sprite moves around on top of the desert background image. The aliens appear in the sky and move around trying to hit the car by firing various missiles. Of course, the car also fires missiles back at the aliens. The score for the game is displayed in the upper right corner of the game screen, along with the number of remaining lives (cars).

Now that you understand the basics of the game, it's important to examine the sprites that it requires. The following is a list of the sprites that go into the Space Out game:

- ▶ Car sprite
- ▶ Alien sprites
- ▶ Missile sprites (from the aliens and the car)
- ▶ Explosion sprites

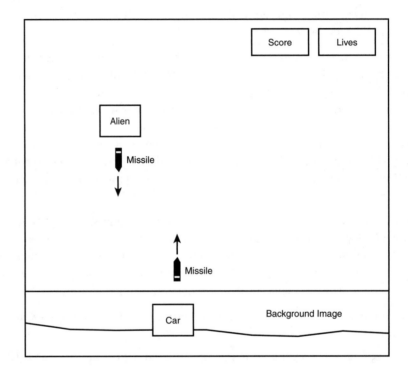

The only type of sprite in this list that I haven't mentioned is the explosion sprite, which is used to show an alien being destroyed by a missile, as well as the car being destroyed by an alien missile. Two different sizes of explosions are actually used in the Space Out game. The larger explosion is used to show an alien or the car being destroyed, whereas the smaller explosion is used to show a missile exploding. This distinction is important because it shows how missiles cause a smaller explosion when they simply crash into the desert, as opposed to hitting the car.

In addition to the sprites, the Space Out game requires several bitmaps. The following are the bitmap images required of the game:

- ▶ Background desert image
- ▶ Car image (see Figure 19.2)
- ▶ Missile image, fired by car (see Figure 19.3)
- ▶ Animated alien images—Blobbo, Jelly, and Timmy (see Figure 19.4)
- ▶ Missile images, fired by each of the three aliens (see Figure 19.5)
- ▶ Animated explosion images, small and large (see Figure 19.6)
- ▶ Small car image (see Figure 19.7)
- ▶ Game over image

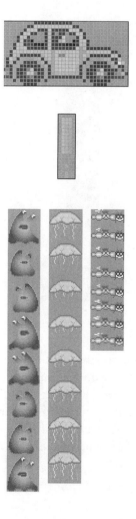

FIGURE 19.2
The car bitmap image consists of a green car facing to the right.

FIGURE 19.3
The player missile bitmap image consists of a missile aiming upward.

FIGURE 19.4
The alien bitmap images are all animated, although they contain varying numbers of frames.

FIGURE 19.5
The alien missile bitmap images are all aimed downward because they appear to drop vertically from top to bottom in the game.

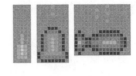

FIGURE 19.6
The large and small explosion bitmap images are both animated.

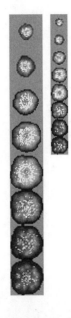

FIGURE 19.7
The small car bitmap image is used to display the number of remaining lives.

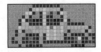

These images flow directly from the design of the game that you've covered thus far, so there hopefully shouldn't be any big surprises here. Perhaps the main thing to point out is that the aliens all rely on animated images (refer to Figure 19.4) to provide them with a more interesting appearance as they move around on the game screen. The only other animated images in the game are the explosion images (refer to Figure 19.6), which go with the explosion sprites.

The score needs to be maintained throughout the game, as well as the number of remaining lives (cars); the game ends when all three of your cars have been destroyed. The difficulty level of the game is stored away in a global variable and gradually increases as the player racks up points and progresses through the game. Another important piece of information is the familiar Boolean variable that keeps track of whether the game is over.

The last global game variable required of Space Out is an input delay variable that helps add some restraint to the player's ability to fire missiles rapidly. Without this input delay variable, it would be too easy to wipe out the aliens by holding down the fire key (spacebar) and raining missiles on the aliens with little effort. By slowing down the number of missiles that can be fired, the player is forced to be more accurate and to evade aliens when they miss. Establishing the appropriate delay is somewhat of a trial-and-error process, and you might decide that the game is more fun with a slightly different value than I use.

To recap, the design of the Space Out game has led us to the following pieces of information that must be managed by the game:

- The number of lives (cars) remaining
- The score
- The difficulty level
- A Boolean game over variable
- A delay variable for firing input

Before diving into the code for the Space Out game, you need to add a new feature to the game engine. Although the game engine is a flexible piece of software, you will likely find yourself adding new features in the future to accommodate the special needs of new games. This is a good thing because you get to reuse those features in any game that you create from then on.

Adding Yet Another Sprite Feature to the Game Engine

The missing feature in the game engine critical to the Space Out game is the capability for a sprite to automatically create another sprite. This might seem like a strange requirement, but think about an alien that is firing a missile at the car in the Space Out game. The missile must be created so that it appears to come from the alien, which means that the missile must know about the alien's position. Not only that, but the missile must be unique to the alien that fired it because each alien fires a different kind of missile. This presents a significant challenge to the current design of the game engine because there isn't a good way to automatically create a new sprite based on the properties of another sprite.

A good solution to this problem involves allowing a sprite to create another sprite whenever it needs to. For example, you can allow the alien sprites to create missile sprites themselves, which makes it very easy to position the missile based on the alien's position—not to mention create the appropriate missile for each different type of alien. The problem with this approach is that it is impossible to add this functionality to the Sprite class in a generic fashion. In other words, the specifics regarding what kind of sprite needs to be created are unique to each game and therefore can't be carried out in the Sprite class. However, the Sprite class can establish the interface that makes this task possible.

An important part of this new "add sprite" feature is a new sprite action called SA_ADDSPRITE. The following code shows how the SA_ADDSPRITE sprite action is added to the existing sprite actions:

```
typedef WORD      SPRITEACTION;
const SPRITEACTION  SA_NONE      = 0x0000L,
                    SA_KILL      = 0x0001L,
                    SA_ADDSPRITE = 0x0002L;
```

If you recall, sprite actions are used to signal to the game engine that some particular action must be taken in regard to a sprite. The SA_ADDSPRITE sprite action simply results in a special method being called on the Sprite object to which the action applies. This method is called AddSprite(), and it looks like this:

```
virtual Sprite* AddSprite();
```

The idea behind the AddSprite() method is that it gets called to enable a sprite to add a new sprite to the game engine; a pointer to the newly created sprite is returned by the AddSprite() method. The specifics of the new sprite are entirely dependent on each individual game. In fact, the version of the AddSprite() method in the Sprite class doesn't do anything, as the following code reveals:

```
Sprite* Sprite::AddSprite()
{
  return NULL;
}
```

This code shows how the base `Sprite::AddSprite()` method doesn't do anything other than return a `NULL` sprite pointer, which reveals that the task of adding a sprite via the `AddSprite()` method is left up to derived sprite classes. Therefore, in order to take advantage of this method, you must derive a sprite class for a particular kind of sprite and then override the `AddSprite()` method with a version that actually creates a sprite.

The `SA_ADDSPRITE` action and `AddSprite()` method enter the picture in the game engine in the `GameEngine::UpdateSprites()` method, which must check for the presence of the `SA_ADDSPRITE` sprite action and then call the `AddSprite()` method on the sprite if the action is set. The return value of the sprite's `AddSprite()` method is passed along to the game engine's `AddSprite()` function, which handles inserting the sprite into the sprite list. This is all that is required of the game engine to support adding a sprite from within another sprite, which is a subtle but critical feature that is useful in many types of games.

Building the Game

The construction of the Space Out game is similar to that of the other games you've developed throughout the book. However, Space Out is slightly more involved simply because it is a more complete game. The next few sections guide you through the development of the game's code and resources.

Writing the Game Code

Although the development of all the previous games in the book began with the header file for the game, Space Out is a little different in that it relies on a custom sprite class. For this reason, the code for the Space Out game begins with the header for this custom sprite class, `AlienSprite`, which is shown in Listing 19.1.

LISTING 19.1 The AlienSprite.h Header File Declares the `AlienSprite` Class, Which Is Derived from `Sprite`

```
#pragma once

//----------------------------------------
// Include Files
//----------------------------------------
#include <windows.h>
#include "Sprite.h"

//----------------------------------------
// AlienSprite Class
//----------------------------------------
```

continues

LISTING 19.1 Continued

```
class AlienSprite : public Sprite
{
public:
  // Constructor(s)/Destructor
          AlienSprite(Bitmap* pBitmap, RECT& rcBounds,
              BOUNDSACTION baBoundsAction = BA_STOP);
  virtual ~AlienSprite();

  // General Methods
  virtual SPRITEACTION  Update();
  virtual Sprite*       AddSprite();
};
```

These two methods primarily give the alien sprite its unique functionality.

The AlienSprite class is not very complex at all, as the listing hopefully reveals.
It's important to notice that AlienSprite derives from Sprite and declares a constructor and destructor. More importantly, however, are the two methods in the
Sprite class that AlienSprite overrides, Update() and AddSprite(). These two
methods are critical to providing the AlienSprite class with its own unique functionality separate from the Sprite class. In case you're wondering exactly what
this functionality is, let me explain.

If you recall from the previous section, one of the problems in the game engine
was that it didn't enable a sprite to create another sprite on its own. You added
code to the game engine, including a method called AddSprite() in the Sprite
class, to allow for this task to be carried out by sprites. However, the version of the
AddSprite() method in the Sprite class doesn't do anything—it's up to derived
Sprite classes to create their own sprites. The AlienSprite class is an example of
one of these derived classes that overrides the AddSprite() method to do something useful.

Before you get to the AlienSprite::AddSprite() method, however, let's take a
quick look at some external global variables that are required of the AlienSprite
class:

```
extern Bitmap* g_pBlobboBitmap;
extern Bitmap* g_pBMissileBitmap;
extern Bitmap* g_pJellyBitmap;
extern Bitmap* g_pJMissileBitmap;
extern Bitmap* g_pTimmyBitmap;
extern Bitmap* g_pTMissileBitmap;
extern int     g_iDifficulty;
```

These global variables are part of the main Space Out game code and are included in the file SpaceOut.h, which you will see in a moment. They must be declared externally in the AlienSprite code because the code references the global variables. Listing 19.2 contains the code for the AlienSprite::AddSprite() method, which makes use of the external global variables to determine what kind of missile sprite to add.

LISTING 19.2 The AlienSprite::AddSprite() Method Adds a Missile Sprite Based on the Alien that Is Firing It

```
Sprite* AlienSprite::AddSprite()
{
  // Create a new missile sprite
  RECT    rcBounds = { 0, 0, 640, 410 };
  RECT    rcPos = GetPosition();
  Sprite* pSprite = NULL;
  if (GetBitmap() == g_pBlobboBitmap)
  {
    // Blobbo missile
    pSprite = new Sprite(g_pBMissileBitmap, rcBounds, BA_DIE);
    pSprite->SetVelocity(0, 7);
  }
  else if (GetBitmap() == g_pJellyBitmap)
  {
    // Jelly missile
    pSprite = new Sprite(g_pJMissileBitmap, rcBounds, BA_DIE);
    pSprite->SetVelocity(0, 5);
  }
  else
  {
    // Timmy missile
    pSprite = new Sprite(g_pTMissileBitmap, rcBounds, BA_DIE);
    pSprite->SetVelocity(0, 3);
  }
  // Set the missile sprite's position and return it
  pSprite->SetPosition(rcPos.left + (GetWidth() / 2), rcPos.bottom);
  return pSprite;
}
```

Blobbo fires the fastest missiles in the game.

Jelly fires medium speed missiles.

Timmy's missiles are downright slow compared to Blobbo's and Jelly's.

Start the missile out just below the position of the alien sprite.

The purpose of this AddSprite() method is to enable an alien sprite to create a missile sprite. The important thing to notice in the AddSprite() method is that it fires a different missile for each kind of alien. To determine what kind of alien is firing the missile, the method checks the bitmap image for the sprite. A missile sprite is then created based on which alien is firing the missile. Finally, the new missile sprite's position is set so that it appears just below the alien, and the sprite is returned from the method so that it can be added to the sprite list in the game engine.

You might have noticed earlier in the `AlienSprite` class that the `Update()` method is also overridden. Listing 19.3 contains the code for the `AlienSprite::Update()` method, which handles randomly setting the `SA_ADDSPRITE` sprite action for the aliens.

LISTING 19.3   The `AlienSprite::Update()` Method Randomly Sets the `SA_SPRITEACTION` Sprite Action so that the Aliens Fire Missiles

```
SPRITEACTION AlienSprite::Update()
{
  // Call the base sprite Update() method
  SPRITEACTION saSpriteAction;
  saSpriteAction = Sprite::Update();

  // See if the alien should fire a missile
  if ((rand() % (g_iDifficulty / 2)) == 0)
    saSpriteAction |= SA_ADDSPRITE;

  return saSpriteAction;
}
```

The likelihood of an alien firing a missile is determined by the difficulty level.

The most important line of code in this method is the call to the base class `Update()` method, which ensures that the sprite is properly updated. The method then uses the `g_iDifficulty` global variable as the basis for randomly setting the `SA_SPRITEACTION` sprite action, which results in the alien firing a missile. This works because the `SA_SPRITEACTION` sprite action causes the `AlienSprite::AddSprite()` method to get called, which creates a new missile sprite and adds it to the game engine.

That wraps up the code for the `AlienSprite` class, which is a crucial component of the *Space Out* game. The core of the *Space Out* game is laid out in the SpaceOut.h header file, which is responsible for declaring the global variables used throughout the game (see Listing 19.4).

LISTING 19.4   The SpaceOut.h Header File Declares Global Variables that Are Used to Manage the Game

```
#pragma once

//-------------------------------------------------
// Include Files
//-------------------------------------------------
#include <windows.h>
#include "Resource.h"
#include "GameEngine.h"
#include "Bitmap.h"
#include "Sprite.h"
#include "Background.h"
```

```
#include "AlienSprite.h"

//---------------------------------.
// Global Variables
//---------------------------------.
HINSTANCE          g_hInstance;
GameEngine*        g_pGame;
HDC                g_hOffscreenDC;
HBITMAP            g_hOffscreenBitmap;
Bitmap*            g_pDesertBitmap;
Bitmap*            g_pCarBitmap;
Bitmap*            g_pSmCarBitmap;
Bitmap*            g_pMissileBitmap;
Bitmap*            g_pBlobboBitmap;
Bitmap*            g_pBMissileBitmap;
Bitmap*            g_pJellyBitmap;
Bitmap*            g_pJMissileBitmap;
Bitmap*            g_pTimmyBitmap;
Bitmap*            g_pTMissileBitmap;
Bitmap*            g_pSmExplosionBitmap;
Bitmap*            g_pLgExplosionBitmap;
Bitmap*            g_pGameOverBitmap;
StarryBackground*  g_pBackground;
Sprite*            g_pCarSprite;
int                g_iFireInputDelay;
int                g_iNumLives, g_iScore, g_iDifficulty;
BOOL               g_bGameOver;

//---------------------------------.
// Function Declarations
//---------------------------------.
void NewGame();
void AddAlien();
```

The bitmaps start to add up quickly when you get into creating more interesting games.

The car sprite is the only sprite you need to keep track of because you need to move it in response to user interactions.

The listing shows that the global variables for the Space Out game largely consist of the different bitmaps used throughout the game. The starry background for the game is declared after the bitmaps, followed by the car sprite that represents the player. Member variables storing the number of remaining lives, the score, and the difficulty level are then declared, followed by the familiar game over Boolean variable.

Similar to the Meteor Defense game in Chapter 17, the Space Out game also relies on a couple of support functions. The first of these, NewGame(), is important because it is used to set up and start a new game. Unlike the GameStart() function, which performs initialization tasks such as loading bitmaps, the NewGame() function handles starting a new game once everything else is in place. The AddAlien() function is used to simplify the task of adding alien sprites to the game. You find out more about how these functions work a little later in the chapter.

The primary setup code for the game takes place in the familiar GameStart()
function, which is shown in Listing 19.5.

LISTING 19.5 The GameStart() Function Initializes the Bitmaps and
Background for the Game and Calls the NewGame() Function

```
void GameStart(HWND hWindow)
{
  // Seed the random number generator
  srand(GetTickCount());

  // Create the offscreen device context and bitmap
  g_hOffscreenDC = CreateCompatibleDC(GetDC(hWindow));
  g_hOffscreenBitmap = CreateCompatibleBitmap(GetDC(hWindow),
    g_pGame->GetWidth(), g_pGame->GetHeight());
  SelectObject(g_hOffscreenDC, g_hOffscreenBitmap);

  // Create and load the bitmaps
  HDC hDC = GetDC(hWindow);
  g_pDesertBitmap = new Bitmap(hDC, IDB_DESERT, g_hInstance);
  g_pCarBitmap = new Bitmap(hDC, IDB_CAR, g_hInstance);
  g_pSmCarBitmap = new Bitmap(hDC, IDB_SMCAR, g_hInstance);
  g_pMissileBitmap = new Bitmap(hDC, IDB_MISSILE, g_hInstance);
  g_pBlobboBitmap = new Bitmap(hDC, IDB_BLOBBO, g_hInstance);
  g_pBMissileBitmap = new Bitmap(hDC, IDB_BMISSILE, g_hInstance);
  g_pJellyBitmap = new Bitmap(hDC, IDB_JELLY, g_hInstance);
  g_pJMissileBitmap = new Bitmap(hDC, IDB_JMISSILE, g_hInstance);
  g_pTimmyBitmap = new Bitmap(hDC, IDB_TIMMY, g_hInstance);
  g_pTMissileBitmap = new Bitmap(hDC, IDB_TMISSILE, g_hInstance);
  g_pSmExplosionBitmap = new Bitmap(hDC, IDB_SMEXPLOSION, g_hInstance);
  g_pLgExplosionBitmap = new Bitmap(hDC, IDB_LGEXPLOSION, g_hInstance);
  g_pGameOverBitmap = new Bitmap(hDC, IDB_GAMEOVER, g_hInstance);

  // Create the starry background
  g_pBackground = new StarryBackground(600, 450);

  // Play the background music
  g_pGame->PlayMIDISong(TEXT("Music.mid"));

  // Start the game
  NewGame();
}
```

*The NewGame()
helper function
isolates the code
required to start
a new game.*

After the GameStart()function finishes loading the bitmaps for the game and creating the starry background, it starts playing the background music. The function
then finishes up by calling the NewGame() function to start a new game. The
GameEnd() function cleans up after the GameStart() function and is called whenever the user exits the game. Since you've seen cleanup code for several games
already, let's skip the details of how this GameEnd() function works.

The game screen in the Space Out game is painted by the GamePaint() function, which is shown in Listing 19.6.

LISTING 19.6   The GamePaint() Function Draws the Background, the Desert Ground Bitmap, the Sprites, the Score, and the Game Over Message

```
void GamePaint(HDC hDC)
{
  // Draw the background
  g_pBackground->Draw(hDC);

  // Draw the desert bitmap
  g_pDesertBitmap->Draw(hDC, 0, 371);

  // Draw the sprites
  g_pGame->DrawSprites(hDC);

  // Draw the score
  TCHAR szText[64];
  RECT  rect = { 460, 0, 510, 30 };
  wsprintf(szText, "%d", g_iScore);
  SetBkMode(hDC, TRANSPARENT);
  SetTextColor(hDC, RGB(255, 255, 255));
  DrawText(hDC, szText, -1, &rect, DT_SINGLELINE | DT_RIGHT | DT_VCENTER);

  // Draw the number of remaining lives (cars)
  for (int i = 0; i < g_iNumLives; i++)
    g_pSmCarBitmap->Draw(hDC, 520 + (g_pSmCarBitmap->GetWidth() * i),
      10, TRUE);

  // Draw the game over message, if necessary
  if (g_bGameOver)
    g_pGameOverBitmap->Draw(hDC, 190, 149, TRUE);
}
```

Although visually the desert image is part of the background, it is drawn separately from the starry background.

If the background fill mode isn't set to TRANSPARENT, a solid colored rectangle would appear behind the score.

The GamePaint() function takes care of drawing all graphics for the Space Out game. The function begins by drawing the starry background, followed by the desert ground image. The sprites are then drawn, followed by the score. The number of remaining lives (represented by small car images) is drawn in the upper-right corner of the screen just right of the score. Finally, the function finishes up by drawing the game over image, if necessary.

The GameCycle() function works hand in hand with the GamePaint() function to update the game's sprites and reflect the changes onscreen. Listing 19.7 shows the code for the GameCycle() function.

LISTING 19.7   The `GameCycle()` Function Randomly Adds New Aliens to the Game

```
void GameCycle()
{
  if (!g_bGameOver)
  {
    // Randomly add aliens
    if ((rand() % g_iDifficulty) == 0)
      AddAlien();

    // Update the background
    g_pBackground->Update();

    // Update the sprites
    g_pGame->UpdateSprites();

    // Obtain a device context for repainting the game
    HWND  hWindow = g_pGame->GetWindow();
    HDC   hDC = GetDC(hWindow);

    // Paint the game to the offscreen device context
    GamePaint(g_hOffscreenDC);

    // Blit the offscreen bitmap to the game screen
    BitBlt(hDC, 0, 0, g_pGame->GetWidth(), g_pGame->GetHeight(),
      g_hOffscreenDC, 0, 0, SRCCOPY);

    // Cleanup
    ReleaseDC(hWindow, hDC);
  }
}
```

The rate at which aliens are added is directly determined by the difficulty level of the game.

Aside from the standard `GameCycle()` code that you're already accustomed to seeing, this function doesn't add much additional code. The new code involves randomly adding new aliens, which is accomplished by calling the `AddAlien()` function after using the difficulty level to randomly determine if an alien should be added.

With the alien sprites squared away, you still have to contend with how the user is going to control the car sprite. This is accomplished via a keyboard interface using the `HandleKeys()` function, which is shown in Listing 19.8.

LISTING 19.8   The `HandleKeys()` Function Allows the User to Control the Car Sprite Using Keys on the Keyboard

```
void HandleKeys()
{
  if (!g_bGameOver)
  {
    // Move the car based upon left/right key presses
    POINT ptVelocity = g_pCarSprite->GetVelocity();
```

```
  if (GetAsyncKeyState(VK_LEFT) < 0)
  {
    // Move left
    ptVelocity.x = max(ptVelocity.x - 1, -4);
    g_pCarSprite->SetVelocity(ptVelocity);
  }
  else if (GetAsyncKeyState(VK_RIGHT) < 0)
  {
    // Move right
    ptVelocity.x = min(ptVelocity.x + 2, 6);
    g_pCarSprite->SetVelocity(ptVelocity);
  }

  // Fire missiles based upon spacebar presses
  if ((++g_iFireInputDelay > 6) && GetAsyncKeyState(VK_SPACE) < 0)
  {
    // Create a new missile sprite
    RECT  rcBounds = { 0, 0, 600, 450 };
    RECT  rcPos = g_pCarSprite->GetPosition();
    Sprite* pSprite = new Sprite(g_pMissileBitmap, rcBounds, BA_DIE);
    pSprite->SetPosition(rcPos.left + 15, 400);
    pSprite->SetVelocity(0, -7);
    g_pGame->AddSprite(pSprite);

    // Play the missile (fire) sound
    PlaySound((LPCSTR)IDW_MISSILE, g_hInstance, SND_ASYNC |
      SND_RESOURCE | SND_NOSTOP);

    // Reset the input delay
    g_iFireInputDelay = 0;
  }
}

// Start a new game based upon an Enter (Return) key press
if (g_bGameOver && (GetAsyncKeyState(VK_RETURN) < 0))
  // Start a new game
  NewGame();
}
```

The car's maximum speed to the left is slower than its maximum speed to the right because it is going in reverse when moving left.

The missile's position is set so that it starts out just above the car's position.

The HandleKeys() function looks to see if any of four keys are being pressed. The following are the meanings of these keys in the context of the Space Out game:

▶ Left arrow—Moves the car left

▶ Right arrow—Moves the car right

▶ Space—Fires a missile

▶ Enter (Return)—Starts a new game (only if the game is over)

By knowing the meanings of these keys, the code in the HandleKeys() function hopefully makes a bit more sense. The function begins by making sure that the game isn't over and then proceeds to check on the status of each of the three keys that have relevance to the game play; the fourth key (Enter) only applies to a game that is over. If the left arrow key is pressed, the HandleKeys() function alters the car sprite's velocity so that it moves more to the left. On the other hand, if the right arrow key is pressed, the car sprite's velocity is set so that it moves more to the right. One interesting thing to note about this code is that the car is capable of moving faster to the right than it is to the left, which is because the car is aiming to the right. In other words, it can't go as fast in reverse as it can moving forward, which adds a subtle touch of realism to the game.

Firing missiles is initiated by the user pressing the Space key (spacebar), but it only takes place if the fire input delay has been triggered. The net effect of the fire input delay is to slow down the firing of missiles so that the player can't go crazy with a barrage of missiles; the game would be too easy if you could fire at that rate. To actually fire a missile, a missile sprite is created and set to a position just above the car sprite, which makes the missile appear to originate from the car. A sound effect is also played to indicate that the missile was fired.

The last section of code in the HandleKeys() function starts a new game in response to the user pressing the Enter (Return) key. The g_bGameOver variable is checked to make sure that the game is over, and the NewGame() function is called to start the new game.

Another important function in the Space Out game is the SpriteCollision() function, which is called in response to sprites colliding (see Listing 19.9).

LISTING 19.9 The SpriteCollision() **Function Responds to Collisions Between Missiles, Aliens, and the Car Sprite**

```
BOOL SpriteCollision(Sprite* pSpriteHitter, Sprite* pSpriteHittee)
{
  // See if a player missile and an alien have collided
  Bitmap* pHitter = pSpriteHitter->GetBitmap();
  Bitmap* pHittee = pSpriteHittee->GetBitmap();
  if ((pHitter == g_pMissileBitmap && (pHittee == g_pBlobboBitmap ¦¦
    pHittee == g_pJellyBitmap ¦¦ pHittee == g_pTimmyBitmap)) ¦¦
    (pHittee == g_pMissileBitmap && (pHitter == g_pBlobboBitmap ¦¦
    pHitter == g_pJellyBitmap ¦¦ pHitter == g_pTimmyBitmap)))
  {
    // Play the small explosion sound
    PlaySound((LPCSTR)IDW_LGEXPLODE, g_hInstance, SND_ASYNC ¦
      SND_RESOURCE);

    // Kill both sprites
    pSpriteHitter->Kill();
    pSpriteHittee->Kill();
```

Check to see if a player missile has collided with an alien.

```
  // Create a large explosion sprite at the alien's position
  RECT rcBounds = { 0, 0, 600, 450 };
  RECT rcPos;
  if (pHitter == g_pMissileBitmap)
    rcPos = pSpriteHittee->GetPosition();
  else
    rcPos = pSpriteHitter->GetPosition();
  Sprite* pSprite = new Sprite(g_pLgExplosionBitmap, rcBounds);
  pSprite->SetNumFrames(8, TRUE);
  pSprite->SetPosition(rcPos.left, rcPos.top);
  g_pGame->AddSprite(pSprite);

  // Update the score
  g_iScore += 25;
  g_iDifficulty = max(80 - (g_iScore / 20), 20);
}

// See if an alien missile has collided with the car
if ((pHitter == g_pCarBitmap && (pHittee == g_pBMissileBitmap ¦¦
  pHittee == g_pJMissileBitmap ¦¦ pHittee == g_pTMissileBitmap)) ¦¦
  (pHittee == g_pCarBitmap && (pHitter == g_pBMissileBitmap ¦¦
  pHitter == g_pJMissileBitmap ¦¦ pHitter == g_pTMissileBitmap)))
{
  // Play the large explosion sound
  PlaySound((LPCSTR)IDW_LGEXPLODE, g_hInstance, SND_ASYNC ¦
    SND_RESOURCE);

  // Kill the missile sprite
  if (pHitter == g_pCarBitmap)
    pSpriteHittee->Kill();
  else
    pSpriteHitter->Kill();

  // Create a large explosion sprite at the car's position
  RECT rcBounds = { 0, 0, 600, 480 };
  RECT rcPos;
  if (pHitter == g_pCarBitmap)
    rcPos = pSpriteHitter->GetPosition();
  else
    rcPos = pSpriteHittee->GetPosition();
  Sprite* pSprite = new Sprite(g_pLgExplosionBitmap, rcBounds);
  pSprite->SetNumFrames(8, TRUE);
  pSprite->SetPosition(rcPos.left, rcPos.top);
  g_pGame->AddSprite(pSprite);

  // Move the car back to the start
  g_pCarSprite->SetPosition(300, 405);

  // See if the game is over
  if (-g_iNumLives == 0)
  {
    // Play the game over sound
    PlaySound((LPCSTR)IDW_GAMEOVER, g_hInstance, SND_ASYNC ¦
      SND_RESOURCE);
    g_bGameOver = TRUE;
```

Check to see if the player's car has collided with an alien missile.

Move the car back to its start position to simulate a new car being created.

continues

LISTING 19.9   Continued

```
    }
  }

  return FALSE;
}
```

The SpriteCollision() function is undoubtedly the heftiest function in the Space Out game and for good reason: The collisions between the sprites in the game completely determine the play of the game. The function begins by checking for a collision between a player missile and an alien. If the collision occurred, the SpriteCollision() function plays a small explosion sound, kills both sprites, and creates a large explosion sprite at the alien's position. The score is also increased to reward the player for taking out an alien. Of course, this also means that the difficulty level is recalculated to factor in the new score.

The other collision detected in the SpriteCollision() function is between an alien missile and the car sprite. If this collision takes place, a large explosion sound is played, and the missile sprite is killed. A large explosion sprite is then created at the car's position, and the car sprite is moved back to its starting position.

The last section of the SpriteCollision() function checks the number of lives to see if the game is over. If so, a game over sound is played and the g_bGameOver variable is set to TRUE.

Another important sprite-related function in the Space Out game is the SpriteDying() function, which is called whenever a sprite is being destroyed. In the case of Space Out, this function is used to create a small explosion sprite any time an alien missile sprite is destroyed. Listing 19.10 shows how this function works.

LISTING 19.10   The SpriteDying() **Function Creates a Small Explosion Whenever an Alien Missile Sprite Is Destroyed**

```
void SpriteDying(Sprite* pSpriteDying)
{
  // See if an alien missile sprite is dying
  if (pSpriteDying->GetBitmap() == g_pBMissileBitmap ||
    pSpriteDying->GetBitmap() == g_pJMissileBitmap ||
    pSpriteDying->GetBitmap() == g_pTMissileBitmap)
  {
```

```
    // Play the small explosion sound
    PlaySound((LPCSTR)IDW_SMEXPLODE, g_hInstance, SND_ASYNC |
      SND_RESOURCE | SND_NOSTOP);

    // Create a small explosion sprite at the missile's position
    RECT rcBounds = { 0, 0, 600, 450 };
    RECT rcPos = pSpriteDying->GetPosition();
    Sprite* pSprite = new Sprite(g_pSmExplosionBitmap, rcBounds);
    pSprite->SetNumFrames(8, TRUE);
    pSprite->SetPosition(rcPos.left, rcPos.top);
    g_pGame->AddSprite(pSprite);
  }
}
```

If an alien sprite is dying, play a small explosion sound and create a small explosion sprite.

The function begins by checking to see if the dying sprite is an alien missile. If so, a small explosion sound is played, and a small explosion sprite is created.

The last two functions in the Space Out game are support functions that are completely unique to the game. The first one is NewGame(), which performs the steps necessary to start a new game (see Listing 19.11).

LISTING 19.11   The NewGame() Function Gets Everything Ready for a New Game

```
void NewGame()
{
  // Clear the sprites
  g_pGame->CleanupSprites();

  // Create the car sprite
  RECT rcBounds = { 0, 0, 600, 450 };
  g_pCarSprite = new Sprite(g_pCarBitmap, rcBounds, BA_WRAP);
  g_pCarSprite->SetPosition(300, 405);
  g_pGame->AddSprite(g_pCarSprite);

  // Initialize the game variables
  g_iFireInputDelay = 0;
  g_iScore = 0;
  g_iNumLives = 3;
  g_iDifficulty = 80;
  g_bGameOver = FALSE;

  // Play the background music
  g_pGame->PlayMIDISong();
}
```

When starting a new game, clear out the sprite list and start with a clean slate.

The difficulty level of the game counts down from 80 as the game progresses; this number indicates the likelihood of a new alien being created, so a smaller value results in aliens being added more rapidly.

The NewGame() function begins by clearing the sprite list, which is necessary because you can't be certain what sprites have been left over from the previous game. The car sprite is then created, and the global game variables are set. The function finishes by starting the background music. Speaking of creating sprites, the AddAlien() function is shown in Listing 19.12, and its job is to add a new alien sprite to the game at a random location.

LISTING 19.12   The AddAlien() Function Adds a New Alien at a Random Position

```
void AddAlien()
{
  // Create a new random alien sprite
  RECT         rcBounds = { 0, 0, 600, 410 };
  AlienSprite* pSprite;
  switch(rand() % 3)
  {
  case 0:
    // Blobbo
    pSprite = new AlienSprite(g_pBlobboBitmap, rcBounds, BA_BOUNCE);
    pSprite->SetNumFrames(8);
    pSprite->SetPosition(((rand() % 2) == 0) ? 0 : 600, rand() % 370);
    pSprite->SetVelocity((rand() % 7) - 2, (rand() % 7) - 2);
    break;
  case 1:
    // Jelly
    pSprite = new AlienSprite(g_pJellyBitmap, rcBounds, BA_BOUNCE);
    pSprite->SetNumFrames(8);
    pSprite->SetPosition(rand() % 600, rand() % 370);
    pSprite->SetVelocity((rand() % 5) - 2, (rand() % 5) + 3);
    break;
  case 2:
    // Timmy
    pSprite = new AlienSprite(g_pTimmyBitmap, rcBounds, BA_WRAP);
    pSprite->SetNumFrames(8);
    pSprite->SetPosition(rand() % 600, rand() % 370);
    pSprite->SetVelocity((rand() % 7) + 3, 0);
    break;
  }

  // Add the alien sprite
  g_pGame->AddSprite(pSprite);
}
```

The X and Y velocity values for Blobbo are randomly chosen in the range -2 to 4.

The X velocity value for Jelly is randomly chosen in the range -2 to 2, whereas the Y component is in the range 3 to 7.

The X velocity value for Timmy is randomly chosen in the range 3 to 9, whereas the Y component is always 0.

The AddAlien() function adds a new alien to the game, which can be one of three types: Blobbo, Jelly, or Timmy. The code for the creation of each type of alien is similar, but each alien has slightly different characteristics. For example, Blobbo is capable of moving around fairly rapidly in any direction, but he bounces off the edges of the game screen. Jelly also bounces off the screen edges, but his velocity is set differently so that he tends to move much more vertically than Blobbo. Finally, Timmy moves entirely horizontally, and he is allowed to wrap off the screen from right to left. The AddAlien() function ends by adding the new alien sprite to the game engine.

You're probably relieved to find out that this wraps up the code for the Space Out game, which means that you're ready to put the resources together and take the game for a test spin.

Construction Cue

> If you're using Visual C++ 6.0, you might need to change the type casts from (DWORD_PTR) to (DWORD) in GameEngine.cpp in order for the Space Out code to compile properly.

Construction Cue

> As with most of the examples in the book, the Space Out program relies on the standard msimg32.lib and winmm.lib libraries. These libraries are included with most Windows compilers, but they aren't automatically linked into programs when you create a new project. If you are using your own project or make files, as opposed to the ones provided on the CD-ROM, make sure that you change the link settings so that these library files are properly linked into the final executable. Refer to the documentation for your specific compiler for how this is done.

Testing the Game

I've already said it numerous times that testing a game is the most fun part, and yet again you've arrived at the testing phase of a completely new game. Similar to the Meteor Defense game, the Space Out game requires a fair amount of testing, simply because a lot of different interactions are taking place among the various sprites in the game. The great thing is that you test a game simply by playing it. Figure 19.8 shows the Space Out game at the beginning with a single alien firing a few missiles at the car below.

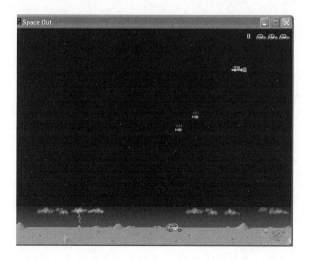

FIGURE 19.8
The Space Out game gets started with an alien firing a few missiles at the car below.

You can move the car left and right using the arrow keys and then fire back at the alien using the Space key (spacebar). Shooting an alien results in a small explosion appearing, as shown in Figure 19.9.

FIGURE 19.9
A small explosion appears when you successfully shoot an alien.

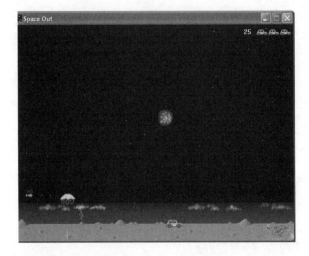

Eventually, you'll venture into dangerous territory and get shot by an alien, which results in a large explosion appearing, as shown in Figure 19.10.

FIGURE 19.10
A large explosion appears when the car gets shot by an alien.

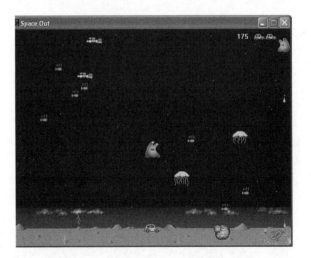

You only have three cars to lose, and the number of remaining cars is shown in the upper-right corner of the game screen next to the score. When you lose all three cars, the game ends, as shown in Figure 19.11.

FIGURE 19.11
When you lose all three cars, the game ends and the game over image is displayed.

The good news about the game ending in Space Out is that you can immediately start a new one by simply pressing the Enter (Return) key.

Summary

Regardless of whether you are a fan of shoot-em-up space games, I hope you realize the significance of the Space Out game that you designed and built in this chapter. In addition to adding yet another fully functioning game to your accomplishments, the Space Out game is important because it represents the most complete game in the book thus far. In other words, it makes the most inclusive usage of the features you've worked so hard at adding to the game engine. Not only that, but the Space Out game is a great game for experimenting with your own ideas, simply because it is the kind of game that can be expanded upon in so many different ways. Before you get too crazy about modifying the Space Out game, however, sit tight because I have a few modifications of my own to throw at you.

This chapter concludes this part of the book, which is admittedly quite short. The next part of the book picks up where you left off by showing you some surefire techniques to add pizzazz to your games. More specifically, you find out how to add interesting features to the Space Out game such as a splash screen, a demo mode, and a high score list.

PART VII

Spicing Up Your Games

CHAPTER 20

Adding Pizzazz to Your Game with a Splash Screen

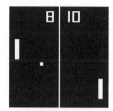

Arcade Archive

If you're a nerd like me, and you grew up playing Dungeons and Dragons, you no doubt have an appreciation for role-playing adventure games. The first video game of this genre to grace arcades was Gauntlet, which was released in 1985 by Atari. Gauntlet was unique among most games of the era because it allowed four-player cooperative play. Each player controlled a unique character with his own special skills, strengths, and weaknesses. Gauntlet later served as the inspiration for countless other adventure games. Interestingly enough, Atari was granted a patent in 1994 for a "multiplayer, multicharacter cooperative play video game with independent player entry and departure." Sounds a lot like Gauntlet to me!

One of the problems with the games you've developed throughout the book thus far is that they don't adequately identify themselves when they first run. Sure, the title bar of the window has the name of the game, but it's important to clearly identify your game when it first starts up. In this way, a game is a lot like a movie in that it should present a title at the beginning. Unlike movies, however, titles in games are referred to as splash screens, and they can contain useful information, such as a copyright notice and directions about how to play the game. This chapter shows you how to spruce up the Space Out game by adding a splash screen.

In this chapter, you'll learn

► Why a splash screen is an important part of just about any game

► What it takes to incorporate a splash screen into a game

► How to add a splash screen to the Space Out game

The Importance of a Splash Screen

Generally speaking, I get annoyed with opening credits in movies because I'm ready for the movie to get started. However, there are a few rare movies whose opening credits are creative and interesting enough to make them enjoyable during the introduction to the movie. A big part of the opening credits for movies is the movie title, which is akin to splash screens used in video games. Similar to a movie title, a splash screen in a video game should convey the theme of the game and possibly provide a sneak preview of what's to come in the game. Of course, it's also possible to deliberately show very little in the splash screen for a game, with the idea being that you want to shroud the game in mystery until the game play actually starts.

Regardless of how much or how little you give away in the splash screen for a game, it's important to at least communicate the title of the game and any other pertinent information, such as the copyright for the game. If a certain action is required to start the game, it's a good idea to mention it on the splash screen as well. No one likes a game that immediately throws you into the action without any warning when the game is launched, so at a bare minimum, the splash screen should give you a chance to initiate the start of game play.

A splash screen is also a good place to include abbreviated instructions for a game, as well as tips and hints about how to play. In the 1980s, when arcade games were the rage, you could often read the splash screen for a game to quickly learn how to play it. This feature isn't as critical in computer games, but it never hurts to provide information that allows people to get started playing a game quickly. One final piece of information to consider for a splash screen is a high score list. This list contains the top scores people have achieved in the game, and it is popular in classic arcade games. Chapter 22, "Keeping Track of High Scores," shows you how to create a high score list that saves high scores for the Space Out game to a file.

Many commercial games these days go far beyond a splash screen by including an introductory animation or video sequence. This "splash animation" is a lot flashier than a simple splash screen, but it often requires a considerable amount of effort to create, especially if it's an actual video. For example, many popular sports games include video clips of the actual sports being played, whereas some story-based games actually provide a thematic introduction that establishes the game's premise. On the other hand, some games just display animation sequences directly from the game, which serves as kind of a demo for the game. You'll find out how to turn a splash screen into a demo mode for the Space Out game in the next chapter. For now, let's continue to dig deeper into basic splash screens and how they work.

Looking Behind a Splash Screen

Although you could certainly dream up a complex approach to creating a splash screen, the easiest way to carry out the task is to simply create a bitmap image for the screen and then display it on the game screen before the game begins. The image for a splash screen can be large enough to fill the entire game screen, or it can be smaller and can be displayed on top of the existing background for the game. The size of the splash screen for your own games is entirely up to you. However, for the Space Out game, I opted to create a splash screen smaller than the game screen. Figure 20.1 shows how the splash screen image is designed to overlay on top of the game background in the Space Out game.

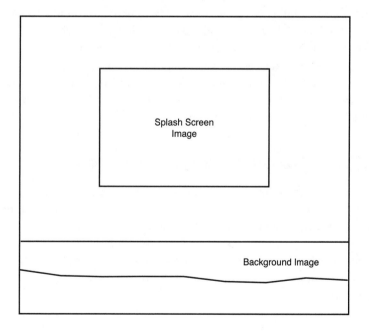

FIGURE 20.1
The splash screen image in the Space Out game is designed to be displayed over the background for the game.

As you can see in the figure, there really isn't anything magical about displaying a splash screen, especially in the Space Out game. The only slightly tricky aspect of adding a splash screen to a game is establishing a separate mode of the game for the splash screen. For example, all the games you've created in the book are always in one of two modes, "game over" or "game not over." These two modes are directly controlled by the g_bGameOver global variable, which has one of two Boolean values, TRUE or FALSE. Although you could associate the splash screen with a game being over, it is more accurate to give it a mode of its own. Therefore, the game will grow to accommodate the following three modes:

▶ Splash screen

▶ Game over

▶ Game not over

Of course, the game is over when the splash screen is displayed, but the "game over" mode is different from the "splash screen" mode because the splash screen isn't displayed.

Giving the splash screen a mode of its own basically means adding a global variable that indicates whether the splash screen should be displayed. This makes sense because you probably don't want to display the splash screen once a game has started and ended. In other words, the splash screen is only shown when the game first starts and then never appears again. You could create a splash screen that is shown in between games, but that's a role better suited to demo mode, which you'll learn about in the next chapter.

Building the Space Out 2 Game

You now know enough about splash screens to take a stab at adding one to the Space Out game. In doing so, you'll be making it more of a complete game with a professional touch. The new version of the Space Out game with a splash screen is called Space Out 2, and it is the focus of the remainder of this chapter. Space Out 2 is very similar to the original Space Out program. In fact, the play of the game doesn't change a bit; all you're doing is adding a splash screen to spruce up the game a bit.

Writing the Game Code

The first step in adding a splash screen to the Space Out 2 game is to add a couple of global variables to the game that store the bitmap for the splash screen, as well as the mode for the splash screen. The following are these variables, which are declared in the Space Out 2 header file, SpaceOut.h:

```
Bitmap* g_pSplashBitmap;
BOOL    g_bSplash;
```

The first variable, g_pSplashBitmap, is pretty straightforward in that it represents the bitmap image for the splash screen (see Figure 20.2). The other global variable, g_bSplash, is a Boolean variable that indicates whether the game is in splash screen mode. More specifically, if the g_bSplash variable is TRUE, the game is in splash screen mode, and the splash screen is displayed; you can't play the game while the splash screen is being displayed. If the g_bSplash variable is FALSE, the game plays normally as if there is no splash screen. So, the idea is to set the g_bSplash variable to TRUE at the beginning of the game and then return it to FALSE after the user starts the game by pressing the Enter key.

FIGURE 20.2
The splash screen bitmap image in the Space Out 2 game contains useful information, such as the title of the game, the copyright notice, and how to start a new game.

As with any global variables, it's important to initialize the splash screen variables. This takes place in the GameStart() function, which is very similar to the previous version. The first change to the GameStart() function is the creation of the splash screen bitmap:

```
g_pSplashBitmap = new Bitmap(hDC, IDB_SPLASH, _hInstance);
```

The only other change is the initialization of the g_bSplash global variable, which must be set to TRUE in order to display the splash screen when the game starts:

```
g_bSplash = TRUE;
```

A big part of making the splash screen work properly is disabling parts of the game when the game is in splash screen mode. Listing 20.1 contains the code for the GameActivate() and GameDeactivate() functions, which check the value of the g_bSplash variable before resuming or pausing the MIDI background music.

LISTING 20.1   The GameActivate() and GameDeactivate() Functions Check the Value of the g_bSplash Variable Before Resuming or Pausing the MIDI Background Music

Only resume the background music if the game isn't in splash screen mode.

```
void GameActivate(HWND hWindow)
{
  if (!g_bSplash)
    // Resume the background music
    g_pGame->PlayMIDISong(TEXT(""), FALSE);
}

void GameDeactivate(HWND hWindow)
{
  if (!g_bSplash)
    // Pause the background music
    g_pGame->PauseMIDISong();
}
```

There isn't too much explanation required for these functions because they simply check the g_bSplash variable to see if the game is in splash screen mode before resuming or pausing the MIDI background music.

Gamer's Garage

You could argue that the background music should be played when the splash screen is visible, but many arcade games operate in silent mode when the game is not in play. Background music could be perceived as an unnecessary annoyance when a game is not being played, which is why I like reserving it for actual game play.

The most important code in the Space Out 2 program in relation to the splash screen is contained in the GamePaint() function, which is where the splash screen is actually drawn. Listing 20.2 contains the code for the GamePaint() function.

LISTING 20.2 The `GamePaint()` Function Draws the Splash Screen
Bitmap When the Game Is in Splash Screen Mode

```
void GamePaint(HDC hDC)
{
  // Draw the background
  g_pBackground->Draw(hDC);

  // Draw the desert bitmap
  g_pDesertBitmap->Draw(hDC, 0, 371);

  if (g_bSplash)
  {
    // Draw the splash screen image
    g_pSplashBitmap->Draw(hDC, 142, 100, TRUE);
  }
  else
  {
    // Draw the sprites
    g_pGame->DrawSprites(hDC);

    // Draw the score
    TCHAR szText[64];
    RECT  rect = { 460, 0, 510, 30 };
    wsprintf(szText, "%d", g_iScore);
    SetBkMode(hDC, TRANSPARENT);
    SetTextColor(hDC, RGB(255, 255, 255));
    DrawText(hDC, szText, -1, &rect, DT_SINGLELINE | DT_RIGHT | DT_VCENTER);

    // Draw the number of remaining lives (cars)
    for (int i = 0; i < g_iNumLives; i++)
      g_pSmCarBitmap->Draw(hDC, 520 + (g_pSmCarBitmap->GetWidth() * i),
        10, TRUE);

    // Draw the game over message, if necessary
    if (g_bGameOver)
      g_pGameOverBitmap->Draw(hDC, 170, 100, TRUE);
  }
}
```

The splash screen image is drawn centered on the game screen.

The change to the `GamePaint()` function involves drawing the splash screen
image if the `g_bSplash` variable is TRUE. If the `g_bSplash` variable is FALSE, the
`GamePaint()` function draws the sprites, score, and remaining lives, which are
only pertinent to a game being played. It's important to notice that the starry
background and desert bitmaps are both drawn, regardless of the value of the
`g_bSplash` variable. This results in the background and desert images being
drawn, even when the splash screen image is drawn; these images are necessary
because the splash screen doesn't fill up the entire game screen.

The last coding change in the Space Out 2 game involves the HandleKeys() function, which you know processes key presses for the game. If you recall, the Enter key is used to start a new game if the current game is over. Because the same key is used to leave the splash screen and start a game, it is necessary to change the value of the g_bSplash variable when the user presses the Enter key. Listing 20.3 shows the new version of the HandleKeys() function with this change in place.

LISTING 20.3 The HandleKeys() Function Changes the Value of the g_bSplash Variable if the Game Is Exiting the Splash Screen to Start a New Game

```
void HandleKeys()
{
  if (!g_bGameOver)
  {
    // Move the car based upon left/right key presses
    POINT ptVelocity = g_pCarSprite->GetVelocity();
    if (GetAsyncKeyState(VK_LEFT) < 0)
    {
      // Move left
      ptVelocity.x = max(ptVelocity.x - 1, -4);
      g_pCarSprite->SetVelocity(ptVelocity);
    }
    else if (GetAsyncKeyState(VK_RIGHT) < 0)
    {
      // Move right
      ptVelocity.x = min(ptVelocity.x + 2, 6);
      g_pCarSprite->SetVelocity(ptVelocity);
    }

    // Fire missiles based upon spacebar presses
    if ((++g_iFireInputDelay > 6) && GetAsyncKeyState(VK_SPACE) < 0)
    {
      // Create a new missile sprite
      RECT  rcBounds = { 0, 0, 600, 450 };
      RECT  rcPos = g_pCarSprite->GetPosition();
      Sprite* pSprite = new Sprite(g_pMissileBitmap, rcBounds, BA_DIE);
      pSprite->SetPosition(rcPos.left + 15, 400);
      pSprite->SetVelocity(0, -7);
      g_pGame->AddSprite(pSprite);

      // Play the missile (fire) sound
      PlaySound((LPCSTR)IDW_MISSILE, g_hInstance, SND_ASYNC |
        SND_RESOURCE | SND_NOSTOP);

      // Reset the input delay
      g_iFireInputDelay = 0;
    }
  }

  // Start a new game based upon an Enter (Return) key press
  if (GetAsyncKeyState(VK_RETURN) < 0)
```

```
    if (g_bSplash)
    {
      // Start a new game without the splash screen
      g_bSplash = FALSE;
      NewGame();
    }
    else if (g_bGameOver)
    {
      // Start a new game
      NewGame();
    }
}
```

Allow a new game to be started from within the splash screen.

Within the code that responds to the Enter (Return) key, you'll find the code that checks to see if the game is leaving splash screen mode. This code first checks to see if the game is in splash screen mode; if so, it then clears the g_bSplash variable and starts a new game. If the game is not in splash screen mode, the function checks to see if the game is over. If the game is over, a new game is started, which is similar to how the HandleKeys() function worked prior to adding the splash screen code.

> If you're using Visual C++ 6.0, you might need to change the type casts from (DWORD_PTR) to (DWORD) in GameEngine.cpp in order for the Space Out 2 code to compile properly.

Construction Cue

> As with most of the examples in the book, the Space Out 2 program relies on the standard msimg32.lib and winmm.lib libraries. These libraries are included with most Windows compilers, but they aren't automatically linked into programs when you create a new project. If you are using your own project or make files, as opposed to using the ones provided on the CD-ROM, make sure that you change the link settings so that these library files are properly linked into the final executable. Refer to the documentation for your specific compiler for how this is done.

Construction Cue

Testing the Finished Product

The Space Out 2 game represents one of the easiest tests you'll ever perform on a game. All you really have to do is run the game and make sure that the splash screen appears properly. Of course, you also need to make sure that the splash screen goes away when you press the Enter key to start a new game, but you get the idea. Figure 20.3 shows the splash screen displayed in the Space Out 2 game when the game first starts.

FIGURE 20.3
The splash screen
in the Space Out 2
game appears
when the game
first starts.

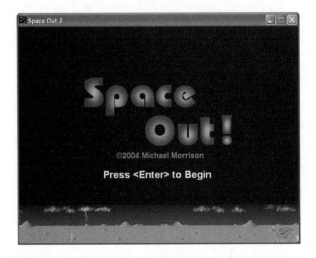

Keep in mind that you are free to get as fancy as you want with the splash screen images for your own games. I chose to keep the Space Out 2 splash screen relatively simple, but you might want to jazz it up to suit your own tastes. The important thing to note about this example is that the splash screen is properly displayed when the game starts.

Summary

This chapter introduced you to an important feature of most games—the splash screen. Not only is the splash screen important in terms of conveying useful information about a game, such as a copyright notice, but it also serves as the player's first glimpse at what your game looks like. You can take advantage of a splash screen to dramatize the theme of your game and even exaggerate the game graphics. For example, it was common for early arcade games to include a fully illustrated splash screen—even though the graphics in the actual games were simpler. This is an engaging way to grab the player's attention and get him interested in the game.

The next chapter builds upon what you learned about splash screens and shows you how to include a demo mode in your games. A demo mode is similar to a splash screen, but its goal is to provide a glimpse at how a game actually plays.

Field Trip

This field trip is, without a doubt, the easiest one in the entire book. It's so simple that you might not even have to move from where you're currently sitting. I want you to find an advertisement for a product and carefully analyze its composition. How is the product being presented? Is it exaggerated for humorous purposes or to otherwise make the pitch more interesting or entertaining? Are the statements within the ad used in such a way as to entice someone to purchase or try the product? These are the questions you should pose to yourself as you construct splash screens for your games. Granted, a splash screen plays a slightly different role than an ad pasted onto a bus stop bench, but the general idea is the same—you're selling something. In this case, you're selling the fun factor of taking the time to play your game. Don't just stop at studying one ad—make it a habit to pay attention to what works and what doesn't because you might be your own target customer. Just do me one favor: Try not to model your splash screens after obnoxious car dealer ads!

CHAPTER 21

Showing Off Your Game with Demo Mode

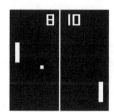

Arcade Archive

If you ever watched any of the old *King Kong* movies or even the recent remake, you can certainly appreciate the excitement of a giant ape roaming around a populated city causing mayhem. This theme forms the basis of the arcade game Rampage, which was released in 1986 by Bally Midway. Rampage added to the King Kong theme by including two other monsters, a giant lizard and a giant wolf, who join forces with a giant ape to carry out as much destruction as possible. One of the neat game play features of Rampage is that three players can play at once cooperatively, with each player controlling one of the monsters. In case you were wondering, the monsters have names: George (the ape), Lizzie (the lizard), and Ralph (the wolf). I suppose that makes them a little more endearing as they stomp buildings and eat helpless people!

In the previous chapter, you learned how important it is to display a splash screen that serves as a title for your game. This chapter continues in the theme of making a game more professional and complete by demonstrating the importance of demo mode. Demo mode is an animated sequence displayed when you're not playing the game that demonstrates how the game is played. Demo mode can be as simple as showing some of the game creatures moving around or as complex as showing an entire simulated game being played. Demo mode is important because it gives a player a glimpse of how a game actually plays, which is a considerable step beyond the role of a splash screen.

In this chapter, you'll learn

- ▶ Why demo mode is useful in showing people how a game works
- ▶ What is involved in adding a demo mode to a game
- ▶ How to add a demo mode to the Space Out game

What Is Demo Mode?

If you've ever been hesitant to buy a product, you might have been offered an opportunity to "try before you buy," which allows you to try out a product before you spend any money on it. This sales technique is particularly useful in the automotive industry, where it is virtually impossible to justify purchasing a product as expensive as a car without taking it for a test drive. In the early days of video games, it was important to convince game players that a game was worthy of spending a quarter for a play, so demo mode was invented. Demo mode is sort of like "try before you buy" applied to video games—you get to see how a game plays before you invest any time or money playing it. In regard to computer games, "try before you buy" now typically involves downloading a limited version of the game that you really can play. However, demo mode is still a useful and worthwhile feature to consider adding to your games.

The main idea behind demo mode is that it goes beyond a splash screen by showing more than just a title or stationary game graphics. Demo mode attempts to show the game actually being played or at least show some of the main characters in the game going through the motions as you'll see them in the game. Demo mode can be as simple or as complex as you choose, but the idea is to provide a hook to convince someone to play the game. In other words, you're attempting to sell the game so that it looks fun and inviting. Demo mode can also be informative, similar to a splash screen. In fact, it's not a bad idea to design demo mode so that it serves as a more interesting splash screen.

Unlike a splash screen, demo mode is not something that appears at the beginning of the game, never to be seen again once the game starts. Instead, demo mode is displayed in between every game and helps fill the space between games with interesting animations from the game. So, when a game ends, there should be a brief pause during which the player is able to take in that the game is actually over, and then the game should return to demo mode. Of course, the game also starts in demo mode. In this way, demo mode replaces the splash screen for a game and also goes a few steps beyond the role of a splash screen.

The Nuts and Bolts of Demo Mode

Similar to a splash screen, demo mode is a distinct mode that a game enters when the game is not underway. This mode is different from the "game over" and "game not over" modes, and it is entered when the game program first starts, as well as in between games. A single Boolean global variable is sufficient to keep track of when a game is in demo mode. This sounds very much like how the splash screen was managed in the previous chapter. Demo mode differs from a splash screen in that it involves demonstrating the game, which means that sprites must be allowed to move around. If you recall, the splash screen for the Space Out 2 game deliberately disallowed sprites to be drawn.

The key to making demo mode work in a game is to simulate the game being played without actually involving a human player. One way to do this is to start up a new game as normal and simulate keystrokes using code that is somehow timed. Of course, this also involves disabling the real keys used in the game so that the player can't suddenly jump into a demo mode game. Although this approach can work very well, and it is ultimately the ideal approach to creating a demo mode because it shows how the player interacts with other characters in a game, it is more difficult to create. The code to replace a human player with a computer player can get tricky and usually involves some degree of artificial intelligence programming. One workaround for this approach is to "record" the keystrokes made by a player during a real game and store them away. You can then "play" the keystrokes back to re-create the demo game. This technique obviously requires some extra work, but it will most likely be a lot simpler than trying to establish realistic AI for the computer player.

> Regardless of how you simulate a human player in demo mode, it's very important that you structure the code in your game so that the human player's character in the game can be controlled by the player or the computer. In other words, make sure that the code to move the player left, for example, can just as easily be called by the computer from demo mode as from the normal game code when the player presses the left arrow key.

Construction Cue

An easier approach to creating a demo mode for a game is to simply show how the characters in the game move around without attempting to simulate a human player in the game. In other words, you aren't actually trying to make it look as if a human player is guiding his character through the game or otherwise interacting with the game. Instead, you're just demonstrating how the computer-controlled characters within the game move around and interact with one another. This approach simplifies things considerably because you aren't in a situation in which you have to try and control an otherwise human player using computer logic. Keep in mind that the whole premise of demo mode is to show off a game and make it look appealing. In many cases, it is sufficient to just show a few characters within the game to achieve this goal.

If you're having trouble figuring out the best approach for structuring a demo mode for your own games, take a look back at how some of the classic arcade games made use of demo mode. Keep in mind that those games had to rely solely on demo mode to lure in potential game players and part them from their quarters, so demo mode was a serious issue. Stop by the Killer List of Video Games Web site at http://www.klov.com/ to learn more about classic video games and get ideas for your own demo mode.

Creating a demo mode that shows a few characters and doesn't actually simulate play is still somewhat of a challenge because you have to create and use sprites just as if you were starting a real game. However, in this case, the idea is to disable any interaction from a human player, other than initiating a new game. If you think about it, creating a demo mode for a game, such as Space Out, involves making several changes throughout the game to allow it to appear as if the game is being played, even though there is no user interaction. The remainder of the chapter focuses on how to add a demo mode to this game.

Building the Space Out 3 Game

You've already learned that in some ways demo mode is similar to a splash screen because it appears in a game when the game is not actually being played. Unlike a splash screen, however, demo mode is responsible for displaying sprites and enabling them to interact to some degree. Adding a demo mode to the Space Out game represents a programming challenge, but one that isn't too terribly difficult to solve. The next few sections lead you through the modifications required in the game to add a demo mode. The new version of the game you'll be creating is called Space Out 3.

Writing the Game Code

The best place to start with the code for the Space Out 3 game is the SpaceOut.h header file, which includes a couple of new global variables. Demo mode for the game requires two new global variables; one of which replaces the g_bSplash global variable that you added in the last chapter for the splash screen. The following are the new global variables necessary to support demo mode in the Space Out 3 game:

```
BOOL g_bDemo;
int  g_iGameOverDelay;
```

The first variable, g_bDemo, is very similar to the g_bSplash variable in the Space Out 2 game from the previous chapter. In fact, it serves virtually the same purpose in this game, except that demo mode impacts more code than did the splash screen. The g_iGameOverDelay global variable is used to provide a delay between when a game ends and when the game enters demo mode. This allows the player to take a moment and realize that the game is over before the game cuts back to demo mode.

The first function of particular interest in the Space Out 3 game is the GameStart() function, which shouldn't come as too much of a surprise. The only change to the GameStart() function is the initialization of the g_bDemo variable.

The GamePaint() function is where the code for the Space Out 3 game starts to diverge more significantly from the Space Out 2 game. However, the change is still somewhat subtle in that all the same code is here; it's just organized a little differently. Take a look at Listing 21.1 to see what I mean.

LISTING 21.1 The GamePaint() Function Draws the Game Graphics While Taking into Consideration Demo Mode

```
void GamePaint(HDC hDC)
{
  // Draw the background
  g_pBackground->Draw(hDC);

  // Draw the desert bitmap
  g_pDesertBitmap->Draw(hDC, 0, 371);

  // Draw the sprites
  g_pGame->DrawSprites(hDC);

  if (g_bDemo)
  {
    // Draw the splash screen image
    g_pSplashBitmap->Draw(hDC, 142, 100, TRUE);
  }
  else
  {
    // Draw the score
    TCHAR szText[64];
    RECT  rect = { 460, 0, 510, 30 };
    wsprintf(szText, "%d", g_iScore);
    SetBkMode(hDC, TRANSPARENT);
    SetTextColor(hDC, RGB(255, 255, 255));
    DrawText(hDC, szText, -1, &rect, DT_SINGLELINE | DT_RIGHT | DT_VCENTER);

    // Draw the number of remaining lives (cars)
    for (int i = 0; i < g_iNumLives; i++)
      g_pSmCarBitmap->Draw(hDC, 520 + (g_pSmCarBitmap->GetWidth() * i),
        10, TRUE);
```

The sprites are drawn regardless of whether the game is in demo mode.

The splash screen is only drawn when the game is in demo mode.

continues

LISTING 21.1 Continued

```
  // Draw the game over message, if necessary
  if (g_bGameOver)
    g_pGameOverBitmap->Draw(hDC, 170, 100, TRUE);
  }
}
```

The GameCycle() function in Space Out 3 looks a lot like its predecessor, but there is a significant change to which you should pay close attention. The change I'm talking about involves the fact that the sprites are drawn regardless of whether the game is in demo mode. In fact, the only thing *not* drawn in demo mode is the score, the number of remaining lives, and the game over message. Also notice that the same splash screen image is displayed when the game is in demo mode, which means that the game is combining demo mode with the splash screen. This isn't a problem; in fact, it's a neat solution in that it enables the game to be demonstrated behind the splash screen image.

The GameCycle() function must be modified to accommodate demo mode as well. More specifically, the GameCycle() function is where the timing delay is established that displays the game over screen for a period of time before reverting back to demo mode when a game ends. Listing 21.2 shows the code for the new version of the GameCycle() function.

LISTING 21.2 The GameCycle() Function Establishes a Timing Delay Before Moving to Demo Mode from the Game Over Screen

```
void GameCycle()
{
  if (!g_bGameOver)
  {
    if (!g_bDemo)
    {
      // Randomly add aliens
      if ((rand() % g_iDifficulty) == 0)
        AddAlien();
    }

    // Update the background
    g_pBackground->Update();

    // Update the sprites
    g_pGame->UpdateSprites();

    // Obtain a device context for repainting the game
    HWND  hWindow = g_pGame->GetWindow();
    HDC   hDC = GetDC(hWindow);

    // Paint the game to the offscreen device context
```

```
  GamePaint(g_hOffscreenDC);

  // Blit the offscreen bitmap to the game screen
  BitBlt(hDC, 0, 0, g_pGame->GetWidth(), g_pGame->GetHeight(),
    g_hOffscreenDC, 0, 0, SRCCOPY);

  // Cleanup
  ReleaseDC(hWindow, hDC);
}
else
  if (--g_iGameOverDelay == 0)
  {
    // Stop the music and switch to demo mode
    g_pGame->PauseMIDISong();
    g_bDemo = TRUE;
    NewGame();
  }
}
```

The game over delay must count down before the game switches into demo mode after a game ends; this gives the player a few seconds to realize that the game is over.

In addition to changing the g_bSplash variable to g_bDemo, the GameCycle() function establishes a timing delay for the game over screen. When this delay finishes counting down, it means that the game over message has been displayed long enough, and it's okay to go ahead and put the game in demo mode. This is accomplished by setting the g_bDemo variable to TRUE and then calling the NewGame() function to add a few alien sprites to demo mode. Notice that the MIDI music isn't actually stopped until the game switches to demo mode, which makes sense when you consider that the game over screen is still a reflection on the last game played.

Demo mode also impacts the HandleKeys() function in the Space Out 3 game, as you can see in Listing 21.3.

LISTING 21.3 The HandleKeys() Function Supports Demo Mode by Changing the Value of the g_bDemo Variable if the Game Is Exiting Demo Mode to Start a New Game

```
void HandleKeys()
{
  if (!g_bGameOver && !g_bDemo)
  {
    // Move the car based upon left/right key presses
    POINT ptVelocity = g_pCarSprite->GetVelocity();
    if (GetAsyncKeyState(VK_LEFT) < 0)
    {
      // Move left
      ptVelocity.x = max(ptVelocity.x - 1, -4);
      g_pCarSprite->SetVelocity(ptVelocity);
    }
    else if (GetAsyncKeyState(VK_RIGHT) < 0)
```

Make sure that the game isn't over and that it isn't in demo mode.

continues

LISTING 21.3 Continued

```
    {
      // Move right
      ptVelocity.x = min(ptVelocity.x + 2, 6);
      g_pCarSprite->SetVelocity(ptVelocity);
    }

    // Fire missiles based upon spacebar presses
    if ((++g_iFireInputDelay > 6) && GetAsyncKeyState(VK_SPACE) < 0)
    {
      // Create a new missile sprite
      RECT   rcBounds = { 0, 0, 600, 450 };
      RECT   rcPos = g_pCarSprite->GetPosition();
      Sprite* pSprite = new Sprite(g_pMissileBitmap, rcBounds, BA_DIE);
      pSprite->SetPosition(rcPos.left + 15, 400);
      pSprite->SetVelocity(0, -7);
      g_pGame->AddSprite(pSprite);

      // Play the missile (fire) sound
      PlaySound((LPCSTR)IDW_MISSILE, g_hInstance, SND_ASYNC |
        SND_RESOURCE | SND_NOSTOP);

      // Reset the input delay
      g_iFireInputDelay = 0;
    }
  }

  // Start a new game based upon an Enter (Return) key press
  if (GetAsyncKeyState(VK_RETURN) < 0)
    if (g_bDemo)
    {
      // Switch out of demo mode to start a new game
      g_bDemo = FALSE;
      NewGame();
    }
    else if (g_bGameOver)
    {
      // Start a new game
      NewGame();
    }
}
```

The only changes in this function involve renaming the g_bSplash variable to
g_bDemo.

The new code in the SpriteCollision() function involves the timing delay for
the game over screen. More specifically, the g_iGameOverDelay variable is set to
150, which means that the game screen will be displayed for 150 cycles before the
game returns to demo mode:

```
if (--g_iNumLives == 0)
{
  // Play the game over sound
  PlaySound((LPCSTR)IDW_GAMEOVER, g_hInstance, SND_ASYNC |
    SND_RESOURCE);
  g_bGameOver = TRUE;
  g_iGameOverDelay = 150;
}
```

The game over delay is set to enable the game over screen to be displayed for a certain length of time before switching to demo mode.

Any idea how much time 150 cycles takes? You know that the frame rate for the game is set at 30 frames per second, which is the same as saying that the game goes through 30 cycles per second. Knowing this, you can divide 150 by 30 to arrive at a delay of 5 seconds for the game over screen. Pretty slick, right?

The SpriteDying()function involves an interesting change related to demo mode that you might not have thought about. Analyze Listing 21.4 and see if you can figure out why the change is necessary.

LISTING 21.4 The SpriteDying() Function Makes Sure Not to Play the Sound of Exploding Alien Missiles When the Game Is in Demo Mode

```
void SpriteDying(Sprite* pSpriteDying)
{
  // See if an alien missile sprite is dying
  if (pSpriteDying->GetBitmap() == g_pBMissileBitmap ||
    pSpriteDying->GetBitmap() == g_pJMissileBitmap ||
    pSpriteDying->GetBitmap() == g_pTMissileBitmap)
  {
    // Play the small explosion sound
    if (!g_bDemo)
      PlaySound((LPCSTR)IDW_SMEXPLODE, g_hInstance, SND_ASYNC |
        SND_RESOURCE | SND_NOSTOP);

    // Create a small explosion sprite at the missile's position
    RECT rcBounds = { 0, 0, 600, 450 };
    RECT rcPos = pSpriteDying->GetPosition();
    Sprite* pSprite = new Sprite(g_pSmExplosionBitmap, rcBounds);
    pSprite->SetNumFrames(8, TRUE);
    pSprite->SetPosition(rcPos.left, rcPos.top);
    g_pGame->AddSprite(pSprite);
  }
}
```

Only play explosion sounds when the game is not in demo mode.

When you think about it, demo mode for a computer game shouldn't be something that annoys you, which means that it's probably best for it to not make a bunch of noise. Because the aliens in demo mode will be firing missiles that explode when they hit the ground, it's necessary to quiet the missiles in the SpriteDying() function so that they don't make noise in demo mode.

Construction Cue

All the other sound effects in the game are related to something happening with the player, the car. Because the car sprite doesn't even exist in demo mode, as you see in a moment, there is no need to "silence" any other sound effects.

The NewGame() function is the last of the functions impacted by the switch to demo mode in the Space Out 3 game, and it's also the most interesting. Listing 21.5 shows the code for the NewGame() function.

LISTING 21.5   The NewGame() Function Adds a Few Aliens to the Game When It Is in Demo Mode

```
void NewGame()
{
  // Clear the sprites
  g_pGame->CleanupSprites();

  // Initialize the game variables
  g_iFireInputDelay = 0;
  g_iScore = 0;
  g_iNumLives = 3;
  g_iDifficulty = 80;
  g_bGameOver = FALSE;

  if (g_bDemo)
  {
    // Add a few aliens to the demo
    for (int i = 0; i < 6; i++)
      AddAlien();
  }
  else
  {
    // Create the car sprite
    RECT rcBounds = { 0, 0, 600, 450 };
    g_pCarSprite = new Sprite(g_pCarBitmap, rcBounds, BA_WRAP);
    g_pCarSprite->SetPosition(300, 405);
    g_pGame->AddSprite(g_pCarSprite);

    // Play the background music
    g_pGame->PlayMIDISong(TEXT("Music.mid"));
  }
}
```

In demo mode, six aliens are created, but there is no car for the player.

Although you might think of the NewGame() function as only being used to start a new game that you're going to play, it is also used to start a new demo game. A demo game is a "game" that includes a few aliens and nothing else. In other words, there is no car, which eliminates the difficulty of trying to simulate a human player in code. Fortunately, the aliens in the Space Out game are interesting enough that they do a pretty good job of conveying the premise of the game without having to throw in the car.

The NewGame() function actually adds six alien sprites to the game engine when the game is in demo mode. One neat thing about this code is that the AddAlien() function is designed to add random aliens, which means that demo mode varies each time the game goes into it; the six aliens added are always different. Granted, this demo mode could have been made more interesting by adding the car sprite and having it fight back with the aliens, but for the sake of simplicity, you can't help but like the approach of just adding a few aliens and letting them cruise around the game screen firing missiles on their own.

Construction Cue

If you're using Visual C++ 6.0, you might need to change the type casts from (DWORD_PTR) to (DWORD) in GameEngine.cpp in order for the Space Out 3 code to compile properly.

Construction Cue

As with most of the examples in the book, the Space Out 3 program relies on the standard msimg32.lib and winmm.lib libraries. These libraries are included with most Windows compilers, but they aren't automatically linked into programs when you create a new project. If you are using your own project or make files, as opposed to using the ones provided on the CD-ROM, make sure that you change the link settings so that these library files are properly linked in to the final executable. Refer to the documentation for your specific compiler for how this is done.

Testing the Finished Product

Testing demo mode in the Space Out 3 game is a little like testing the splash screen in Space Out 2—just launch the game and watch it go! Figure 21.1 shows the Space Out 3 demo mode with the aliens flying around having a good time.

As you can see, the aliens in demo mode help to demonstrate how the game is played, even though they aren't interacting directly with a simulated player through the car sprite. Like I said, the car sprite would be a very nice improvement for demo mode, but the idea here is to keep things simple. Any time you can achieve a desired effect with less time and code, and therefore less complexity, it is a good thing.

Figure 21.2 shows a game that has just ended in Space Out 3. In this figure, the game over screen is shown while the time delay is ticking away.

The game over screen in Space Out 3 is displayed for a few seconds before the game goes back to demo mode, as shown in Figure 21.3.

FIGURE 21.1
Demo mode in the
Space Out 3 game
involves several
aliens flying around
the game screen
behind the splash
screen image.

FIGURE 21.2
When a game fin-
ishes in Space Out
3, the game over
screen is displayed
for a few seconds.

I'm showing a shot of demo mode one more time just to demonstrate how it
varies each time the game goes into it. If you compare Figure 21.3 with Figure
21.1, you'll notice that the aliens are distributed a little differently. This is a subtle
detail of demo mode that makes the game a bit more interesting.

FIGURE 21.3
After the game over
screen has been
shown for a few
seconds, the Space
Out 3 game reverts
back to demo
mode, with each
demo mode being
a little different.

Summary

This chapter demonstrated an interesting feature of many commercial games that
you now know how to add to your own games. I'm referring to demo mode,
which enables a game to present to the game player a glimpse of how the game
plays. Demo mode was a critical feature in arcade games, where a game needed
to sell itself in order to convince someone to spend a quarter on a play. Computer
games don't rely as heavily on demo mode because they don't live on quarters,
but it's nonetheless an important touch for a game that might otherwise do nothing in between plays.

The next chapter wraps up this part of the book by showing you a game feature
that we've all grown to love: the high score list. The high score list was an important part of most classic video games because it provided a means of measuring
your skill at a game and saving it for others to see.

Extreme Game Makeover

Demo mode is cool; there's no doubt about it. But in regard to the Space Out 3
game, demo mode could stand to be improved to some extent. More specifically,
demo mode in Space Out 3 is missing the player's car, which is useful in not only

conveying what kinds of characters exist in the game, but also how the player interacts with those characters. So, this makeover involves adding a simulated player to demo mode to battle it out with the aliens. Keep in mind that once you add a player car to demo mode and it begins firing at the aliens, both the car and the aliens are capable of being destroyed, which means that demo mode has to account for this somehow. The easiest solution is to quickly create a new car and aliens to replace the destroyed ones. Here are the steps to carry out the demo mode upgrade on the Space Out 3 game:

1. Change the `NewGame()` function so that the car sprite is created regardless of whether the game is in demo mode; still leave the `PlayMIDISong()` call inside the else clause.

2. Break the car movement and firing code out of the `HandleKeys()` function into separate functions called `MoveCarLeft()`, `MoveCarRight()`, and `FireCarMissile()`. These generic car move and fire functions are now called from within `HandleKeys()`, and they are also available for being called from elsewhere to simulate a game being played in demo mode.

3. Add a section of code to the `GameCycle()` function that randomly calls `MoveCarLeft()`, `MoveCarRight()`, and `FireCarMissile()`, but only if the game is in demo mode.

4. Change the `SpriteCollision()` function so that when an alien is killed by a player missile, the `AddAlien()` function is called to immediately add a new alien in the dead alien's place.

5. Change the `SpriteCollision()` function so that when an alien missile collides with the car, the test to adjust the number of lives and see if the game is over is only made when the game isn't in demo mode.

These changes might seem a bit tricky at first, but they are actually fairly straightforward once you get into the code. The end result of having the player simulated in demo mode is subtle, but significant in that the true play of the game is better represented.

CHAPTER 22

Keeping Track of High Scores

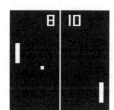

Arcade Archive

Back in the 1980s, *Saturday Night Live* ran a great skit about kids who were addicted to arcade games. The kids would panhandle on the street for quarters to play games and feed their addiction. When you think of game addiction, it's hard not to think about Tetris, the smashingly successful puzzle game by Atari that was released in 1988. In case you've never played it, in Tetris, you must maneuver falling blocks of different shapes so that they interlock at the bottom of the screen and form complete lines. As the game progresses, the blocks fall faster, making it increasingly difficult to place them properly. The game is highly addictive, which also means that it is quite fun. The background artwork on the Tetris game depicts Russian buildings and dancers because the game was designed by a Russian programmer, Alexei Pazhitnov.

Unless you grew up during the heyday of arcade games in the 1980s, you might not have an appreciation for the sense of nerd accomplishment associated with a top spot on a game's high score list. The high score list in arcade games serves as a public acknowledgement of who has the time, skills, and quarters to be the best of the best. If you think I'm dramatizing this a bit, keep in mind that a major plot device within an episode of *Seinfeld* involved George Castanza attempting to move a Frogger game across a busy street while connecting it to a temporary battery supply to keep his high score from being lost. Even if you don't have a large nerd ego, it can be rewarding to know that you placed within the upper ranks of those who have played a game before you. This chapter shows you how to develop a high score list that is saved to disk so that high scores are retained between games.

In this chapter, you'll learn

▶ Why it's important to keep track of high scores

▶ How to represent high score data in a game

▶ How to store and retrieve high score data using a file

▶ How to add a high score list to the Space Out game

The Significance of Keeping Score

When you think of video games, the word "achievement" might not be the first thing that comes to mind. You might not approach video games with the idea that you could be the best player of a particular game, but there are people out there who do. In fact, the concept of a professional "cyber athlete" is alive and real—companies are paying the best of the best video game players to test and promote their games. If you aspire to such a unique career, I must warn you that thousands of hours of game play await you.

I brought up the issue of "cyber athletes" because it has a lot to do with the topic of this chapter—keeping track of high scores. Nowadays, the best video game players are determined in national tournaments where people get together and compete head-to-head. However, in years past, the best players were known only by their three initials that appeared in the high score lists of arcade games. The high score list in a classic arcade game was quite important to many early gamers because it was the only way to show off their gaming achievements.

It's really kind of sad that high score lists aren't as popular as they once were, but we can't lament advances in technology. On the other hand, it doesn't mean that high scores are entirely things of the past. For example, many popular games, such as the Tony Hawk Pro Skater series, still rely on a score to indicate how well a player performed. So, the idea of using a numeric score to measure your video game playing prowess is still valid. What has changed is that the shift away from arcade games has made it less of an issue to keep track of high scores. However, I still like the idea of a high score list—even if it's only shared between friends.

This chapter focuses on adding a high score list to the Space Out game that you've worked on in previous chapters. A high score list presents a new challenge to you as a game programmer because you must store away the scores so that they can be retrieved even when a game program is closed. This requires storing the scores to disk and then reading them back later, which is a unique discipline in game programming. The first step is to figure out how to model the high score data, which means that you need to determine what you're going to keep up with and how.

Modeling High Score Data

I would love to tell you that I'm going to show you how to create a classic arcade game high score feature in which you get to enter your name or initials and then see them displayed for all to see. Unfortunately, the seemingly simple task of allowing a player to enter his name or initials is fairly complex from a game programming perspective. More accurately, it requires a significant enough side step from the topic at hand that I don't want to burden you with the details. Therefore, you're instead going to focus on a high score list that simply keeps up with the top five scores for a game, without any personalization associated with the scores. Although this approach to keeping track of a high score list doesn't give credit for each score, it's still a useful means of keeping up with the top five scores for a game.

Because you aren't going to worry with storing the name of the person for each score, you only have to contend with storing away five numbers. At this point, you have to consider how many digits you need to represent the maximum possible score for a game. In the case of the Space Out game, it's virtually impossible to score beyond four digits, which means that you can safely make a five-digit score the maximum. This also means that each score in the high score list is capable of having five digits. Of course, the number of digits in an integer in the game isn't really a critical factor; the number of digits enters the picture when it comes time to store the scores to disk and then read them back.

The maximum number of digits in a high score is important because you're going to store that many digits for a score, even if it doesn't need that many. This makes the scores much easier to read after you've written them to disk. Therefore, as an example, if the highest score is 1250, you obviously only need four digits to represent the score. However, the score needs to be stored on disk as 01250 to make it fit within a five-digit storage space. Each of the numbers in the high score list is stored this way.

Getting back to the specifics of high scores and the Space Out game, after the high scores are read from disk, they are treated as normal integers. In fact, a simple array of integers is sufficient to represent the high score list. So, the process of reading and writing the high score list involves initializing and then storing away an array of integers. The next section gets into more detail about exactly how you use the Win32 API to read and write data using files.

Storing and Retrieving High Score Data

Before you learn about the specific Win32 API functions used to read and write files, let's go over exactly what happens to the array of high score integers when they are read from and written to a file. You've already learned that each number in the array of integers gets converted to five digits. However, I didn't mention that these digits aren't actually numbers, but instead, are text characters. In other words, the number 1250 gets converted to 01250 before being written to a file. This process is known as *streaming* the high score data to a file because you are converting the numeric data into a stream of characters. Figure 22.1 shows what the streaming process looks like.

FIGURE 22.1
Streaming the high scores involves padding the numbers to five digits and converting them to a stream of characters.

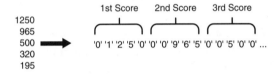

As the figure reveals, the five high scores are converted to a stream of five-digit characters during the streaming process. Along with making it very straightforward to store the numbers to a file, streaming the numbers also makes it much easier to read them back in. More specifically, you just read five digits of characters at a time and then convert the character string into an integer number.

I've talked about how to read and write files in general terms, but I haven't given you any specifics. All file input and output in Windows involves a small set of Win32 API functions. The most important of these functions is `CreateFile()`, which looks like this:

```
HANDLE CreateFile(
    LPCTSTR szFileName,
    DWORD dwDesiredAccess,
    DWORD dwShareMode,
    LPSECURITY_ATTRIBUTES pSecurityAttributes,
    DWORD dwCreationDisposition,
    DWORD dwFlagsAndAttributes,
    HANDLE hTemplateFile);
```

The `CreateFile()` function is important because it is used to both create and open files. Although it takes quite a few arguments, not all of them apply to basic reading and writing; you don't need to worry about some of the arguments unless you're performing more advanced file input and output. Knowing this, I want to point out the arguments relevant to reading and writing high scores. The first argument, szFileName, is used to provide the name of the file to be created or opened. The second argument, dwDesiredAccess, determines what you want to do with the file, such as read from or write to it. The fifth argument, dwCreationDisposition, determines whether you want to open an existing file or create a new file. Finally, the sixth argument, dwFlagsAndAttributes, allows you to control various other aspects of opening or creating a file, such as whether you want to limit access to read-only.

Rather than have you memorize the arguments to the CreateFile() function, I'd rather just show you how to use it to open and create files. The following is an example of using the CreateFile() function to create a new file ready for writing:

```
HANDLE hFile = CreateFile(TEXT("HiScores.dat"), GENERIC_WRITE, 0, NULL,
  CREATE_ALWAYS, FILE_ATTRIBUTE_NORMAL, NULL);
```

In this example, the new file is called HiScores.dat, and it is created and ready to be written to using the file handle returned from the CreateFile() function. The hFile handle is what you'll use with a write function later to actually write data to the file. For now, let's take a quick look at how you open a file for reading:

```
HANDLE hFile = CreateFile(TEXT("HiScores.dat"), GENERIC_READ, 0, NULL,
  OPEN_EXISTING, FILE_ATTRIBUTE_READONLY, NULL);
```

As you can see, the CreateFile() function is called in a similar manner as it is called for writing, with a few small changes. The second argument indicates that this is a read operation, whereas the fifth argument indicates that an existing file should be opened, as opposed to creating a new one. Finally, the sixth argument specifies that the file is read-only, which prevents you from writing to it using the provided file handle, even if you want to.

Now that you have a file handle that can be used for reading or writing, depending on how you call the CreateFile()function, you're ready to find out how to write data to a file and then read it back. The Win32 API function used to write data to a file is called WriteFile(), and it looks like this:

```
BOOL WriteFile(
  HANDLE hFile,
  LPCVOID pBuffer,
  DWORD dwNumberOfBytesToWrite,
  LPDWORD pNumberOfBytesWritten,
  LPOVERLAPPED pOverlapped);
```

As with the `CreateFile()` function, not every argument to `WriteFile()` is critical for our purposes. You obviously need to provide the file handle in the first argument, which you got from calling `CreateFile()`, as well as a data buffer from which the data is written. It's also important to specify the number of bytes to write, as well as a pointer to a `DWORD` that is to receive the number of bytes actually written. The last argument is the one that you don't need to worry about. To show you how easy it is to use the `WriteFile()` function, the following is code to write a five-digit high score to a file:

```
DWORD dwBytesWritten;
WriteFile(hFile, &cData, 5, &dwBytesWritten, NULL);
```

This code assumes that the high score has already been converted from an integer into a five-character string that is stored in the `cData` variable. Notice that the number of bytes to write is specified as 5, which makes sense considering that the score consists of five characters (digits).

Reading from a file is similar to writing to a file, except that it involves the `ReadFile()` function, instead of `WriteFile()`. The following is the `ReadFile()` function as it is defined in the Win32 API:

```
BOOL ReadFile(
  HANDLE hFile,
  LPVOID pBuffer,
  DWORD dwNumberOfBytesToRead,
  LPDWORD pNumberOfBytesRead,
  LPOVERLAPPED pOverlapped);
```

As you can see, the `ReadFile()` function actually takes the same arguments as the `WriteFile()` function. However, it uses the arguments a little differently because data is being read into the buffer, instead of being written from it. The following is an example of reading an individual high score from a file using the `ReadFile()` function:

```
char  cData[6];
DWORD dwBytesRead;
ReadFile(hFile, &cData, 5, &dwBytesRead, NULL);
```

It's important for the array of characters that holds each score to be null-terminated, which is why the `cData` variable is declared as being six characters long, instead of just five. In this code, the `ReadFile()` function reads five characters from the file and stores them in the `cData` variable.

When you're finished reading from or writing to a file, it's important to close the file. This is accomplished with the `CloseHandle()` Win32 function, which is called like this:

```
CloseHandle(hFile);
```

You now have the fundamental knowledge required to store and retrieve high score data to and from a file on disk, which is what you need to add a high score feature to the Space Out game.

Building the Space Out 4 Game

The final version of the Space Out game that you create in this book is called Space Out 4, and it completes the game by including a high score list that is stored to a file on disk. You've learned enough about high scores and file I/O in this chapter to handle the task of adding a high score list to the game. So, let's get started!

Writing the Game Code

The Space Out 4 game requires only one new global variable, which is the array of integers that stores the high score list. The following is the g_iHiScores variable as it appears in the SpaceOut.h header file:

```
int g_iHiScores[5];
```

This variable is pretty straightforward in that it stores away five integers that represent the top five scores for the game. The scores are arranged in order of greatest to least. Notice that these scores are integer scores, which means that they aren't yet formatted as characters for writing to a file. However, keeping them as integers is important because it's much easier to compare scores and determine if a new score is high enough to make the list.

Several new functions are required to successfully update, read, and write the high score list in the Space Out 4 game:

```
void UpdateHiScores();
BOOL ReadHiScores();
BOOL WriteHiScores();
```

The UpdateHiScores() function is used to determine if a new score has made it into the high score list. If so, the function makes sure to insert the score in the correct position and slide the lower scores down a notch to make room for the new score. The ReadHiScores() and WriteHiScores() functions use the g_iHiScores array as the basis for reading and writing the high score list from and to the HiScores.dat file. You'll learn how each of these functions work a little later in the chapter, but for now, it's important to see how they are used in the context of the game.

The GameStart() function is responsible for initializing the game, which now includes reading the high score list. The only change to this function is the new call to the ReadHiScores() function:

```
ReadHiScores();
```

This call makes sure that the high score list is properly initialized before the game attempts to draw the scores later in the GamePaint() function.

The GameEnd() function cleans up resources used by the game and serves as a great place to write the high score list to a file. A simple addition to this function is all that is required to write the high score list:

```
WriteHiScores();
```

Of course, the high score list wouldn't be of much use if the game didn't display it for all to see. This takes place in the GamePaint() function, which is shown in Listing 22.1.

LISTING 22.1 The GamePaint() Function Draws the High Score List if the Game Is in Demo Mode

```
void GamePaint(HDC hDC)
{
  // Draw the background
  g_pBackground->Draw(hDC);

  // Draw the desert bitmap
  g_pDesertBitmap->Draw(hDC, 0, 371);

  // Draw the sprites
  g_pGame->DrawSprites(hDC);

  if (g_bDemo)
  {
    // Draw the splash screen image
    g_pSplashBitmap->Draw(hDC, 142, 20, TRUE);
```

```
    // Draw the hi scores
    TCHAR szText[64];
    RECT  rect = { 275, 250, 325, 270};
    SetBkMode(hDC, TRANSPARENT);
    SetTextColor(hDC, RGB(255, 255, 255));
    for (int i = 0; i < 5; i++)
    {
      wsprintf(szText, "%d", g_iHiScores[i]);
      DrawText(hDC, szText, -1, &rect, DT_SINGLELINE | DT_CENTER | DT_VCENTER);
      rect.top += 20;
      rect.bottom += 20;
    }
  }
  else
  {
    // Draw the score
    TCHAR szText[64];
    RECT  rect = { 460, 0, 510, 30 };
    wsprintf(szText, "%d", g_iScore);
    SetBkMode(hDC, TRANSPARENT);
    SetTextColor(hDC, RGB(255, 255, 255));
    DrawText(hDC, szText, -1, &rect, DT_SINGLELINE | DT_RIGHT | DT_VCENTER);

    // Draw the number of remaining lives (cars)
    for (int i = 0; i < g_iNumLives; i++)
      g_pSmCarBitmap->Draw(hDC, 520 + (g_pSmCarBitmap->GetWidth() * i),
        10, TRUE);

    // Draw the game over message, if necessary
    if (g_bGameOver)
      g_pGameOverBitmap->Draw(hDC, 170, 100, TRUE);
  }
}
```

The location of this rectangle ensures that the high scores are drawn centered on the game screen.

The high score list is drawn just after the splash screen image by looping through each score and drawing it a little below the previous score. Notice that the high score list is only drawn if the game is in demo mode, which makes sense when you consider that the high score list is something you want to see in between games.

The last game function impacted by the high score list is the SpriteCollision() function, which is important because it detects when a game ends. Listing 22.2 contains the code for the SpriteCollision() function.

LISTING 22.2 The SpriteCollision() Function Updates the High Score List Whenever a Game Ends

```
BOOL SpriteCollision(Sprite* pSpriteHitter, Sprite* pSpriteHittee)
{
  // See if a player missile and an alien have collided
  Bitmap* pHitter = pSpriteHitter->GetBitmap();
  Bitmap* pHittee = pSpriteHittee->GetBitmap();
```

continues

LISTING 22.2   Continued

```cpp
if ((pHitter == g_pMissileBitmap && (pHittee == g_pBlobboBitmap ¦¦
  pHittee == g_pJellyBitmap ¦¦ pHittee == g_pTimmyBitmap)) ¦¦
  (pHittee == g_pMissileBitmap && (pHitter == g_pBlobboBitmap ¦¦
  pHitter == g_pJellyBitmap ¦¦ pHitter == g_pTimmyBitmap)))
{
  // Play the small explosion sound
  PlaySound((LPCSTR)IDW_LGEXPLODE, g_hInstance, SND_ASYNC ¦
    SND_RESOURCE);

  // Kill both sprites
  pSpriteHitter->Kill();
  pSpriteHittee->Kill();

  // Create a large explosion sprite at the alien's position
  RECT rcBounds = { 0, 0, 600, 450 };
  RECT rcPos;
  if (pHitter == g_pMissileBitmap)
    rcPos = pSpriteHittee->GetPosition();
  else
    rcPos = pSpriteHitter->GetPosition();
  Sprite* pSprite = new Sprite(g_pLgExplosionBitmap, rcBounds);
  pSprite->SetNumFrames(8, TRUE);
  pSprite->SetPosition(rcPos.left, rcPos.top);
  g_pGame->AddSprite(pSprite);

  // Update the score
  g_iScore += 25;
  g_iDifficulty = max(80 - (g_iScore / 20), 20);
}

// See if an alien missile has collided with the car
if ((pHitter == g_pCarBitmap && (pHittee == g_pBMissileBitmap ¦¦
  pHittee == g_pJMissileBitmap ¦¦ pHittee == g_pTMissileBitmap)) ¦¦
  (pHittee == g_pCarBitmap && (pHitter == g_pBMissileBitmap ¦¦
  pHitter == g_pJMissileBitmap ¦¦ pHitter == g_pTMissileBitmap)))
{
  // Play the large explosion sound
  PlaySound((LPCSTR)IDW_LGEXPLODE, g_hInstance, SND_ASYNC ¦
    SND_RESOURCE);

  // Kill the missile sprite
  if (pHitter == g_pCarBitmap)
    pSpriteHittee->Kill();
  else
    pSpriteHitter->Kill();

  // Create a large explosion sprite at the car's position
  RECT rcBounds = { 0, 0, 600, 480 };
  RECT rcPos;
  if (pHitter == g_pCarBitmap)
    rcPos = pSpriteHitter->GetPosition();
  else
    rcPos = pSpriteHittee->GetPosition();
  Sprite* pSprite = new Sprite(g_pLgExplosionBitmap, rcBounds);
```

```
    pSprite->SetNumFrames(8, TRUE);
    pSprite->SetPosition(rcPos.left, rcPos.top);
    g_pGame->AddSprite(pSprite);

    // Move the car back to the start
    g_pCarSprite->SetPosition(300, 405);

    // See if the game is over
    if (--g_iNumLives == 0)
    {
      // Play the game over sound
      PlaySound((LPCSTR)IDW_GAMEOVER, g_hInstance, SND_ASYNC |
        SND_RESOURCE);
      g_bGameOver = TRUE;
      g_iGameOverDelay = 150;

      // Update the hi scores
      UpdateHiScores();
    }
  }

  return FALSE;
}
```

A single call to the UpdateHiScores() function is all it takes to update the high score list with the new score, if necessary.

When a game ends, the SpriteCollision() function plays a game over sound
and sets the game over delay, which you already know about. However, what you
don't already know about is the line of code that calls the UpdateHiScores()
function to give the game a chance to insert the new score in the high score list.
You don't have to worry about whether the score is high enough to make the
high score list because this is determined by the UpdateHiScores() function,
which is shown in Listing 22.3.

LISTING 22.3 The UpdateHiScores() **Function Checks to See if a High
Score Should Be Added to the High Score List and Adds It, if Necessary**

```
void UpdateHiScores()
{
  // See if the current score made the hi score list
  int i;
  for (i = 0; i < 5; i++)
  {
    if (g_iScore > g_iHiScores[i])
      break;
  }

  // Insert the current score into the hi score list
  if (i < 5)
  {
    for (int j = 4; j > i; j--)
    {
```

Break out of the loop so that you'll know where to insert the new score.

continues

Slide the lesser scores down the list to make room for the new score.

LISTING 22.3 Continued

```
    g_iHiScores[j] = g_iHiScores[j - 1];
  }
  g_iHiScores[i] = g_iScore;
}
}
```

Set the new high score in the list.

Although the code for the UpdateHiScores() function looks a little tricky at first, it really isn't too bad. The first loop checks to see if the score is higher than any of the existing high scores. If so, the second loop is entered, which handles the task of inserting the score in the correct position in the list, as well as sliding down the lower scores in the list. You might notice that the list is looped through in reverse, which enables it to easily move scores down the list to make room for the new score. After a space has been made, the new score is placed in the high score list.

The high scores are written to a data file in the WriteHiScores() function, which is shown in Listing 22.4.

LISTING 22.4 The WriteHiScores() Function Writes the High Score List to the File HiScores.dat

```
BOOL WriteHiScores()
{
  // Create the hi score file (HiScores.dat) for writing
  HANDLE hFile = CreateFile(TEXT("HiScores.dat"), GENERIC_WRITE, 0, NULL,
    CREATE_ALWAYS, FILE_ATTRIBUTE_NORMAL, NULL);
  if (hFile == INVALID_HANDLE_VALUE)
    // The hi score file couldn't be created, so bail
    return FALSE;

  // Write the scores
  for (int i = 0; i < 5; i++)
  {
    // Format each score for writing
    CHAR cData[6];
    wsprintf(cData, "%05d", g_iHiScores[i]);

    // Write the score
    DWORD dwBytesWritten;
    if (!WriteFile(hFile, &cData, 5, &dwBytesWritten, NULL))
    {
      // Something went wrong, so close the file handle
      CloseHandle(hFile);
      return FALSE;
    }
  }

  // Close the file
  return CloseHandle(hFile);
}
```

If the HiScores.dat file doesn't already exist, a new one is created and opened.

Each score is written using five digits, regardless of whether the score actually requires five digits.

Most of this code should look familiar to you because it is very similar to the code you saw earlier in the chapter when you learned how to create a new file and write a score using the CreateFile() and WriteFile() functions. A new HiScores.dat file is first created with a call to the CreateFile() function; even if the file already exists, a new one is created to replace it. After the file is created, the function prepares to write to the file by looping through the high scores. Each score must be formatted into a five-digit character string before it can be written. The score is then written to the file with a call to the WriteFile() function. If an error occurs during the write, the file handle is closed with a call to CloseHandle(). If all goes well and the data is successfully written, the function finishes by closing the file with a call to CloseHandle().

Not surprisingly, the ReadHiScores() function works similarly to WriteHiScores(), except everything happens in the reverse. Listing 22.5 contains the code for the ReadHiScores() function.

LISTING 22.5 The ReadHiScores() Function Reads the High Score List from the File HiScores.dat

```
BOOL ReadHiScores()
{
  // Open the hi score file (HiScores.dat)
  HANDLE hFile = CreateFile(TEXT("HiScores.dat"), GENERIC_READ, 0, NULL,
    OPEN_EXISTING, FILE_ATTRIBUTE_READONLY, NULL);
  if (hFile == INVALID_HANDLE_VALUE)
  {
    // The hi score file doesn't exist, so initialize the scores to 0
    for (int i = 0; i < 5; i++)
      g_iHiScores[i] = 0;
    return FALSE;
  }

  // Read the scores
  for (int i = 0; i < 5; i++)
  {
    // Read the score
    char  cData[6];
    DWORD dwBytesRead;
    if (!ReadFile(hFile, &cData, 5, &dwBytesRead, NULL))
    {
      // Something went wrong, so close the file handle
      CloseHandle(hFile);
      return FALSE;
    }

    // Extract each integer score from the score data
```

If the HiScores.dat file doesn't exist, the high score list is initialized with scores of 0.

continues

LISTING 22.5   Continued

The character high [
score is converted
to an integer score
with a call to the
standard atoi()
function.

```
    g_iHiScores[i] = atoi(cData);
  }

  // Close the file
  return CloseHandle(hFile);
}
```

The ReadHiScores() function reads the high score list from the HiScores.dat file. The CreateFile() function is again used to obtain a file handle, but this time an existing file is opened, as opposed to creating a new file. If there is an error reading the file, such as if the file doesn't exist, the high score array is simply filled with scores of 0. This code is very important because the first time you play the game, there won't be a high score file.

If the file is opened okay, the function starts a loop to read each score from the file. Each score is then read by calling the ReadFile() function. Simply reading the scores from the file isn't sufficient to place them in the high score list because the scores are read as five-digit character strings. Each score must be converted to an integer number before you can add it to the high score array. After reading and converting all the scores, the ReadFile() function finishes by calling the CloseHandle() function to close the file.

Construction Cue

> If you're using Visual C++ 6.0, you might need to change the type casts from (DWORD_PTR) to (DWORD) in GameEngine.cpp in order for the Space Out 4 code to compile properly.

Construction Cue

> As with most of the examples in the book, the Space Out 4 program relies on the standard msimg32.lib and winmm.lib libraries. These libraries are included with most Windows compilers, but they aren't automatically linked into programs when you create a new project. If you are using your own project or make files, as opposed to using the ones provided on the CD-ROM, make sure that you change the link settings so that these library files are properly linked into the final executable. Refer to the documentation for your specific compiler for how this is done.

Testing the Finished Product

Similar to a few of its predecessors, the Space Out 4 game is quite simple to test. In fact, it's also a fun test to perform because you need to play the game a few times and build up some scores on the high score list. Figure 22.2 shows the high score list in the game upon playing the game for the first time, which means that the list is filled with scores of 0.

FIGURE 22.2
Prior to playing the Space Out 4 game for the first time, the high score list is full of zero scores.

Keep in mind, in this figure, the game still tried to read the high scores from a file, but the file didn't exist, so the scores were zeroed out. After you play a few games, the list will start looking better as it fills out with new high scores. Whenever you exit the game, the high score list gets stored to a file. Upon restarting the game, the high score list is restored by reading the scores from the same file. Figure 22.3 shows a high score list that has just been restored from a file.

FIGURE 22.3
The high score list is read from a file, which causes it to persist between games.

The high score list really is a useful enhancement to the Space Out game because it allows you to keep track of the best games you've played, potentially over a long period of time. Keep in mind that you can easily clear out the high score list by simply deleting the HiScores.dat file.

Summary

This chapter explored a facet of games that you might have overlooked—the high score list. Granted, high score lists aren't as popular these days because arcades aren't as important as they were in the early days of video games, but that doesn't necessarily mean that players don't like to know what their highest gaming achievements are. High score lists provide a great way to remember the best games you've played, and also serve as a means for competitive gamers to share a high score with friends. Although a high score list isn't necessary in all games, you should consider adding one to games where it makes sense. The Space Out game is a good example of a game that benefits from keeping track of high scores.

This chapter is the last chapter in this part of the book, but it's only a prelude to what lies ahead. Coming up next in Part VIII is a chapter devoted to scrolling backgrounds, along with another complete game that allows you to finish up the book with a bang by putting all of your game programming knowledge to good use.

Field Trip

This could very well be the toughest field trip of the book. Like George Costanza in the classic Frogger episode of *Seinfeld*, you need to use your mastery of video games to leave a mark on an arcade game's high score list. It doesn't matter what game it is, but go to your local arcade and play a game until you're able to obtain a score high enough to make the list. Not only will this give you bragging rights to point out your accomplishment to friends and family members, but also it will help add some real-world impact to the high score list you added to the Space Out 4 game in this chapter. Who knows? It might even inspire you to enhance Space Out 4 so that it allows players to enter their initials when they achieve a high score.

PART VIII

One for the Road

CHAPTER 23

Changing Perspective with Scrolling Backgrounds

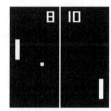

Arcade Archive

Whether or not you're a fan of fighting games, it's hard to ignore the impact of the first hugely successful arcade fighting game, Mortal Kombat. Released in 1992 by Midway, Mortal Kombat was a highly controversial game because of its realistic violence and reliance on gore to show the effects of brutal fighting moves. Not surprisingly, this controversy only served to make the game more popular. Mortal Kombat is unique in that it is one of the first video games to be made into a movie. If you happen to get a chance to play the original Mortal Kombat game, pay close attention to the glowing moon that appears in the scene of the game where you're fighting on a stone platform above spikes. The game's creators included randomly appearing silhouettes of some humorous characters flying past the moon, including Peter Pan, a witch on a broomstick, and even Santa Claus.

Dating all the way back to the original Ultima series of games on Apple II computers, scrolling backgrounds have been an important part of the video game experience. If Ultima isn't very familiar to you, look no further than a modern strategic war simulator to find a scrolling background of some sort. Although specific approaches to developing a scrolling background might vary, the basic idea is the same—provide the game player with a limited view of a much larger world than could possibly fit on her monitor. You create a background map that is as large as you want, and then the game screen serves as a window onto that map. Instead of moving a character around on a static background, you typically move a scrolling background around while keeping the main character centered on the screen. This chapter beefs up the game engine with support for scrolling backgrounds.

In this chapter, you'll learn

▶ What types of games benefit from scrolling backgrounds

▶ How scrolling backgrounds work

▶ How to add support for scrolling backgrounds to the game engine

▶ How to use a scrolling background to create an adventure simulation

What Is a Scrolling Background?

A scrolling background is a background that is somehow moved around on the game screen in response to a user interaction or simply as an indication of the passing of time. The movement of a scrolling background can be as simple as the background scrolling from right to left to simulate a character moving from left to right, as in the popular Super Mario Bros. games, or it can be a more complex effect, such as quickly moving the background image back and forth to simulate an earthquake in a game.

Side-Scrolling Backgrounds

The Super Mario Bros. example is important because it represents an entire genre of games known as "side scrollers." Side-scrolling games allowed game developers to present a much larger world to the game player because things could be outside of the view of the immediate game screen; you had to move and scroll the screen to see more. Figure 23.1 shows how the background is moved in a side-scrolling game.

FIGURE 23.1
In a side-scrolling game, the background is scrolled horizontally from one side of the screen to the other.

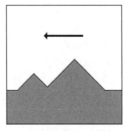

It's worth pointing out that the background image isn't necessarily larger than the game screen in a side scroller. As long as the image is created to wrap properly at the edges, it's possible to scroll an image that is exactly the same size as the game screen.

Vertical-Scrolling Backgrounds

In addition to side-scrolling games, there are also vertical-scrolling games, which include space shooters in which you appear to travel vertically through space and some older driving games (see Figure 23.2), not to mention games that enable the background to scroll in any direction. Most early adventure games fall into this latter category, where a world map is much larger than the game screen (see Figure 23.3). You control a character that can roam around on the map, interact with creatures, and discover things. The "virtual map" in these kinds of games dictates how large the virtual world actually is; in most cases, it's large enough to give the effect that there is no border.

FIGURE 23.2
In a vertical-scrolling game, the background is scrolled vertically from the top or bottom of the screen.

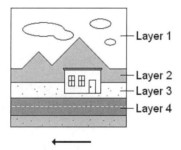

Layer 1

Layer 2

Layer 3

Layer 4

FIGURE 23.3
In a game that uses a scrolling map, the background is usually much larger than the game screen, with only a small portion capable of being viewed at any given time.

Even if your game doesn't rely on a map or virtual world, it could still potentially benefit from a scrolling background purely for the visual effect. For example, consider how a scrolling background might add interest to the Roids example from earlier in the book. Instead of displaying a stationary background of twinkling stars, you could scroll a background of twinkling stars to give the effect that the ship is traveling in an endless expanse of space. In this case, the scrolling background isn't really serving any critical role in the strategy or play of the "game," but it is providing a compelling sensory effect to make the simulation more interesting.

Parallax-Scrolling Backgrounds

Another type of scrolling background worth mentioning here is a parallax-scrolling background. This type of background actually involves multiple layers that move at varying speeds. The idea is that each layer of the background represents a different distance away from the player's perspective, so the furthest layer is scrolled at a slower speed than the closest layer. The end result is that parallax-scrolling backgrounds provide an element of realism and depth not possible with a simple one-layer scrolling background. Figure 23.4 shows how parallax scrolling makes it possible to simulate depth in a scrolling background. Parallax scrolling is typically used in only one dimension, so it is usually only applicable to side- or vertical-scrolling backgrounds. However, it is technically possible to get an interesting parallax-scrolling effect even with a top-view map background, as you'll find out later in the chapter in the Wanderer example.

FIGURE 23.4
By using multiple layers moving at varying speeds, parallax-scrolling backgrounds simulate depth as it applies to a player's movement within a game.

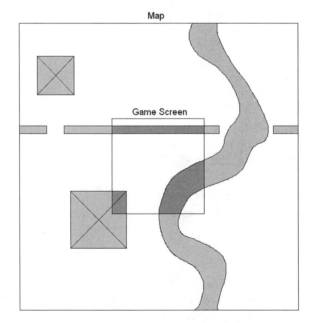

Understanding How Scrolling Backgrounds Work

Although the net effect of scrolling backgrounds can certainly be dramatic, the details of how they work are actually relatively simple. First, it's important to point out that I'll be discussing scrolling backgrounds purely in terms of images, meaning that I'll always be referring to a background image being scrolled. It's possible to render a background from information other than an image, but that's beyond the scope of this book. Knowing that you'll always be scrolling an image, the key to creating a scrolling background is deciding exactly how it will scroll.

The easiest type of scrolling background to create is one that only scrolls in a single direction and in which scrolling is unaffected by user interactions. A star field that scrolls from the top of the screen to the bottom, regardless of what the user does, is a good example of this kind of scrolling background. In this scenario, the background image could be the same size as the game screen, or it could be taller if you want more variance in the scrolling pattern. Either way, you basically set the scrolling effect in motion when the game first starts, and then you never have to worry about it again.

You probably already understand that in order for a scrolling background image to yield the scrolling effect, it must be designed so that it wraps in the direction or directions you want it to scroll. For example, a vertical-scrolling background image must be designed to wrap vertically. This means that the top and bottom of the image must blend perfectly so that they can be drawn seamlessly next to each other. Figure 23.5 shows how a scrolling background image gets "stitched" together to create a scrolling effect.

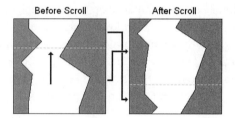

Before Scroll   After Scroll

FIGURE 23.5
To achieve a scrolling effect, scrolling background images are actually sliced into two pieces and "stitched" together.

As the figure reveals, the background image is sliced into two pieces, which are then reattached along their top and bottom edges. It helps to understand this effect by picturing the image scrolling off one edge of the game screen (the top) and reappearing on the other (the bottom). The portion of the image that scrolls off the screen makes up one of the sliced pieces, whereas the remaining portion of the image is the other piece. By constantly sliding, slicing, and redrawing the background image, you get the effect of a scrolling background.

Figure 23.5 shows an example of a scrolling background image that is the same size as the game screen. It can be even more useful to take advantage of a background image that is larger than the game screen. In this case, the image is only sliced and stitched in two pieces when the viewing area is wrapping from one side to the other. The concept of a viewing area will become increasingly important as you get into the code for a scrolling background class shortly. I refer to the viewing area of a scrolling background as its viewport. Just as a telescope provides a view into space, a viewport provides a view into your background image. Scrolling the background then just becomes a matter of moving the viewport.

You now understand that a background image can be virtually any size and that a viewport provides the means of viewing a particular portion of a large background image. What I haven't mentioned yet is how a scrolling background can consist of multiple layers. Knowing that images can have transparent areas, consider a scrolling background consisting of multiple layers that can scroll independently of each other. The background images stack on top of each other similar to how sprites are drawn within the game engine, but in this case, they are all part of the background. By allowing a scrolling background to consist of multiple layers, you open up the possibilities for interesting scrolling effects, such as parallax scrolling, in which an illusion of depth is achieved by varying the speeds of each background layer.

From a technical perspective, the neat thing about a layered scrolling background is that it takes very little extra code to develop than a single-layer scrolling background. All that really takes place when layers are introduced is that you are updating and drawing multiple background images, but nothing's really complicated or tricky about that. The only thing to be careful about when layers enter the scrolling background picture is making sure that the layers are created in the proper order so that they draw on top of each other correctly.

Adding Scrolling Background Support to the Game Engine

In order to make scrolling backgrounds an option for all of your games, it's a good idea to go ahead and place the support for them into the game engine that you've been busily constructing throughout the book. Support for scrolling backgrounds actually requires two different classes thanks to the fact that you're going to include the capability of creating scrolling backgrounds with multiple layers.

So, in the next couple of sections, you'll create a class for a background layer, as well as a class for a scrolling background made up of background layers. These two new classes will work in concert to take the game engine to a whole new level in terms of making your game backgrounds considerably more interesting.

Creating a Background Layer Class

The BackgroundLayer class represents a single layer within a scrolling background. More specifically, the BackgroundLayer class keeps track of the bitmap image for a particular layer, along with the layer's viewport, speed, and direction. That's right: Each layer in a scrolling background has its own viewport, speed, and direction, and here's how they work:

▶ Viewport—A rectangle that identifies what portion of the layer image is currently in view

▶ Speed—A positive integer number that indicates how fast (in pixels) the layer is being scrolled for each game cycle

▶ Direction—A constant directional value (up, right, down, left) that indicates which direction the layer is being scrolled

The viewport for a background layer should be familiar to you from the earlier discussion in this chapter. The speed and direction of the layer work together to determine exactly how the layer is scrolled over time. The header source code file for the BackgroundLayer class (BackgroundLayer.h) specifies exactly what values to use for the direction component of a layer:

```
typedef WORD        SCROLLDIR;
const SCROLLDIR     SD_UP     = 0,
                    SD_RIGHT  = 1,
                    SD_DOWN   = 2,
                    SD_LEFT   = 3;
```

Listing 23.1 contains the code for the BackgroundLayer class, which reveals its overall design.

LISTING 23.1 The BackgroundLayer Class Represents a Layer Within a Scrolling Background

```
class BackgroundLayer : Bitmap  ⌉
{
protected:
  // Member Variables
```

The BackgroundLayer class is derived from the Bitmap class.

continues

The viewport deter-mines what part of the background is actually drawn to the game screen.

These two con-structors allow you to create a back-ground layer from a bitmap file or resource.

LISTING 23.1 Continued

```
RECT      m_rcViewport;
int       m_iSpeed;
SCROLLDIR m_sdDirection;

public:
// Constructor(s)/Destructor
BackgroundLayer(HDC hDC, LPTSTR szFileName, int iSpeed,
  SCROLLDIR sdDirection);
BackgroundLayer(HDC hDC, UINT uiResID, HINSTANCE hInstance, int iSpeed = 0,
  SCROLLDIR sdDirection = SD_LEFT);

// General Methods
virtual void  Update();
virtual void  Draw(HDC hDC, int x, int y, BOOL bTrans = FALSE,
  COLORREF crTransColor = RGB(255, 0, 255));
void          SetSpeed(int iSpeed)   { m_iSpeed = iSpeed; };
void          SetDirection(SCROLLDIR sdDirection)
  { m_sdDirection = sdDirection; };
void          SetViewport(RECT& rcViewport)
  { CopyRect(&m_rcViewport, &rcViewport); };
};
```

Perhaps the most striking revelation in the code for the BackgroundLayer class is that it is derived from the Bitmap class. Although this might seem like a surprise at first, it makes complete sense when you think about it—a background layer is really nothing more than a specialized bitmap image. In fact, the specialization consists mainly of adding to the bitmap information about its viewport, speed, and direction. Of course, the two BackgroundLayer() constructors are modified from the original Bitmap() constructors so that they accept speed and direction parameters.

The remaining methods in the BackgroundLayer class consist of an overloaded Update() method, an overloaded Draw() method, and several "setter" methods for the member variables. The Update() method is overloaded because an "update" for a background layer is very different from an "update" for a normal bitmap. In the case of a background layer, an "update" consists of sliding the viewport according to the speed and direction of the layer. The Draw() method must also be overloaded so that the layer knows how to properly draw itself based on the viewport; remember from earlier in the chapter (refer to Figure 23.5) that it is often necessary for a scrolling layer to slice itself into two parts and draw them separately.

Now that you have an understanding of how the BackgroundLayer class is structured, you can take a look at the specific code that makes it work. Listing 23.2 shows the code for the BackgroundLayer() constructors.

LISTING 23.2 The `BackgroundLayer::BackgroundLayer()` Constructors Are Used to Create Background Layers

```
// Create a background layer from a bitmap file
BackgroundLayer::BackgroundLayer(HDC hDC, LPTSTR szFileName,
  int iSpeed, SCROLLDIR sdDirection)
  : Bitmap(hDC, szFileName), m_iSpeed(iSpeed), m_sdDirection(sdDirection)
{
  // Set the viewport to the entire layer image by default
  m_rcViewport.left = m_rcViewport.top = 0;
  m_rcViewport.right = m_iWidth;
  m_rcViewport.bottom = m_iHeight;
}

// Create a background layer from a bitmap resource
BackgroundLayer::BackgroundLayer(HDC hDC, UINT uiResID, HINSTANCE hInstance,
  int iSpeed, SCROLLDIR sdDirection)
  : Bitmap(hDC, uiResID, hInstance), m_iSpeed(iSpeed),
  m_sdDirection(sdDirection)
{
  // Set the viewport to the entire layer image by default
  m_rcViewport.left = m_rcViewport.top = 0;
  m_rcViewport.right = m_iWidth;
  m_rcViewport.bottom = m_iHeight;
}
```

By default, the viewport is set to the full layer size.

The constructors for the `BackgroundLayer` class are pretty straightforward in that they simply initialize the viewport for the layer to the default setting (the entire image size). The two constructors allow you to create a background layer from either a bitmap file or resource.

The `Update()` method in the `BackgroundLayer` class handles the chore of moving the viewport to scroll the layer. More specifically, the method uses the speed and direction of the layer to slide the viewport a certain number of pixels. The only tricky piece of business in this method is making sure that the viewport wraps around to the other side of the image when it fully scrolls off one side. Listing 23.3 contains the code for the `BackgroundLayer::Update()` method.

LISTING 23.3 The `BackgroundLayer::Update()` Method Handles Updating a Background Layer

```
void BackgroundLayer::Update()
{
  switch (m_sdDirection)
  {
  case SD_UP:
    // Move the layer up (slide the viewport down)
    m_rcViewport.top += m_iSpeed;
    m_rcViewport.bottom += m_iSpeed;
    if (m_rcViewport.top > m_iHeight)
    {
```

continues

LISTING 23.3   Continued

If the viewport has wrapped completely off the bottom of the bitmap, move it to the top of the bitmap.

```
      m_rcViewport.bottom = m_rcViewport.bottom - m_rcViewport.top;
      m_rcViewport.top = 0;
    }
    break;

  case SD_RIGHT:
    // Move the layer right (slide the viewport left)
    m_rcViewport.left -= m_iSpeed;
    m_rcViewport.right -= m_iSpeed;
    if (m_rcViewport.right < 0)
    {
      m_rcViewport.left = m_iWidth - (m_rcViewport.right - m_rcViewport.left);
      m_rcViewport.right = m_iWidth;
    }
    break;

  case SD_DOWN:
    // Move the layer down (slide the viewport up)
    m_rcViewport.top -= m_iSpeed;
    m_rcViewport.bottom -= m_iSpeed;
    if (m_rcViewport.bottom < 0)
    {
      m_rcViewport.top = m_iHeight - (m_rcViewport.bottom - m_rcViewport.top);
      m_rcViewport.bottom = m_iHeight;
    }
    break;

  case SD_LEFT:
    // Move the layer left (slide the viewport right)
    m_rcViewport.left += m_iSpeed;
    m_rcViewport.right += m_iSpeed;
    if (m_rcViewport.left > m_iWidth)
    {
      m_rcViewport.right = (m_rcViewport.right - m_rcViewport.left);
      m_rcViewport.left = 0;
    }
    break;
  }
}
```

If the viewport has wrapped completely off the left side of the bitmap, move it to the right side of the bitmap.

You'll notice that the code in the Update() method is fairly repetitive, performing virtually the same task in each of the four scrolling directions (up, right, down, and left). All the method does is shift the viewport over a number of pixels equal to the speed of the layer and then check to make sure that the viewport hasn't wrapped to the other side of the layer image. If it has, the viewport is just moved to the other side of the image.

The method that works hand in hand with the Update() method is the Draw() method, which is responsible for drawing a background layer while taking into account its viewport. Brace yourself because the Draw() method is an absolute beast! Listing 23.4 contains the code for the hefty BackgroundLayer::Draw() method.

LISTING 23.4 The BackgroundLayer::Draw() **Method Handles Drawing a Background Layer Based on Its Viewport**

```
void BackgroundLayer::Draw(HDC hDC, int x, int y, BOOL bTrans,
  COLORREF crTransColor)
{
  // Draw only the part of the layer seen through the viewport
  if (m_rcViewport.top < 0 && m_rcViewport.left < 0)
  {
    // Draw the split viewport wrapping top to bottom AND left to right
    DrawPart(hDC, x, y,
      m_iWidth + m_rcViewport.left, m_iHeight + m_rcViewport.top,
      -m_rcViewport.left, -m_rcViewport.top,
      bTrans, crTransColor);
    DrawPart(hDC, x - m_rcViewport.left, y,
      0, m_iHeight + m_rcViewport.top,
      m_rcViewport.right, -m_rcViewport.top,
      bTrans, crTransColor);
    DrawPart(hDC, x, y - m_rcViewport.top,
      m_iWidth + m_rcViewport.left, 0,
      -m_rcViewport.left, m_rcViewport.bottom,
      bTrans, crTransColor);
    DrawPart(hDC, x - m_rcViewport.left, y - m_rcViewport.top,
      0, 0,
      m_rcViewport.right, m_rcViewport.bottom,
      bTrans, crTransColor);
  }
  else if (m_rcViewport.top < 0 && m_rcViewport.right > m_iWidth)
  {
    // Draw the split viewport wrapping top to bottom AND right to left
    DrawPart(hDC, x, y,
      m_rcViewport.left, m_iHeight + m_rcViewport.top,
      m_iWidth - m_rcViewport.left, -m_rcViewport.top,
      bTrans, crTransColor);
    DrawPart(hDC, x + (m_iWidth - m_rcViewport.left), y,
      0, m_iHeight + m_rcViewport.top,
      m_rcViewport.right - m_iWidth, -m_rcViewport.top,
      bTrans, crTransColor);
    DrawPart(hDC, x, y - m_rcViewport.top,
      m_rcViewport.left, 0,
      m_iWidth - m_rcViewport.left, m_rcViewport.bottom,
      bTrans, crTransColor);
    DrawPart(hDC, x + (m_iWidth - m_rcViewport.left), y - m_rcViewport.top,
      0, 0,
      m_rcViewport.right - m_iWidth, m_rcViewport.bottom,
      bTrans, crTransColor);
  }
  else if (m_rcViewport.bottom > m_iHeight && m_rcViewport.left < 0)
  {
    // Draw the split viewport wrapping bottom to top AND left to right
```

If the viewport is wrapping off the top and left of the bitmap, draw the wrapped image in four pieces.

continues

LISTING 23.4 Continued

```
    DrawPart(hDC, x, y,
      m_iWidth + m_rcViewport.left, m_rcViewport.top,
      -m_rcViewport.left, m_iHeight - m_rcViewport.top,
      bTrans, crTransColor);
    DrawPart(hDC, x - m_rcViewport.left, y,
      0, m_rcViewport.top,
      m_rcViewport.right, m_iHeight - m_rcViewport.top,
      bTrans, crTransColor);
    DrawPart(hDC, x, y + (m_iHeight - m_rcViewport.top),
      m_iWidth + m_rcViewport.left, 0,
      -m_rcViewport.left, m_rcViewport.bottom - m_iHeight,
      bTrans, crTransColor);
    DrawPart(hDC, x - m_rcViewport.left, y + (m_iHeight - m_rcViewport.top),
      0, 0,
      m_rcViewport.right, m_rcViewport.bottom - m_iHeight,
      bTrans, crTransColor);
  }
  else if (m_rcViewport.bottom > m_iHeight && m_rcViewport.right > m_iWidth)
  {
    // Draw the split viewport wrapping bottom to top AND right to left
    DrawPart(hDC, x, y,
      m_rcViewport.left, m_rcViewport.top,
      m_iWidth - m_rcViewport.left, m_iHeight - m_rcViewport.top,
      bTrans, crTransColor);
    DrawPart(hDC, x + (m_iWidth - m_rcViewport.left), y,
      0, m_rcViewport.top,
      m_rcViewport.right - m_iWidth, m_iHeight - m_rcViewport.top,
      bTrans, crTransColor);
    DrawPart(hDC, x, y + (m_iHeight - m_rcViewport.top),
      m_rcViewport.left, 0,
      m_iWidth - m_rcViewport.left, m_rcViewport.bottom - m_iHeight,
      bTrans, crTransColor);
    DrawPart(hDC, x + (m_iWidth - m_rcViewport.left),
      y + (m_iHeight - m_rcViewport.top),
      0, 0,
      m_rcViewport.right - m_iWidth, m_rcViewport.bottom - m_iHeight,
      bTrans, crTransColor);
  }
  else if (m_rcViewport.top < 0)
  {
    // Draw the split viewport wrapping from top to bottom
    DrawPart(hDC, x, y,
      m_rcViewport.left, m_iHeight + m_rcViewport.top,
      m_rcViewport.right - m_rcViewport.left, -m_rcViewport.top,
      bTrans, crTransColor);
    DrawPart(hDC, x, y - m_rcViewport.top,
      m_rcViewport.left, 0,
      m_rcViewport.right - m_rcViewport.left, m_rcViewport.bottom,
      bTrans, crTransColor);
  }
  else if (m_rcViewport.right > m_iWidth)
  {
    // Draw the split viewport wrapping from right to left
    DrawPart(hDC, x, y,
```

If the viewport is wrapping off the top of the bitmap, draw the wrapped image in two pieces.

```
    m_rcViewport.left, m_rcViewport.top,
    m_iWidth - m_rcViewport.left, m_rcViewport.bottom - m_rcViewport.top,
    bTrans, crTransColor);
  DrawPart(hDC, x + (m_iWidth - m_rcViewport.left), y,
    0, m_rcViewport.top,
    m_rcViewport.right - m_iWidth, m_rcViewport.bottom - m_rcViewport.top,
    bTrans, crTransColor);
}
else if (m_rcViewport.bottom > m_iHeight)
{
  // Draw the split viewport wrapping from bottom to top
  DrawPart(hDC, x, y,
    m_rcViewport.left, m_rcViewport.top,
    m_rcViewport.right - m_rcViewport.left, m_iHeight - m_rcViewport.top,
    bTrans, crTransColor);
  DrawPart(hDC, x, y + (m_iHeight - m_rcViewport.top),
    m_rcViewport.left, 0,
    m_rcViewport.right - m_rcViewport.left, m_rcViewport.bottom - m_iHeight,
    bTrans, crTransColor);
}
else if (m_rcViewport.left < 0)
{
  // Draw the split viewport wrapping from left to right
  DrawPart(hDC, x, y,
    m_iWidth + m_rcViewport.left, m_rcViewport.top,
    -m_rcViewport.left, m_rcViewport.bottom - m_rcViewport.top,
    bTrans, crTransColor);
  DrawPart(hDC, x - m_rcViewport.left, y,
    0, m_rcViewport.top,
    m_rcViewport.right, m_rcViewport.bottom - m_rcViewport.top,
    bTrans, crTransColor);
}
else
  // Draw the entire viewport at once
  DrawPart(hDC, x, y,
    m_rcViewport.left, m_rcViewport.top,
    m_rcViewport.right - m_rcViewport.left,
    m_rcViewport.bottom - m_rcViewport.top,
    bTrans, crTransColor);
}
```

If the viewport doesn't wrap at all, just draw it as a single image.

Okay, now that I've scared you with this enormous chunk of code, let me explain that it isn't critical for you to understand exactly what's going on here. The complexity of the code stems from the fact that there are several different exceptional cases that you must handle when it comes to the viewport wrapping around to the other side of the layer image. Each of these cases requires its own approach to drawing the layer based on the specific wrapping of the viewport. More specifically, when the viewport wraps to the other side of the layer image, the image must be drawn in multiple steps (slices). As an example, if the viewport wraps off the top edge of the image, the layer must be drawn as one slice along the top edge of the image plus another slice that picks up a portion of the bottom edge of the image. If you go back and study Figure 23.5, this will make more sense. If the viewport happens to wrap off both a horizontal edge and a vertical edge at the same time, it takes four slices to assemble the resulting viewport image.

I can tell you from experience that this kind of code is difficult to debug, and it can often take several attempts to get working correctly. As I write this, I'm staring at several pieces of paper with sketches on them for all the possible exceptions involved in a viewport wrapping around the layer image. Fortunately, I've done the hard work for you, so let's move on and find out how the BackgroundLayer class is used in the context of the ScrollingBackground class.

Creating a Scrolling Background Class

The BackgroundLayer class is certainly interesting, but by itself, it isn't of much use—the ScrollingBackground class is what makes it possible to incorporate layers into a scrolling background. Similar to other background classes that you've seen and used throughout the book, the ScrollingBackground class is derived from the familiar Background class. In fact, the ScrollingBackground class is very similar to the Background class, except that its focus is on managing, updating, and drawing background layers, as opposed to a single background image or color.

Listing 23.5 contains the code for the ScrollingBackground class, which reveals its member variables and methods.

LISTING 23.5   The ScrollingBackground **Class Is Used to Create a Multilayered Scrolling Background**

```
class ScrollingBackground : Background
{
protected:
  // Member Variables
  int              m_iNumLayers;
  BackgroundLayer* m_pLayers[10];

public:
  // Constructor(s)/Destructor
        ScrollingBackground(int iWidth, int iHeight);
  virtual ~ScrollingBackground();

  // General Methods
  virtual void  Update();
```

A maximum of 10 layers is allowed on a scrolling background, but you can always increase this number if you really think you need more layers.

```
virtual void  Draw(HDC hDC, BOOL bTrans = FALSE,
   COLORREF crTransColor = RGB(255, 0, 255));
 void         AddLayer(BackgroundLayer* pLayer);
};
```

The AddLayer() *method is used to add individual layers to a scrolling background.*

The two member variables in the ScrollingBackground class store away the number of background layers, along with pointers to each layer; each layer is of type BackgroundLayer. You'll notice that the array of layer pointers is fixed at 10 layers, which is mainly a convenience because I didn't want to have to deal with a vector or linked list that could shrink and grow. More importantly, it would be extremely inefficient for you to use more than a few background layers, so capping the layers at 10 isn't unreasonable.

The constructor and destructor for the ScrollingBackground class are primarily placeholders for the class, and they don't really add any functionality beyond what is provided in Background base class. The ScrollingBackground() constructor does initialize the m_iNumLayers member variable to 0, but other than that, there isn't much to see in the constructor and destructor code.

The Update() and Draw() methods are where the ScrollingBackground class gets more interesting, not to mention the entirely new AddLayer() method. The Update() method is responsible for updating the layers that make up the background, whereas the Draw() method is responsible for drawing the layers. The AddLayer() method is used to add new layers to the background; this is the sole means of adding new layers to a scrolling background. Listing 23.6 contains the code for all three methods.

LISTING 23.6 The ScrollingBackground::Update(),
ScrollingBackground::Draw(), and
ScrollingBackground::AddLayer() Methods are Used to Update, Draw,
and Add Layers to a Scrolling Background

```
void ScrollingBackground::Update()
{
  // Update the layers
  for (int i = 0; i < m_iNumLayers; i++)
    m_pLayers[i]->Update();
}

void ScrollingBackground::Draw(HDC hDC, BOOL bTrans,
  COLORREF crTransColor)
{
  // Draw the layers
  for (int i = 0; i < m_iNumLayers; i++)
```

continues

LISTING 23.6   Continued

```
    m_pLayers[i]->Draw(hDC, 0, 0, bTrans, crTransColor);
}

void ScrollingBackground::AddLayer(BackgroundLayer* pLayer)
{
  // Add the new layer (maximum of 10)
  if (m_iNumLayers < 10)
    m_pLayers[m_iNumLayers++] = pLayer;
}
```

The Update() method takes care of updating the layers in the scrolling background, which simply involves looping through each background layer and calling its respective Update() method. The Draw() method for the ScrollingBackground class is very similar in that it simply loops through the background layers and calls the Draw() method on each of them. Finally, the AddLayer() method is responsible for adding new layers to the scrolling background. This method accepts a pointer to a BackgroundLayer object, and as long as there are fewer than 10 layers in the background, a new layer is added. As the code for these three methods reveals, the ScrollingBackground class delegates the majority of the scrolling background work to the BackgroundLayer class, which simplifies the scrolling background code considerably.

Building the Wanderer Example

You now have a shiny new game engine with support for scrolling backgrounds, so of course, we need to take this new feature for a test spin. The remainder of this chapter is devoted to the development of an example called Wanderer, which is somewhat of an adventure simulator in which you control a character around a scrolling map. Although the Wanderer example isn't technically a game, it could be transformed into an adventure game without too much additional effort. The key to the Wanderer example is that it uses an oversized map capable of being scrolled in any direction. Your character stays anchored in the middle of the game screen, and he has the appearance of movement because the map scrolls under him.

To show how you can often use game engine features to get unique results, the Wanderer example makes use of two different scrolling backgrounds. In actuality, one of them is a background and one is a foreground, which means that one is drawn behind the character and one is drawn on top of the character. Why on Earth would you want to draw a "background" in front of a character in a game?

In this case, the reason is to add some realism via clouds that appear to be floating by above the character. By creating the clouds as a scrolling foreground, the effect is much better than simply creating a few cloud sprites and moving them around.

You might be slightly disappointed to learn that the Wanderer example only makes use of one layer in the scrolling background and foreground. However, you'll get to see several background layers in action in the next chapter when you create the last game of the book, Stunt Jumper.

Writing the Program Code

The Wanderer program begins with the Wanderer.h header file, which declares global variables that are important to the program. Take a look at Listing 23.7 to see these variables.

LISTING 23.7 The Wanderer.h Header File Imports Several Header Files and Declares Global Variables Required for the Scrolling Background and Foreground

```
#pragma once

//———————————————————————————————————————·
// Include Files
//———————————————————————————————————————·
#include <windows.h>
#include "Resource.h"
#include "GameEngine.h"
#include "Bitmap.h"
#include "Sprite.h"
#include "ScrollingBackground.h"
#include "PersonSprite.h"


//———————————————————————————————————————·
// Global Variables
//———————————————————————————————————————·
HINSTANCE              g_hInstance;
GameEngine*            g_pGame;
HDC                    g_hOffscreenDC;
HBITMAP                g_hOffscreenBitmap;
BackgroundLayer*       g_pBGLandscapeLayer;
BackgroundLayer*       g_pFGCloudsLayer;
ScrollingBackground*   g_pBackground;
ScrollingBackground*   g_pForeground;
Bitmap*                g_pPersonBitmap;
PersonSprite*          g_pPersonSprite;
int                    g_iInputDelay;
```

Admittedly, it is a little strange using two scrolling backgrounds, but in this example, its usage makes perfect sense.

The first variables of importance to the Wanderer example are the two BackgroundLayer pointers, g_BGLandscapeLayer and g_FGCloudsLayer. The g_BGLandscapeLayer variable stores a pointer to the background layer for the main landscape map, whereas g_FGCloudsLayer stores away the foreground layer for the clouds. Of course, these background layers require scrolling backgrounds in order to be successfully incorporated into the example. These backgrounds are stored as ScrollingBackground pointers in the g_pBackground and g_pForeground variables. The remaining member variables represent the bitmap image for the person (character), the person sprite, and an input delay to make the keyboard and joystick interface respond smoothly.

Figure 23.6 shows the person bitmap image, where you can see that the image consists of two animation frames. These two frames provide a rudimentary illusion of walking as you move the person around on the landscape map. The person sprite is of type PersonSprite, which is a sprite class you'll learn about later in the chapter.

FIGURE 23.6
The animated person sprite consists of two animation frames that provide a simple walking effect as you move the person around.

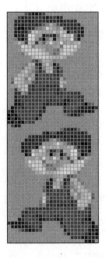

The required functions for the Wanderer example begin with the GameStart() function, which is where the scrolling background, foreground, and layers are created, along with the person bitmap and sprite. Listing 23.8 shows the code for this function.

LISTING 23.8 The `GameStart()` Function Initializes the Landscape Background and Clouds Foreground, as Well as the Person Sprite

```
void GameStart(HWND hWindow)
{
  // Create the offscreen device context and bitmap
  g_hOffscreenDC = CreateCompatibleDC(GetDC(hWindow));
  g_hOffscreenBitmap = CreateCompatibleBitmap(GetDC(hWindow),
    g_pGame->GetWidth(), g_pGame->GetHeight());
  SelectObject(g_hOffscreenDC, g_hOffscreenBitmap);

  // Create the scrolling background and landscape layer
  HDC hDC = GetDC(hWindow);
  g_pBackground = new ScrollingBackground(256, 256);
  g_pBGLandscapeLayer = new BackgroundLayer(hDC, IDB_BG_LANDSCAPE, g_hInstance);
  RECT rcViewport = { 352, 352, 608, 608 };
  g_pBGLandscapeLayer->SetViewport(rcViewport);
  g_pBackground->AddLayer(g_pBGLandscapeLayer);

  // Create the scrolling foreground and clouds layer
  g_pForeground = new ScrollingBackground(256, 256);
  g_pFGCloudsLayer = new BackgroundLayer(hDC, IDB_BG_CLOUDS, g_hInstance);
  rcViewport.left = rcViewport.top = 64;
  rcViewport.right = rcViewport.bottom = 320;
  g_pFGCloudsLayer->SetViewport(rcViewport);
  g_pForeground->AddLayer(g_pFGCloudsLayer);

  // Create and load the person bitmap
  g_pPersonBitmap = new Bitmap(hDC, IDB_PERSON, g_hInstance);

  // Create the person sprite
  RECT rcBounds = { 115, 112, 26, 32 };
  g_pPersonSprite = new PersonSprite(g_pPersonBitmap, rcBounds, BA_STOP);
  g_pPersonSprite->SetNumFrames(2);
  g_pPersonSprite->SetPosition(115, 112);
  g_pGame->AddSprite(g_pPersonSprite);

  // Play the background music
  g_pGame->PlayMIDISong(TEXT("Music.mid"));
}
```

The viewport is initially set so that it shows the center of the landscape bitmap.

After the first section of code in the `GameStart()` function, which should be very familiar to you by now, the scrolling background and its landscape layer are created. The background is created 256 pixels wide and 256 pixels high, which matches the size of the game screen. The landscape layer is created from a bitmap resource, and its viewport is set to the center of the layer image. Figure 23.7 shows the landscape layer image, which is 960 pixels wide by 960 pixels high.

FIGURE 23.7
The background
landscape layer
image is 960x960
in size, which pro-
vides plenty of
scrolling room for
the 256x256 view-
port of the scrolling
background.

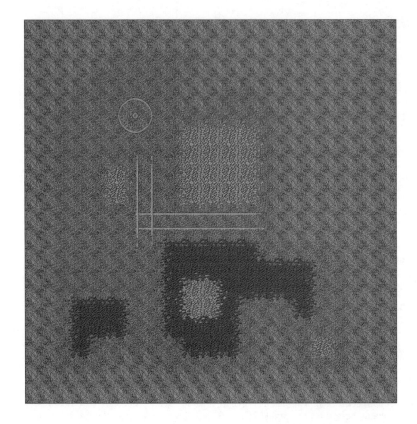

As the figure reveals, the landscape layer image is plenty large enough to give the illusion of a large virtual world because the game screen (therefore, the viewport) is significantly smaller. Figure 23.8 shows the clouds layer image, which is 384 pixels wide by 384 pixels wide and provides a similar effect as the landscape layer image.

In the clouds layer image, you'll notice that there are large transparent areas, which are very much necessary because this layer is part of the foreground, and therefore, it appears on top of the person in the example. Without transparent areas, the clouds layer would hide both the person sprite and the landscape background.

After creating the landscape background and clouds foreground, the GameStart() function creates the person sprite and starts up the background music. Notice that the person sprite is created as a PersonSprite object; you'll learn more about the PersonSprite class a bit later in the chapter.

FIGURE 23.8
The clouds foreground layer image is 384x384 in size, which provides enough scrolling room to make the clouds appear varied within the 256x256 viewport of the scrolling foreground.

The GameEnd() function is responsible for cleaning up when the Wanderer application is closed. Listing 23.9 shows the code for the GameEnd() function.

LISTING 23.9 The GameEnd() Function Cleans Up the Background, Foreground, and Person Sprite

```
void GameEnd()
{
  // Close the MIDI player for the background music
  g_pGame->CloseMIDIPlayer();

  // Cleanup the offscreen device context and bitmap
  DeleteObject(g_hOffscreenBitmap);
  DeleteDC(g_hOffscreenDC);

  // Cleanup the bitmaps
  delete g_pPersonBitmap;

  // Cleanup the scrolling background and landscape layer
  delete g_pBackground;
  delete g_pBGLandscapeLayer;

  // Cleanup the scrolling foreground and clouds layer
  delete g_pForeground;
  delete g_pFGCloudsLayer;

  // Cleanup the sprites
  g_pGame->CleanupSprites();

  // Cleanup the game engine
  delete g_pGame;
}
```

You must clean up both the scrolling background object and its individual layer.

The GameEnd() function doesn't hold too many surprises—it's sole function is freeing up the memory taken by the various objects used in the example.

The actual game screen in the Wanderer example is drawn in the GamePaint() function, which takes care of drawing both the background and foreground, as well as the person sprite. Listing 23.10 reveals how the GamePaint() function works.

LISTING 23.10 The GamePaint() Function Draws the Scrolling Background, the Sprites, and Then the Scrolling Foreground

```
void GamePaint(HDC hDC)
{
  // Draw the scrolling background
  g_pBackground->Draw(hDC);

  // Draw the sprites
  g_pGame->DrawSprites(hDC);

  // Draw the scrolling foreground
  g_pForeground->Draw(hDC, TRUE); // draw with transparency
}
```

It is critical that the foreground is drawn after the background and the sprites in order for it to appear above them.

The most significant thing to note about the GamePaint() function is the order of the drawing that it does. More specifically, the scrolling background is drawn first, followed by the sprites, followed by the scrolling foreground. This drawing order is what ensures that the clouds appear over the person sprite, which in turn appears over the landscape background. Also notice that the landscape background is drawn without transparency because there are no transparent areas on the landscape image, whereas the clouds foreground is drawn with transparency.

The last two functions of importance in the Wanderer example are related to user input: HandleKeys() and HandleJoystick(). These two functions end up being very similar because they essentially provide the same controls over moving the person sprite. The HandleKeys() function is shown in Listing 23.11.

LISTING 23.11 The HandleKeys() Function Takes Care of Processing Keyboard Input and Using It to Control the Person Sprite and Scroll the Background and Foreground

```
void HandleKeys()
{
  // Move the landscape/cloud layers based upon arrow key presses
  if (g_iInputDelay++ > 1)
  {
    if (GetAsyncKeyState(VK_LEFT) < 0)
    {
      // Make the person walk
      g_pPersonSprite->Walk();
```

```
  // Move the landscape layer to the right
  g_pBGLandscapeLayer->SetSpeed(16);
  g_pBGLandscapeLayer->SetDirection(SD_RIGHT);
  g_pBGLandscapeLayer->Update();
  g_pBGLandscapeLayer->SetSpeed(0);

  // Move the cloud layer to the right
  g_pFGCloudsLayer->SetSpeed(4);
  g_pFGCloudsLayer->SetDirection(SD_RIGHT);
  g_pFGCloudsLayer->Update();
  g_pFGCloudsLayer->SetSpeed(0);
}
else if (GetAsyncKeyState(VK_RIGHT) < 0)
{
  // Make the person walk
  g_pPersonSprite->Walk();

  // Move the landscape layer to the left
  g_pBGLandscapeLayer->SetSpeed(16);
  g_pBGLandscapeLayer->SetDirection(SD_LEFT);
  g_pBGLandscapeLayer->Update();
  g_pBGLandscapeLayer->SetSpeed(0);

  // Move the cloud layer to the left
  g_pFGCloudsLayer->SetSpeed(4);
  g_pFGCloudsLayer->SetDirection(SD_LEFT);
  g_pFGCloudsLayer->Update();
  g_pFGCloudsLayer->SetSpeed(0);
}
else if (GetAsyncKeyState(VK_UP) < 0)
{
  // Make the person walk
  g_pPersonSprite->Walk();

  // Move the landscape layer down
  g_pBGLandscapeLayer->SetSpeed(16);
  g_pBGLandscapeLayer->SetDirection(SD_DOWN);
  g_pBGLandscapeLayer->Update();
  g_pBGLandscapeLayer->SetSpeed(0);

  // Move the cloud layer down
  g_pFGCloudsLayer->SetSpeed(4);
  g_pFGCloudsLayer->SetDirection(SD_DOWN);
  g_pFGCloudsLayer->Update();
  g_pFGCloudsLayer->SetSpeed(0);
}
else if (GetAsyncKeyState(VK_DOWN) < 0)
{
  // Make the person walk
  g_pPersonSprite->Walk();

  // Move the landscape layer up
  g_pBGLandscapeLayer->SetSpeed(16);
  g_pBGLandscapeLayer->SetDirection(SD_UP);
  g_pBGLandscapeLayer->Update();
```

To make the person appear to be moving left, you must move the background and foreground to the right.

continues

LISTING 23.11   Continued

```
      g_pBGLandscapeLayer->SetSpeed(0);

      // Move the cloud layer up
      g_pFGCloudsLayer->SetSpeed(4);
      g_pFGCloudsLayer->SetDirection(SD_UP);
      g_pFGCloudsLayer->Update();
      g_pFGCloudsLayer->SetSpeed(0);
    }

    // Reset the input delay
    g_iInputDelay = 0;
  }
}
```

Although there is a fair amount of code in the HandleKeys() function, it is all very straightforward. What basically happens is this: Each time a key is pressed, the landscape background's speed and direction are set, the background is updated to make it scroll, and then its speed is set back to 0. The same steps are taken for the clouds foreground except that the speed is always less, which results in the clouds moving slower. Also notice that the background and foreground are moved in the opposite direction of the person; this is necessary to provide the illusion that the person is moving.

The other thing taking place in the HandleKeys() function is the person sprite being moved, thanks to a call to the Walk() method. It's worth pointing out that the Walk() method isn't actually moving the position of the person sprite; it's just altering the animation frame so that the person appears to be walking as the background scrolls by. You'll find out exactly how the Walk() method works in just a moment.

The HandleJoystick() function is virtually identical to the HandleKeys() function. In fact, you could argue that I should've broken the code out into a third helper function to eliminate repetitive code, but in this case, I opted for simplicity over code reduction. Listing 23.12 contains the code for the HandleJoystick() function.

LISTING 23.12   The HandleJoystick() Function Uses Joystick Input to Control the Person Sprite and Scroll the Background and Foreground

```
void HandleJoystick(JOYSTATE jsJoystickState)
{
  if (++g_iInputDelay > 2)
  {
    // Check horizontal movement
    if (jsJoystickState & JOY_LEFT)
```

```
{
  // Make the person walk
  g_pPersonSprite->Walk();

  // Move the landscape layer to the right
  g_pBGLandscapeLayer->SetSpeed(16);
  g_pBGLandscapeLayer->SetDirection(SD_RIGHT);
  g_pBGLandscapeLayer->Update();
  g_pBGLandscapeLayer->SetSpeed(0);

  // Move the cloud layer to the right
  g_pFGCloudsLayer->SetSpeed(4);
  g_pFGCloudsLayer->SetDirection(SD_RIGHT);
  g_pFGCloudsLayer->Update();
  g_pFGCloudsLayer->SetSpeed(0);
}
else if (jsJoystickState & JOY_RIGHT)
{
  // Make the person walk
  g_pPersonSprite->Walk();

  // Move the landscape layer to the left
  g_pBGLandscapeLayer->SetSpeed(16);
  g_pBGLandscapeLayer->SetDirection(SD_LEFT);
  g_pBGLandscapeLayer->Update();
  g_pBGLandscapeLayer->SetSpeed(0);

  // Move the cloud layer to the left
  g_pFGCloudsLayer->SetSpeed(4);
  g_pFGCloudsLayer->SetDirection(SD_LEFT);
  g_pFGCloudsLayer->Update();
  g_pFGCloudsLayer->SetSpeed(0);
}
else if (jsJoystickState & JOY_UP)
{
  // Make the person walk
  g_pPersonSprite->Walk();

  // Move the landscape layer down
  g_pBGLandscapeLayer->SetSpeed(16);
  g_pBGLandscapeLayer->SetDirection(SD_DOWN);
  g_pBGLandscapeLayer->Update();
  g_pBGLandscapeLayer->SetSpeed(0);

  // Move the cloud layer down
  g_pFGCloudsLayer->SetSpeed(4);
  g_pFGCloudsLayer->SetDirection(SD_DOWN);
  g_pFGCloudsLayer->Update();
  g_pFGCloudsLayer->SetSpeed(0);
}
else if (jsJoystickState & JOY_DOWN)
{
  // Make the person walk
  g_pPersonSprite->Walk();
```

continues

LISTING 23.12 Continued

```
      // Move the landscape layer up
      g_pBGLandscapeLayer->SetSpeed(16);
      g_pBGLandscapeLayer->SetDirection(SD_UP);
      g_pBGLandscapeLayer->Update();
      g_pBGLandscapeLayer->SetSpeed(0);

      // Move the cloud layer up
      g_pFGCloudsLayer->SetSpeed(4);
      g_pFGCloudsLayer->SetDirection(SD_UP);
      g_pFGCloudsLayer->Update();
      g_pFGCloudsLayer->SetSpeed(0);
    }

    // Reset the input delay
    g_iInputDelay = 0;
  }
}
```

Like I said, this function is virtually indistinguishable from its keyboard counterpart, other than the specific tests used to see which direction the joystick was pushed. In case you're wondering, an input delay is used in both functions to help regulate the speeds of the scrolling background and foreground. Feel free to tinker with the g_iInputDelay variable if you want to further speed up or slow down the user input.

The last code component of the Wanderer example that you've yet to see is the PersonSprite class, which is a sprite class derived from the familiar Sprite class you've used throughout the book. The only reason for deriving a new class for the person sprite is because the general Sprite class doesn't provide a means of carefully controlling the animation frames. More specifically, you need to be able to manually alter the animation frames of the person to make it look like he's walking in response to user input. There just isn't a good way to do this with the Sprite class alone. Listing 23.13 shows how the PersonSprite class is structured.

LISTING 23.13 The PersonSprite Class Is Used to Create a Sprite Whose Animation Frames Are Used to Simulate Walking

```
class PersonSprite : public Sprite
{
public:
  // Constructor(s)/Destructor
          PersonSprite(Bitmap* pBitmap, RECT& rcBounds,
            BOUNDSACTION baBoundsAction = BA_STOP);
  virtual ~PersonSprite();

  // Helper Methods
```

```
virtual void  UpdateFrame();

  // General Methods
  void Walk();
};
```

The UpdateFrame() method must be overridden to interrupt the default updating of animation frames.

Beyond the boilerplate constructor and destructor, the PersonSprite class only defines two methods: an overridden UpdateFrame() method and a new method named Walk(). The new UpdateFrame() method is required because the UpdateFrame() method in the Sprite class is where the animation frame is automatically updated. By overriding it here, you are able to prevent the default updating process. The Walk() method simply provides a means of manually updating the animation frame so that the person sprite appears to walk. If you're bracing yourself for some complex code with these two methods, brace no more because Listing 23.14 shows how painfully simple they actually are.

LISTING 23.14 The PersonSprite::UpdateFrame() and PersonSprite::Walk() **Methods Override the Default Sprite Behavior So that the Person Sprite Can Be Manually Animated**

```
inline void PersonSprite::UpdateFrame()
{
}

void PersonSprite::Walk()
{
  // Toggle between the two frames to give the illusion of walking
  m_iCurFrame = 1 - m_iCurFrame;
}
```

Brutally simple might have been a better description of these methods! The UpdateFrame() method actually contains no code at all because its sole purpose is to defuse the default behavior in the Sprite::UpdateFrame() method. The Walk() method simply toggles the current animation frame between 0 and 1. You could just as easily add more detailed animation frames to provide a more realistic walking effect, in which case the Walk() method would cycle through the frames.

You've now taken in all the code for the Wanderer example, so let's move on to seeing how it looks in action.

If you're using Visual C++ 6.0, you might need to change the type casts from (DWORD_PTR) to (DWORD) in GameEngine.cpp in order for the Wanderer code to compile properly.

Construction Cue

Construction Cue

As with most of the examples in the book, the Wanderer program relies on the standard msimg32.lib and winmm.lib libraries. These libraries are included with most Windows compilers, but they aren't automatically linked into programs when you create a new project. If you are using your own project or make files, as opposed to using the ones provided on the CD-ROM, make sure that you change the link settings so that these library files are properly linked into the final executable. Refer to the documentation for your specific compiler for how this is done.

Testing the Finished Product

Even though it isn't technically a game with a start and a finish, the Wanderer example is actually one of the most interesting examples in the book—at least in my humble opinion. The effect of being able to control a character and wander around a virtual world is quite interesting. Take a look at Figure 23.9 to see the little wanderer person being guided around the cloudy landscape in the Wanderer example.

FIGURE 23.9
The scrolling landscape background and clouds foreground provide an immersive environment for the user-controlled person character in the Wanderer program.

As with all of the animated examples in the book, you can't quite get the effect from looking at a static image on a printed page, so I encourage you to run the Wanderer program and experiment with it. You'll notice that the virtual world feels much larger than it really is because it scrolls back on itself. The clouds add a unique effect in that they are capable of hiding the person at times. Keep in mind that both the landscape background and clouds foreground were created with a tiny amount of code in the Wanderer example; this is yet another example of how the game engine removes the burden of coding from games by supporting cool features internally.

I have to make a small apology for not taking the Wanderer example to its logical conclusion as a complete adventure game. However, I didn't want to distract from the main point of the example, which was to demonstrate how to use a scrolling background as a world map. So, I'll leave it to you to add other characters and objects and expand the Wanderer example into your own adventure game. Keep in mind that you could easily plug in different graphics to create an entirely different looking game—maybe a water background and a ship, instead of the person, and suddenly you'd have a naval game!

Summary

Seeing as how you mastered them much earlier in the book, backgrounds were nothing new to you entering this chapter. However, you had yet to tackle the most interesting background of all, the scrolling background. This chapter introduced the concept of a scrolling background and what it takes to make one work. You also took the concept a bit farther by exploring what is required to support multiple layers within a scrolling background. Moving from concept to reality, you saw how to add support to the game engine for layered scrolling backgrounds. Finally, the chapter culminated with the creation of an adventure simulation involving a scrolling background and foreground.

Although the next chapter is focused solely on the development of a complete game, in many ways, it is a continuation of the scrolling background discussion. This is because you learn how to build a game that uses the scrolling background support in the game engine to create a multilayered parallax-scrolling background. All this takes place within the context of a motorcycle jumping game!

Extreme Game Makeover

In truth, the Wanderer example isn't designed very efficiently because it tends to hog a lot of memory due to the fact that you're dealing with one huge image for the background. A better design would involve tiles of smaller bitmaps that could be arranged in varying patterns to form a larger, continuous background. Not only is this design more efficient from a memory perspective, but it also gives you more flexibility in generating unique backgrounds on-the-fly. However, as is usually the case with additional flexibility in game code, there is additional complexity. The following are the steps required to develop a tiled background class for the Wanderer example that relies on multiple smaller tile images arranged in an array, as opposed to a single large background image:

1. Change the background layer array in the `ScrollingBackground` class so that it is a three-dimensional array; the first dimension is the layer depth, whereas the second and third dimensions are the background layer tiles at each X and Y position of the background.

2. Modify the code for the `ScrollingBackground::Update()` method so that it updates all the background layer tiles.

3. Change the `ScrollingBackground::Draw()` method so that it draws all the background layer tiles in their appropriate positions.

4. Modify the code for the `ScrollingBackground::AddLayer()` method so that it accepts an XY tile position for the new layer; the default action can be to append the tile layer to the end of the last row in the tile layer array.

The nice thing about the original designs of the `BackgroundLayer` and `ScrollingBackground` classes is that they are already set up to accommodate a viewport that works regardless of whether you're dealing with a single layer image or a two-dimensional array of layer tiles. Such a design enables you to carry out the tiled background layer makeover without as much complex coding as you might have expected.

CHAPTER 24

Example Game: Stunt Jumper

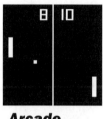

Arcade Archive

Widely regarded as one of the best driving games ever made, if not the best driving game ever made, Daytona USA was introduced in 1994 by Sega. The game made a major leap forward from other driving games by incorporating realistic physics into the driving experience, which could be felt by the driver through a force-feedback steering wheel. The game graphics were stunning for its time, and included an incredible range of detail. The Daytona USA game is still alive today in Daytona USA 2: Power Edition, which supports up to 40 players in simultaneous play. This is the one game that even non-gamers can appreciate. I know this firsthand because my wife absolutely loves banging fenders against me in this game, and she generally avoids all other video games.

This chapter embarks yet again on the development of another complete game. The game is called Stunt Jumper, and in many ways it represents a culmination of everything you've learned about game programming throughout the book. The Stunt Jumper game is a horizontal-scrolling motorcycle jumping game loosely based on the Stunt Cycle game released by Atari in 1976. The Stunt Cycle game was released during the height of the popularity of Evel Knievel, "The King of Stuntmen," the legendary motorcycle stunt jumper who attempted such incredible jumps as the Snake River Canyon in Idaho. While the Atari video game didn't enjoy the success of later Atari hits, such as Asteroids, it was still a very fun game. The Stunt Jumper game you develop in this chapter is similar to Stunt Cycle in that you must carefully control the speed of a motorcycle jumper to help him launch over a line of buses.

In this chapter, you'll learn

▶ About the basic premise behind the Stunt Jumper game

▶ How to design the Stunt Jumper game

▶ About the nuts and bolts of constructing the Stunt Jumper game

▶ How to catch big air on a motorcycle without risking serious injury

How Does the Game Play?

If you weren't old enough to remember the excitement surrounding Evel Knievel back in the 1970s, let me tell you that he set the standard for modern day daredevils. It's not such a big deal to see a guy jumping hundreds of feet on a motorcycle these days, thanks to the X-Games, but Evel Knievel pioneered stunt jumping. Unlike modern motorcycle jumping, Evel Knievel always had a flair for the dramatic and made his jumps more interesting by jumping over objects whose size immediately conveyed the scale of the jump. Buses were the most popular items to be jumped in the golden era of stunt jumping, so I decided to use buses as the basis for stunt jumping in the Stunt Jumper game.

Gamer's Garage

If you've ever heard the term "jumping the shark," it refers to the height of a phenomenon before it begins to fade away in success/popularity. The term comes from a popular episode of *Happy Days* in which the hip character, The Fonz, jumps a motorcycle over a great white shark. That particular episode was considered the beginning of the end of the show, and the term is now applied to everything from television shows to companies to technologies. Check out `http://www.jumptheshark.com/` for more on the topic.

In Stunt Jumper, you are a stunt-loving motorcycle rider who just loves to blast big air jumping over buses lined up in a row. Having some background in bicycle stunt jumping myself, I can tell you that it's a bad idea to jump anything big without having a reasonably inclined landing area. In other words, you would never launch from a big jump and land on a flat surface—you would crash pretty badly. The answer is a landing ramp, which is simply another ramp turned the other way that provides a soft landing. You can jump surprisingly high and yet have a smooth landing if you properly hit a landing ramp. However, that can be a big "if."

One of the challenges facing any jumper is determining the appropriate speed so that you clear your obstacle, but not overshoot the landing ramp. If you have too little speed, you'll crash into an obstacle, whereas too much speed will result in you overshooting the landing ramp and crashing from a hard landing. The challenge in playing the Stunt Jumper game is to quickly alter the speed of the motorcycle to match the distance you're jumping, which changes after each successful jump. More specifically, the number of buses changes after each jump, so you constantly have to gauge the required speed and adjust accordingly. You alter the speed of the motorcycle in the game by pressing the left (slow down) and right (speed up) arrow keys on the keyboard or by using a joystick and moving the handle left (slow down) and right (speed up).

Graphical objects in the Stunt Jumper game consist of the motorcycle jumper, the buses, and the launch and landing ramps. In addition to these objects that directly impact the play of the game, a parallax-scrolling background is a useful addition to help provide some added visual interest. This background consists of several layers that scroll by at different speeds to provide the illusion of movement and depth.

Gamer's Garage

In case you've forgotten from earlier discussions in the book, a parallax-scrolling background is one that consists of multiple layers scrolling at different speeds. The idea is that the different layers represent objects at different distances, so mountains in the distance appear to go by slower than trees that are nearer. This provides a terrific illusion of depth.

The motorcycle jumper in the game is always moving horizontally across the game screen. Although you can slow him down and speed him up, you can never bring him to a complete stop. This makes the game a bit more challenging because you don't have much time to think between jumps; once you land one jump, you have to immediately begin adjusting your speed for the next one. The game ends when you gauge your speed wrong and land short of or overshoot the landing ramp.

Designing the Game

With a basic understanding of the Stunt Jumper game in your mind, let's move on to addressing a few details regarding the design of the game. First, the trickiest part of this game is making the motorcycle's movements appear realistic. Animating a motorcycle cruising across the screen horizontally is no big deal, but when a motorcycle jumps in the real world, it doesn't stay level. In fact, just riding up the launch ramp should make the motorcycle tilt so that it appears to actually be riding, not just sliding up the ramp. Furthermore, as the motorcycle flies through the air, its tilt should vary so that it arcs upward and then downward. Think about a real motorcycle jumping and visualize it arcing through the air. All this motorcycle tilt business can be handled using animation frames within the motorcycle sprite, but it will take some creative thinking to make it happen. More on this in a moment.

The launch ramp, landing ramp, and buses are all suitable for being created as sprites because you need to be able to vary their placement and detect collisions between them and the motorcycle jumper; all the sprites, except the motorcycle, are stationary. The parallax-scrolling background is purely an aesthetic detail that can be accomplished entirely through a multilayered scrolling background, which is easily handled by the ScrollingBackground class you developed in the previous chapter. Figure 24.1 brings together the various elements in the Stunt Jumper game to show you what the game screen looks like in terms of graphical objects.

FIGURE 24.1
The Stunt Jumper game consists of a parallax-scrolling background, a motorcycle jumper, a launch ramp, buses, and a landing ramp.

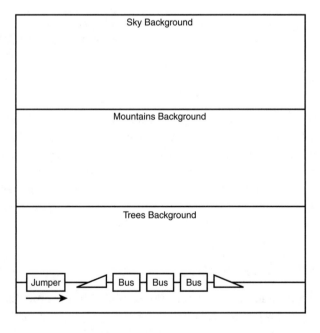

In terms of sprites, the interactions in the game consist of the motorcycle sprite hitting the launch ramp to initiate a jump. Any collision with a bus results in an unsuccessful jump, as does missing the landing ramp. So, a successful jump involves clearing the buses, but not overshooting the landing ramp. You can see how this functionality can be carried out through simple collision detection between the different sprites. To recap, the following are the sprites used in the Stunt Jumper game:

▶ Motorcycle jumper sprite

▶ Launch ramp sprite

▶ Landing ramp sprite

▶ Bus sprites

In addition to sprites, the Stunt Jumper game relies on several different bitmap images. The most interesting of these images is the one for the motorcycle jumper, which consists of several animation frames to account for the various tilt positions of the motorcycle. Before you see this image, take a look at the following list of bitmap images used throughout the game:

▶ Background sky image (see Figure 24.2)

▶ Background mountains image (see Figure 24.3)

▶ Background trees image (see Figure 24.4)

▶ Background road image (see Figure 24.5)

▶ Animated motorcycle jumper image (see Figure 24.6)

▶ Launch ramp image (see Figure 24.7)

▶ Landing ramp image (see Figure 24.8)

▶ Bus image (see Figure 24.9)

▶ Splash screen image

▶ Game over image

FIGURE 24.2
The sky background bitmap image consists of clouds on a blue sky with a transparent area below.

FIGURE 24.3
The mountains background bitmap image consists of mountains with a transparent area above.

FIGURE 24.4
The trees background bitmap image consists of trees with transparent areas above and below.

FIGURE 24.5
The road background bitmap image consists of a road with a transparent area above.

FIGURE 24.6
The animated motorcycle jumper bitmap image contains several animation frames to show the motorcycle at varying tilts.

FIGURE 24.7
The launch ramp bitmap image contains a ramp that is approached from the left.

FIGURE 24.8
The landing ramp bitmap image contains a ramp that is landed on from the left.

FIGURE 24.9
The bus bitmap image contains the front of a bus so that the bus appears to be parked perpendicular to the jump direction.

These images flow directly from the design of the game that you've covered thus far, so there hopefully shouldn't be any big surprises here. One detail worth taking a closer look at is the animation frames for the motorcycle jumper image (refer to Figure 24.6), which is the only animated image in the game. If you notice, each frame shows the motorcycle rotated at a different angle, which is intended to show the motorcycle tilted at different angles as it jumps through the air. The neutral position of the motorcycle, where it is perfectly level, is visible in the seventh frame. There are then 6 animation frames for each direction of tilt, resulting in a total of 13 animation frames for the motorcycle image. It's fairly obvious that you can't simply cycle through these animation frames indiscriminately in the game, so you'll be creating a custom sprite class for the motorcycle jumper to help manage the animation frames intelligently.

Unlike most of the other games you've created throughout the book, the Stunt Jumper game doesn't keep track of a difficulty level and doesn't get harder as the game progresses. In fact, the game doesn't really progress, other than changing the number of buses being jumped with each pass of the motorcycle across the screen. For these reasons, I also decided not to keep score for this game. You can certainly add a score variable and even additional lives if you want to put the traditional bells and whistles on the game, but I find it to be plenty of fun just seeing how fast you can react and jump the never ending line of buses.

Because no score is being kept and no extra lives are available, the global variables for the game consist primarily of those required for the bitmap images and sprites. Of course, it's still handy to use an input delay variable to regulate the responsiveness of the keyboard and joystick. You also need a couple of Boolean variables to keep track of whether the game is over and the splash screen should be displayed. Other than that, no other game-specific global variables are required.

You now have a good enough feel for the design of the Stunt Jumper game to delve into the code and find out exactly how it works. As with all the games you've developed throughout the book, keep in mind that, in many ways, the Stunt Jumper game represents version 1.0 of the game, meaning that you should experiment with improving it and making it more interesting and fun. So consider possible changes and enhancements you might want to make as you work through the code for the game.

Building the Game

The code for the Stunt Jumper game is relatively straightforward thanks to the many features you've built into the game engine over the course of the book. Even so, I think you'll find that the game leads you through a few interesting twists and turns with the code that you haven't necessarily encountered in other games. The next few sections guide you through the development of the Stunt Jumper game's code and resources.

Writing the Game Code

Because the entire Stunt Jumper game revolves around the motorcycle jumper and its capability to fly through the air realistically, I want to lead off the code for the game by first tackling the motorcycle jumper sprite. As you know, the motorcycle jumper relies on a bitmap that has 13 animation frames—with the image of the motorcycle on level residing directly in the middle of the frames. The trick to the motorcycle sprite is figuring out how to cycle through the animation frames so that the motorcycle tilts realistically during a jump. There are a variety of different approaches you could use to control the tilt of the motorcycle, and I hope I settled on one of the simplest—you can be the judge of that when you find out how it works in just a moment.

Before getting into the code that makes the motorcycle tilt, first take a look at the header file for the MotorcycleSprite class, which is shown in Listing 24.1.

LISTING 24.1　The MotorcycleSprite.h Header File Declares the MotorcycleSprite Class, Which Is Derived from Sprite

```
#pragma once

//--------------------------------.
// Include Files
//--------------------------------.
#include <windows.h>
#include "Resource.h"
#include "Sprite.h"

//--------------------------------.
// MotorcycleSprite Class
//--------------------------------.
class MotorcycleSprite : public Sprite
{
protected:
```

continues

LISTING 24.1   Continued

```
// Member Variables
const int m_iMINSPEED, m_iMAXSPEED;
const int m_iHANGTIME;
BOOL      m_bJumping;
int       m_iJumpCounter;
BOOL      m_bLandedSafely;

public:
// Constructor(s)/Destructor
        MotorcycleSprite(Bitmap* pBitmap, RECT& rcBounds,
          BOUNDSACTION baBoundsAction = BA_STOP);
virtual ~MotorcycleSprite();

// Helper Methods
virtual void  UpdateFrame();

// General Methods
void IncreaseSpeed();
void DecreaseSpeed();
void StartJumping();
void LandedSafely();
BOOL HasLandedSafely() { return m_bLandedSafely; };
};
```

The hang time constant determines how long the motorcycle is in the air while jumping; you can think of it as controlling gravity in the game.

The StartJumping() method triggers the motorcycle to begin jumping, which involves changing both its velocity and appearance.

The MotorcycleSprite class might have more member variables and methods than you expected. Fortunately, the class still isn't too complex, despite using several member variables and methods. The following is a list of the member variables defined in the MotorcycleSprite class, along with their usage:

▶ m_iMINSPEED—The minimum speed of the motorcycle (constant)

▶ m_iMAXSPEED—The maximum speed of the motorcycle (constant)

▶ m_iHANGTIME—A number that controls how long the motorcycle stays in the air during each jump (constant)

▶ m_bJumping—A Boolean value indicating whether the motorcycle is jumping

▶ m_iJumpCounter—A counter that keeps track of how long the motorcycle stays in the air during each jump

▶ m_bLandedSafely—A Boolean value indicating whether the motorcycle has landed safely

The m_iMINSPEED and m_iMAXSPEED member constants determine the minimum and maximum speeds of the motorcycle, respectively. You can alter these values to change how fast the motorcycle is capable of going, and therefore how far it can jump, along with how slow it can go. You'll see in a moment that the m_iMINSPEED variable isn't set to zero so that the player doesn't have time to stop and plan each jump. The m_iHANGTIME member constant is used to determine how much hang time the motorcycle has when it jumps. You can think of the m_iHANGTIME member as being sort of like an antigravity value in that higher values for it result in the motorcycle jumping higher. The value I settled on for it (6) was arrived at through trial and error, so you might want to experiment with it yourself.

The m_bJumping member variable stores the jumping status of the motorcycle, whereas the m_bLandedSafely member variable keeps up with whether the motorcycle has successfully jumped and landed safely. At first glance, it might seem that these two variables are redundant, but you'll see why it is necessary to have both when you get into the jumping code for the motorcycle. The last member variable in the MotorcycleSprite class is m_iJumpCounter, which is a counter used to control how long each jump lasts. The m_iJumpCounter variable is set to a value when a jump begins based on the motorcycle's velocity and the m_iHANGTIME constant, and it counts down to zero as the jump progresses. Without the m_iJumpCounter variable, you would have no way of knowing how long to show the motorcycle flying through the air.

Moving right along, you probably noticed that the MotorcycleSprite class derives from Sprite and declares a constructor and destructor. More importantly, however, is the method in the Sprite class that MotorcycleSprite overrides, UpdateFrame(). This method is critical in that it controls how the motorcycle's animation frame is altered to give the illusion of jumping. What it actually does is use the jump counter as the basis for determining which animation frame to use for the motorcycle, which enables the tilt of the motorcycle to change as the jump progresses. Listing 24.2 contains the code for the MotorcycleSprite::UpdateFrame() method.

LISTING 24.2 The MotorcycleSprite::UpdateFrame() Method Changes the Default Updating of the Animation Frames So that the Motorcycle Tilts as It Jumps

```
void MotorcycleSprite::UpdateFrame()
{
  if (m_bJumping)
  {
    // Start jumping
    if (m_iJumpCounter— >= 0)
    {
      // See if the motorcycle is on the way up
```

continues

LISTING 24.2 Continued

```
                    if (m_iJumpCounter > (m_ptVelocity.x * m_iHANGTIME / 2))
                    {
                      // Change the frame to show the motorcycle tilt upward
                      m_iCurFrame = min(m_iCurFrame + 1, 12);

                      // Change the vertical velocity to cause the motorcycle to ascend
                      if (m_iJumpCounter % (m_iHANGTIME / 2) == 0)
                        m_ptVelocity.y++;
                    }
                    // See if the motorcycle is on the way down
                    else if (m_iJumpCounter <= (m_ptVelocity.x * m_iHANGTIME / 2))
                    {
                      // Change the frame to show the motorcycle tilt downward
                      m_iCurFrame = max(m_iCurFrame - 1, 0);

                      // Change the vertical velocity to cause the motorcycle to descend
                      if (m_iJumpCounter % (m_iHANGTIME / 2) == 0)
                        m_ptVelocity.y++;
                    }
                  }
                  else
                  {
                    // Stop the jump and level the motorcycle
                    m_bJumping = FALSE;
                    m_iCurFrame = 6;
                    m_ptVelocity.y = 0;

                    // See if the motorcycle overshot the landing ramp
                    if (!m_bLandedSafely)
                    {
                      // Play the crash sound
                      PlaySound((LPCSTR)IDW_CRASH, g_hInstance, SND_ASYNC |
                        SND_RESOURCE);

                      // End the game
                      m_ptVelocity.x = 0;
                      g_bGameOver = TRUE;
                    }
                  }
                }
              }
            }
```

Increment the frame so that the motorcycle tilts upward in a wheelie.

Decrement the frame so that the motorcycle tilts downward in an endo.

Level out the motorcycle so that it has no tilt.

Keep in mind that the UpdateFrame() method is called on the motorcycle sprite once every game cycle to update the appearance of the sprite. The first thing the UpdateFrame() method does is check to see if the motorcycle is jumping. If so, the jump counter is decremented and checked to make sure that it is still greater than zero; this indicates that the motorcycle is still in flight. The next check is to see if the motorcycle is on the way up or on the way down because the Y component of the motorcycle's velocity must be altered in each case. If the motorcycle is on the way up, the animation frame is incremented because the tilt of the motorcycle increases in the upward direction from the middle frame to the end frame.

Conversely, for the downward part of the jump, the animation frame is decremented because the motorcycle's tilt angles downward from the middle frame to the first frame; don't forget that the middle animation frame is where the motorcycle is level. The other thing to notice in the jump code in this part of the UpdateFrame() method is how the m_iHANGTIME constant is used to determine if the Y component of the motorcycle's velocity needs to be adjusted; this code determines the "hang time" of the jump. I realize that this jumping code is a bit tricky to follow the first time through, but take your time and think about the mechanics of what must take place in order to make the motorcycle sprite appear to fly through the air smoothly.

The latter part of the UpdateFrame() method kicks in once a jump is over. The m_bJumping flag is set back to FALSE, and the animation frame is set back to the middle frame so that the level motorcycle is displayed. Additionally, the motorcycle's vertical velocity is set to zero so that it returns to cruising across the screen on the road. The m_bLandedSafely flag is then checked to see if the motorcycle indeed landed safely. If not, the crash sound is played, and the game is ended.

The m_bLandedSafely flag works like this: When the motorcycle first starts jumping, the flag is cleared to indicate that it has yet to land safely. If the motorcycle lands safely (hits the landing ramp), the flag is set to TRUE. This is the only way to register a safe landing and continue along in the game. Otherwise, the m_bLandedSafely flag will remain FALSE, and the code in the UpdateFrame() method that you just saw will catch the crash landing and end the game. The StartJumping() and LandedSafely() methods are used to help control this functionality, as shown in Listing 24.3.

LISTING 24.3 The MotorcycleSprite::StartJumping() and MotorcycleSprite::LandedSafely() Methods Help Control the Jumping Logic in the Motorcycle Sprite

```
void MotorcycleSprite::StartJumping()
{
  if (!m_bJumping)
  {
    // Start the motorcycle jumping
    m_iJumpCounter = m_ptVelocity.x * m_iHANGTIME;
    m_ptVelocity.y = -m_ptVelocity.x;
    m_bJumping = TRUE;
    m_bLandedSafely = FALSE;
  }
}

void MotorcycleSprite::LandedSafely()
{
  // Flag the motorcycle as having landed safely (hit the landing ramp)
  m_bLandedSafely = TRUE;
}
```

The jump counter is calculated based on the velocity and hang time constant and counts down to control the length of the jump.

The StartJumping() method begins by making sure that the motorcycle isn't already jumping. To get the jump started, the method calculates the starting value of the jump counter, which is based on the value of the m_iHANGTIME constant and the current speed of the motorcycle. To cause the motorcycle to actually take off on the jump, its vertical velocity is set to the inverse of its horizontal velocity. The vertical velocity must be negative because graphics coordinates in Windows increase as you go down the screen. In this case, the motorcycle is jumping up the screen, which means that its Y position is decreasing in value. The StartJumping() method finishes up by setting the m_bJumping flag and clearing the m_bLandedSafely flag. Finally, the LandedSafely() method simply sets the m_bLandedSafely flag to TRUE, which indicates a safe landing.

Construction Cue

Since the m_iJumpCounter variable counts down to determine how long the motorcycle jump lasts, you can easily use it to calculate a real hang time for each jump. The frame rate for the game is set to 30, which means that there are 30 game cycles per second. So, to determine how much hang time the motorcycle has for each jump, divide the jump counter by 30.

The remaining methods in the MotorcycleSprite class are the IncreaseSpeed() and DecreaseSpeed() methods, which are simply used to alter the speed of the motorcycle as it races across the game screen. Listing 24.4 contains the code for these methods.

LISTING 24.4 The MotorcycleSprite::IncreaseSpeed() and MotorcycleSprite::DecreaseSpeed() Methods Control the Speed of the Motorcycle Sprite

```
void MotorcycleSprite::IncreaseSpeed()
{
  if (!m_bJumping)
    // Increase the horizontal speed of the motorcycle
    m_ptVelocity.x = min(m_ptVelocity.x + 1, m_iMAXSPEED);
}

void MotorcycleSprite::DecreaseSpeed()
{
  if (!m_bJumping)
    // Decrease the horizontal speed of the motorcycle
    m_ptVelocity.x = max(m_ptVelocity.x - 1, m_iMINSPEED);
}
```

These two methods are relatively straightforward in that they increment and decrement the horizontal velocity of the motorcycle sprite. It is worth noting that the m_iMAXSPEED and m_iMINSPEED constants are used to establish minimum and maximum speeds for the sprite.

That wraps up the code for the motorcycle sprite, which you'll find represents a great deal of the code for the game as a whole. The rest of the Stunt Jumper game is laid out in the StuntJumper.h header file, which is responsible for declaring the global variables used throughout the game (see Listing 24.5).

LISTING 24.5 The StuntJumper.h Header File Declares Global Variables that Are Used to Manage the Game

```
#pragma once

//---------------------------------.
// Include Files
//---------------------------------.
#include <windows.h>
#include "Resource.h"
#include "GameEngine.h"
#include "Bitmap.h"
#include "Sprite.h"
#include "ScrollingBackground.h"
#include "MotorcycleSprite.h"

//---------------------------------.
// Global Variables
//---------------------------------.
HINSTANCE               g_hInstance;
GameEngine*             g_pGame;
HDC                     g_hOffscreenDC;
HBITMAP                 g_hOffscreenBitmap;
Bitmap*                 g_pSplashBitmap;
BackgroundLayer*        g_pBGRoadLayer;
BackgroundLayer*        g_pBGTreesLayer;
BackgroundLayer*        g_pBGMountainsLayer;
BackgroundLayer*        g_pBGSkyLayer;
Bitmap*                 g_pJumperBitmap;
Bitmap*                 g_pBusBitmap;
Bitmap*                 g_pRampBitmap[2];
Bitmap*                 g_pGameOverBitmap;
ScrollingBackground*    g_pBackground;
MotorcycleSprite*       g_pJumperSprite;
Sprite*                 g_pLaunchRampSprite;
Sprite*                 g_pLandingRampSprite;
Sprite*                 g_pBusSprite[7];
int                     g_iInputDelay;
BOOL                    g_bGameOver;
BOOL                    g_bSplash;

//---------------------------------.
// Function Declarations
//---------------------------------.
void NewGame();
void NewJump(int iNumBuses);
```

These four layers are used in concert to carry out a parallax-scrolling effect.

The listing shows that the global variables for the Stunt Jumper game largely consist of the different bitmaps and background layers used in the game. The splash screen bitmap is first declared, followed by the four background layers and various other bitmaps. The scrolling background is then declared, followed by the motorcycle, launch ramp, landing ramp, and bus sprites. An array of seven bus sprites is declared, which means that a maximum of seven buses can be arranged between the launch and landing ramps. The familiar integer input delay, Boolean game over, and Boolean splash screen variables are declared last.

Similar to some of the other games you've built throughout the book, the Stunt Jumper game also relies on a couple of support functions. The first of these, NewGame(), is important because it is used to set up and start a new game. Unlike the GameStart() function, which performs initialization tasks, such as loading bitmaps, the NewGame() function handles starting a new game once everything else is initialized. The NewJump() function is used to simplify the task of rearranging the ramps and placing the bus sprites. You'll find out more about how these functions work a little later in the chapter.

The primary setup code for the game takes place in the familiar GameStart() function, which is shown in Listing 24.6.

LISTING 24.6 The GameStart() Function Initializes the Bitmaps and Scrolling Background for the Game

```
void GameStart(HWND hWindow)
{
  // Seed the random number generator
  srand(GetTickCount());

  // Create the offscreen device context and bitmap
  g_hOffscreenDC = CreateCompatibleDC(GetDC(hWindow));
  g_hOffscreenBitmap = CreateCompatibleBitmap(GetDC(hWindow),
    g_pGame->GetWidth(), g_pGame->GetHeight());
  SelectObject(g_hOffscreenDC, g_hOffscreenBitmap);

  // Create and load the bitmaps
  HDC hDC = GetDC(hWindow);

  g_pSplashBitmap = new Bitmap(hDC, IDB_SPLASH, g_hInstance);
  g_pJumperBitmap = new Bitmap(hDC, IDB_JUMPER, g_hInstance);
  g_pBusBitmap = new Bitmap(hDC, IDB_BUS, g_hInstance);
  g_pRampBitmap[0] = new Bitmap(hDC, IDB_RAMPLEFT, g_hInstance);
  g_pRampBitmap[1] = new Bitmap(hDC, IDB_RAMPRIGHT, g_hInstance);
  g_pGameOverBitmap = new Bitmap(hDC, IDB_GAMEOVER, g_hInstance);

  // Create the scrolling background and layers
  g_pBackground = new ScrollingBackground(750, 250);
```

```
g_pBGSkyLayer = new BackgroundLayer(hDC, IDB_BG_SKY, g_hInstance, 1, SD_LEFT);
g_pBackground->AddLayer(g_pBGSkyLayer);
g_pBGMountainsLayer = new BackgroundLayer(hDC, IDB_BG_MOUNTAINS, g_hInstance,
  2, SD_LEFT);
g_pBackground->AddLayer(g_pBGMountainsLayer);
g_pBGTreesLayer = new BackgroundLayer(hDC, IDB_BG_TREES, g_hInstance,
  3, SD_LEFT);
g_pBackground->AddLayer(g_pBGTreesLayer);
g_pBGRoadLayer = new BackgroundLayer(hDC, IDB_BG_ROAD, g_hInstance);
g_pBackground->AddLayer(g_pBGRoadLayer);

// Set the splash screen variable
g_bSplash = TRUE;
g_bGameOver = TRUE;
}
```

Because the sky is the layer farthest in the distance, its speed is set slower than the other moving layers at 1.

The road layer doesn't need to move, so it has no speed or direction at all.

After the GameStart() function finishes loading the bitmaps for the game and creating the parallax-scrolling background, it sets the splash and game over variables. Notice that each background layer must be added to the scrolling background via a call to the AddLayer() method. Also, remember that the order in which you add layers to the scrolling background is critical—always add the back layer first and the closest layer last.

The game screen in the Stunt Jumper game is painted by the GamePaint() function, which is shown in Listing 24.7.

LISTING 24.7 The GamePaint() Function Draws the Splash Screen Image, the Parallax-Scrolling Background, the Sprites, and the Game Over Message

```
void GamePaint(HDC hDC)
{
  // Draw the scrolling background
  g_pBackground->Draw(hDC, TRUE);

  if (g_bSplash)
  {
    // Draw the splash screen image
    g_pSplashBitmap->Draw(hDC, 175, 15, TRUE);
  }
  else
  {
    // Draw the sprites
    g_pGame->DrawSprites(hDC);

    // Draw the game over message, if necessary
    if (g_bGameOver)
      g_pGameOverBitmap->Draw(hDC, 175, 15, FALSE);
  }
}
```

Even with all that's going on with the parallax-scrolling background, a single call to the Draw() method is all that is required from the game side of things.

The GamePaint() function takes care of drawing all graphics for the Stunt Jumper game. The function begins by drawing the scrolling background for the game, followed by the splash screen image if the game is in splash mode. If not, the sprites are drawn. The function finishes up by drawing the game over image, if necessary.

The GameCycle() function works hand in hand with the GamePaint() function to update the game's background and sprites and reflect the changes onscreen. Listing 24.8 shows the code for the GameCycle() function.

LISTING 24.8   The GameCycle() Function Updates the Background and Sprites and Checks to See if the Motorcycle Has Crossed the Game Screen

```
void GameCycle()
{
  if (!g_bGameOver)
  {
    // Update the background
    g_pBackground->Update();

    // Update the sprites
    g_pGame->UpdateSprites();

    // Obtain a device context for repainting the game
    HWND  hWindow = g_pGame->GetWindow();
    HDC   hDC = GetDC(hWindow);

    // Paint the game to the offscreen device context
    GamePaint(g_hOffscreenDC);

    // Blit the offscreen bitmap to the game screen
    BitBlt(hDC, 0, 0, g_pGame->GetWidth(), g_pGame->GetHeight(),
      g_hOffscreenDC, 0, 0, SRCCOPY);

    // Cleanup
    ReleaseDC(hWindow, hDC);

    // See if the motorcycle has crossed the screen
    RECT& rc = g_pJumperSprite->GetPosition();
    if (rc.right > g_pGame->GetWidth())
      // Create another jump (maximum of 7 buses)
      NewJump(rand() % 7 + 1);
  }
}
```

If the motorcycle has made it across the screen, set up a new jump.

In addition to updating the scrolling background and sprites, the GameCycle() function is responsible for determining when to create a new jump. The idea is that the game creates a new jump for each pass of the motorcycle across the screen, which means that the creation of a new jump is triggered by the motorcycle wrapping from the right side of the screen back to the left. Creating a new jump simply involves altering the number of buses being jumped and repositioning the buses and the ramps. The jump creation is handled by the NewJump() function, which you'll learn about in a moment.

User input in the Stunt Jumper game consists of both keyboard and joystick input. The keyboard portion of the user input equation takes place within the HandleKeys() function, which is shown in Listing 24.9.

LISTING 24.9   The HandleKeys() Function Allows the User to Control the Speed of the Motorcycle Jumper Using Keys on the Keyboard

```
void HandleKeys()
{
  if (!g_bGameOver)
  {
    // Move the jumper based upon left/right key presses
    POINT ptVelocity = g_pJumperSprite->GetVelocity();
    if (g_iInputDelay++ > 1)
    {
      if (GetAsyncKeyState(VK_LEFT) < 0)
      {
        // Play the brake sound
        PlaySound((LPCSTR)IDW_BRAKES, g_hInstance, SND_ASYNC |
          SND_RESOURCE);

        // Decrease speed
        g_pJumperSprite->DecreaseSpeed();          ⌐──────────────── The left arrow key
                                                                      decreases the speed
        // Reset the input delay                                     of the motorcycle.
        g_iInputDelay = 0;
      }
      else if (GetAsyncKeyState(VK_RIGHT) < 0)
      {
        // Play the engine sound
        PlaySound((LPCSTR)IDW_ENGINE, g_hInstance, SND_ASYNC |
          SND_RESOURCE);

        // Increase speed
        g_pJumperSprite->IncreaseSpeed();          ⌐──────────────── The right arrow
                                                                      key increases the
        // Reset the input delay                                     speed of the
        g_iInputDelay = 0;                                           motorcycle.
      }
    }
  }

  // Start a new game based upon an Enter (Return) key press
  if (GetAsyncKeyState(VK_RETURN) < 0)
```

continues

LISTING 24.9   Continued

*The Enter
(Return) key
starts a new game.*

```
if (g_bSplash)
{
  // Start a new game without the splash screen
  g_bSplash = FALSE;
  NewGame();
}
else if (g_bGameOver)
{
  // Start a new game
  NewGame();
}
}
```

The HandleKeys() function looks to see if any of three keys are being pressed. The following are the meanings of these keys in the context of the Stunt Jumper game:

▶ Left arrow—Decreases the motorcycle's speed

▶ Right arrow—Increases the motorcycle's speed

▶ Enter (Return)—Starts a new game (only if the game is over)

The HandleKeys() function begins by making sure that the game isn't over and then proceeds to check on the status of the two keys that have relevance to the game play; the third key (Enter) only applies to a game that is over. If the left arrow key is pressed, the HandleKeys() function plays a brake sound and decreases the motorcycle sprite's velocity with a call to the sprite's DecreaseSpeed() method. On the other hand, if the right arrow key is pressed, the motorcycle sprite's velocity is increased with a call to the sprite's IncreaseSpeed() method.

The last section of code in the HandleKeys() function starts a new game in response to the user pressing the Enter (Return) key. The g_bGameOver variable is checked to make sure that the game is over, and the NewGame() function is called to start a new game. Notice that if the splash screen is currently being displayed, it is turned off in order to start a new game.

The HandleJoystick() function is very similar to the HandleKeys() function, except it focuses on trapping and responding to joystick input. Listing 24.10 contains the code for the HandleJoystick() function.

LISTING 24.10 The `HandleJoystick()` Function Allows the User to Control the Speed of the Motorcycle Jumper Using the Joystick

```
void HandleJoystick(JOYSTATE jsJoystickState)
{
  if (!g_bGameOver)
  {
    // Move the jumper based upon left/right joystick movement
    POINT ptVelocity = g_pJumperSprite->GetVelocity();
    if (g_iInputDelay++ > 1)
    {
      if (jsJoystickState & JOY_LEFT)
      {
        // Play the brake sound
        PlaySound((LPCSTR)IDW_BRAKES, g_hInstance, SND_ASYNC |
          SND_RESOURCE);

        // Decrease speed
        g_pJumperSprite->DecreaseSpeed();

        // Reset the input delay
        g_iInputDelay = 0;
      }
      else if (jsJoystickState & JOY_RIGHT)
      {
        // Play the engine sound
        PlaySound((LPCSTR)IDW_ENGINE, g_hInstance, SND_ASYNC |
          SND_RESOURCE);

        // Increase speed
        g_pJumperSprite->IncreaseSpeed();

        // Reset the input delay
        g_iInputDelay = 0;
      }
    }
  }

  // Start a new game based upon the first joystick button
  if (jsJoystickState & JOY_FIRE1)
    if (g_bSplash)
    {
      // Start a new game without the splash screen
      g_bSplash = FALSE;
      NewGame();
    }
    else if (g_bGameOver)
    {
      // Start a new game
      NewGame();
    }
}
```

As you can see, this code is virtually identical to the HandleKeys() code in that it allows the user to increase and decrease the speed of the motorcycle, along with starting a new game. The only difference is that this function responds to left and right joystick directions, instead of the left and right arrow keys. Furthermore, pressing the fire button on the joystick takes the place of pressing the Enter (Return) key on the keyboard to start a new game.

Another important function in the Stunt Jumper game is the SpriteCollision() function, which is called in response to sprites colliding (see Listing 24.11).

LISTING 24.11 The SpriteCollision() Function Responds to Collisions Between the Motorcycle, Bus, and Ramp Sprites

```
BOOL SpriteCollision(Sprite* pSpriteHitter, Sprite* pSpriteHittee)
{
  Bitmap* pHitter = pSpriteHitter->GetBitmap();
  Bitmap* pHittee = pSpriteHittee->GetBitmap();
  // Only check for collision between sprites that aren't hidden
  if (!pSpriteHitter->IsHidden() && !pSpriteHittee->IsHidden())
  {
    // See if the motorcycle has hit the launch ramp
    if ((pHitter == g_pJumperBitmap) && (pHittee == g_pRampBitmap[0]))
    {
      // Start jumping
      g_pJumperSprite->StartJumping();
    }
    // See if the motorcycle has hit the landing ramp
    else if ((pHitter == g_pJumperBitmap) && (pHittee == g_pRampBitmap[1]))
    {
      if (!g_pJumperSprite->HasLandedSafely())
      {
        // Play the celebration sound
        PlaySound((LPCSTR)IDW_CELEBRATION, g_hInstance, SND_ASYNC |
          SND_RESOURCE);

        // Indicate that the motorcycle landed safely
        g_pJumperSprite->LandedSafely();
      }
    }
    // See if the motorcycle has hit a bus
    else if ((pHitter == g_pJumperBitmap) && (pHittee == g_pBusBitmap))
    {
      // Play the crash sound
      PlaySound((LPCSTR)IDW_CRASH, g_hInstance, SND_ASYNC |
        SND_RESOURCE);

      // End the game
      g_bGameOver = TRUE;
    }
  }

  return FALSE;
}
```

A collision between the motorcycle and the launch ramp indicates that the motorcycle should start jumping.

A collision between the motorcycle and the landing ramp indicates that the motorcycle has landed safely.

A collision between the motorcycle and a bus isn't good!

The `SpriteCollision()` function begins by checking for a collision between the motorcycle sprite and the launch ramp sprite. If a collision is detected, it indicates that the motorcycle should start jumping. On the other hand, if the motorcycle sprite collides with the landing ramp, it means that the motorcycle has landed a successful jump. Finally, if the motorcycle collides with a bus, it can only mean a crash and therefore the end of the game.

The last two functions in the Stunt Jumper game are support functions that are completely unique to the game. The first one is `NewGame()`, which performs the steps necessary to start a new game (see Listing 24.12).

LISTING 24.12 The `NewGame()` Function Gets Everything Ready for a New Game

```
void NewGame()
{
  // Clear the sprites
  g_pGame->CleanupSprites();

  // Initialize the game variables
  g_iInputDelay = 0;
  g_bGameOver = FALSE;

  // Create the ramp and bus sprites
  RECT rcBounds = { 0, 0, 750, 250 };
  g_pLaunchRampSprite = new Sprite(g_pRampBitmap[0], rcBounds);
  g_pGame->AddSprite(g_pLaunchRampSprite);
  g_pLandingRampSprite = new Sprite(g_pRampBitmap[1], rcBounds);
  g_pGame->AddSprite(g_pLandingRampSprite);
  for (int i = 0; i < 7; i++)
  {
    g_pBusSprite[i] = new Sprite(g_pBusBitmap, rcBounds);
    g_pGame->AddSprite(g_pBusSprite[i]);
  }

  // Create the motorcycle jumper sprite
  g_pJumperSprite = new MotorcycleSprite(g_pJumperBitmap, rcBounds, BA_WRAP);
  g_pJumperSprite->SetNumFrames(13);
  g_pJumperSprite->SetVelocity(4, 0);
  g_pJumperSprite->SetPosition(0, 200);
  g_pGame->AddSprite(g_pJumperSprite);

  // Setup the first jump (maximum of 3 buses)
  NewJump(rand() % 3 + 1);

  // Play the background music
  g_pGame->PlayMIDISong(TEXT("Music.mid"));
}
```

A maximum of seven buses can be jumped at any one time in the game.

The initial jump can't be more than three buses in length.

The `NewGame()` function begins by clearing the sprite list, which is necessary because you can't be certain what sprites have been left over from the previous game. The ramp and bus sprites are then created, followed by the motorcycle jumper sprite. The NewJump() function is called to get the initial jump ready, and the background music is started up. Notice that the call to the NewJump() function is structured so that a maximum of three buses are used in the first jump of the game. This keeps the player from having to tackle a huge jump to begin the game.

The NewJump() function is shown in Listing 24.13, and its job is to create a new jump for the motorcycle to launch.

LISTING 24.13   The NewJump() Function Arranges the Buses and Repositions the Ramps for a New Jump

```
void NewJump(int iNumBuses)
{
  // Set the position of the launch ramp
  int iXStart = (g_pGame->GetWidth() / 2) - (iNumBuses * 40);
  g_pLaunchRampSprite->SetPosition(iXStart, 215);

  // Set the positions and visibility of the buses
  for (int i = 0; i < 7; i++)
  {
    if (i < iNumBuses)
    {
      // Arrange and show these buses
      g_pBusSprite[i]->SetPosition(iXStart + g_pRampBitmap[0]->GetWidth() +
        5 + i * g_pBusBitmap->GetWidth(), 200);
      g_pBusSprite[i]->SetHidden(FALSE);
    }
    else
    {
      // Hide these buses
      g_pBusSprite[i]->SetPosition(0, 0);
      g_pBusSprite[i]->SetHidden(TRUE);
    }
  }

  // Set the position of the landing ramp
  g_pLandingRampSprite->SetPosition(iXStart + g_pRampBitmap[0]->GetWidth() +
    5 + iNumBuses * g_pBusBitmap->GetWidth() + 5, 215);
}
```

The launch ramp is carefully positioned to leave room for the buses and the landing ramp.

Although there are always seven bus sprites in the game, only the ones being jumped are positioned and made visible.

The remaining buses are hidden out of the way.

The NewJump() function accepts a parameter that indicates the number of buses being jumped. The function assumes that this number is in the range of one to seven. Depending on the number of buses being jumped, the launch ramp is first positioned to provide ample room for the motorcycle to approach while leaving enough space for the buses and landing ramp to the right of the launch ramp. The buses are then positioned and made visible, with any extra buses positioned away from the jumping area and hidden. Finally, the landing ramp is positioned to the right of the buses. That's all it takes to create a new jump!

This wraps up the code for the Stunt Jumper game, which means that you're ready to take the game for a test spin.

> If you're using Visual C++ 6.0, you might need to change the type casts from `(DWORD_PTR)` to `(DWORD)` in GameEngine.cpp in order for the Stunt Jumper code to compile properly.

Construction Cue

> As with most of the examples in the book, the Stunt Jumper program relies on the standard msimg32.lib and winmm.lib libraries. These libraries are included with most Windows compilers, but they aren't automatically linked into programs when you create a new project. If you are using your own project or make files, as opposed to the ones provided on the CD-ROM, make sure that you change the link settings so that these library files are properly linked into the final executable. Refer to the documentation for your specific compiler for how this is done.

Construction Cue

Testing the Game

I've said it time and time again that testing a game is the most fun part. For the last time in this book, you've arrived at the testing phase of a completely new game. Thanks to the trickiness of the motorcycle sprite's animation code, the Stunt Jumper game requires a fair amount of testing. For example, it required a fair amount of testing to arrive at the constants I used to control the motorcycle's hang time and minimum and maximum speeds. The neat thing is that you get to play a game while testing it, so testing is rarely a bad experience. Since I've already done the tough testing of the Stunt Jumper game, you can just have fun playing the game.

Upon starting the Stunt Jumper game, you'll see the splash screen shown in Figure 24.10.

Once you start a game, the motorcycle immediately takes off across the game screen, as shown in Figure 24.11.

You must quickly adjust the speed of the motorcycle jumper to prepare for the first jump. When the motorcycle hits the launch ramp, it is immediately launched into the air over the buses, as shown in Figure 24.12. If you've adjusted to the correct speed, the motorcycle will hit part of the landing ramp on the way down. Notice in all these figures how the parallax-scrolling background is changing. Admittedly, this effect is best witnessed in person by running the game on your computer, but the figures still provide a glimpse.

FIGURE 24.10
The Stunt Jumper splash screen contains a stylized version of the motorcycle jumping over a couple of buses.

FIGURE 24.11
When the game first starts, the motorcycle jumper immediately begins approaching the first jump.

FIGURE 24.12
If you dial in your speed properly, you can successfully sail over the first jump.

Notice in the figure how the motorcycle isn't level because it is flying through the air. As long as you continue to successfully land jumps, you will be presented with a never ending sequence of jumps with varying numbers of buses. Sooner or later, you will encounter the biggest jump in the game, a seven-bus jump, as shown in Figure 24.13.

Eventually, you will miscalculate your speed a bit and either under- or over-jump—in which case, the motorcycle will crash and the game will end. Figure 24.14 shows the game over image that is displayed when a game ends.

FIGURE 24.13
Successfully clear-
ing the biggest
jump in the game
requires adjusting
the motorcycle
jumper to the per-
fect speed.

FIGURE 24.14
Overshooting the
landing ramp or col-
liding with a bus
results in the game
ending and the
game over mes-
sage being dis-
played.

Since the Stunt Jumper game only gives you one chance to screw up per game, you'll likely be starting new games rather frequently. All you have to do to start a new game is press the Enter (Return) key or press the primary fire button on the joystick.

Summary

Whether or not you grew up idolizing Evel Knievel and his outlandish motorcycle jumping stunts, hopefully, you can appreciate the Stunt Jumper game and its unique usage of the game engine that you've developed throughout the book. You could argue that the Stunt Jumper game isn't the most complex game in the book, but it probably includes the most interesting sprite class that you've seen in the motorcycle sprite. Not only does the motorcycle sprite intelligently update its animation frames, but it also manages to determine how to alter its speed so that it follows an arc that imitates the effects of gravity as it flies through the air. Hopefully, you'll figure out some innovative ways to build on the motorcycle sprite to create your own sprites with even more interesting characteristics.

For better or worse, this chapter concludes the book. If you're hungering for more game programming knowledge, plenty of other books pick up where this book leaves off. More likely, you're ready to get busy using the knowledge and code gained from this book to embark on your own game development projects. Either way, I wish you the best of luck in your game programming endeavors. Feel free to stop by my Web site and share your game ideas on the Forum for this book— `http://www.michaelmorrison.com/`.

Extreme Game Makeover

My first inclination for the makeover of the Stunt Jumper game was for you to change the buses to a body of water with sharks swimming around. Although the "jump the shark" idea certainly has some merit, I wanted to see you twist the game into something uniquely different. One particularly interesting makeover that isn't immediately obvious is to turn the Stunt Jumper game into a tank game where two players fire cannons at each other over some kind of mountainous obstacle in the middle of the screen. The tie-in to the Stunt Jumper game is that you can use the same code for the motorcycle's jump to control the arc of the mortar being fired by each tank. Again, the idea is to have a tank on each side of the screen facing toward the middle, where a mountain is located. Each tank raises and lowers its cannon to alter the trajectory of the shot and then fires over the mountain. The scrolling background is less of an issue in this game, but you might keep the clouds moving in the background for some visual interest. The following are the general steps required to turn Stunt Jumper into Mountain Fodder:

1. Create new game graphics that include several different animation frames for a tank with the turret angled at various degrees (from 30 degrees to 60 degrees, for example). You also need graphics for a large mountain, tank mortar (preferably round), and explosion animation frames.

2. Create an animated sprite class called `Tank` that includes methods for controlling the tank's position, such as `MoveLeft()` and `MoveRight()`, and another function for altering the turret angle, such as `AimTurret()`.

3. Modify the `HandleKeys()` function so that one of the tanks is moved and its turret's aim is altered in response to the arrow keys so that it fires in response to the Return (Enter) key. Include code to create (launch) a mortar sprite.

4. Modify the HandleJoystick() function so that one of the tanks is moved and its turret's aim is altered in response to joystick movements so that it fires in response to the primary fire button. Include code to create (launch) a mortar sprite.

5. Modify the NewGame() code so that the mountain sprite is created; get rid of the ramp and bus sprites.

6. Change the SpriteCollision() function so that collisions are detected between the mortar and the tanks, making sure to end the game and announce the winner when a collision occurs. You'll also need to detect a collision between a tank and the mountain, which results in the tank being stopped, as well as between mortar and the mountain—in which case, the mortar is destroyed.

7. No doubt, this game makeover is the most ambitious makeover of the entire book. But, what do you expect? You're almost done! Hopefully, you'll find that turning a motorcycle stunt jumping game into a war game without having to reinvent the wheel is an interesting enough challenge to render this extreme game makeover worthwhile.

Field Trip

For your last field trip in the book, I want you to sit back, relax, close your eyes, and daydream for several minutes. Okay, make it several hours if you want. The goal of this field trip is to dream up an original idea for a game of your own. The book has made mention of your own game plans as you've progressed through the examples and expanded upon your game programming knowledge, but now it's time to put those plans into action. So take a field trip into the depths of your psyche and turn one of your own ideas into something we can all play and enjoy!

PART IX

Appendixes on CD-ROM

Index

NOTE: Page numbers preceded by *CD:* are located on the accompanying CD-ROM. For example, an index entry followed by *CD:559* would be located on page 559 on the CD-ROM.

Symbols

A

B

How can we make this index more useful? Email us at indexes@samspublishing.com

G

How can we make this index more useful? Email us at indexes@samspublishing.com

How can we make this index more useful? Email us at indexes@sampublishing.com

MoveChicken() function, 258, 265-266, 308-309

MoveToEx() function, 73-74, 83

Ms. Pac-Man, 273

msimg32.lib library, 123, 439

multiple initialization compiler error, 140, 192, 290

Multiple Instrument Digital Interface. *See* MIDI

multiple joysticks, supporting, 163

music. *See* sound

Musical Instrument Digital Interface. *See* MIDI

N

Namco Galaga, 199

naming variables, CD:572

ND_ASYNC flag, 285

nesting expressions, CD:561

NewGame() function, 430, 437

    Light Cycles game, 180, 185-186

    Meteor Defense game, 382-383, 389-390

    Space Out 3 game, 463, 466

    Stunt Jumper game, 541-542

NewJump() function, 542

Nintendo Donkey Kong, 231

not operator, CD:567

O

object-oriented programming. *See* OOP

objects

    cleaning up, CD:579-580

    initializing, CD:579-580

OffsetRect() function, 83

OOP (object-oriented programming), 22-26, CD:556

opening MIDI synthesizers, 297-299

operands, CD:561

operators

    addition, CD:568

    and, 118, CD:568

    assignment, CD:564

    bang, CD:567, CD:569

    decrement, CD:577

    extractor, CD:563

    increment, CD:577

    infix, CD:568-569

    not, CD:567

    or, CD:568

    postfix, CD:577-578

    precedence, CD:561

    prefix, CD:577-578

    prefix unary, CD:568

    relational, CD:568-569

    scope resolution, CD:579

or (||) operator, CD:568

origin (coordinate systems), 62

Q-R

V